Conflict resolution theory and practice

Integration and application

To the post-Cold-War generations of scholars, researchers, practitioners, and students of conflict resolution

Conflict resolution theory and practice

Integration and application

edited by
Dennis J.D. Sandole *and* Hugo van der Merwe

Foreword by Herbert C. Kelman

Manchester University Press
Manchester and New York

Distributed exclusively in the USA and Canada by St. Martin's Press

Published by Manchester University Press
Oxford Road, Manchester M13 9PL, UK
and Room 400, 175 Fifth Avenue,
New York, NY 10010, USA

Distributed exclusively in the USA and Canada
by St. Martin's Press, Inc.,
175 Fifth Avenue, New York, NY 10010, USA

British Library Cataloguing-in-Publication Data
A catalogue record for this book is available from the British Library

Library of Congress Cataloging-in-Publication Data
Conflict resolution theory and practice : integration and application
/ edited by Dennis J. D. Sandole and Hugo van der Merwe, forward by
Herbert C. Kelman.
        p.   cm.
    Includes index.
    ISBN 0-7190-3747-6. — ISBN 0-7190-3748-4 (paper)
    1. Conflict management.   2. Mediation.   3. Social conflict.
    4. Pacific settlement of international disputes.   I. Sandole,
Dennis J. D., 1941– .   II. Merwe, Hugo van der, 1965–
HD42.C674   1993
303.6'9–dc20   92-2493

ISBN 0 7190 3747 6 *hardback*
ISBN 0 7190 3748 4 *paperback*

Reprinted in paperback 1994

Typeset in Great Britain
by Williams Graphics, Llanddulas, N. Wales
Printed in Great Britain
by Redwood Books, Trowbridge

Contents

Contents

Contents

Foreword

In the past two decades or so we have witnessed the development and proliferation of a variety of new approaches to conflict resolution, which together amount to a new field of theory and practice. The precise boundaries of this emerging field are very difficult to draw and participants in this new movement differ in their view of what is to be included and what excluded. Not surprisingly, a number of writers have been distinguishing between sub-categories of the field, although different writers draw their lines in different places.

Practitioners of conflict resolution work at different levels, ranging from the interpersonal to the international. They operate in different domains, such as the court system, public policy, labor—management relations, inter-ethnic relations, or international diplomacy. They derive their ideas from a variety of sources, such as law, psychotherapy, management theories, group dynamics, peace research, decision theory, the study of conflict resolution in traditional societies, and theoretical models based in the entire range of social-science disciplines. Despite the diversity in level, domain, and intellectual origin that characterizes the work in this field, there are certain common threads — shared insights and approaches to practice — that run through all of its manifestations. Thus, it can probably be said that, with different degrees of emphasis, all of them call for a non-adversarial framework for conflict resolution, an analytic approach, a problem-solving orientation, direct participation by the parties in conflict in jointly shaping a solution, and facilitation by a third party trained in the process of conflict resolution.

Agreement on these general principles still leaves considerable room for differences in theoretical assumptions and in philosophy and style of practice. Moreover, the level at which and the domain in which practitioners operate inevitably influence their goals, methods, and overall approach. The inter-action among practitioners differing in the level and domain of conflict that they address is very stimulating and instructive and contributes significantly to the refinement of theory and technique. But, as one who has worked at the level of international and intercommunal conflict, I am very conscious of the need to be knowledgeable about and experienced with the particular features and issues of conflict at these levels, and of the danger of direct transfer of experiences from the interpersonal and interorganizational level to the international arena. Thus, the application of general principles requires sensitivity to the unique features of the context in which they are applied.

In the development of this multifaceted new field of conflict resolution that I have been describing, the Institute for Conflict Analysis and Resolution at George Mason University has played a unique and central role. George Mason has been one of the earliest institutions to establish a program in this field, which eventually became ICAR. It remains one of a handful of institutions that offers systematic training in conflict resolution at the MA and Ph.D. levels. The core faculty at ICAR, faculty from other departments or units of the University who have an association with ICAR, and several organizations affiliated with ICAR, work at different levels and in different domains of conflict resolution. Together, they help to build a theoretical base for the field and to provide the students with opportunities to gain practical experience and to reflect on that experience. The present volume derives from and epitomizes the special role of ICAR in the field. As the editors explain in their introduction, the book has its origins in a course on the integration of theory and practice in conflict resolution. Some of the chapters are based on faculty presentations in that seminar, and all were written by scholar/practitioners associated with ICAR – as core faculty, associated faculty, visiting faculty, or members of affiliated organizations. Thus, the volume reflects the contribution that ICAR has made and continues to make to the field through training, practice, and the development of theory and research.

What stands out as I read the chapters that follow is both the diversity and the continuity that this volume represents. There is a rich and varied array of philosophical assumptions, theoretical approaches, research methodologies, levels of analysis, and styles of practice. Moreover, there is controversy in these pages. Not only do different chapters approach the issues from divergent vantage points, but some authors explicitly debate each other across the chapters about their philosophical or theoretical differences. For example, a pervasive presence in this volume in John Burton – and rightly so, given his seminal role in the development of the field and of ICAR itself. Apart from his own contribution to the book, some three quarters of the chapters refer to Burton's writings. Some work specifically within his framework or extend that framework. Others are clearly influenced by the issues he has identified and the way in which he has formulated them. Still others, however, express disagreement with Burton's formulations and argue with him. I believe, incidentally, that some of these conflicts could be resolved – if only I were given the opportunity to act as the third party in the conflict between Burton and some of his colleagues. But, no matter. What counts is that there is no party line in this book and the occasional disagreements add a sense of vitality and intellectual excitement.

And yet, with all the diversity, the differences, and even the disagreements that this book displays, there is also a great deal of continuity. It seems to me that there are several common elements in the way in which most, if not all, of the chapters approach conflict and its resolution. Even chapters that disagree about some important assumptions − such as the biological versus cultural basis of human needs, or the role of power in conflict resolution − impress me as agreeing at a deeper level about the nature of the conflicts they address, of the solutions they envisage, and of the process they propose.

First, the conflicts addressed throughout the book are, or are analyzed as, protracted conflicts around identity, security, and other deep-rooted needs that are unmet or severely threatened. Such conflicts are necessarily 'cultural' conflicts in the sense that the parties bring to their relationship important differences in values, in the assignment of meaning, and in the definition of what the conflict is about. Furthermore, they are 'structural' conflicts in the sense that power deficiencies of one or both parties within the organization, community, state, or region hamper or threaten their ability to satisfy basic needs.

Second, the solutions envisaged throughout the book entail structural changes in the conflict system and transformation of the relationship between the conflicting parties. Thus, the goal of conflict resolution is to shape new political and social arrangements that will empower the parties, meet their vital needs for identity and security, and lay the foundation for a stable, cooperative relationship consistent with the welfare and development of each party. Such changes imply some redistribution of power, as well as the gradual creation of a new culture shared by the former adversaries (without, of course, abandoning their separate cultures).

Third, the process of conflict resolution favored throughout the book is an interactive process, in which the conflicting parties engage in analytic problem-solving, designed to generate mutually satisfactory solutions, usually with the facilitation of a professional third party whose role is quite different from that of neutral technicians.

In one way or another, all of the chapters address the relationship between theory and practice, which is the theme of the volume as a whole. These relationships may be of different kinds and go in both directions, as Chris Mitchell points out in his chapter and Dennis Sandole recaps in his epilogue. First, theory is *used* in practice: different chapters show the ways in which theoretical formulations either provide the underpinnings for practice or guide specific decisions in the course of practice. Second, theory is *tested* by practice: insofar as practice is based on theoretical hypotheses, it allows us to assess the reasonableness and power of these hypotheses. Finally, theory is *generated* by practice; practice provides unique opportunities for observing the dynamics of conflict and developing new insights that enrich our theoretical formulations.

Foreword

The theory that this volume relates to practice is of two interconnected types: theory about practice, i.e., about the techniques of conflict resolution; and theory about conflict, i.e., about the causes, the escalation, and the perpetuation of conflict, as well as about its management, resolution, and prevention. The essays assembled in this volume demonstrate the rich array of theoretical models and concepts, from a variety of disciplinary sources, that have informed the practice of conflict resolution. At the same time, they show how much practice − and reflection upon practice − can teach us about the nature of conflict and conflict resolution and thus contribute to generating new hypotheses and refining our theoretical models.

Herbert C. Kelman

Preface

This volume had its genesis in the context of a postgraduate course on the integration of theory and practice in conflict resolution, offered by one of us (Sandole) during the Fall of 1990, as part of the academic programs of the Institute for Conflict Analysis and Resolution (ICAR) at George Mason University. The idea was to have each of the core faculty plus colleagues from affiliate organizations, come into the course and provide the students with his or her 'angle' on the meaning of the integration of theory and practice.

The idea was expanded to include tape-recording each guest presentation and feeding it back to the presenter to use as a basis for a written version of the presentation, each of which could go into a volume on the integration of theory and practice in conflict resolution. It was our belief that there was a need for such a volume as many of the books in the field dealt with conflict/conflict resolution theory *or* conflict resolution practice, but not with the *integration* of theory and practice.

The idea was expanded further to include contributions from other colleagues who teach for ICAR from time to time or who are otherwise connected with its programs. What we ended up with was a volume comprised of contributions from theorists, researchers, and practitioners in conflict and conflict resolution, each of whom is noteworthy not only because of his or her own reputation in various aspects of the field, but also because each is, or has been, involved in some way with ICAR: as *core faculty* (Mary Clark, Christopher Mitchell, Richard Rubenstein, and Dennis Sandole); *members of affiliate organizations* (Marcelle DuPraw, John Murray, and Wallace Warfield); *members of the Faculty Liaison Committee* (Kevin Avruch, Peter Black, Benjamin Broome, Brack Brown, and Joseph Scimecca); *visiting professors* (Elise Boulding, John Burton, Daniel Druckman, and John Warfield); *senior associates* (Joseph Montville and John McDonald); and *student* (Hugo van der Merwe).

By bringing together the views of such a unique group of theorists, researchers, and practitioners on the integration of theory and practice, the book is designed to contribute to, and shape the rapidly developing field of conflict and peace studies (CAPS) and, by implication, to increase the capability of conflict *analysts* to better understand, and conflict resolution *practitioners* to better deal with, the major problem of conflict – particularly protracted, violent conflict – at all levels, worldwide.

The volume is intended for theorists, researchers, practitioners, teachers/trainers, students, and others interested in better understanding and dealing with conflict.

Summary descriptions of the various contributions appear in the annotated table of contents.

Dennis J. D. Sandole
Hugo van der Merwe
Institute for Conflict Analysis and Resolution
George Mason University
Fairfax, Virginia
June 1992

Acknowledgements

A number of people have facilitated the completion of this volume, for instance, Anne Bonanno and Mary Blackwell of George Mason University's Computing Support Services who are responsible for the 'camera-ready' diagrams in the chapters by Christopher Mitchell and Wallace Warfield, and Michael Fitch, freelance copy editor at Durness, Scotland. We are also indebted to the decision-making process at the Institute for Conflict Analysis and Resolution that brought us together – during academic year 1990–1991, Hugo van der Merwe was Dennis Sandole's graduate research assistant. We also appreciate the support and encouragement of Richard Purslow, Editorial Director, and Celia Ashcroft, Editorial Assistant, of Manchester University Press. Needless to say, without our contributors (including Herbert Kelman, who kindly consented to write the foreword), there would have been no book at all. Finally, each of us thanks our respective families, without whose support, encouragement *and* patience there would have been no book at all – at least, not edited by us!

Part I

Generic theory and practice in conflict resolution

Paradigm, theories, and metaphors in conflict and conflict resolution: Coherence or confusion?

Introduction

Any attempt to 'map' the field(s) of conflict and conflict resolution becomes more than an intellectual exercise as one contemplates conflicts where the parties seem more intent on continuing and escalating their violence and destruction than in taking advantage of efforts by various third parties, e.g., the European Community, former Soviet President Mikhail Gorbachev, the UN, and others to broker cease-fires, perhaps as preliminary steps to initiating problem-solving approaches to conflict resolution.

The question arises: Do we – conflict analysts, conflict resolution theorists and practitioners, peace researchers, and 'concerned others' – have anything to say about, or to offer the parties in, protracted violent conflict situations? This suggests a preliminary question: What do (or *should*) we know that is relevant and communicable to the parties in these situations?

Alternative realities in conflict and conflict resolution

In his landmark assault on the 300-year reign of the Cartesian dogma of 'immaculate perception', Thomas Kuhn (1970) tells us that the 'realities' perceived by the 'high priests of truth', scientists, are a function of their collective, internalized 'maps' (or *paradigms*). Different paradigms, different mappings of the 'same thing,' mean different 'realities' – different descriptions and explanations of the 'same thing', plus a different sense of problems appropriate to that 'thing' and of methods relevant to solving them – whether for members of different communities at one point in time or for members of the same community undergoing radical change over time.

Clearly, whatever applies to scientists must apply to the rest of us as well since, as Sir Karl Popper (1959, p. 22) tells us, scientific knowledge is 'common-sense knowledge writ large'. That there may be multiple, and indeed, even *competing conceptions/reconstructions of 'reality'*, even (but clearly, not only) in the sciences, makes the concept of 'paradigms' particularly relevant to conflict and conflict resolution where parties are quite prepared to die and to kill to defend their *competing* worldviews.

There are at least four paradigms relevant to conflict and conflict resolution at *all* levels, from the interpersonal to international: (1) Political Realism (*Realpolitik*), (2) Political Idealism (*Idealpolitik*), (3) Marxism, and (4) what I call 'Non-Marxist Radical Thought' (NMRT).

The first two, the subject of 'The Great Debates' recounted by Carr (1939), are polar opposites; indeed, each can be viewed as a reaction to the other. Political Realism (*Realpolitik*), which tends to be the dominant system (see Sandole, 1984), can be viewed as having three component parts:

(1) *Descriptive Realism*: The view that the world is always a potential, and often an actual battleground;
(2) *Explanatory Realism*: The belief that the reasons for this state of affairs are:
  (a) Primary: at all levels the core genotypic basis of human behavior is a *negative human nature*, a flaw with which we are born (see Koestler's *The Ghost in the Machine*, 1967); and
  (b) Secondary: especially at the international level, but elsewhere as well, there is an absence of appropriate conflict resolution mechanisms. As Waltz (1959, p. 232), in his discussion of Rousseau, tells us, 'wars occur because there is nothing to prevent them'; and
(3) *Prescriptive Realism*: If especially a negative biological determinism but also a lack of appropriate problem-solving mechanisms are the reasons for the deplorable states of violence at all levels, then we – as decision-makers – must do anything and everything we can to defend our basic interests: to maintain the *survival* of the Self, role, and/or group (the Nation). The 'only morality' is *successful* defense of those interests.

The *Realpolitik*-defined world is clearly a bleak one, encouraging the use of what Morton Deutsch (1973) refers to as 'competitive' processes of conflict resolution: power-based, adversarial, confrontational, zero-sum, 'win–lose' approaches to dealing with conflict. *Realpolitik* was the determinative *Weltanschauung* of superpower decision-makers during the Cold War. It has dominated the perceptions and behavior of Serbs and Croats during their wars in Croatia and Bosnia-Hercegovina and of Armenians and Azerbaijanis in (and over) Nagorno-Karabakh, and continues to dominate perceptions and behavior elsewhere (e.g., Northern Ireland, Palestine, Sri Lanka). It is not surprising, therefore, that *Realpolitik* and the corresponding *competitive* processes are associated with *destructive* outcomes.

Proponents of Political Idealism (*Idealpolitik*), on the other hand, may be in agreement with 'Realists' about the alarming frequency and intensity of violence ('Descriptive Realism') but disagree with them over the reasons for such ('Explanatory Realism') and how we should respond to the problem ('Prescriptive Realism'). For 'Idealists', violent conflict can be the result of many contributory factors, including *learned* responses to *frustrated* goal-seeking behavior. The range of responses to violence is fairly broad, including 'counter-violence' (in self-defense), but also nonviolent means for bringing about change in political, social, economic, and other systems to eliminate causes and conditions of violent conflict.

Idealism encourages the use of Deutsch's 'cooperative' processes of conflict resolution: nonadversarial, nonconfrontational, non-zero-sum (positive-sum), 'win–win' approaches to dealing with conflict. Idealism, therefore, tends to be associated with *constructive* outcomes.

The basic difference between *Realpolitik* and *Idealpolitik* is, quite simply, 'nature vs. nurture': While one stresses 'containing', 'deterring', and making the best of a basically negative, biologically determined situation, the other emphasizes the *changeability* of environment and, therefore, of behavior. As Waltz (1959) indicates, one orientation is clearly pessimistic in outlook while the other is optimistic.

The two remaining paradigms relevant (for our purposes) to conflict and conflict resolution represent various combinations of Political Realism and Idealism. Like Realism, Marxism stresses the inevitability of conflict (between socioeconomic classes). Marxism is also like Idealism, however, in its emphasis on structural change, especially in the system of ownership of the means of production, as the way to bring about behavioral change. Hence, Marxism, like Idealism, has a variable conception of human nature, which is dependent on environment, in contrast to Realism's fixed conception of human nature (irrespective of environment).

What I have called Non-Marxist Radical Thought (NMRT) is like Realism in that it recognizes the potency of our biological nature (e.g., the 'power of human needs in world society' – see Coate and Rosati, 1988), but like Idealism in that it stresses structural change to bring social, political, economic, and other institutions more in line with *basic human needs*. NMRT is also very much like Marxism in its recognition that the changes necessary to (re)align institutions with needs – environment with 'human nature' – are often radical and, therefore, attempts to effect such change, coupled with the 'role-defense' response to such by supporters of a threatened status quo (see Burton, 1979), are likely to generate and sustain violent conflict cycles.

Both Marxism and NMRT are like Realism in that they see *competitive* processes of conflict resolution (and often destructive outcomes) characterizing the efforts of disenfranchised, disempowered, needs-violated persons and minority outgroups generally, attempting to redefine their relationships with resistant supporters of a status quo which benefits only the ingroup. NMRT also shares with Idealism, however, a sense of the validity, power, and rationality of *cooperative* processes (and constructive outcomes) as the only way to achieve fair, long-lasting, durable solutions to problems underlying manifest conflict. The paradox (for Marxist as well as NMRT thinkers and doers) is that the use of competitive processes, intentionally or ostensibly to clear the

5

way for structural change and cooperative processes, may generate *self-perpetuating violent conflict systems* which fall right into the Realist category (a fate which could befall Idealists as well, who become involved in 'wars to end war').

Accordingly, there are at least four different orientations to conflict (Realism, Idealism, Marxism, and NMRT) and two different approaches to dealing with conflict (competitive and cooperative). Although analytically distinct as *static* points of departure, there is sufficient overlap among the four conflict orientations to blur their fine points of distinction once static conditions become overwhelmed by *dynamic* processes of conflict escalation and 'controlled maintenance' over time. What is important to realize here is that, although parties to conflict may wind up killing each other, they may have come to that point from different 'start-up conditions' (*equifinality!*). What is also important is that conflict analysts, conflict resolution theorists and practitioners, peace researchers, and others can embody (or otherwise use) any of the conflict and conflict resolution perspectives (or some combination of them), in order to make sense of, and to deal with conflict.

My own preference is to combine the (4 + 2) perspectives into an overall basis for looking at a wide range of causes and conditions of conflict, plus strategies for dealing with such. In what follows, I conduct such a 'multi-paradigm'-based examination of the literature, especially on the 'causes and conditions', with implications for conflict resolution. But as a preliminary step, I define some of the basic terms addressed by those perspectives.

Basic terms: Conflict, MCP, and AMCP

Conflict, as I have indicated elsewhere (Sandole, 1980, 1986), is 'a dynamic phenomenon, ..., a *manifest conflict process (MCP)*, comprised of phases of initiation, escalation, controlled maintenance, abatement, and termination/resolution'. More specifically, an MCP is: 'a situation in which at least two actors, or their representatives, try to pursue their perceptions of mutually incompatible goals by undermining, directly or indirectly, the goal-seeking capability of one another'.

There is nothing inherently wrong with conflict in this sense. As John Burton (1972, pp. 137–138) put it some time ago:

Conflict, like sex, is an essential creative element in human relationships. It is the means to change, the means by which our social values of welfare, security, justice, and opportunities for personal development can be achieved. ... The existence of a flow of conflict is the only guarantee that the aspirations of society will be attained. Indeed, conflict, like sex, is to be enjoyed.

What does concern me, however, is whether the parties to conflict employ competitive means for dealing with it. Even if they elect to use competitive processes *within* the context of Political Idealism or NMRT, the chances are enhanced for transforming MCPs into AMCPs (*aggressive manifest conflict processes*):

situations in which at least two actors, or their representatives, try to pursue their perceptions of mutually incompatible goals by physically damaging or destroying the property and high-value symbols of one another; and/or psychologically or physically injuring, destroying, or otherwise forcibly eliminating one another (Sandole, 1980, 1986).

To return to our original question, what do we know that may be relevant to understanding and dealing with protracted, violent conflict? In effect, what do theory and research tell us about the transition from MCPs to AMCPs?

Theory and research in conflict and conflict resolution

To help manage an otherwise confusing welter of information in seeking answers to these questions, it is useful to employ an appropriate framework. One useful candidate is Waltz's (1959) system which comprises the following dimensions:

(1) The Individual Level (image I);
(2) The Societal/National Level (image II); and
(3) The Trans-Societal/International Level (image III).
(4) The Global Level (image IV) has been added by Robert North (1990) and Nazli Choucri (Choucri and North, 1990), to capture those events, processes, and systems (natural and social) that are truly 'global' either as effects of the first three images and/or as sources of influence on them – e.g., destruction of the world's rain forests, depletion of the ozone layer, the greenhouse effect, the AIDS pandemic, and other global problems in need of solution.

The individual level

Many theorists and researchers have worked at this level, producing such variety that I have subdivided it into four subcategories: (1) biological, (2) physiological, (3) learning, and (4) dissonance.

Biological   Both the *biological* and *physiological* subcategories are concerned with 'human nature', the former tending to reflect the work of philosophers, theologians, and others who discuss the 'nature of the Beast' without necessarily attempting or being able to measure or otherwise systematically observe aspects of that nature. The *physiological*, on the other hand, reflects the work of physiologists, psychologists and others who *have* attempted to measure or otherwise systematically observe aspects of human nature.

Among the *biological* theorists and researchers are the classic Realist thinkers. For Hans Morgenthau (1973), the Realist 'supremo' during the

Cold War period, 'power politics' (*Machtpolitik*) – the defense, increase, or demonstration of power, in pursuit of 'interest defined as power' (i.e., survival) – 'is governed by objective laws that have their roots in human nature' (p. 4). Morgenthau's fellow Realist, the Protestant theologian Reinhold Niebuhr (1940, 1953), conceived of humans as corrupted by original sin and capable, therefore, of evil behavior, especially given their 'will-to-live'/'will-to-power' which encourages them to seek security (and to reduce failure-generated anxiety) by enhancing their power, usually at the expense of others.

Earlier thinkers, such as St. Augustine (1948), also argued that negative human behavior was a function of original sin. Spinoza (1951), on the other hand, argued that violence was the result of passion overwhelming reason.

Following the end of World War I, Sigmund Freud (1922, 1959, 1961) viewed human destructiveness as the result of a 'dialectical struggle' between two opposing forces, one associated with life (*Eros*) and the other with death (*Thanatos*). When Eros dominates, aggression tends to be directed outward ('explosion'), whereas when Thanatos is in the ascendancy, aggression tends to be directed inward ('implosion'). This energy is always present and always seeking release, if not externally, then internally. Hence:

the recurrence of war and conflict becomes a necessary periodic release by which groups preserve themselves through diverting their self-destructive tendencies to outsiders (Dougherty and Pfaltzgraff, 1990, p. 277).

Another group in the *biological* subcategory are the ethologists, especially Konrad Lorenz (1967). Although Lorenz believed that aggression was innate to humans as well as to other forms of life, he also believed that, *within species*, it tended not to be lethal *and* to have survival value (e.g., to prevent bunching-up of a species within its habitat). Among humans, however, this observation breaks down: Because their rate of technological/cultural evolution has surpassed their rate of phylogenetic evolution, especially in the 'natural' development of mechanisms of *ritualized aggression* and inhibitions to lethal aggression found in other species, aggression among humans has tended *not* to have survival value; indeed, to be clearly lethal and dysfunctional.

Given the location of Political Realists in the *biological* subcategory, and that the remaining thinkers there share the assumption that violent human behavior is a function of a biologically-determined human nature, the biological subcategory lends itself easily to a *Realpolitik* view of conflict and conflict resolution.

Physiological Again, this subcategory applies to theorists and researchers who deal with efforts to measure or otherwise systematically observe 'symptoms' of human nature: specifically, those who actually intervene into parts of the organism to explore the effects of certain interventions. John

Paul Scott (1958), for example, has argued that humans have 'an internal physiological mechanism which has only to be stimulated to produce fighting' (pp. 62–63). The mechanism, therefore, is not spontaneous; also, the form of its expression is dependent on *learning*: 'we find that motivation for fighting is strongly increased by success, and that the longer success continues, the stronger the motivation becomes' (p. 126). In effect, Scott's theory locates the physiological sources of aggressive behavior within a *multi-factor framework* which allows for the *interaction* between the organism ('nature') and its environment ('nurture') – 'we must not forget that in any real situation behavior will be the result of factors *from all levels* (p. 2, emphasis added).

Paul MacLean (1975, 1978) has advanced the thesis that humans have a 'triune brain', comprised of (a) reptilian, (b) limbic, and (c) cerebral cortex subsystems which correspond to progressive levels of phylogenetic evolution (with the 'reptilian' subcomponent being the most primitive part). In animals other than humans, stimulation of either of two parts of the brain 'concerned primarily with self- and species-preservation' (Restak, 1979, p. 41) – the *hypothalamus* in the reptilian section or the *amygdala* in the limbic section – produces physiological reactions associated with 'preparation for attack' (e.g., hissing, pupil dilation, arching of the back, salivation) (see Hilgard *et al.*, 1979, p. 321; Restak, 1979, p. 46). By observing reptilian- and limbic-dominant behaviors in other animals (reptiles and subhuman mammals, respectively), MacLean believes that we can have a glimpse of *paleopsychic processes* – ancient forms of behavior that we have inherited from our reptilian and mammalian antecedents (Restak, 1979, p. 36). But humans are also characterized by the cerebral cortex, which 'is more highly developed in human beings than in any other organism' (Hilgard *et al.*, 1979, p. 42); hence, we might expect human behavior to be more governed by the cerebral cortex than by the reptilian and limbic brains.

MacLean tells us that in any particular social situation, 'all three brains [reptilian, limbic, and neocortical] would be experiencing the same thing [but, as in the case of *competing paradigms*] each in a different way' (Restak, 1979, p. 51), and that the experiences mediated by one or two of these brains might be in conflict with those mediated by the remaining brain(s). In this regard, MacLean has developed the concept of *schizophysiology* to refer to the conflict between *feelings* (the limbic brain) and *thinking* (the neocortical brain). If the limbic brain gains the ascendancy in such ('inter-brain') conflicts, and starts to control and dictate behavior, then actors may 'feel' strongly about something but be completely in error. Such powerful feelings 'may be the basis for some forms of paranoid psychosis: a schizophysiology where *believing is seeing rather than seeing is believing*' (ibid., p. 52). (Wittingly or otherwise, MacLean may have provided a physiological basis for Spinoza's thesis that violence is the result of reason being overwhelmed by passion.)

The argument that, under stress, reptilian and limbic 'rationality' may not be under the control of what 'common sense' might dictate, neocortical 'rationality,' is compatible with Arthur Koestler's (1978) argument 'that there is a flaw, some potentially fatal engineering error built into ... the circuits of our nervous system'. 'The Ghost in the Machine' that drives all this for Koestler is MacLean's *schizophysiology* between the limbic and neocortical brains (Koestler, 1967, pp. 281–282).

Implicit in Koestler's argument are *basic needs*, e.g., the need for belongingess: the 'excessive capacity and urge' among humans 'to become identified with a tribe, nation, church, or cause' (Koestler, 1978). He identifies these *integrative, self-transcending* tendencies, rather than the *self-assertive* ones, as major factors contributing to violence throughout human history (Koestler, 1967, p. 234):

the crimes of violence committed for selfish, personal motives are historically insignificant compared to those committed ... out of a self-sacrificing devotion to a flag, a leader, a religious faith or a political conviction.

In Koestler's scheme, 'war is a ritual, a deadly ritual, not the result of aggressive self-assertion, but of self-transcending identification' (ibid., p. 253), where, in the process of transcending the Self, one *identifies* with a tribe, church, flag, or ideal and then one may experience 'vicarious ... violent emotions on behalf of the entity' (ibid., pp. 244, 245); where one also surrenders responsibility for one's behavior to the entity, thereby encouraging acting 'with ruthless cruelty towards the enemy or victim of the [entity]' (ibid., pp. 248, 251). Personal hating is not part of this process: 'The individual victim ... is punished not as an individual, but as a symbolic representation of [the 'enemy'] (ibid., pp. 252, 253). This is all evidence of 'The Ghost', the 'fatal flaw', the schizophysiology between the limbic and neocortical brains – a sort of physiological support for the doctrine of original sin!

Koestler's general pessimism, plus his particular reconstruction of MacLean's work, not only renders that work as compatible with *Realpolitik*, but further encourages its use by Realists *as evidence* that their assumption of a violence-prone, flawed human nature, is valid.

Learning Albert Bandura (1973), like John Paul Scott, sees aggression as a function of the *interaction* between a physiological mechanism, stimulation of that mechanism, and learning. Whereas Scott 'roots the aggressive impulse in physiological processes, but demands a stimulus from the environment' (Dougherty and Pfaltzgraff, 1990, p. 278), Bandura bases his theory

not on inner impulses or drives, but on social learning, social contexts and roles, response feedback influences, modeling and reinforcement, and the learned ability to assess the rewarding and punishing consequences of any given action (ibid., p. 288).

Given MacLean's observation that the limbic system dominates the cerebral cortex in stressful situations, if a 'schizophysiology' produces a violent response to a stressful stimulus – perhaps a response 'modeled' on the behavior of someone else or others in a similar situation – and should that violent response succeed in containing, destroying, or otherwise eliminating the stimulus as a threat, then the organism may 'learn' a particular relationship between a certain stimulus (x) and response (y). This is 'discriminant learning'. Once the connection has been made and begins to serve as a *norm* for the individual, to be used in similar situations, and further successes are experienced, then the successive experiences of 'positive reinforcement' of the x–y connection may have the effect of virtually 'wiring' the connection into his or her nervous system. As this 'response generalization' occurs over time, it will become progressively more difficult to undermine that internalized x–y connection, even in cases where it no longer applies.

This may explain why, in cases of perceived threats to security, *Realpolitik* is so compelling a normative guide to action: why it (perhaps as a limbic-dominated framework) tends to dominate behavior in international (and other) conflict situations where 'wars [seem to] occur because there is nothing to prevent them'.

Accordingly, learning can play a powerful role in conflict, especially in the escalation and perpetuation of violent conflict systems. On the assumption that what is learned can be *unlearned*, however, learning theorists in conflict and conflict resolution tend to be optimistic and, therefore, identified with *Idealpolitik*.

Dissonance   This subcategory concerns violence as a reaction to felt discrepancies between *preferred* and *actual* states of affairs. I derived it from Leon Festinger's (1962) concept of *cognitive dissonance*, which *is* about discordant relationships between preferred and actual states of affairs – between our beliefs and values, behavior, and/or environment as they actually are and as we think or prefer them to be. 'Dissonance', which is experienced as anxiety (which plays a role in Niebuhr's 'Realism'), can be managed, if not reduced and eliminated by avoiding further dissonance-provoking situations, and/or by making appropriate changes in our beliefs and values, behavior, and/or environment, to reach new equilibria between the preferred and actual. Dissonance-management/reduction behavior can be expressed violently, either internally or externally (especially if the limbic dominates the neocortical brain).

A number of theorists and researchers belong here, starting with Johan Galtung, whose *structural violence* (1969) still ranks as one of the most provocative contributions to conflict and peace studies (CAPS). Defined as a *structurally* based discrepancy between actual and potential states of somatic and mental well-being, it need not be perceived by its 'victims' or involve *physical* violence. What it does constitute, however, is a system of differential, unequal access to the means for closing the gap between the actual and the potential, where those at 'the bottom' of some hierarchically structured relational system, cannot – by reason of *involuntary membership* in certain ethnic, class, religious, and/or other groups — obtain fair access to the social, economic, political, educational, legal, and/or other resources typically enjoyed, and presided over by the mainstream. Structural violence is what exists in situations of institutionalized racism within, and imperialism across, societies: 'Above all the *power to decide over the distribution of resources is unevenly distributed*' (ibid., p. 171).

When structural violence makes the transition from the objective to the subjective realms — when it gets to be perceived by those who have been suffering, or are about to suffer, from it — the limbic system may, indeed, become exercised, predisposing actors toward violent reactions against those (or surrogates of those) who have been oppressing them, or are about to attempt to oppress them.

Ted Robert Gurr (1970) has conceptualized one variation on the perceived structural violence theme, *relative deprivation (RD)*, as a perceived discrepancy between 'value expectations' (VE) (resources to which one feels entitled) and 'value capabilities' (VC) (resources which one feels capable of acquiring and keeping). The greater the 'average degree' of perceived discrepancy between VE and VC, the greater the RD; the greater the intensity and scope of RD among members of some collectivity, the greater the potential for collective violence, including political violence (Gurr, 1970, Chaps. 2, 3, 6, 8; and pp. 360–367).

Galtung's *rank disequilibrium* (1964) refers to discordant locations of actors along various indicators of socioeconomic (and other) measurement. One may, for example, be high on some indicators (e.g., education), but low on others (employment, income, housing). In Galtung's scheme, it is not the actor who is low across all indicators, but the one who is *mixed* between 'topdog' and 'underdog' statuses, who is most likely to respond violently to the perceived source of the imbalance (Galtung, 1964, in Smith, 1971, p. 275):

Aggression is most likely to arise in social positions in rank-disequilibrium. In a system of individuals it may take the form of crime, in a system of groups the form of revolutions, and in a system of nations the form of war. But these extreme forms of aggression are unlikely to occur unless (1) other means of equilibration towards a complete topdog configuration have been tried, and (2) the culture has some practice in violent aggression.

When *perceived* structural violence — whether conceptualized as Gurr's 'relative deprivation' or Galtung's 'rank-disequilibrium' — leads to the contemplation or manifestation of *violence* as a means to *change* one's situation, then *frustration–aggression* may be involved.

According to John Dollard and his colleagues, whose *Frustration and Aggression* (1939) 'has stimulated more empirical research than any other theory of aggression' (Megargee and Hokanson, 1970, p. 22), *frustration* is the 'interference with the occurrence of an instigated goal-response at its proper time in the behavior sequence' (Dollard *et al.*, 1939, p.7). According to the original formulation, frustration was both a *necessary* and a *sufficient condition* of aggression (ibid., p.1):

This study takes as its point of departure the assumption that *aggression is always a consequence of frustration*. More specifically the proposition is that the occurrence of aggressive behavior always presupposes the existence of frustration and contrariwise, that the existence of frustration always leads to some form of aggression.

This fairly tight causal connection between frustration and aggression was facilitated by the comprehensive, multidimensional formulation of aggression put forward by Dollard and his colleagues: Aggression could be overt or non-overt, direct or indirect (in the latter case, involving *object-* and/or *response*-displacement), physical or ideational, conscious or unconscious, external or internal.

Whatever forms of aggression occur (if any) are a function of a complex interplay between the *strength of instigation to aggression* and the *inhibition of acts of aggression*:

The strength of instigation to aggression varies directly with the amount of frustration. Variation in the amount of frustration is a function of three factors: (1) strength of instigation to the frustrated response; (2) degree of interference with the frustrated response; and (3) the number of response sequences frustrated (Dollard *et al.*, 1939, in Megargee and Hokanson, 1970, p.29).

But if, through prior learning, the frustrated individual associates *punishment* with certain acts committed against certain objects, then, depending upon whether the weight comes down more on one side than on the other in the instigation-to-aggression/anticipation-of-punishment relationship (the 'ITA: AOP ratio'), he or she may be *inhibited*, deterred from behaving in certain ways toward certain objects. This 'interference' with an instigation to aggression sets up further frustrations (in addition to the original frustration), which can fuel a *frustration – aggression – interference with aggression – more frustration* etc. cycle, 'manageable' to some extent through object and/or response displacement: the frustrated individual can substitute targets and/or means in his or her attempts to reduce the instigation to aggression, and to experience *catharsis*. Depending upon circumstances, object displacement may include self-punishment: 'the tendency to self-aggression is stronger both when the individual believes himself, rather than an external agent, to be responsible for the original frustration and when direct aggression is restrained by the self rather than by an external agent' (ibid., in Megargee and Hokanson, 1970, p.32).

Over the years, in part because of reformulations by the Dollard group and critiques by others (e.g., Bandura and Walters, 1963), frustration has, for many, including myself, taken on the status of a *contributory condition* of aggression. But, in any case, what is it in the 'Self' that is being *frustrated* that can cause conflict to be expressed *violently*?

13

James Chowning Davies (1962, 1973, 1986) makes an explicit theoretical connection between the Dollard group's formulation of frustration–aggression and his (Davies's) modification of the 'hierarchy of needs' developed by Abraham Maslow (1987). For Davies, it is the *frustration* of *substantive* (physical, social-affectional, self-esteem, and self-actualization) or *implemental needs* (security, knowledge, and power) that can facilitate the transition from MCPs to AMCPs: 'Violence ... is produced when certain innate needs or demands are deeply frustrated' (Davies, 1973, p. 251).

John Burton (1979, 1990a, 1990b) has hypothesized a link between *frustration* and *basic needs* for identity, security, recognition, autonomy, dignity, and bonding:

Human needs theory argues ... that there are certain ontological and genetic needs that *will* be pursued, and that socialization processes, if not compatible with such human needs, far from socializing, will lead to frustrations, and to disturbed and anti-social personal and group behaviors. Individuals cannot be socialized into behaviors that destroy their identity and other need goals and, therefore, must react against environments that do this. ... Behaviors that are a response to frustration of such human needs will often seem aggressive and counterproductive, but they are understandable in this context (Burton, 1990a, pp. 33–34).

All four of the conflict paradigms are reflected in the 'dissonance' sub-category: Structural violence (including relative deprivation and rank disequilibrium), especially when it is manifested as institutionalized racism or imperialism, can easily find a niche under Political Idealism, Marxism, and NMRT; however, it can also find a home under Political Realism (e.g., in a *hegemonic* balance-of-power system). Frustration–aggression can clearly be subsumed under all four. And while basic needs are explicitly linked (at least by me) to NMRT, they are certainly implied in the other three orientations as well; e.g., a need for security, especially a frustrated one, will always make sense to 'Realists'.

Whether one's focus is violent conflict at the interpersonal, intergroup, interorganizational, international, or other levels, the actors in each case, at each level, are impacted by factors at other levels. This is part of the value of Waltz's (now modified, four-image) framework (although he was concerned specifically with the causes and conditions of international war): it forces us to take into account John Paul Scott's (1958, p. 2) proposition, 'that in any real situation behavior will be the result of factors from all levels'. We move on, therefore, from the content-rich first image of the individual to the second image of the societal (national) level.

The societal level
Much of what applies at the individual level has been or can be applied at the societal level and beyond. While there are clear differences of scale and appearance between, say, a divorcing couple and an international war,

individuals are still involved across the spectrum of different levels of analysis, as *decision-makers*; by implication, so are individual-level causes and conditions. This is why, for John Burton, the individual is the *unit of explanation*, the generic, cross-level independent variable: 'the basis of an explanation of social change and of the consequences of resistance to social change' (Burton, 1984, p. 19). This is not, however, an argument in favor of reductionism (in this regard, see Kelman, 1965, pp. 5–6): the causes and conditions of marital strife will not transfer automatically to the causes and conditions of war (although there may be similarities, e.g., in the processes of initiation and escalation).

One particular societal/intersocietal application of individual/interpersonal processes can be found in the studies conducted by Robert North and his colleagues of the crisis which escalated into World War I. Using content analysis to transform qualitative information into quantitative data, the researchers explored relationships between perceptions and actions, and uncovered evidence to support the following:

If perceptions of anxiety, fear, threat, or injury are great enough, even the perception of one's own inferior capability will fail to deter a nation from going to war (Zinnes, North, and Koch, 1961); and
In situations of high involvement, actors will tend to
- *overperceive* the level of violence in the actions of their adversary; and to
- *overreact* to the actions of the adversary (Holsti, North, and Brody, 1968).

Overperception of, and overreaction to threatened or actual attacks: these findings are compatible with Spinoza's thesis that violence is the result of the passions overwhelming reason; and with MacLean's schizophysiology – that under the stress of threatened or actual attacks, the limbic will dominate the neocortical brain, thereby increasing the probability of an emotional (e.g., violent) response to the threatened or actual *frustration* of *basic needs*, e.g., for security.

When two or more actors are so characterized, their conflict relationship may become transformed into an apparently *deterministic*, escalatory spiral, outside of their control to halt or reverse. Lewis Richardson (1939) has attempted, with his action–reaction models, to capture mathematically the dynamics of such processes, which he believed occur when people do not stop to think. (My own view is that people, especially men, do 'stop to think' during periods of conflict escalation, but within the context of the (limbic-dominated) *Realpolitik* framework.)

If such dynamics are occurring *within* a society, between the defenders and attackers of the political status quo, the defenders may elect to operationalize what I call the 'oldest hypothesis in politics' – 'when the natives are restless, threaten to go to war!' Georg Simmel (1955, p. 98) even prescribed

15

that elites in 'certain groups ... see to it that there be some enemies in order for the unity of the members to remain effective and for the group to remain conscious of this unity as its vital interest'.

That one should *invent* enemies in order to protect and preserve one's Self, role, and 'identity group', is reminiscent of Freud's theory: to avoid a *Thanatos*-driven 'implosion', actors may have to engineer an *Eros*-dominant 'explosion' and externalize their hostilities onto others. This is also compatible with Vamik Volkan's (1985, 1987) thesis that there is a *need for enemies* as well as allies, fulfillment of which is essential to the development of one's identity.

The idea (and perhaps *drive*) to externalize aggression, *at all levels*, in order to maintain one's Self and/or 'ingroup', may be an expression of *ethnocentrism*, which William Graham Sumner (1906) thought was a universal human trait: where 'each group nourishes its own pride and vanity, boasts itself superior, exalts its own divinities, and looks with contempt on outsiders' (ibid., pp. 12−13; LeVine and Campbell, 1972, p. 8).

The tendency to bifurcate people into 'them' and 'us' and to reserve most of our wrath for 'them', may, according to John Pfeiffer (1984, p. 92) 'have been inherited from times past and wired in from birth'. Edward Wilson (1979, pp. 122−123) tells us that, 'Our brains do appear to be programmed to the following extent: we are inclined to partition other people into friends and aliens, ... [and] we tend to fear deeply the actions of strangers and to solve conflict by aggression'. The 'problem is that our built-in universe was formed largely in prehistoric ... times [when] the sight of a stranger ... meant real trouble − and triggered swift, generally violent action' (Pfeiffer, 1984, p. 92). Nowadays, 'large-scale violence may be a throwback', something that made sense in earlier times, but not now.

This apparently universal tendency for conflict *within* to spill over *without* is compatible with Burton's (1984, pp. 3, 6−7) thesis 'that the major sources of potential conflict [*between* capitalism and socialism] are the shortcomings *within each system* that render each insecure, even without any external threat' (emphasis added): 'shortcomings' such as ethnic conflicts, race riots, high levels of street violence, high levels of unemployment and growing inequalities of income and opportunity. The Serbian−Croatian wars in Croatia and Bosnia−Hercegovina and Armenian−Azerbaijani hostilities in (and over) Nagorno−Karabakh are just two examples of 'system failures and inadequacies' in the post-Cold War era, capable of spilling over and drawing in other societies (see Sandole, 1991).

As Burton suggests, the 'shortcomings' within social systems may concern the nature of a society's economic system. John Hobson (1965), for example, argued that imperialism was the result of maladjustments in capitalism: (a) overproduction on the part of a wealthy elite and (b) underconsumption on the part of an impoverished majority. Such a structural inequity can clearly be an 'objective' condition of Galtung's structural violence *within* a society.

Borrowing from Hobson and others, Lenin (1939) argued that imperialism was the inevitable consequence of 'the highest stage of capitalism', in which the world's more powerful capitalist states, requiring ever more resources to sustain further economic growth, would compete for cheap sources of raw materials and labor, and guaranteed markets. In a world of shrinking colonial opportunities, relationships between the competing capitalist states would resemble a *perpetual state of potential (and often, actual) war*, while relationships between the 'exploiting' and the 'exploited' would constitute objective conditions for structural violence *between* societies. For Lenin, therefore, an international system dominated basically by capitalist states would be rife with international conflict.

Similarly, Nazli Choucri and Robert North (1975) have argued that increases in population and in corresponding demands for resources to sustain further economic growth, against a background of advances in technology, can lead to 'lateral pressures' for societies to move beyond their borders to get what they want. A good deal of conflict potential inheres in lateral pressures, especially if, as in the portrait of imperialism painted by Hobson and Lenin, potential sources of the desired resources are less and less available. This means that, more and more, states might attempt to get want they want *by force*. Choucri and North did, in fact, find relationships between domestic growth, national expansion, military expenditures, alliances, and international violence.

The international level

The more the international environment reflects the 'Hobbesian black hole of international anarchy', the more it is what Rapoport (1974, p. 175) refers to as an 'exogenous' (in contrast to an 'endogenous') conflict environment:

Endogenous conflicts are ... those wherein the conflicting systems are parts of a larger system that has its own mechanisms for ... controlling or resolving conflict [vs. *exogenous* conflicts, where there are no such mechanisms].

Hence, the more 'exogenous' the conflict environment, the more that 'wars [will] occur because there is nothing to prevent them' (Waltz, 1959, p. 232).

'Nothing' in this context means *nothing of any significance*, 'with teeth', to enforce decisions made 'beyond the nation-state'. As the 'Realists' would be the first to argue, the 'buck' of national security stops being passed at the level of a nation-state's decision-makers. Hence, Waltz's argument that, although the international level (image III) 'is a *permissive* or underlying cause of war ... the *immediate*, or efficient, causes of war ... are contained in the first [*individual-*] and second [societal-level] images' (ibid., emphasis added).

The war-'permissive' or -facilitative function of the international environment can vary, depending on the extent to which its various international political systems are, among other things, *bipolar* or *multipolar*. Karl Deutsch

17

and J. David Singer (1964), for instance, have equated multipolarity in the international system with increased 'interaction opportunities', pluralistic possibilities for cross-cutting loyalties, stability, and therefore, less war (in terms of frequency and intensity). Kenneth Waltz (1967), on the other hand, has argued that bipolarity means simplicity, predictability, manageability, stability and therefore, less war.

Attempts to resolve the *system polarity—stability* debate in other than a theoretical way (e.g., see Rosecrance's 'bimultipolarity', 1966), have led to *empirical* inconclusiveness, to match the state of affairs in *theory*: One of the participants in the theoretical debate, J. David Singer, and one of his main co-workers in the Correlates-of-War (COW) project, Melvin Small (Singer and Small, 1968), found that bipolarity (as well as alliance aggregation) correlated *negatively* with war (whether measured 'by number of wars, the nation-months involved, or battle deaths incurred' (ibid., p. 283)) in the nineteenth century, but *positively* with war in the twentieth century. In terms of Singer's own COW results, therefore, his and Deutsch's theoretical multipolarity—stability argument is valid only for the twentieth century (up to 1945), whereas Waltz's bipolarity—stability argument holds for the nineteenth century.

Since the ending of the Cold War in 1989—91, the replacement of the bipolar, East—West relationship with 'creeping' multipolarity has been accompanied by a resurrection in ethnic conflict and nationalist sentiments in Eastern Europe and the former Soviet Union, developments which have caused concern for some (e.g., U.S. Deputy Secretary of State Lawrence Eagleburger, cited in Tarnoff, 1989; and John Mearsheimer, 1990a, 1990b), including Robert Hunter (1989) who has commented that, 'we have more chance of a [European] war now than we have had during the last thirty years'.

Further suggestions that the 'new multipolarity' might be a harbinger of more intense as well as more frequent warfare can be found in the evidence documenting the *proliferation* of nuclear as well as chemical, biological and even conventional weapons of mass destruction, plus missile technology. Just looking at trends in nuclear proliferation (see Spector, 1987; *The Economist*, 1992; Budiansky, 1992; Robbins, 1992), the international environment seems to be moving in the direction of Morton Kaplan's (1957) 'unit veto state', where many, most, or all states have the capacity to destroy everyone else − a very *unstable* state of affairs, indeed!

One reason for proliferation is that it may allow the developing world (the South) to compensate partially (in a military sense) for the massive economic disparity it suffers from in its relationship with the North. According to the first Brandt Commission Report (1980), one-fourth of the world's population (the North) has four-fifths of the world's income, while three-fourths of the world's population (the South) has one-fifth of the world's income. Also:

In the North, the average person can expect to live for more than seventy years; he or she will rarely be hungry, and will be educated at least up to secondary level. In the countries of the South the great majority of people have a life expectancy of closer to fifty years; in the poorest countries one out of every four children dies before the age of five; one-fifth or more of all the people in the South suffer from hunger and malnutrition; fifty per cent have no chance to become literate (ibid., p. 32).

Arguably, these data fit neatly into a Marxist (but also an Idealist, NMRT, or Realist) framework and constitute 'objective' conditions of Galtung's structural violence on a grand scale and, according to Willy Brandt (1980, p. 7), the 'great social challenge of our time. [Hence,] the two decades ahead of us may be fateful for mankind.'

The Global Level

The 'fourth, or global image', as Robert North (1990, p. 25) defines it, 'distinquishes between natural and social environments and allows for the systematic investigation of the ways they interact on land, in the sea, and in space and for the outcomes'. North is particularly concerned about the outcomes of the first three images on the global level:

the planet and the delicate balances of its natural features. Even relatively minor alterations in natural environment ... could make our survival difficult, if not impossible.
Meanwhile, our expanding activities and interests exert increasingly threatening
pressures on both social and natural environments.

In a very important sense, the fourth, or global, level is under assault by the 'lateral pressures' discussed earlier (Choucri and North, 1975), that 'are directly traceable to the growth of human populations, the advancement of their technologies (including organizations), and their search for resources' (North, 1990, p. 188). As one example of how all this can translate into violent conflict, Jessica Mathews (1992) tells us about what I call the 'Malthusian nightmare revisited':

Poverty and environmental decline are tightly linked. Neither is conducive to stable
democracy. Where the land's capacity to produce is ebbing under the pressure of
rapidly growing numbers of people who have no alternative means of survival, the
result is economic stagnation or decline. This in turn can lead to *frustration, resentment, political turmoil and violence* (Mathews, 1992, emphasis added).

Although this 'new' level of analysis is less 'invisible' now than it was, say, twenty years ago, it still does not command the attention of the political and industrial elites, or of the numbers of people in general which the problems it addresses would seem to demand, partly for emotional–ideological and partly for cognitive–conceptual reasons. As North (1990, p. 24) puts it: 'the fourth image, or global system, has not been extensively developed or widely accepted as an analytical concept, even though there seems to be an increasing need for it'. Hence, his book, as well as Mary Clark's 'search for new modes of thinking' (1989) – to encourage necessary reconceptualizations of global problems in need of solution, if we and the planet are to survive.

Conceptual integration or confusion: Generic theory or disparate 'islands of theory'?

Returning to our original question, do we have anything to say about, or to offer the parties in, protracted, violent conflict situations? And if so, is it 'coherent'?

Given the discussion thus far (which does *not*, by any means, represent an *exhaustive* account of theory and research on the matter), it would seem that we do have something *relevant* to say to parties to violent conflicts. I would also say that this knowledge is 'coherent', which facilitates 'communicability'.

Beginning with the prescriptions of both John Paul Scott and Kenneth Waltz to employ a framework that recognizes and allows for the potential contribution of factors from *all levels* to the development of conflict, including violent conflict, the following would seem to 'cohere' into the basis of a *generic theory* on the initiation and escalation of violent conflict, with implications for conflict resolution:

(1) There does appear to be a *physiological mechanism* (inclusive of, e.g., the hypothalamus and amygdala) that requires some kind of stimulation to be activated to produce violent reactions, which can be influenced by *learning* (Scott; Bandura).

(2) During periods of threatened or actual violations of an actor's *basic needs* for *security*, identity, and the like, elements of this physiological mechanism (specifically, the *limbic system*) may come to dominate the actor's neocortical rationality (MacLean's *schizophysiology*), increasing the probability of a violent response to the perceived source (or a surrogate of the source) of the *frustrated* needs (Davies; Burton; Dollard *et al.*).

(3) Frustration can be fed by perceived *structural violence* (Galtung) at various levels of the actor's external environment, e.g., *rank disequilibrium* (Galtung) or *relative deprivation* (Gurr).

(4) The frustration-of-needs/aggression nexus is both stimulated by, and in turn stimulates, *ethnocentrism* (Sumner) and *Realpolitik*.

(5) When two or more actors so characterized are parties to a conflict, then frustration-of-needs/aggression can generate a quasi-deterministic spiral, reflective of Richardson's *action–reaction* processes (where, again, 'men' in particular do 'stop to think', but in terms of *Realpolitik*), where the more involved in the process the actors become, the more they will tend to *overperceive* and to *overreact* to threatened and actual assaults to needs (North *et al.*), thereby fueling the spiral (and MacLean's *schizophysiology/*

Koestler's 'Ghost in the Machine') even further, and increasing the probability of generating what I call *negative self-fulfilling prophecies (NSFPs)* (Sandole, 1984, 1986, 1987).
(6) 'Conflicts as process' (as well as 'conflicts as start-up conditions', e.g., relative deprivation) can be further exacerbated by environmental 'shocks' and uncertainties associated with developments at the international and global levels (e.g., *proliferation* of weapons of mass destruction (Kaplan) and the *Malthusian nightmare revisted* (Choucri and North; Clark; Mathews)).
(7) 'Conflict as process' is where third parties enter the scene, and their 'trick' is to create the 'magic' by which *Realpolitik*-driven *competitive* processes can be replaced (or supplemented) by *Idealpolitik*-based *cooperative* processes of conflict resolution.

Weaving these elements into a 'fuller-blown' tapestry of integrated theory and practice must await a later time. For the time being, however, the following chapters will help to 'fill in' some of the 'blanks'.

References

Bandura, A. (1973), *Aggression: A Social Learning Analysis*, Prentice-Hall, Englewood Cliffs, New Jersey.

Bandura, A. and Walters, R.H. (1963, 1973), 'Reinforcement patterns and social behavior: Aggression'. Abridged from *Social Learning and Personality Development*, Holt, Rinehart and Winston, New York, in E.I. Megargee and J.E. Hokanson, eds, *The Dynamics of Aggression: Individual, Group, and International Analyses*, Harper and Row, New York and London.

Brandt Commission Report (1980), *North-South: A Programme for Survival*, Report of the Independent Commission on International Development Issues, Pan Books, London and MIT Press, Cambridge, Massachusetts.

Brandt, W. (1980), 'A plea for change: peace, justice, jobs – an introduction', Brandt Commission Report (ibid.).

Budiansky, S. (1992), 'The nuclear epidemic', *Newsweek*, 16 March, pp. 40–44.

Burton, J.W. (1972), *World Society*, Cambridge University Press, Cambridge and New York.

Burton, J.W. (1979), *Deviance, Terrorism and War: The Process of Solving Unsolved Social and Political Problems*, Martin Robertson, Oxford and St. Martin's Press, New York.

Burton, J.W. (1984), *Global Conflict: The Domestic Sources of International Crisis*, Wheatsheaf Books, Brighton.

Burton, J.W. (1990a), *Conflict: Resolution and Provention*, Macmillan, London and St. Martin's Press, New York.

Burton, J.W. (ed.) (1990b), *Conflict: Human Needs Theory*, Macmillan, London and St. Martin's Press, New York.

Carr, E.H. (1939), *The Twenty Years Crisis, 1919–1939: An Introduction to the Study of International Relations*, Macmillan, London and Harper and Row, New York.

Choucri, N. and North, R.C. (1975), *Nations in Conflict: National Growth and International Violence*, W.H. Freeman, San Francisco.

Choucri, N. and North, R.C. (1990), 'Global environmental change: Toward a framework for decision and policy'. Paper prepared for the Annual Meeting of the International Studies Association (ISA), Washington, D.C., 10–14 April.

Clark, M.E. (1989), *Ariadne's Thread: The Search for New Modes of Thinking*, Macmillan, London and St. Martin's Press, New York.

Coate, R.A. and Rosati, J.A. (eds) (1988), *The Power of Human Needs in World Society*, Lynne Rienner Publishers, Boulder, Colorado, and London.

Davies, J.C. (1962), 'Toward a theory of revolution,' *American Sociological Review*, 27, pp. 5–19.

Davies, J.C. (1973), 'Aggression, violence, revolution, and war', in J.N. Knutson, ed., *Handbook of Political Psychology*, Jossey-Bass, San Francisco and London.

Davies, J.C. (1986), 'Roots of political behavior', in M.G. Hermann, ed., *Political Psychology: Contemporary Problems and Issues*, Jossey-Bass, San Francisco and London.

Deutsch, K.W. and Singer, J.D. (1964), 'Multipolar power systems and international stability', *World Politics*, 16, pp. 390–406.

Deutsch, M. (1973), *The Resolution of Conflict: Constructive and Destructive Processes*, Yale University Press, New Haven, Connecticut and London.

Dollard, J., Doob, L.W., Miller, N.E., Mowrer, O.H., and Sears, R.R. (1939), *Frustration and Aggression*, Yale University Press, New Haven, Connecticut and London.

Dougherty, J.E. and Pfaltzgraff, Jr, R.L. (1990), *Contending Theories of International Relations: A Comprehensive Survey*, 3rd edition, Harper Collins, New York.

The Economist (1992), 'Bombs for all?', 14 March, pp. 15–16, 45–47.

Festinger, L. (1962), *A Theory of Cognitive Dissonance*, Stanford University Press, Stanford, California.

Freud, S. (1922), *Beyond the Pleasure Principle*, Hogarth Press, London.

Freud, S. (1959), 'Why war?' A letter from Sigmund Freud to Albert Einstein, written in 1932. Text in E. Jones, ed., *The Collected Papers of Sigmund Freud*, Vol. 5, Basic Books, New York.

Freud, S. (1961), *Civilization and Its Discontents*, W.W. Norton, New York.

Galtung, J. (1964), 'A structural theory of aggression', *Journal of Peace Research*, 1, pp. 95–119.

Galtung, J. (1969), 'Peace, violence and peace research', *Journal of Peace Research*, 6, pp. 167–191.

Gurr, T.R. (1970), *Why Men Rebel*. Princeton University Press, Princeton, New Jersey.

Hilgard, E.R., Atkinson, R.L., and Atkinson, R.C. (1979), *Introduction to Psychology*, 7th edition, Harcourt Brace Jovanovich, New York.

Hobson, J.A. (1965), *Imperialism: A Study*, University of Michigan Press, Ann Arbor.

Holsti, O.R., North, R.C., and Brody, R.A. (1968), 'Perception and action in the 1914 crisis', in J.D. Singer, ed., *Quantitative International Politics*, Free Press, New York and Collier-Macmillan, London.

Hunter, R. (1989), 'Political stability in Europe: The dynamics of the East-West relationship'. Seminar on Implications of CFE (Conventional Armed Forces in Europe Treaty) for Political and Military Stability in Europe. Science Applications International Corporation (SAIC), McLean, Virginia, 9 November.

Kaplan, M. A. (1957), *System and Process in International Politics*, John Wiley, New York.

Kelman, H. C. (1965), 'Social-psychological approaches to the study of international relations', in H. C. Kelman, ed., *International Behavior: A Social-Psychological Analysis*, Holt, Rinehart and Winston, New York.

Koestler, A. (1967), *The Ghost in the Machine*, Macmillan, New York.

Koestler, A. (1978), 'The brain explosion', *Observer* (London), 15 January, p. 25.

Kuhn, T. S. (1970), *The Structure of Scientific Revolutions*, 2d Edition, University of Chicago Press, Chicago and London.

Lenin, V. I. (1939), *Imperialism: The Highest Stage of Capitalism*, International Publishers, New York.

LeVine, R. A. and Campbell, D. T. (1972), *Ethnocentrism: Theories of Conflict, Ethnic Attitudes and Group Behavior*, John Wiley, New York and London.

Lorenz, K. (1967), *On Aggression*, Bantam Books, New York.

MacLean, P. (1975), 'On the evolution of three mentalities', in S. Arieti and G. Chrzanowski, eds, *New Dimensions in Psychiatry: A World View*, Vol. 2, John Wiley, New York.

MacLean, P. (1978), 'A mind of three minds: Educating the triune brain', in *Education and the Brain*, 77th Yearbook of the National Society for the Study of Education, Part II, University of Chicago Press, Chicago.

Maslow, A. H. (1987), *Motivation and Personality*, 3rd edition, Harper and Row, New York and London.

Mathews, J. (1992), 'The greater threat to democracy', *Washington Post*, 13 March, p. A25.

Mearsheimer, J. J. (1990a), 'Back to the future: Instability in Europe after the Cold War', *International Security*, 15, pp. 5−56.

Mearsheimer, J. J. (1990b), 'Why we will soon miss the Cold War', *The Atlantic*, August, pp. 35−50.

Megargee, E. I. and Hokanson, J. E. (eds) (1970), *The Dynamics of Aggression: Individual, Group, and International Analyses*, Harper and Row, New York and London.

Morgenthau, H. J. (1973), *Politics Among Nations: The Struggle for Power and Peace*, 5th edition, Alfred A. Knopf, New York.

Niebuhr, R. (1940), *Christianity and Power Politics*, Charles Scribner's Sons, New York.

Niebuhr, R. (1953), *Christian Realism and Political Problems*, Charles Scribner's Sons, New York.

North, R. C. (1990), *War, Peace, Survival: Global Politics and Conceptual Synthesis*, Westview Press, Boulder, Colorado and Oxford.

Pfeiffer, J. (1984), 'Human nature: The universe inside your skull', *Science Digest*, 92, p. 92.

Popper, K. R. (1959), *The Logic of Scientific Discovery*, Hutchinson, London.

Rapoport, A. (1974), *Conflict in Man-Made Environment*, Penguin Books, Harmondsworth (England) and New York.

Restak, R.M. (1979), *The Brain: The Last Frontier*, Doubleday, Garden City, New York.

Richardson, L.F. (1939), 'Generalized foreign politics: A study in group psychology', *British Journal of Psychology, Monograph Supplements*, 7.

Robbins, C.A. (1992), 'The x factor in the proliferation game: The former Soviet Union's explosive potential', *Newsweek*, 16 March, pp. 44–51.

Rosecrance, R.N. (1966), 'Bipolarity, multipolarity, and the future', *Journal of Conflict Resolution*, 10, pp. 314–327.

St. Augustine (1948), *The City of God*, translated by Marcus Dods, Hafner, New York.

Sandole, D.J.D. (1980), 'Economic conditions and conflict processes', in P. Whiteley, ed., *Models of Political Economy*, Sage, London and Beverly Hills, California.

Sandole, D.J.D. (1984), 'The subjectivity of theories and actions in world society', in M. Banks, ed., *Conflict in World Society: A New Perspective on International Relations*, Wheatsheaf, Brighton and St. Martin's Press, New York.

Sandole, D.J.D. (1986), 'Traditional approaches to conflict management: Short-term gains vs. long-term costs,' *Current Research on Peace and Violence*, 9, pp. 119–124.

Sandole, D.J.D. (1987), 'Conflict management: Elements of generic theory and practice', in D.J.D. Sandole and I. Sandole-Staroste, eds, *Conflict Management and Problem Solving: Interpersonal to International Applications*, Frances Pinter, London and New York University Press, New York.

Sandole, D.J.D. (1991), 'The Conflict Prevention Centre and cooperative conflict resolution in Europe', *Peace and the Sciences*, June, pp. 9–18.

Scott, J.P. (1958), *Aggression*, University of Chicago Press, Chicago and London.

Simmel, G. (1955), *Conflict and the Web of Group Affiliations*, Free Press, New York and Collier-Macmillan, London.

Singer, J.D. and Small, M. (1968), 'Alliance aggregation and the onset of war, 1815–1945', in J.D. Singer, ed., *Quantitative International Politics: Insights and Evidence*, Free Press, New York and Collier-Macmillan, London.

Smith, C.G. (ed.) (1971), *Conflict Resolution: Contributions of the Behavioral Sciences*, University of Notre Dame Press, Notre Dame, Indiana.

Spector, L.S. (1987), *Going Nuclear*, Ballinger, Cambridge, Massachusetts.

Spinoza, B. (1951), *The Chief Works of Benedict de Spinoza*, translated by R.H.M. Elwes, Dover, New York.

Sumner, W.G. (1906), *Folkways*, Ginn, New York.

Tarnoff, P. (1989), 'A bizarre nostalgia for the Cold War', *New York Times*, 19 September, p. A25.

Volkan, V.D. (1985), 'The need to have enemies and allies: A developmental approach', *Political Psychology*, 6, pp. 219–245.

Volkan, V.D. (1987), *The Need to Have Enemies and Allies: From Clinical Practice to International Relationships*, Jason Aronson, Northvale, New Jersey and London.

Waltz, K.N. (1959), *Man, the State, and War: A Theoretical Analysis*, Columbia University Press, New York and London.

Waltz, K.N. (1967), 'International structure, national force, and the balance of world power', *Journal of International Affairs*, 21, pp. 215–231.

Wilson, E.O. (1979), *On Human Nature*, Bantam Books, New York.

Zinnes, D.A., North, R.C., and Koch, Jr, H.E. (1961), 'Capability, threat and the outbreak of war', in J.N. Rosenau, ed., *International Politics and Foreign Policy: A Reader in Research and Theory*, Free Press, New York and Collier-Macmillan, London.

An analytical research agenda for conflict and conflict resolution

In this chapter we identify issues from the literature on conflict and conflict resolution that can be clarified through experimental research. The discussion is organized in terms of a framework consisting of four parts: the structure of conflict, processes of conflict, influences on conflict behavior, and the broader contexts for conflict. These distinctions highlight issues that have been the bases for programmatic research on interpersonal, intergroup, and interorganizational conflict. They also call attention to the next steps that are part of a research agenda needed to provide further clarification of the issues. Both the accomplishments to date and the needed research are summarized. While focusing primarily on a research agenda, we also consider key conceptual and methodological concerns raised by each part of the framework. The discussion of these concerns is organized in terms of the variables found to contribute to sources of conflict and influences on attempts to resolve conflicts. Examples of important studies illustrate the prevailing paradigm used to explore effects and, in some sections, key findings are summarized. The research agendas that emerge from each section are highlighted as a menu of research challenges in a concluding section.

Structure of Conflict

The structure of conflict refers to the sources of differences among individuals or groups. Three sources or types of conflict have been the subject of experimental research: interests, understanding, and ideology or beliefs. Each source has been a focus of studies designed to investigate the effects of the *size* of conflict on attempts by disputants to resolve their differences. While size or intensity of conflict is the primary independent variable in the studies, it is defined differently for each source due largely to differences in experimental paradigms used in the investigations. Each paradigm is discussed in turn.

Daniel Druckman

Conflict of interest

A conflict of interest is a discrepancy in preferred outcomes to self and other and is often manifest in a competition for tangible resources or rewards. The extreme case of conflict is when one person's gains are directly proportional to another's losses, referred to as zero-sum outcomes and illustrated by the game of poker. The opposite situation is when one's gains are equal to those of another, referred to as positive-sum outcomes and illustrated by the game of charades. Most situations can, however, be depicted to lie between these extremes where there are elements of both competition and cooperation, referred to as mixed-motive and illustrated by the well-known matrix game of prisoner's dilemma. By varying the amount of conflict present in a situation, it is possible to explore the effects of size of conflict on behavior intended to resolve the differences. This relationship has been explored in a number of experiments.

A variety of games have been used as experimental tasks within which the size of conflicting interests is manipulated. These include the popular matrix games where opposing players make choices between alternative payoffs over the course of many plays (Axelrod, 1970), the Acme—Bolt trucking game where varying route lengths are translated into potential differences in the earnings of the opposing players (Deutsch *et al.*, 1971), and resource-distribution problems where allocation decisions are made within wide or narrow ranges creating potential discrepancies in outcomes that are either large or small (Thibaut, 1968; Zechmeister and Druckman, 1973). In each of these situations, size of conflict is defined in terms of a range of outcomes where the possible differences between players is large, moderate, or small. Of particular interest in these studies is the relationship between three types of variables: (a) the way conflict is created by manipulating the structure of the situation, (b) perceptions of players (e.g., the extent to which they view the situation as competitive), and (c) the players' behavior which may be indexed, for example, as the number of cooperative or competitive choices made, whether agreement is reached, or the amount of compromise in decisions made at the end (outcomes) or during the process of interacting.

Results obtained from these studies indicate clearly that the larger the potential discrepancy in outcomes, the more the conflict is viewed as being intense or competitive, and the more difficult it is to resolve through bargaining. People respond to situations in expected ways; larger conflicts, defined in terms of the structure of the situation, are more difficult to resolve than smaller conflicts. Less is known, however, about the precise relationships between these variables: How much change in the amount of conflict is needed to alter perceptions and behavior? Are there threshold effects such that a certain minimum change in the situation is needed to produce corresponding changes in perceptions and behavior? Little is also known about the possible countervailing effects of shared interests in other areas: Do shared or cross-cutting interests facilitate the resolution of conflicts on other

26

issues? How many shared interests are needed to offset the intensifying effects of conflicts on other issues? The variable of shared interests suggests the importance of broader relationships between parties in conflict: Do positive long-term relationships facilitate the resolution of conflicts on particular issues? And, are similar results obtained in studies of other types of conflict? We turn now to that question.

Conflict of understanding

Disagreements between self and other over the best way to accomplish a shared goal is a conflict of understanding or of alternative cognitions. Unlike conflicts of interest, the parties agree on the goal or desire the same outcome. Rather than arguing over *who* should 'get more', the parties argue about how *both* can 'get more'. Considered by some to be the major source of international conflict in the twentieth century, cognitive differences have been the focus of innovative research conducted by Kenneth Hammond and his colleagues. The intractability of these conflicts has been demonstrated in studies that sought to relate the size of conflict to conflict-resolution behavior. Size of conflict is defined in this paradigm as the amount of discrepancy between parties in the cues used to predict events: examples of problems used in the studies are predicting the level of democratic institutions from such cues as the amount of state control and free elections; stock performance from cues such as the growth rate, debt, and price/earnings ratio; and type of ammunition for a police department based on the stopping power and amount of injury caused by a bullet. (See Brehmer and Hammond, 1977, for a review of these studies.) In these studies, larger discrepancies in cue usage led to more difficulty in resolving the differences between parties in their predictions of events. Subjects were reluctant to compromise or change their reliance on the original cues, leading to impasses in the bargaining or debate process. And, this effect seems to generalize across a variety of cultures (Hammond and Brehmer, 1973).

The question of interest is how to produce the cognitive change needed to reach agreements. Among the suggestions that derive from the research completed to date are that thinking intuitively, rather than analytically, about the problem (Rappoport, 1965) and adopting a problem-solving (rather than a competitive) approach to the discussion of differences (Summers, 1968) results in more compromise and cognitive change. Larger changes have been shown to occur with various technological aids based on computer graphics. Hammond and his colleagues demonstrated that the aids increased each party's understanding of the other's positions, or at least clarified the differences that existed, leading to the cognitive changes needed for resolution. These are important findings. They address the kinds of conflicts that often occur between scientists or 'experts' over the interpretation of data (e.g., Ozawa and Susskind, 1985). These kinds of differences can harden into ideologies not amenable to resolution with the help of technology or other forms of mediation. The challenge for further research on this topic is to understand the conditions under which cognitive differences translate into differences of ideology or belief. The translation from one type of conflict to another highlights the problem of effects on conflict resolution of interacting sources of conflict. Such connections have been explored in recent research.

Conflicting ideologies

There is little doubt that contrasting ideological perspectives are unresolvable through bargaining. A long tradition of work on the sociology of conflict makes evident the intractable features of ideological conflict (Simmel, 1955; Coser, 1956). A more interesting research issue is the way that differences in ideology interact with interests and understanding in the process of conflict resolution. Coser's (1956) elaboration of Simmel's proposition concerning the objectifying influence of ideological commitment on conflict of interest was the basis for a program of research on the interplay between ideologies (or values) and interests. Hammond's (1965) caution about the dangers of a 'hardening' of cognitive differences called attention to another type of interplay, between cognitive and ideological differences. Each of these themes is summarized in turn.

Results from several experiments provide evidence for the propositions that, (a) conflicts of interest linked to differences in ideology are more difficult to resolve than conflicts that do not derive from contrasting ideological orientations, and, (b) the more polarized the parties in ideological orientation, the more difficult it is to resolve a related conflict of interest (Druckman and Zechmeister, 1970; Zechmeister and Druckman, 1973; Druckman *et al.*, 1974, 1977). These effects are quite robust across a variety of subject populations and conditions, although the interests are more difficult to negotiate when representatives are strongly committed to the underlying ideologies and when monetary incentives for resolving the conflict are not part of the task (Druckman, 1971a). Of interest, then, is the question of how to facilitate the resolution of these conflicts. One strategy is to 'delink' the ideologies or values from the interests. Another is to explore the differences in values or ideologies in prenegotiation workshop sessions. Both strategies have been shown to be effective: both led to more agreements than a condition where interests derived explicitly from ideologies without a prenegotiation workshop (Druckman *et al.*, 1988). Interestingly, however, the workshop condition produced more cooperation during the bargaining process than either of the other conditions. This was shown to be a result of *both* increased familiarity *and* liking produced by the workshop (Druckman and Broome, 1991).

A number of issues have been suggested for further research in this paradigm. One set of issues concerns the strength of the link between the interests and ideologies, the relative intensity of the two sources of conflict, and their relative impact on future interactions between the parties. Another issue concerns the conditions that produce cooperative versus competitive bargaining processes and the implications of these processes for the long-term relationship between the parties. A third issue deals with the relative importance of the two sources of conflict in the resolution process. Preliminary findings suggest that the relative emphasis placed on one or the other type of conflict depends on the issue area or institutional context within which the conflicts occur: for example, ideologies are important in areas where policy issues are still in dispute and programs have yet to be institutionalized; interests are emphasized more in areas where policies have been established (Druckman *et al.*, 1977). And, finally, it would be useful to conduct case studies that parallel the experiments. Serving to document the interplay between these conflicts as they occur in real-world situations, the case studies would provide a basis for evaluating the generality of the experimental findings. (An example is provided by the Druckman and Green, 1990, study of regime—insurgent negotiations in the Philippines.)

Ideological differences add a competitive dimension to conflicts caused by differences of understanding. Results obtained from a cognitive conflict experiment showed that when the differences were viewed in ideological terms – as a difference between social-change and system-maintenance perspectives – the conflict was more difficult to resolve than when the differences were only matters of understanding (Druckman, 1970). Further analyses conducted recently elucidate some differences in perceptions between the conditions. Subjects who viewed the conflict in ideological terms also perceived the bargaining process as being more like an arms race, and this perception correlated with their being less willing to compromise, viewing their opponent as being less willing to compromise, and being less satisfied with the outcome. The 'arms-race' metaphor (discovered from answers to questions about similarity to other situations) illustrates the importance of 'mental models' in the negotiation process. Some models, or analogies, may lead subjects to cooperate in seeking an agreement; others may lead them to compete for advantage. We need to learn more about the way such imagery influences conflict behavior, leading toward or away from satisfactory resolutions. This would seem to be a fruitful line of work to be placed on our research agenda.

Processes of conflict

The two processes receiving the most attention in the experimental literature on conflict are bargaining and debate. The bargaining process has been construed in terms of concession making: Most of the experimentation has concentrated on factors that influence the amount and rate of concessions made by bargainers. The process of debate has emphasized the role of verbal behavior and persuasion in negotiation. The research has focused on the way negotiators communicate or disguise their intentions and the arguments used to influence the other's positions. Each of these processes is discussed in turn.

Bargaining

Stimulated by the early research conducted by Siegel and Fouraker (1960), investigators have concentrated on discovering a 'best' concession-making strategy. Does it pay to be tough, soft, or have a mix of these strategies? The answer is that it depends on a number of factors in the situation: A bargainer's concession strategy is one of several influences on the other's concessions; it interacts with such variables as time pressures, the initial offer, perceived relative defensibility of positions, perceived similarity between bargaining opponents, and the pressures of being a representative. (See Druckman, 1971b, for a review of the evidence.) But, responding to another's moves is unlikely to be automatic, as in tit-for-tat. It is a more complex process involving expectations, evaluations, and adjustments (Coddington, 1968; Druckman, 1977b). Such cognitive processes accompanying bargaining moves have been the focus of recent research.

The information-processing aspects of bargaining are highlighted in the research on responsiveness. Bargainers compare their own concessions to those made by their opponent, a process referred to as the monitoring function in negotiation (Druckman, 1978). Referred to as 'threshold-adjustment', the monitoring leads to decisions to alter one's pattern usually in the direction – either tougher or softer – of the other's concessions: The largest adjustments occur when there is a noticeable discrepancy between one's own and the other's concession pattern. This form of responsiveness has been shown to depict a variety of international negotiations (Druckman and Harris, 1990) and can lead either to impasses (Druckman, 1986) or agreements (Hopmann and King, 1976) depending on the direction of the adjustment.

Further implications for a theory of responsiveness come from the literature on cognitive social psychology. The central idea in that literature is that responses derive from attributions about why the other behaves as he or she does. (See Druckman, 1990, for a review.) Three questions in particular would guide future research: (a) How do bargainers use the other's moves to infer intentions about the kind of 'game' (cooperative or competitive) the other is playing? (b) What variables, in addition to his or her moves, influence these attributions? (c) How does one's attributions of the other's intentions affect one's own moves or tactics? These questions can be refined by adding the dimension of time. The attributional process may evolve during the course of a negotiation, having different implications for decisions at different junctures: When does a bargainer have sufficient information to infer intentions? At which point(s) in the process do the inferred intentions lead one to change one's strategy? Answers to these questions would contribute to a more differentiated conception of negotiation than currently exists. They would distinguish between types of information processing that occur during different stages of an extended process.

Debating

The debate aspects of negotiation are captured by content-analysis codings of the 'give-and-take' exchanges. The coding systems have evolved from those designed to analyze problem-solving behavior in small groups (Bales, 1950; Landsberger, 1955) to those intended to capture processes that occur in negotiations (Walcott *et al.*, 1977). The value of these systems is evidenced by findings obtained in a variety of case studies, including the Partial Test-Ban talks (Hopmann and Smith, 1977), the Seabed Arms Control negotiations (Hopmann, 1974), the Mutual and Balanced Force Reductions talks (see Druckman and Hopmann, 1989), and the military base-rights negotiations between Spain and the United States (Druckman, 1986). Contributions have also been made to understanding relationships between process and outcome as these vary in repeated runs of simulation experiments (Zechmeister and Druckman, 1973; Hopmann and Walcott, 1977).

Content analysis has been used to evaluate techniques designed to increase understanding of the other's positions in order to produce better outcomes. The approach receiving the most attention is role-reversing exercises where opposing negotiators learn to distinguish between similarities and differences in their positions and interests (Rapoport, 1960). Three conclusions from these evaluations are that, (a) most applications of role reversal increase understanding but do not result in better outcomes (Hammond *et al.*, 1966; Druckman, 1968; Muney and Deutsch, 1968), (b) effectiveness is enhanced if the techniques are executed accurately, if compromises are proposed during the exercise, and if participants perceive the interactions as being 'warm' (Johnson, 1971), and (c) the increased understanding achieved may reveal certain incompatibilities that reduce the chances of achieving agreements (Johnson, 1967). King's (1976) attempt to document role reversal in the extended debate of an international negotiation showed that it occurred infrequently due, apparently, to the competitive postures taken by the national representatives. Another avenue is to use the content-analysis techniques to distinguish between problem-solving and competitive behaviors that occur during the debate, gauging the impact of these behaviors on the outcome, and identifying aspects in the situation that influence the frequency of the one or the other type of rhetoric. Rather than concentrating on a particular technique, this approach would identify various factors that encourage either cooperative or competitive postures that have implications for outcomes as agreements or impasses (McGillicuddy *et al.*, 1987).

The progress made to date suggests several paths for further work. One path is the merging of new conceptions of the negotiating process with new coding systems. The systems should capture the way negotiators develop packages of issues, the discussions leading to the forming of coalitions in multilateral conferences, and the way that organizational structures are reflected in the negotiating process. The systems should also reflect the substantive complexity of negotiations, including subtle meanings communicated between the parties, and be able to distinguish between critical events or turning points and events of less consequence.

Another path is further development of the theories upon which the coding categories are based. A step in this direction was taken by Hopmann and Walcott in their work on Bargaining Process Analysis. The categories for coding verbal behavior are defined on the basis of theoretical conceptions of the negotiating process, from theories of influence to theories of small-group dynamics. New applications to real-world transcripts will aid in the refining of the methodology, but this should be done within a tradition that highlights theoretical perspectives. Methods have, to date, outpaced theory and many perspectives are put forth without the accompanying empirical work. Future research should reflect a self-conscious merging of theory and method.

Influences on conflict

By 'influences on conflict' we refer to the distinction made between person, role, and situational variables. Of all the issues raised by social psychologists, none is more central to the discipline than the relative importance of these factors as determinants of behavior. Of all the settings in which this issue has been explored, none is more relevant than negotiation. Negotiators are individuals, they usually represent constituencies, and their behavior is influenced by the negotiating situation. The negotiation literature has addressed this issue. Key findings and research issues are summarized in this section.

Person variables

The idea of person by situation interactions pervades the literatures of personality and social psychology. The research on this subject has yet to produce clear results on the way that these factors interact. One approach construes the issue in terms of moderating and enhancing effects of the situation on such person variables as attitudes, values, or cultural styles (Druckman, 1971b). Contrast, for example, (a) situations where negotiators can choose between alternative strategies each leading to the same outcome, or the very early phases of an interaction before negotiators become familiar with the 'rules of the game', with (b) situations where certain strategies are particularly salient, or the later phases of an interaction when structural aspects of the situation overtake any initial differences between persons or cultures. Person variables are likely to have less impact on conflict behavior in the latter situations. They are also likely to have limited impact in threatening or stressful situations or when roles have clearly prescribed obligations. Thus, while some situations moderate the impact of these variables, other situations (as noted above) can enhance their impact. Or, they may appear as influences on behavior in subtle, non-obvious ways (Druckman, 1977b).

Several studies suggest that culture is an important influence on behavior. (See Chapter 9 by Avruch and Black in this volume.) However, we have not accumulated enough empirical studies to claim that culture is the primary determinant of conflict behavior. Nor have we developed a conceptualization that would guide research toward an understanding of complex interactions between the enduring and changing aspects of culture. Whelen's (1979) study of Soviet diplomacy is a start. His cultural imperatives are broad constraints within which a wide range of diplomatic behaviors can occur. Negotiating behavior is sensitive to circumstances and historical time periods that are themselves shaped by traditions, ideologies, and institutions. Many possibilities exist in any culture; which is chosen depends on the situation. Clues to the motives for particular moves are to be found in the interplay between the enduring (cultural) and changing (situational) aspects of diplomacy (see also Druckman and Hopmann, 1989). This is a fertile area for research.

Role obligations

Systematic analytical work has identified a number of components of the representative's role, showing strong effects on conflict behavior. Further work would examine the relative importance of these components as well as extend the range of variation in the definitions of them. Examples of research issues are the following: extent of accountability to constituents versus the amount of latitude in decision-making; differing amounts of responsibility for the outcome, comparing sole versus shared responsibility and equal versus unequal responsibility among teammates, and the effects of different types of constituencies on negotiating behavior (teammates, interest groups, organizations, nations, abstract ideologies).

An important concept is the boundary role conflict, which refers to the competing demands made by one's own and other parties as well as the demands on negotiators made by multiple constituencies and opponents as these align and realign in the context of shifting coalitions in multilateral conferences (Walton and McKersie, 1965; Druckman, 1977b). An interesting research issue concerns the advantages and disadvantages of involving constituents (those who delegate authority to negotiators) in the negotiation process. On the one hand, involving constituents makes it easier to 'sell' the outcome; on the other hand, not involving them may make it easier to achieve an agreement. Concession-making is easier in private but harder to sell to constituents kept out of the process that led to decisions to make the concessions. These competing hypotheses can be subjected to experimental evaluation.

Situational influences

We refer here to aspects of the situation other than those that define a negotiating representative's role. Effects of many aspects can be evaluated through experiments. The following are some of the variables that have received attention in the literature to date.

(a) Prenegotiation experience: the way that negotiators prepare for a negotiation has been shown to influence the process and outcomes. Earlier work separated the way bargainers prepared for a negotiation from whether they discussed the issues with opponents (Bass, 1966; Druckman, 1968). The importance of the prenegotiation phase is emphasized in recent case studies of international negotiations − as processes for 'getting to the table' (Stein, 1989). On the other hand, these processes have been conceived as 'workshops' for resolving conflicts without formal negotiation (Rothman, 1990).

(b) Communication opportunities: the physical arrangement of parties during negotiation has been shown to contribute to the intensity of the conflict. Separating opponents fosters competitiveness detrimental to achieving agreements. For example, negotiating over a 'hot line' is unlikely to lead to agreements. Seeing and hearing an opponent is conducive to agreement, with hearing being more important than seeing (Wichman, 1970). Practical implications have been developed in the context of the debate over a hot line between the superpowers: videotape is best, followed by telephone and, worst of all, teletype or fax. Further work might explore the issue of what it is about isolation that is detrimental to reaching agreements.

(c) Tactics: as situational influences, we are interested in the other's use of tactics on a negotiator's behavior. Examples are commitments (placing the burden of concession-making on the other), casuistry (creating the perception of benefits for the other who has offered a concession), saving face, and manipulating concession rates. One issue is how to distinguish between moves that are tactical or manipulative from those intended to communicate actual positions. Another issue is the consequences of asymmetrical versus symmetrical use of these tactics: Does the former lead to one-sided agreements, the latter to deadlocks?

(d) Incentives: high stakes may lead negotiators to define the situation as one requiring collusive-type cooperation (to gain large joint payoffs); low stakes may lead them to define the situation as game-like competition where winning is the goal. The way a negotiation is framed may suggest a particular orientation similar to the effects of alternative instructions used to introduce laboratory bargaining games (Druckman, 1971b).

(e) Time pressures: deadlines have been shown to produce powerful end-effects − a rush to agreement. They present negotiators with a decision dilemma such that they must choose between getting an agreement or settling for their alternative. Further research could explore ways in which time pressures bring about the decision dilemma, analyzing when it occurs and how it is resolved. (Note the distinction between negotiations that are time-sensitive and those where time is irrelevant as in negotiating for 'side-effects'.)

(f) Structural complexity: multilateral negotiations are complex, requiring careful monitoring for tracking progress. Similarly, multi-layered delegations require monitoring as disagreements occur both within and between delegations. Suggested research might concentrate on coalition-building, examining the ways that various cross-cutting cleavages among factions within delegations serve to produce agreement both within (for positions) and between (for treaties) delegations. (See Evan and MacDougall, 1967, for an example of the use of simulation to explore issues of cleavages within and between parties.)

The context for conflict

By 'context' we refer both to broad systemic influences and to more immediate interventions in conflict by third parties. Systemic influences are the domestic, regional, and international politics surrounding a negotiation. Each of these levels suggests issues that can be addressed by research. Intervention is treated as part of the context for conflict. Placing the disputants' behavior at the center of our attention, the mediator is construed in this framework as being one of several 'external' factors affecting their attempts to resolve the conflict. The wide variety of intervention approaches suggests a long agenda of research issues.

Domestic, regional, and international politics

From a conflict-resolution perspective, a key issue of domestic politics is under what conditions are disputes between powerholders and challengers settled through peaceful means. One research question is under what conditions will opposition groups (including insurgencies) negotiate with government leaders? Another question concerns the effects of domestic constituencies on representatives' negotiating postures: Under what conditions do constituent demands decrease bargaining flexibility and when do they encourage flexible negotiating behavior?

In regional politics, key issues concern negotiation processes and ongoing relationships between neighboring countries. Hypotheses about differences in negotiation processes between *cooperative* (attempts are made to resolve cognitive conflicts), *competitive* (attempts are made to adjust the balance of power), and *transforming* (attempts are made to confront differences in values) systems have been suggested (Druckman, 1980). These hypothesized connections between structure and process can be tested in the context of negotiations within such regional organizations as the Association of Southeast Asian Nations (ASEAN), the Caribbean Community (CARICOM), the European Community (EC), the Organization of African Unity (OAU), and the Organization of American States (OAS). International politics are intertwined with negotiation processes. Of particular interest are relationships between events outside negotiations and interaction within negotiations.

35

What are some effects of cooperative or competitive exchanges between national leaders on moves made in negotiations between national representatives? What are the effects of agreements or impasses in negotiations on events in the international system? We have only begun to explore these questions with codes of soft and tough negotiating behavior and codes of cooperative or competitive events data in the area of arms control (Hopmann and Smith, 1977; Hopmann and Walcott, 1977). These issues have implications for the issue of whether negotiations are a microcosm of international politics or should be treated as distinct analytical processes.

The resolution of conflicts in complex settings turns on the relationship between structures (e.g., types of regional systems) and behaviors (e.g., soft or hard bargaining). Foremost among our concerns are the structural bases for change in strategy from a competitive (negotiations over redistribution) to a cooperative orientation where parties attempt to develop a new relationship through problem-solving (innovation negotiations). This issue can be explored with data from diverse cases, varying in terms of structural dimensions.

Third-party intervention

This topic covers a wide array of approaches, ranging from traditional mediation or arbitration to problem-solving workshops. We have a better conceptual understanding of these approaches than an understanding based on empirical analysis. The considerable body of writing and teaching on the subject includes only a small number of experimental studies among which there are even fewer designed to identify the underlying mechanisms responsible for observed effects caused by the interventions. (See Fisher's 1983 survey, where he concludes that of the thirty-seven studies reviewed only five used control-group designs.) The conceptual progress made to date can serve as a framework that organizes the needed research.

One relevant distinction among approaches is between those intended to alter the psychology of relationships and those that produce convergence on issues through a bargaining process. The former include attempts to change perceptions of actors and situations; they also include programs dealing with the underlying sources of conflict. The latter treat conflict as a game which can be altered through technical manipulations of processes and procedures. A challenge posed by this approach is to determine just when to intervene in order to produce desired effects. Both types of intervention can occur at the prenegotiation, negotiation, or postnegotiation stages of a conflict. Issues raised at each of these stages can be clarified by research. A sampling of those issues follows.

Many of the prenegotiation interventions focus on building relationships that can be sustained over the long term. Getting the parties to the table is one goal (Stein, 1989); resolving conflicts without negotiation is another (Rothman, 1990). Research issues concern discovering procedures that increase trust, liking, and familiarity between the parties; for example: What is the relative importance of positive sentiments and enhanced understanding of the other's positions for willingness to compromise? (Druckman and Broome, 1991). What are the conditions that lead to cooperative or competitive processes and how do these relate to short- and long-term outcomes? (Druckman *et al.*, 1988). Other interventions at the prenegotiation stage emphasize propitious circumstances or ripe moments for negotiation (Zartman, 1986). The key issue is how to identify these moments to prevent missed opportunities. What are the indicators in process or relationship that would encourage parties to seize the moment?

Issues concerning intervention during the negotiation process raise the following research issues: What are the conditions under which requests for third-party help are made? What are the differences between various forms of process mediation such as passive, active, and educational interventions? What are the differences between various forms of content mediation such as facilitating concessions, altering limits, and releasing parties from commitments? What are the differences between alternative tactics such as conducting shuttle diplomacy or joint sessions? What are some differences between alternative third-party styles, such as being appropriately assertive or giving the appearance of neutrality? (See also Pruitt's 1981 discussion of these issues.)

With regard to postnegotiation processes, research has focused on issues surrounding the anticipation of intervention. For example, what are the conditions for 'chilling' and 'hastening' − that is, discouraging or encouraging concessions − effects of anticipating later intervention? Differences between binding arbitration and final-offer arbitration by package or by issue are likely to have different effects on concession-making (Schellenberg and Druckman, 1986). Under certain conditions, bargainers may actually favor an arbitrated solution: For example, if they fear looking weak by conceding, if they expect a split-the-difference solution, if they are familiar with the arbitrator or with his or her procedures, if they choose the arbitrator. Disputants do not like to have their fate taken out of their hands, except when they have reason to believe that it will be a better decision as in the circumstances noted above. On the other hand, the threat of arbitration will hasten concession making when bargainers fear a biased or less-favorable decision. While some progress has been made on these issues, the work to date has not probed sufficiently for underlying mechanisms that cause the observed chilling or hastening effects of the interventions (e.g., McGillicuddy *et al.*, 1987).

Conclusions

The issues discussed in this chapter form the basis for an analytical research agenda. That agenda consists of next steps in the accumulation of knowledge about the external (influences and context) and internal (structure and processes) aspects of conflict. The knowledge has consisted of findings from experimental studies or from the systematic analysis of cases. Continuing in this methodological tradition, results from the suggested studies will enlarge our understanding of each part of the framework. They are less likely to contribute to the larger task of synthesizing diverse findings toward a larger model of conflict. The agenda of research projects includes both further analytical work and attempts at synthesis. These projects are summarized as follows.

Structure of conflict

Much remains to be learned about the way that different sources of conflict interact over time and in various policy-making contexts. One task consists of determining the relative importance of ideological differences and conflicting interests as these occur in different issue areas. Another consists of examining the interplay between these sources of conflict through time; for example, how unresolved conflicts of interest can lead to polarized ideologies between groups, and how converging ideologies within groups can produce increased conflict between groups. A third research issue would address the impact of 'mental models' or analogies aroused by certain dimensions of a conflict situation on conflict reduction or intensification.

Processes of conflict

The role of information processing in bargaining needs to be clarified: for example, how intentions are inferred from the other's moves or other information available to a bargainer, how the attributed intentions affect the bargainer's own moves, and how these thought processes change through time with new information. Further work is also needed on ways to encourage problem-solving behavior in competitive bargaining situations. An understanding of the way that debate and bargaining processes interact to produce outcomes would contribute to that task; for example, intervening early when issues are being defined through debate, and before bargaining occurs, may prove to be effective.

Influences on conflict

Four issues would benefit from further research. One concerns an understanding of the enhancing and moderating effects of the situation on the expression of person variables. Another consists of developing a conception of cultural influences that separates its enduring from its changing aspects as these impact on negotiating behavior. A third project would examine the impact of constituents on the negotiating process; for example, when to keep them at a distance and when to involve them in the 'give-and-take' discussions. And a fourth area of interest would analyze the relative effects of different aspects of the conflict situation: Which situational variables have the strongest impact on flexibility at different stages of the process?

Two broad themes are treated in the section on context. One concerns the ways that external factors (structures or events) impact on internal processes: Emphasized in this research agenda are the way that broader relationships between conflicting parties are reflected in the process and the way that domestic conflicts between groups that differ in power can be managed to prevent civil wars. The other theme concerns third-party intervention. When and how to intervene are challenges that suggest distinctions between stages of an extended process (prenegotiation, negotiation, and postnegotiation process) as well as between interventions designed to alter the psychology of relationships or to produce convergence in a bargaining process. Equally important is the challenge of identifying the underlying mechanisms responsible for observed effects of the interventions.

The parts of the framework are presented as analytical categories for organizing research. They reflect the distinction between processes (issues, bargaining, debating) and influences (immediate situation, broader context) on the one hand, and between external and internal factors on the other. As such, they are *interacting* variables during the course of a conflict or negotiation. A more sophisticated version of the framework would be a model of the way these parts interact in determining the outcome of diverse cases. It would build on the earlier synthetic work of Sawyer and Guetzkow (1965), whose model of the interacting elements of negotiation served to guide empirical studies (Bonham, 1971; Ramberg, 1977; Druckman, 1977a). Whether these models also capture resolution processes other than negotiation remains to be determined.

References

Axelrod, R. (1970), *Conflict of Interest*, Markham, Chicago.
Bales, R. F. (1950), *Interaction Process Analysis: A Method for the Study of Small Groups*, Addison-Wesley, Reading, Massachusetts.
Bass, B. M. (1966), 'Effects on the subsequent performance of negotiators of studying issues or planning strategies alone or in groups', *Psychological Monographs*, Whole No. 614.
Bonham, G. M. (1971), 'Simulating international disarmament negotiations', *Journal of Conflict Resolution*, 15, pp. 299–315.
Brehmer, B. and Hammond, K. R. (1977), 'Cognitive factors in interpersonal conflict', in D. Druckman, ed., *Negotiations: Social-Psychological Perspectives*, Sage, Beverly Hills, California.
Coddington, A. (1968), *Theories of the Bargaining Process*, Aldine, Chicago.
Coser, L. (1956), *The Functions of Social Conflict*, The Free Press, New York.
Deutsch, M., Canavan, D., and Rubin, J. (1971), 'The effects of size of conflict and sex of experimenter upon interpersonal bargaining', *Journal of Experimental Social Psychology*, 7, pp. 258–267.
Druckman, D. (1968), 'Prenegotiation experience and dyadic conflict resolution in a bargaining situation', *Journal of Experimental Social Psychology*, 4, pp. 367–383.

Druckman, D. (1970), 'Position change in cognitive conflict as a function of the cue-criterion relationship and the initial conflict', *Psychonomic Science*, 20, 91–93.

Druckman, D. (1971a), 'Understanding the operation of complex social systems: Some uses of simulation design', *Simulation and Games*, 2, 173–195.

Druckman, D. (1971b), 'The influence of the situation in interparty conflict', *Journal of Conflict Resolution*, 15, pp. 523–554.

Druckman, D. (ed.) (1977a), *Negotiations: Social-Psychological Perspectives*, Sage, Beverly Hills, California.

Druckman, D. (1977b), 'Boundary role conflict: Negotiation as dual responsiveness', *Journal of Conflict Resolution*, 21, pp. 639–662.

Druckman, D. (1978), 'The monitoring function in negotiation: Two models of responsiveness', in H. Sauermann, ed., *Contributions to Experimental Economics: Bargaining Behavior*, J.C.B. Mohr, Tübingen, Germany.

Druckman, D. (1980), 'Social-psychological factors in regional politics', in W.J. Feld and G. Boyd, eds, *Comparative Regional Systems*, Pergamon, New York.

Druckman, D. (1986), 'Stages, turning points, and crises: Negotiating military base-rights, Spain and the United States', *Journal of Conflict Resolution*, 30, pp. 327–360.

Druckman, D. (1990), 'The social psychology of arms control and reciprocation', *Political Psychology*, 11, pp. 553–581.

Druckman, D. and Broome, B.J. (1991), 'Value differences and conflict resolution: Familiarity or liking?', *Journal of Conflict Resolution*, 35, pp. 571–593.

Druckman, D. and Green, J. (1990), 'Playing two games: Internal negotiations in the Philippines'. Paper prepared for the project on Internal Security Negotiations, Paul H. Nitze School of Advanced International Studies, Johns Hopkins University.

Druckman, D. and Harris, R. (1990), 'Alternative models of responsiveness in international negotiation', *Journal of Conflict Resolution*, 34, 234–251.

Druckman, D. and Hopmann, P.T. (1989), 'Behavioral aspects of mutual security negotiations', in P. Tetlock *et al.*, eds, *Behavior, Society, and Nuclear War*, Oxford University Press, New York.

Druckman, D. and Zechmeister, K. (1970), 'Conflict of interest and value dissensus', *Human Relations*, 23, pp. 431–438.

Druckman, D., Broome, B., and Korper, S. (1988), 'Value differences and conflict resolution: Facilitation or delinking?', *Journal of Conflict Resolution*, 32, pp. 489–510.

Druckman, D., Rozelle, R., and Zechmeister, K. (1977), 'Conflict of interest and value dissensus: Two perspectives', in D. Druckman, ed., *Negotiations: Social-Psychological Perspectives*, Sage, Beverly Hills, California.

Druckman, D., Rozelle, R., Krause, R., and Mahoney, R. (1974), 'Power and utilities in a simulated interreligious council: A situational approach to interparty conflict', in J. Tedeschi, ed., *Perspectives on Social Power*, Aldine, Chicago.

Evan, W.M. and MacDougall, J.A. (1967), 'Interorganizational conflict: A labor-management bargaining experiment', *Journal of Conflict Resolution*, 11, pp. 398–413.

Fisher, R.J. (1983), 'Third party consultation as a method of interparty conflict resolution: A review of studies', *Journal of Conflict Resolution*, 27, pp. 301–334.

Hammond, K.R. (1965), 'New directions in research on conflict resolution', *Journal of Social Issues*, 11, pp. 44–66.

Hammond, K. R. and Brehmer, B. (1973), 'Quasi-rationality and distrust: Implications for international conflict', in L. Rappoport and D. A. Summers, eds, *Human Judgment and Social Interaction*, Holt, Rinehart, and Winston, New York.

Hammond, K. R., Todd, F. J., Wilkins, M., and Mitchell, T. O. (1966), 'Cognitive conflict between persons: Application of the "lens model" paradigm', *Journal of Experimental Social Psychology*, 12, pp. 343–360.

Hopmann, P. T. (1974), 'Bargaining in arms control negotiations: The Seabeds Denuclearization Treaty', *International Organization*, 28, pp. 313–343.

Hopmann, P. T. and King, T. D. (1976), 'Interaction and perceptions in the test-ban negotiations', *International Studies Quarterly*, 20, pp. 105–142.

Hopmann, P. T. and Smith, T. C. (1977), 'An application of a Richardson process model: Soviet-American interactions in the test-ban negotiations, 1962–1963', *Journal of Conflict Resolution*, 21, pp. 701–726.

Hopmann, P. T. and Walcott, C. (1977), 'The impact of external stresses and tensions on negotiations', in D. Druckman, ed., *Negotiations: Social-Psychological Perspectives*, Sage, Beverly Hills, California.

Johnson, D. W. (1971), 'Effects of warmth of interaction, accuracy of understanding, and the proposal of compromises on listener's behavior', *Journal of Counseling Psychology*, 18, pp. 207–216.

Johnson, D. W. (1967), 'The use of role reversal in intergroup competition', *Journal of Personality and Social Psychology*, 7, pp. 135–42.

King, T. D. (1976), 'Role reversal debates in international negotiations: The partial test-ban case'. Paper presented at the annual meeting of the International Studies Association, Toronto.

Landsberger, H. A. (1955), 'Interaction process analysis of the mediation of labor-management disputes', *Journal of Abnormal and Social Psychology*, 51, pp. 552–559.

McGillicuddy, N. B., Welton, G. L., and Pruitt, D. G. (1987), 'Third-party intervention: A field experiment comparing three models', *Journal of Personality and Social Psychology*, 53, pp. 104–112.

Muney, B. F. and Deutsch, M. (1968), 'The effects of role reversal during the discussion of opposing viewpoints', *Journal of Conflict Resolution*, 12, pp. 345–356.

Ozawa, C. P. and Susskind, L. (1985), 'Mediating science-intensive policy disputes', *Journal of Policy Analysis and Management*, 5, 23–29.

Pruitt, D. G. (1981), *Negotiation Behavior*, Academic Press, New York.

Ramberg, B. (1977), 'Tactical advantages of opening positioning strategies: Lessons from the Seabeds Arms Control Talks, 1967–1970', *Journal of Conflict Resolution*, 21, pp. 685–700.

Rapoport, A. (1960), *Fights, Games, and Debates*, University of Michigan Press, Ann Arbor.

Rappoport, L. (1965), 'Interpersonal conflict in non-competitive and uncertain situations', *Journal of Experimental Social Psychology*, 1, pp. 323–333.

Rothman, J. (1990), 'A prenegotiation model: Theory and testing', Policy Studies No. 40, The Leonard Davis Institute for International Relations, The Hebrew University of Jerusalem.

Sawyer, J. and Guetzkow, H. (1965), 'Bargaining and negotiation in international relations', in H. C. Kelman, ed., *International Behavior: A Social-Psychological Analysis*, Holt, Rinehart, and Winston, New York.

Daniel Druckman

Schellenberg, J. A. and Druckman, D. (1986), 'Bargaining and gaming', *Society*, 23, pp. 65–71.

Siegel, S. and Fouraker, L. E. (1960), *Bargaining and Group Decision Making: Experiments in Bilateral Monopoly*, McGraw-Hill, New York.

Simmel, G. (1955), *Conflict and the Web of Group Affiliations*, The Free Press, Glencoe, Illinois.

Stein, J. G. (ed.) (1989), *Getting to the Table*, Johns Hopkins University Press, Baltimore.

Summers, D. A. (1968), 'Conflict, compromise, and belief change in a decision making task', *Journal of Conflict Resolution*, 12, pp. 215–221.

Thibaut, J. (1968), 'The development of contractual norms in bargaining: Replication and variation', *Journal of Conflict Resolution*, 12, pp. 102–112.

Walcott, C., Hopmann, P. T., and King, T. D. (1977), 'The role of debate in negotiation', in D. Druckman, ed., *Negotiations: Social-Psychological Perspectives*, Sage, Beverly Hills, California.

Walton, R. E. and McKersie, R. B. (1965), *A Behavioral Theory of Labor Negotiations*, McGraw-Hill, New York.

Whelen, J. G. (1979), *Soviet Diplomacy and Negotiating Behavior: Emerging New Context for U.S. Diplomacy*, U.S. Government Printing Office, Washington, D.C.

Wichman, H. (1970), 'Effects of isolation and communication in a two-person game', *Journal of Personality and Social Psychology*, 16, pp. 114–120.

Zartman, I. W. (1986), 'Ripening conflict, ripe moment, formula, and mediation', in D. B. Bendahmane and J. W. McDonald, eds, *Perspectives on Negotiation: Four Case Studies and Interpretations*, Foreign Service Institute, U.S. Department of State, U.S. Government Printing Office, Washington, D.C.

Zechmeister, K. and Druckman, D. (1973), 'Determinants of resolving a conflict of interest: A simulation of political decision making', *Journal of Conflict Resolution*, 17, pp. 63–88.

3   *Mary E. Clark*

Symptoms of cultural pathologies:
A hypothesis[1]

Let me begin with an observation on a society whose people, according to present Western social thinking, *should* be experiencing a sense of ongoing improvement in their lives. The country is one of those widely proclaimed as an 'economic miracle' – South Korea:

'There is nothing in it for us', Lee So Sun answered without hesitation when we asked her what benefits high-speed industrialization had brought to Korean workers. Her conviction was founded on painful experience. In November 1970, her son Jeon Tae-Il, a pioneering organizer of garment workers in Seoul, set himself on fire with the cry, 'Do not mistreat the young girls'.

Jeon's fiery gesture touched off an extraordinarily energetic and heroic effort to organize Korea's working class. His mother picked up Jeon's banner and endured arrests and repeated jailings to become the symbol of the determination of Korean labor. When Korean workers launched over 7,000 strikes between 1987 and 1990 – or 6.5 per day, probably a world record for a labor force the size of Korea's – they were carrying on Jeon's heroic tradition. When thousands of workers armed with Molotov cocktails battled 10,000 riot policemen for control of the strategic Hyundai shipyard in Ulsan in late April 1990, they were affirming Jeon's uncompromising stance.

Korea's workers are the secret of their country's so called 'economic miracle'. They work an average of 54 hours a week, the longest of any country surveyed by the International Labor Organization. They also suffer the world's highest rate of industrial accidents, with an average of five workers killed daily and another 390 injured. This record of exploitation produced a sizzling nine percent GNP growth rate in the 1980s, but it also resulted in a worsening distribution of income and wealth, as the top 20 percent of the population cornered almost 44 percent of the national income and a minuscule five percent monopolized 65 percent of all private land-holdings nationwide.

The wave of insurrectionary strikes since the summer of 1987, when popular pressure forced an easing of repression, has put South Korea's rulers and the huge conglomerates or *chaebol* that control the Korean economy on notice that labor demands its share of the economic miracle and will no longer tolerate a pattern of high growth achieved through harsh exploitation (Bello and Rosenfeld, 1990).[2]

43

Why has this supposed 'model for the future' gone sour, creating massive social discontent in a country whose political, economic, and cultural futures have all become highly uncertain, made newly vulnerable to forces far beyond the control of ordinary people? The promised 'miracle' has become, instead, disempowerment and a loss of traditional patterns of living that, if not materially lush, provided stability and meaning to people's lives. The newly installed institutions have brought disillusionment, alienation, and violence; in short, they are *pathological*.

Nor is South Korea the only place where attempts to replace old social patterns with new ones — often prescribed from outside — have led to social chaos. It recurs, in various forms, throughout the Third World, which has been rife with local eruptions of violence. But this kind of social alienation is by no means limited to 'developing' nations; it occurs increasingly in many 'rich' countries of the North, where an ever-growing fraction of the population is being excluded from meaningful economic, political, and cultural participation. And even those still in the 'mainstream' often find their lives less and less meaningful. Throughout rich societies, we see growing social unrest, in the forms of family violence, child abuse, drugs, crime, street gangs, and other forms of disruptive behaviors that are consuming more and more of the total social energy for dealing with them. A form of institutionalized disempowerment is gradually encircling the planet and is inimical to the biologically grounded psychic needs of the human animal. It is this notion of a pathological social environment, arising out of cultural deficiency, that I wish to explore.

For the moment, I can only outline the task. This job will require creative work in two areas: (1) formation of a general theory of the attributes of psychologically healthy societies, and (2) an analysis of the processes of cultural change and evolution. In the remainder of this chapter, I propose briefly to examine the components comprised by such a general theory, and its consequences for the field of conflict resolution.

Components of a theory of healthy societies

My hypothesis comprises at least three important concepts about culture: (1) how we 'think'; (2) what we 'need'; and (3) how we 'adapt'. These build, one upon the other.

Worldviews: The basis of cultures

How we 'think' — in terms of biochemical phenomena in the brain — is no doubt uniform from culture to culture, but what we think about, is clearly not. It is now widely agreed that cognition involves the internal mapping of external information, and this mapping process is an abstraction. Since we cannot possibly deal with *all* the information impinging upon our senses, we necessarily *select* what we choose to store. From this selective process, over time, we build up an *interpretation* of our environment. This whole process is deeply affected by what our environment, and particularly our culture, tells us it is important to notice. This means that the *same, identical* set of information will be interpreted and stored differently by persons from different cultures. None is necessarily 'wrong' in any scientific sense; each holds part of what is 'out there' in reality, but they are different snapshots of that reality, emphasizing different parts of it, and valuing those parts in different degrees.

Here I wish to propose two central propositions concerning our worldview, both of which may be regarded as somewhat speculative. First, one becomes emotionally attached to one's worldview. Our inner world *is* our reality, and to have that reality questioned is enormously threatening. Being 'right' is not so much a matter of winning or losing a dispute, but of maintaining one's sense of security in a strange place. If the world is not what I think it is, then I am lost. Thus, changing worldviews is *not* something that people undertake lightly. Furthermore, out of our worldviews, all of our shared social institutions emerge and are legitimized; changing the worldview of an entire culture means changing all the expected patterns of daily personal interaction and all the institutions that make up social life.

Second, not *all* worldviews are equally adaptive. The information excerpted, and the way that selected information is interpreted may, in fact, lead either to destruction of the natural environment or to the destruction of the social fabric; in some cases, both are endangered, but here we are focusing mainly on social disruption. When a worldview generates social pathologies of the sort that were mentioned at the outset, we get a combination of centrifugal alienation and violence, on the one hand, and of authoritarian coercion on the other. Eventually, the system collapses under its self-created overheads.

Obviously we have a difficult dilemma here. If worldviews, even those causing cultural pathologies, are difficult to change, then how can we ever correct them? This may be the central question for our species if it is to survive into the future. Of course, cultural paradigms are *always* changing, but throughout most of the past, the *rate* of change was such that adjustments to shared visions of reality were barely perceived, and were soon embodied into the traditional myths as though they had always existed. But the rate of change that may be necessary for the pathological cultures of today, if we are to avoid widespread suffering and violence, is of a different order of magnitude. We need a new process for cultural rethinking, and that is the purpose of the general theory being addressed here.

Identifying 'healthy' worldviews

Clearly, this brings us to the task of identifying what a 'healthy' worldview consists of. It must be simultaneously adaptive to the natural environment on which all cultures ultimately depend, and it must meet certain needs within the human psyche. The latter is the more difficult to assess, and the tendency

45

has been to try to apply Western psychological theory in defining this aspect of human needs. This is likely, however, to be a too narrow, and perhaps even a mistaken, approach. Western psychological theory has largely been developed from observations of Western individuals, whose culture exhibits many of the pathological institutions that we have been discussing. Yet that theory has seldom if ever looked at the *culture* as the source of 'deviant' or 'anti-social' behavior, instead attempting to analyze the problem at the level of the individual alone. And even if we identify a particular culture that *can* be categorized as 'healthy', there is no reason to suppose it would be unique in being able to satisfy human needs. Thus, we need to seek a broader, more inclusive set of criteria, one that permits us an external reference point that can be used to assess all cultures – and for this we can turn to biology.

Here we have a major source of evidence in recent studies carried out on other social primates. For a long time, behaviorists and sociobiologists studied primates as other behaviorists had studied rats, in circumscribed enclosures, deprived of opportunities for behaving as they would normally. Indeed, many of these subjects had been born and raised in captivity, and were completely innocent of the kinds of cultural patterns that are experienced by free-living members of their own species. In other cases, animals in the wild were studied for brief periods, either at a distance or where the observer's presence affected the group's behavior. The conclusion reached by these (almost wholly male) observers, was that competition for mates predominated, that males dominated females, and that it was physical power that determined group organization.[3]

These observations, it turns out, tell us nothing about healthy primate behavior. For that one must look at primates in undisturbed social settings of long standing, and for that we now have considerable long-term data, collected over decades of patient and detailed observation by, interestingly enough, primarily women: in particular, Jane Goodall's (1986) work on the chimpanzees of Gombe in Tanzania and Shirley Strum's (1987) on baboon troops in Kenya. A short summary of findings includes the existence of reciprocal bonding among members of the whole group, which is essential to the survival of all. This is attained not through aggression and coercion, as had been supposed (although there are dominant members of both sexes), but through the development of trusted friendships. Among baboons, rape does *not* occur (contrary to earlier belief), nor does the most aggressive male get the nubile female. She often saunters off into the bush with a long-time friendly ally, while the two hot-blooded males are locked in combat! These observations overturn most of the cherished Western dogmas about the origins of human nature. When we actually *see* how other social primates behave, we discover that the essence of social life is being accepted; it is 'belonging'. Social life is sought after, desired; isolation and rejection are painful and are avoided.

This is how it must have been for early humans, and must still be for us!

Evolution, even of the most rapid sort, does not produce major changes in the sort of brain patterns that are necessary to establish such universal behaviors. Biologically, we are hard-wired for the emotions of bonding, affection, and reciprocal grooming common to all social primates. We now are beginning to understand that, like other primates, our limbic system, connected to the hypothalamus on the one hand and to the cortex on the other, is the determinant of all the affective relations that make us human. And these feelings, far from being 'animal-like' are more highly developed in humans than in any other species of primate; no other primates can signal as clearly as we their feelings of affection, dismay, anger, fear, joy, and so on; no other animal overtly laughs or cries! We are the emotion-displaying species, *par excellence*, and those emotions are designed to ensure social bonding.

This information is further substantiated if we consider that for the first three or four million years of pre-human existence, emotionally based social bonding must have been highly adaptive, for it permitted the eventual evolution of a generalist species with a large cerebral cortex, which in turn allowed adaptation to a wider range of environments – the signature of human evolutionary 'success'. But achieving a bigger brain meant producing ever more helpless, precocious offspring, whose enlarged heads could still squeeze through the mother's birth canal. And this in turn, entailed an even stronger degree of social bonding than other primates exhibit, to ensure the survival of these helpless newborns. We must conclude that social bonding and the emotional ties of the limbic system preceded such cortical functions as abstract thought, self-awareness, language, and all the other so-called 'human' traits. These aspects of our brain's wiring are still very much with us, and must be understood as we think about what a 'healthy' culture for humans would look like.

Beyond the simple drive for bonding, emerging from our limbic–cortical connections, the growing cortex provided us a new set of 'needs' that are not experienced by other primates. These are the needs that arise out of self-awareness and self-consciousness – particularly the need for *sacred meaning*. We presume that other animals are not aware of the meaning of death and of the concept of 'purpose' – yet at some point in human evolution, certainly by 200,000 years ago when our modern species arose, this need must have emerged with the final enlargement of the cortex.

We thus have a *pair* of biologically, physiologically, and psychologically based needs that, together, constitute the special needs of the human species: **social bonding** and **sacred meaning**, *both* of which can only be fulfilled in a social context. Indeed, *all* our needs find their satisfaction within this social context – food, shelter, personal identity, security, creativity – and these are woven as 'woof and warp' into the overall tapestry of shared social meaning. There is no rigid hierarchy of needs – they are all woven together.

47

We have thus begun to define the kinds of needs that a 'healthy' society must provide for its members. Beyond the strictly biological needs, I want to linger briefly on this need for shared sacred meaning, because it harks back to our deep attachment to an articulated and culturally defined world-view – mental map – mentioned above. It is this mental map of the world and our place in it to which we cling with extraordinary ferocity, and which, ideally, rewards us with contentment and fulfillment and meaning, but all too often today stands in the way of these things more than it facilitates them. Not *all* worldviews, no matter how loyally defended, are equally satisfying of human needs. We begin, I hope, to glean a feeling for how we might set about establishing *culture-free criteria* for distinguishing between pathological and healthy cultural worldviews. (As Jerome Bruner (1990) and other cultural anthropologists have pointed out, it is easier to assume the existence of culture-free universals in human nature than it is to identify them specifically, especially when the traits in question have to do with such tacit qualities as needs for affection, identity, autonomy, and the like. It is far easier to find culture-free data supporting common human needs for tangibles like food, water, shelter, and so forth. But these, being shared with fellow creatures, are not specifically **human psychic** needs, yet the latter surely exist.)

Understanding cultural adaptation

There is, in the West, the general view that cultures that do not change over long periods are somehow unworthy. The term used to describe them is 'stagnant', a pejorative term implying lack of progress, backwardness, even decay. Periods of history in which societies changed but little are also called 'stagnant', as though nothing interesting happened then and peoples' lives were deadly dull. In the modern Western worldview, lack of change is taken as a sign of cultural failure.

By contrast, the West worships what it deems as 'progress', a process of cultural – and particularly technological – change that it deems as generally 'good', and if not perfectly good, at least as inevitable. The overall process of biological (and by implication, of cultural) evolution is labelled as 'progress' from 'the lower' to 'the higher'. Whatever is 'new' is, by definition 'better'. And because the West is certainly at present leading the world in technical change and complexity, it automatically is 'ahead', and hence 'better'. Thus, the Western vision of change is powerfully self-legitimizing, and is regularly used to recommend that others pattern not only their technology, but all their social institutions on the Western model.

As a biologist, I must challenge this view of 'progress' in human cultural evolution. It is based on some widely held, yet erroneous, beliefs about evolution generally. One is the notion that Darwin's ideas about natural selection and survival of the fittest imply 'winning' in a giant competition for scarce resources: food, nesting sites, mates. Such an interpretation argues that individuals and cultures that fall by the wayside are 'less fit' because they lose out to 'superior' persons or societies. Indeed, defining the 'fittest' as those who 'win' allows us to justify the most pathological social institutions of Western society, since the fault is placed on the victims' supposed 'inadequacies', not on the social institutions in which they are embedded.

Now I am not denying that competition occurs in Nature, but it is a far from complete explanation of fitness. In the words of evolutionist George Gaylord Simpson (1949, pp. 221–222), we would do better to think of fitness in far broader terms as 'fitting in' with one's surroundings:

To generalize that natural selection is over-all and even in a figurative sense the outcome of struggle is quite unjustified ... Struggle is sometimes involved, but it usually is not, and when it is, it may even work against rather than toward natural selection. Advantage in ... reproduction is usually a peaceful process in which the concept of struggle is really irrelevant. It more often involves such things as better integration into the ecological situation ... more efficient utilization of food, better care of the young, elimination of intra-group discords ... that might hamper reproduction, [and] exploitation of environmental possibilities that are not the objects of competition or are less effectively exploited by others.

An even more suspect assumption about evolution is that it is linear: that Nature began with something simple and proceeded by adding increments of complexity to produce ever-more 'fit' species. There is a clear presumption of historical 'progress', with humans seen as the end-point in a race for complex cleverness. As Stephen Jay Gould has pointed out, however, it is not at all clear that 'fitness' or 'better adaptation', is mainly responsible for the emergence and survival of a species. As often as not, so far as paleontologists can tell, sheer chance is involved.[4] Yet Gould agrees that such accidental determinism is not the whole story. Selection of better-adapted variants *does* occur — yet that, too, is a matter of chance. Being there — *before* the next environmental crisis — with the right genes to survive in a strange new environment, is essential, but again, which particular oddball genes will be most useful in an unknown future world cannot be specified ahead of time. It is a matter of chance.

Going even further, we now know that a multitude of complex species burst forth 570 million years ago, at the very *outset* of multicellular animals, long before vertebrates, let alone dinosaurs or mastodons, had appeared! But from all this multiplicity of body forms, only a few types survived, and one of them — apparently by sheer chance — happened to be the tiny chordates that led to modern vertebrates, including humans. If that small, insignificant group had gone extinct, our ancestors would never have arisen.

Thus, from a Darwinian point of view, there is nothing predestined about evolution. Humans, with their big brains, were *not* an inevitable outcome of a carefully directed process. Yet, our peculiar search for extraterrestrial intelligence is based on just such a belief: wherever life occurs in the cosmos, it is *bound* eventually to produce sentient, thinking beings. But, as Gould shows, evolution is *not* a directional process: it is a contingent process.

49

Furthermore, it occurs in fits and starts, with sudden blossomings of new, often 'bizarre' forms of which most die out – sometimes for cause, other times by chance. The surviving types sometimes diversify within their own lines, as the insects have done, but sometimes they branch into only one or two species and may persist unchanged for millions of years, like our East coast horseshoe crab. By what criteria, however, shall we evaluate the relative 'success' of these two lines?

My point is this: the *more* we know about evolution the less correct seem our Western assumptions about what constitutes 'fitness' and about the meaning of 'progress' in evolution. To the extent that we persist in those assumptions, and especially in applying them to our assessment of 'success' in human cultural change, we blind ourselves to the real causes of our difficulties. Fortunately, unlike genetic evolution, cultural evolution is reversible, but only if we escape the straitjacket of our linear thinking about evolution and reconstruct our ideas about 'progress' and 'success'. As Gould (1989, p. 320) concludes in his recent book:

Arguments [like those I have presented] lead me to the conclusion that biology's most profound insight into human nature, status, and potential lies in the simple phrase, the embodiment of contingency. *Homo sapiens* is an entity, not a tendency.

To the extent that our future survival is due to our own behavior – our own adaptiveness – and not to chance forces beyond our control (or which we have already unleashed, such as climate warming and its possible consequences), to that extent we have the option to *rethink* our ideas about what kinds of human behavior and human cultural institutions *are* adaptive.

Consequences for conflict resolution

So how might we set about developing a sound theory of what constitutes an adaptive culture? Aside from environmental adaptiveness (living sustainably within one's annual income from Nature), each culture must meet the psychic needs shared by all humans for social bonding and sacred meaning if it is to cohere without coercion. (By the way, 'coerce' originally meant pressing together!) It is learning how to identify the degree to which a given culture meets these needs that is the first trick; the second will be learning the processes of *conscious* cultural change.

Before addressing these questions, a caveat is needed. This theory, and the field of conflict resolution generally, is being formed largely out of the ideas and disciplines of Western intellectual thought – and we must constantly keep this caveat in mind as we proceed, remaining open to, indeed, actively seeking, inputs and corrections from other intellectual traditions. There is no reason to suppose that there is only *one* cultural solution to our human needs for social bonding and sacred meaning – and there clearly will be different cultural approaches to living within local environments, since they differ so widely. Therefore, to assume that one or another culture or worldview is 'ahead' or 'behind' is not only invidious, but serves no positive purpose. There is no single, linear spectrum of worldviews, ranging like the electro-magnetic spectrum along a single continuum, in our case, from 'backward' to 'cutting-edge' – or even from totally 'pathological' to totally 'healthy'. We must instead learn to treasure cultural diversity as we do species diversity – as a vast source of information and ideas. As each culture struggles to perfect itself (which goal of course is never wholly attained, since adaptation goes on indefinitely for humans!), each one also serves as a reservoir for others.

Learning to analyze cultural 'fitness'
If cultural fitness implies not 'winning' in a competition, but 'fitting in' with one's surroundings, with the uncompromising 'given' of the situation, then we need first to define the given – human nature and environmental limits. This – at least regarding human nature – I have already tried to sketch out. Second, we need a means for assessing how well the social institutions of a particular culture meet these needs, although the actual assessing of a culture must ultimately be carried out from within, if it is to undertake adaptive change. While environmental issues *are* beginning to be addressed, albeit with a great deal of foot-dragging, human needs are all but ignored. Instead, there is a lot of talk about human 'rights', which are not the same thing. The dominant Western assumption has been that people are infinitely plastic and can (if only they apply themselves) adapt to any kind of social order. Yet, as I suggested at the outset, the rising incidence of social pathologies of all sorts gives the lie to this assumption.

As a species, we are only at the beginning of *consciously and deliberately* learning how to make the connections between cultural values, cultural institutions, and cultural health. We in the West, for instance, are just becoming aware of the huge benefits of making education a cooperative, social process.[5] A few people (e.g., Etzioni, 1988; Waring, 1988; Daly and Cobb, 1989) are suggesting incorporating moral valuations into our economic calculus, and so on. But these are only timid beginnings to asking the bigger questions, such as 'What is education *for*?' and 'What is an economy *for*?'. Only then will we get to the heart of the assumptions which underlie our worldview, and cause so many of our pathologies.

This kind of questioning, to be effective, cannot be left to cloistered intellectuals, but must become part of the public dialogue. And here we run into two major hurdles. One of these I have already alluded to, namely the need we all have for a worldview, a culturally defined cognitive map by which we make sense of our lives. Raising questions about the validity of that map – even when we suspect it is not a very good one – causes most of us a degree of psychic discomfort that can be highly unsettling. Thus, our public dialogue must take this into account – recognizing that total threats to 'bad' cognitive maps may do as much harm as good. (This, of course, is what is tersely expressed by the popular bumperstickers: 'America: Love It or Leave It.') The more a society as a whole has introspective awareness of what the process of self-analysis entails, the less danger will there be of creating a backlash of psychic uncertainty and anger.

A second, less profound but perhaps more powerful, hurdle facing cultural self-examination will be the resistance from those who gain most from the status quo. These often include persons who control the economic and political power in a society, and those who otherwise benefit from the institutions that are causing social pathologies. People upholding particular religious ideals may also be involved; they are, after all, the guardians of a shared sacred meaning. Because such groups often control the means of both coercion and persuasion – the military, the media, and the means to salvation – they can effectively block the sort of public dialogue that is needed for successful cultural change. In many countries, they threaten – and even 'disappear' – students and faculty who are often in the vanguard of such dialogue, thus closing off any avenue for nonviolent social reform.

It thus becomes apparent that, difficult though it is, the process of analyzing a culture's fitness – of critiquing its health – is easy compared to actually implementing change.

Learning how to change deliberately

Cultures – and the social institutions that emerge from them – are *not* the metaphorical equivalent of a set of clothes, to be put on and off at will. (This fact probably explains why revolutions so seldom succeed in creating lasting social change.) Indeed, it is this process of institutional change that 'politics' is theoretically about. Yet the political institutions of very few societies today are actually functioning as effective vehicles for the social process that I call 'critique–create'.[6] Their ineffectiveness is largely due to the second factor above that prevents public dialogue – namely, entrenched power blocs – but general apathy and resistance to change, and to the uncertainty it brings, also contribute.

Fortunately, in many places, particularly in the Western 'democracies', although access to the formal centralized strongholds of power is precluded, enormous opportunity exists for action at the grassroots, community level. Indeed, this has been and remains possible to some degree through underground networks in other, less 'free', societies. Local politics, leading to new local institutions of all sorts – from local barter economies,[7] to local self-policing, to local housing and food-growing and sewage treatment[8] – can all emerge. TOES (The Other Economic Summit), held each year in conjunction with the G–7 economic summit (annual meetings of the heads of the seven major industrial powers), brings growing numbers of these creative people together; they comprise Green party members from Europe and North America, environmentalists, peace groups, ethnic minorities, and others who seek to change present institutions. There are others. Their strategy is not to topple 'bad' institutions head-on, but to execute an 'end-run' around them by creating viable local alternatives.

Even so, there is a great, unmet need for learning, *as a whole society*, about the need for critique/create and the processes for bringing it about. In the first half of this century, America had a prophet, the educator John Dewey, who understood that for deep cultural change to occur, there needs to be *participatory* society, where everyone is trained in the skills of becoming informed, organizing her or his thoughts, and dialoguing patiently and repeatedly with others. This is the only way that meaningful, uncoerced change *can* occur. Unfortunately, at present, we refuse to hear Dewey's message.

In closing, it is my view, as a biologist, that our society has forgotten that *talking* and *listening* are what we are designed to do best. Our brains evolved for speaking and listening; they work best when we engage in conversation (a word that shares the same root as 'convert', and literally means to turn or evolve together – thus to generate a cohesive group). All the talking by politicians and experts, and all the listening by TV viewers, is no substitute for face-to-face conversation. This activity *must* become an integral part of *all* healthy cultures in the future. The role of conflict resolvers will be to facilitate such conversations.

Notes

1. Originally prepared for the 19th Annual Conference of COPRED, 'Unity in Diversity', Ohio, 5–9 September 1990.
2. The authors go on to analyze the growing social unrest and cultural disruption in South Korea, Taiwan, and Singapore.
3. Critiques of these earlier studies are to be found in the references cited in the following paragraph.
4. Stephen Jay Gould has written a number of popular books in which the ideas expressed here occur. His recent and most explicit in this context is *Wonderful Life: The Burgess Shale and the Nature of History* (1989).
5. See the numerous references to the work of David and Roger Johnson, cited by Alfie Kohn (1988, pp. 236–237).
6. The idea of 'critique–create' as a social process that has occurred at various times in history, and is very much needed now, is argued in my book, *Ariadne's Thread: The Search for New Modes of Thinking* (1989). See especially Chapter 8, 'On acquiring a worldview'.
7. For information on the ideas and practice of 'alternative' trading systems, see Hellman (1987), Henderson (1988, Chapter 13) and Kennedy (1988). This last book is available only direct from publishers for DM 12 (see references for address). For information on Local Exchange Trading Systems (LETS), write Michael Linton, c/o Landsman Community Services Ltd., 304 576 England Ave., Courtenay, BC, V9N 5M7, Canada.
8. A new, ecologically based self-help program is evolving in the impoverished sections

of Mexico City, with the goal of teaching people how to create their own food-growing gardens, to recycle their own refuse, and to build their own houses from rammed earth and recycled bricks, bottles and, cans. For information, write Urban Ecology, P.O. Box 10144, Berkeley, California 94709, and ask about the work of Jesus Arias Chavez and Alfonso Gonzalez Martinez.

References

Bello, W. and Rosenfeld, S. (1990), 'Dragons in distress: The economic miracle unravels in South Korea, Taiwan, and Singapore', *Food First Action Alert*, Spring/Summer.

Bruner, J. (1990), *Acts of Meaning*, Harvard University Press, Cambridge, Massachusetts.

Clark, M.E. (1989), *Ariadne's Thread: The Search for New Modes of Thinking*, St. Martin's Press, New York and Macmillan, London.

Daly, H.E. and Cobb, J.B., Jr. (1989), *For the Common Good: Redirecting the Economy toward Community, the Environment, and a Sustainable Future*, Beacon Press, Boston.

Etzioni, A. (1988), *The Moral Dimension: Toward a New Economics*, The Free Press, New York.

Goodall, J. (1986), *The Chimpanzees of Gombe: Patterns of Behavior*, Belknap Press, Cambridge, Massachusetts.

Gould, S.J. (1989), *Wonderful Life: The Burgess Shale and the Nature of History*, W.W. Norton, New York.

Hellman, R. (1987), *Henry George Reconsidered*, Carlton Press, New York.

Henderson, H. (1988), *Politics of the Solar Age*, 2nd edition, Knowledge Systems, Inc., Indianapolis, Indiana.

Kennedy, M. (1988), *Interest and Inflation Free Money: How to Create an Exchange Medium that Works for Everybody*, Permakultur Institut e.V., Ginsterweg 5, Steyerberg D–3074, Germany.

Kohn, A. (1986), *No Contest: The Case against Competition*, Houghton Mifflin, Boston.

Simpson, G.G. (1949), *The Meaning of Evolution*, Yale University Press, New Haven, Connecticut.

Strum, S. (1987), *Almost Human: A Journey into the World of Baboons*, Random House, New York.

Waring, M. (1988), *If Women Counted: A New Feminist Economics*, Harper and Row, New York.

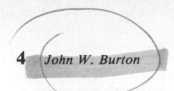

4 John W. Burton

Conflict resolution as a political philosophy

Conflict resolution is a recent concept. It is still not part of any consensual understanding. Indeed, the terms *disputes* and *conflicts* are used interchangeably, as are *settlement* and *resolution*. In the emerging literature on conflict resolution these terms have distinctive meanings. 'Disputes' involve negotiable interests, while 'conflicts' are concerned with issues that are not negotiable, issues that relate to ontological human needs that cannot be compromised. Accordingly, 'settlement' refers to negotiated or arbitrated outcomes of disputes, while 'resolution' refers to outcomes of a conflict situation that must satisfy the inherent needs of all. Hence we have *dispute settlement* and *conflict resolution*.

I wish to emphasize these precise uses of terms because clarifying their meanings goes to the heart of the problem we are discussing, that is, the separate but generic nature of disputes and of conflicts. If there were no difference between disputes and conflicts, if, that is, all human relationships could be regulated and controlled by an authoritative third party, then with sufficient courts and alternative means of settlement, and with sufficient means of enforcement, we could be assured of harmonious relationships domestically and internationally. History shows us that this is not the case: there are situations, both domestic and international, that are not subject to authoritative or coercive settlements.

For example, we are experiencing ethnic and alienation conflicts that are threatening the social stability of even the most developed of societies, including the United States. These are evidence that the person or group, when deprived of some essential human needs, cannot be socialized or induced to behave according to the dictates of law. The greatest military power in history could not in the 1960s subdue a small post-colonial Asian nation that was seeking its autonomy. There are such conflicts at all societal levels, that is, situations in which ontological needs of identity and recognition, and associated human developmental needs, are frustrated. These conflicts cannot long be contained, controlled, or suppressed, but can be resolved and prevented by the satisfaction of such needs.

Associated with confusion in the use of terms, and the underlying conceptual confusion, is the tradition of treating domestic and international disputes and conflicts as separate phenomena. It has been assumed that there is no distinction between disputes and conflicts; it has been reasonable to treat international situations, often far more devastating than domestic ones, as more serious, inviting the stronger term 'conflict'. But the two phenomena are generic: there are both domestic and international disputes and conflicts.

The assumptions lurking behind the confusion in terms have led to major policy mistakes. Underlying the assumption that all domestic disputes can be handled by central authorities, which are supposed to have a monopoly of power with which to enforce peaceful relationships, is a hidden assumption that there are no domestic conflicts, as we have defined the term: there are no situations within a nation-state that are not subject to such coercive control. This thinking has reasonably led to attempts to introduce into the international system some form of central authority based on this domestic model. The United Nations Charter reflected this thinking; e.g., there was to be a standing international force at the disposal of the Security Council with which to enforce its decisions. Fortunately members have not contributed such forces. But in its absence some great powers have sought to head the United Nations in this direction, and we had the example of the Korean war.

But now we face the reality that the domestic model was a fiction inherited from a past of false assumptions and coercive central authorities. In so far as conflict was avoided, it was by repression for limited periods of time. The majority of conflicts in the global society are internal ones, in many cases spilling over into the international system. We are forced to the conclusion that conflict is a generic phenomenon that knows no system boundaries. Whether we are dealing with interpersonal, community, ethnic, or international relations, we are dealing with the same ontological needs of people, requiring the same analytical processes of conflict resolution. Indeed, the international model of separate entities that cooperate on a functional basis may be a model for many states that have within them separate ethnic and identity groups, each seeking autonomy within a wider system of relationships.

The distinction between disputes and conflicts provides us with two conceptual frames: on the one hand, situations that are negotiable, and, on the other, those in which there can be no compromise. These distinctive conceptions imply two very different means of treatment. The first are subject to judicial and arbitrated processes, but the second require analytical problem-solving. Our language as commonly employed has not as yet provided us with means of making these distinctions. Because we have not made these distinctions we are not able to tackle problems appropriately, and far less are we able to predict conflict situations, and follow policies designed to prevent conflicts occurring.

Power-political realism versus behavioral realism

It is useful to look back a few decades and to see where these different conceptual frames emerged. Among the most perceptive of contributions is an article by Michael Banks, 'The International Relations Discipline: Asset or Liability for Conflict Resolution?' (1986). In it he traces the development of practice and thought from feudal times to the present, noting that what was called 'political realism' is proving to be far removed from realities, and what has been termed 'idealism' is proving in practice to be less self-defeating and more realistic than the traditional power approach.

What is clear in retrospect is that what was termed 'political realism' was realistic only in the limited sense that it was practice. From early feudalism to the present day practice has been to govern through coercion. There was no theory that justified this political realism. Failures, such as revolutions and wars, could not be explained except by failure to employ sufficient power. There being no theory, there was no explanation of conflicts, and no basis of prediction of future conflicts. Political realism as practice has now been shown to be unrealistic in behavioral theory, and self-defeating in practice.

The traditional idealists also lacked a theory. There was a belief system based on a desire for cooperative relationships, but no theory that could explain conflict, still less justify alternative policies.

The result has been an alarming void: power politics has failed domestically and internationally, but no alternative has been articulated and applied as policy. This is the bankrupt state of civilization at the end of the twentieth century.

From subjectivity to theory-based objectivity

The absence of any theory becomes apparent when, once again, we examine the use of terms. Without a theory or explanation of human behaviors, only subjective meanings can be given to the concepts of the idealists such as 'justice', 'the social good', and 'human rights'. Furthermore, the institutional means of achieving these subjective goals reflect ignorance of the nature of justice, the social good, and human rights. 'Democracy', for example, has had the meaning of majority government, but when applied to class and ethnic minorities such government is experienced as unjust, not in the social good, a denial of human rights, and, furthermore, a major source of conflict. Only an adequate theory of behavior can eliminate this subjectivity in the use of important concepts.

We have taken the power-political track following Morgenthau (1948) and Schwarzenberger (1964) in the 1930s, a track still followed by the majority of political scientists and all strategists. We now have to find a theory of behavior that explains conflicts, and deduce from this theory the appropriate means of handling them.

A start was made in Berlin in 1979 when an international group discussed the nature of the person that would be the subject of analysis if there were no separate constructs such as economic man, legal man, psychological man, and sociological man. Their book was called *Needs Theory* (Lederer, 1980). They described the essential attributes of this difficult real person whose ontological needs prevent him or her being socialized and coerced into behaviors convenient to political leaders or academics.

This study reflected a growing disquiet in behavioral sciences. In the 1960s scholars had been challenging the assumptions of their disciplines, and discovering the real person. In industrial relations Blake, Shepard and Mouton (1964) challenged the assumptions underlying employer–employee relationships. In sociology Steven Box (1971) challenged the assumptions that were then basic to contemporary thinking about deviance. A few years later Paul Sites (1971) focused on the way in which human-needs deprivation forced the individual to act in ways that would otherwise not be chosen.

There has emerged as a consequence the beginnings of a new conceptual orientation, still perceived unclearly, and not yet part of conventional wisdom: a realization that there are human ontological factors to take into account. Because they are ontological they cannot be subjected to authoritative controls. Whether we are dealing with children, street gangs, ethnic communities, or nations of peoples, we are finding that there are human problems to be solved, and that no amount of coercion or repression can for long contain human developmental aspirations. The U.S. Department of State Foreign Service Institute (FSI) refers to 'track two diplomacy', the second track being the analytical and problem-solving one (see McDonald and Bendahmane, 1987). This is at least an important first step. The second and perhaps vital step is to move toward the second track as the main one.

The alternative to power politics, that is the behavioral approach that assumes certain human needs must be satisfied if conflict is to be resolved, is at long last being articulated and understood at least within that still limited academic population concerned with conflict resolution. A library is emerging (see Burton, 1990a, b; Burton and Dukes, 1990a, b). Courses are being taught (e.g., the MS and Ph.D. programs in Conflict Analysis and Resolution at George Mason University). We have the beginnings of practice, and the appropriate procedures are being spelled out.

This theory of behavior does provide us with an objective basis on which to define concepts. 'Justice', 'the social good', and 'democracy' relate to conditions that satisfy human needs of identity, recognition, and autonomy, all of which imply equity.

As with any paradigm shift, however, there are resistances from both scholars and practitioners. This is understandable, especially in this case. We are experiencing a paradigm shift, a fundamental one touching on the foundations of political philosophy. It challenges the traditional notion that the person can be socialized into the requirements of institutions, and asserts that institutions must accommodate in a continuing way to certain inherent and universal human needs.

Political experience

Recent events in Eastern Europe have alerted us to these realities. But as yet we have not been prepared to apply such lessons to our own societies. As yet there seems to be little understanding that what has happened in Eastern Europe is part of a historical process, driven by the ontological struggle of needs satisfaction, that must take place in all societies where authoritative controls and inequitable institutions fail to cater to human needs. Rationalizing policy on the basis of human rights that are defined conveniently to fit existing cultures and institutions cannot for long prevent the assertion of human needs.

We have gone through colonialism and imperialism of various kinds, but societies have as yet not been prepared to apply the lessons of the failure of power to their own internal problems. Drug violence and gang warfare are symptoms of social deprivations, and can be tackled only by dealing with such deprivations. Ethnic conflicts are a symptom of lack of recognition and autonomy, and can be avoided only by constitutional and perhaps boundary changes. And there are even deeper problems associated with the personalities of leaders whose corrupt and violent behaviors reflect insecurities that require appropriate constitutional safeguards that can ensure limitations on the decision-making of all power elites.

Problem-solving conflict resolution

Academia now faces a major challenge. We must go back to fundamental assumptions and reexamine them. In particular we must move from institutions to persons as the units of analysis, and deduce a political theory on this basis. From such a political theory we must then deduce policies, and then move to application. At this stage, if we encounter problems, there is new material to be fed back into our consideration of hypotheses.

This is the course of problem-solving conflict resolution. As a result it is now beginning to come up with theory and policy, and the testing of practice.

The procedures are readily deduced. First there must be a careful analysis of parties and issues. Second it is necessary to bring those two parties whose relationships are most affected into a facilitated interactive situation in which relationships are analyzed in depth. Other parties and issues are dealt with in due course in the same way. At this stage no proposals are entertained, nor is there any bargaining or negotiation. When there is an agreed definition of the problem, and a full assessment of the costs of existing policies based on a knowledge of responses to the denial of human needs, there can be exploration of positive options. These steps are set out in detail in a handbook devoted to the subject (Burton, 1987).

John W. Burton

Conflict provention

Resolving one conflict, however, does not prevent the next one. Conflict resolution, unlike dispute settlement, is not primarily or even mainly concerned with particular cases. Its processes are analytical and problem-solving, and its approach is within a theoretical framework or explanation of conflict. Its main thrust is, therefore, not merely in conflict prevention, in isolating and removing the sources of conflict, but also in conflict 'provention': promoting the conditions that create cooperative relationships (see Burton, 1990a, b; Burton and Dukes, 1990a, b).

In this sense conflict resolution is a fundamentally different exercise from any settlement processes: it is concerned with prediction and with policy formation based on a political philosophy that asserts that the satisfaction of human needs that are universal must be the ultimate goal of survivable societies.

Let us take as an example the situation in South Africa, or Fiji, or Sri Lanka, or Cyprus, or Northern Ireland, or the (former) USSR. In South Africa there is a minority of whites concerned to maintain their autonomy, just as the minorities in these other cases seek to achieve their separate identities. One-man-one-vote in South Africa would put minorities in the same situation as are these other minorities now seeking separation elsewhere. Why then should we be supporting one-man-one-vote in South Africa rather than some altered constitutional form that also satisfied the concerns of the minority?

In a power-bargaining situation, and with foreign support, it could be that this form of 'democracy' could be forced on the whites in South Africa. Most would leave the country with whatever resources they could take with them. Their presence could in other circumstances be valuable to the development of the economy. A problem-solving process could lead to constitutional relationships that could preserve their legitimate needs, and also those of other minorities, including some African groups which wish to achieve their separate autonomy. This would not be a federation, for federation also rests on the numbers game. It would be a functional arrangement amongst equals, not unlike the international system.

The same considerations apply at all societal levels. Studies of members of 'gangs' show very clearly that members are persons deprived of relationships, desperately seeking them in what appear to be the only means available. The works of sociologists like Box (1971) and Sites (1971) demonstrate that behaviors that are illegal and blatantly anti-social are adopted frequently, if not mostly, in the absence of viable alternatives.

Alternative dispute resolution

At this stage I wish to make some comments on what has come to be known as 'Alternative Dispute Resolution' or ADR, and to separate problem-solving conflict resolution from it.

By 'alternative' in the ADR context is meant alternative to courts. Indeed, institutionally many ADR practices are an adjunct of courts, and sometimes required by courts before cases are referred to them. The assumption is that if disputes cannot be arbitrated or mediated, then they must be adjudicated. Underlying this assumption is the unstated one referred to above: that all situations, whether disputes or conflicts, can be managed by reference to legal norms or by some form of negotiation.

It is true that ADR is confined usually to disputes over compensation or some negotiable issue. But frequently there are hidden elements touching on non-negotiable human needs. In Australia recently there has been an air pilots' strike. It was assumed to be over wages. Courts, politicians and unions could not bring it to an end. In fact it was about status, and the changing status of pilots. No longer are they the rare and respected captains of former times. There were non-negotiable issues involved that required careful analysis and treatment. So it is with many, if not most, industrial and other matters with which ADR deals. What are required are not adjuncts to courts, but real alternatives that can provide the analytical problem-solving approach that courts cannot provide.

The danger is that ADR will be captured by the more powerful whose influence in the creation of the legal system has waned, and who could more readily manipulate this emerging adjunct alternative.

Having made this observation one must go further. If problem-solving processes are to be institutionalized they must impinge upon judicial processes. If legal norms based on precedents cannot resolve problems, then there must be changes in legal norms. Courts must also move toward an understanding of the realities of human needs. Legal processes are well established, and there cannot be a solution to domestic or international problems just by bypassing them or finding alternatives. The legal fraternity itself must play its part in bringing about the paradigm shift that is required if civilizations are to cope with escalating conflicts and violence.

Members of societies globally, even those of the most affluent, are demonstrating by protest, by the deviant behaviors of their members, by exposing deprivations of minorities and underprivileged sections, the need for changes in institutions and policies designed to provide for the satisfaction of human aspirations and needs. If legal processes, ADR and others, were to pursue problem-solving rather than coercive or deterrent strategies, in time there could be knowledge of adjustments required. But such a shift in orientation would require a substantial change in professional training and practices in many fields, as well as in perceived longer-term interests.

Crises in capitalism and communism

I am led to my final observation. Civilizations are at a critical stage, perhaps more critical than at any past stage. The past, from feudal times to modern industrial society, has been a consistent one of power politics. Indeed, even in the United States there has not been as yet the movement required to abolish the essence of slavery. It has merely altered in form. There is no need any more for entrepreneurs to own and lock up slaves. They are there in their thousands in ghettos throughout the country, available at rates far below that which would be required to avoid malnutrition. They cannot run away, there is nowhere to go. Those who try to break out of the ghetto, by stealing or as entrepreneurs peddling drugs, are locked up in prison. It is important to place present conditions in a human perspective: serfdom in one of its many forms is still with us. Until we can get rid of it there will be violence and conflict.

Capitalism has in this sense failed us. It has constructively provided incentives for personal gain, and these have led to major exploitations of resources and development as measured by GNP and resource use. But unrestrained capitalism has led entrepreneurs to undervalue the social good: gross inequalities of income have given rise to serious social and economic problems. They have also undervalued the longer-term ecological good: resource exploitation has been at the expense of the future. Attempts to curb these trends by so-called 'left-wing' governments have been impossible because any success would destroy the system. The degree and type of government intervention within a free-enterprise system remains a contentious issue. Projecting into the future there is no reason for optimism about quality of life even in the most affluent of private-enterprise societies. The future of societies that are not yet economically developed is no less bleak than that of the underprivileged within affluent societies.

Communism has also failed as can clearly be seen. The idealist anticipation of an individual capacity to be motivated, not by reward, but by promoting the social good, has proved to be limited. While there is a demand for consumer goods, there is resistance to work-rewarding demands made on people to provide these goods.

Both systems have necessarily been authoritarian systems with their privileged classes in control. Given the inherent problems of each this is inevitable. In capitalist societies demands for unearned social and economic benefits have to be resisted. In many countries the problems within the free-enterprise system have stimulated revolt, leading often to military dictatorships. In communist societies demands for consumer goods and services, and freedom to choose occupations, have had to be repressed.

Both make the same assumption, that the person is wholly malleable and can be socialized or coerced into required behaviors. No increase in courts, police, or alternative dispute-settlement processes can make up for the inherent deficiencies of these systems.

Neither system has the means of dealing with its problems or the conflicts they create within or between nations. This seems to be the common failing of both systems, and of any others that have been tried, such as fascism. The reason is that political systems so far experienced have rarely had means of system change, other than system overthrow by violent means. Conflict is a symptom of the need for system change. Conflict resolution processes and conflict prevention policies could be the means for peaceful change.

Conflict resolution as a political system

The question I wish to pose is whether, and to what extent, analytical problem-solving processes, widely applied, can promote the means of continuing change and contribute to an alternative political system.

This may seem a strange question to ask in the context of a discussion on conflict resolution. But let us look again at the nature of the problem of conflict and its resolution.

Disputes that are over negotiable interests will always exist, as will problems of management amongst persons who have common goals and values. But both can be dealt with by applying consensus norms and by management techniques. Here ADR has an important contribution to make. Quite simple training can lead to greatly improved management techniques, and appropriate institutional forms of mediation can deal with interest disputes if there are no other underlying issues.

When we come to conflicts, however, it is not sufficient to deal with particular cases and institutionalize means of dealing with them. There must be policies that prevent situations of conflict arising, and that promote cooperative relationships. 'Prevention' becomes the main task. Conflict resolution thus is part of the field of political philosophy. It is relevant to all systems, capitalist, communist and others. Problem-solving processes and conflict prevention policies are the missing ingredients in dealing with systems as we have experienced them, inadequate and subject to crisis and failure.

Such problem-solving is outside any ideologial concept. It is neither 'right' nor 'left'. It is applicable to all systems, and it is a process and philosophy that brings systems together.

A summary

Let me summarize. Management problems and disputes over negotiable interests are not a major problem. Too little has been done about them in the past because systems have been elitist and authoritarian, but good progress has been made in recent years in dispute-settlement techniques. In due course courts and legal processes can be expected to alter norms and procedures to involve far more of the parties in dispute.

Conflict resolution, on the other hand, has been a neglected subject. It is

63

a challenge to all existing capitalist, communist, or other systems. It is a process that can deal with complex situations, both national and international. Its interactive analytical problem-solving processes have been tested and show enormous promise. But the resolution of particular conflicts is just a small beginning. While it helps to provide insights into the nature of conflict and conditions that stimulate conflict, by itself it does not deal with the problem of conflict. Conflict provention is the goal. Both are part of a process of system change, and their theoretical framework points political systems in the directions required.

References

Banks, M. (1986), 'The international relations discipline: Asset or liability for conflict resolution', in E. A. Azar and J. W. Burton, eds, *International Conflict Resolution*, Wheatsheaf.

Blake, R. R., Shepard, H. A., and Mouton, J. S. (1964), *Managing Intergroup Conflict in Industry*, Gulf Publishing Co., Houston, Texas.

Box, S. (1971), *Deviance Reality and Society*, Holt, Rinehart and Winston, New York.

Burton, J. W. (1987), *Resolving Deep-Rooted Conflict: A Handbook*, University Press of America, Lanham, Maryland.

Burton, J. W. (ed.) (1990a), *Conflict: Human Needs Theory*, St. Martin's Press, New York.

Burton, J. W. (1990b), *Conflict: Resolution and Provention*, St. Martin's Press, New York.

Burton, J. W. and Dukes, F. (1990a), *Conflict: Readings in Management and Resolution*, St. Martin's Press, New York.

Burton, J. W. and Dukes, F. (1990b), *Conflict: Practices in Management, Settlement and Resolution*, St. Martins Press, New York.

Lederer, K. (ed.) (1980), *Human Needs: A Contribution to the Current Debate*, Oelgeschlager, Gunn and Hain, Cambridge, Massachusetts.

McDonald, J. W. and Bendahmane, D. B. (1987), *Confict Resolution: Track Two Diplomacy*, U.S. Department of State, Foreign Service Institute, Washington, D.C.

Morgenthau, H. (1948), *Politics among Nations: The Struggle for Power and Peace*, A. A. Knopf, New York.

Schwarzenberger, G. (1964), *Power Politics: A Study of World Society*, Stevens, London.

Sites, P. (1971), *Control, the Basis of Social Order*, Dunellen Publishers, New York.

Complexity and cognitive equilibrium: experimental results and their implications*

In working with complex issues, cognitive equilibrium (Zeleny, 1989a, b, c, 1991a, b) is prerequisite to emotional equilibrium; and both are prerequisite to a state of serenity and harmony within which human beings can enjoy coexistence, mutual respect, and constructive interdependence.

The importance of the foregoing proposition lies in the fact that in these times, society faces many complex, high-stakes issues (Perrow, 1984; Salk, 1985; Warfield, 1990). Typically these are dealt with by people educated in relatively narrow disciplines whose content is far lower than that required to cope with such issues. Two of the primary attributes of these problems are:

(a) their scale (as measured by the number of people who are or may be significantly affected by them); and
(b) the need to have people work together diligently in order to
  (i)   describe these issues in sufficient depth and breadth,
  (ii) discover superior approaches to their resolution or amelioration, and
  (iii) implement one of these approaches across institutional or international boundaries.

Such issues are so well publicized today that details concerning them can be ignored in deference to discussions of coping with them.

One of the key factors that is often overlooked or inadequately dealt with in working with such issues is the challenge to get people to agree on potential resolutions and then act on them. In seeking to get agreement, it is especially important to devote more attention to methodology for group activity, and to give less allegiance to pure metaphysical approaches that are

---

* This paper (with minor differences) was presented at the 1991 Annual Meeting of the American Association for the Advancement of Science (AAAS) in the Alexandria Room of the Washington, D.C., Sheraton Hotel, on February 19, 1991. Also it was published in *Human Systems Management*, 10, 1991, pp. 195–202. It appears here (with minor alterations) with permission of the Editor of that journal, Dr. Milan Zeleny.

heavily promoted. More attention needs to be devoted to collecting data on processes that are used in applications in order to permit continuous improvement to take place in using such processes, and less allegiance needs to be given to conflicting expert opinions about what ought to work but which is unsupported by scientific evidence.

Objective of this chapter

This chapter is intended to shed significant light on the conditions surrounding group work, and especially to present and interpret empirical data drawn from several years of conduct and observation of group activity in working with complex, high-stakes issues. This activity has ranged over a wide variety of groups. All of the cases involved have shared these factors:

(a) a complex, high-stakes issue as the focal point of the work,
(b) a group of people (typically a mix of staff and middle-management) who are knowledgeable about and motivated to resolve the issue,
(c) two key methodologies (to be described later) that were used in all the group work,
(d) documentation of the conduct and products of the group work.

Prior studies

Prior studies relevant to group activity can be categorized as lying in four areas. The areas are:

(a) Individual behavioral features that are transferable to a group setting
(b) Groups engaged in tasks
(c) Organizational problem-solving behavior
(d) Conflict studies

Individual behavior
Most of the available relevant data are generally limited to the first of these, and relate to individual capacity to manage information (G. Miller, 1956; Simon, 1974).

Group behavior
Data coming from research on groups engaged in tasks are often inadequate because of the situation that the experimental design is forced to accommodate, such as having students working for pay on non-complex, non-high-stakes issues; or having military people on leave similarly engaged. What seem most valuable from research on behavior in groups are the categories that have arisen for describing and interpreting such behavior. For example, Bales (1951) introduced the categories of emotional behavior and task-oriented behavior to describe individual behavior in groups. Tuckman (1965) introduced

his famous sequence of forming, storming, norming, and performing to describe unregulated group behavior. Janis (1982) elaborated on the 'group-think' phenomenon to show dysfunctional performance of individuals in groups.

Organizational behavior

Simon enriched the language by introducing the term 'satisficing' to represent the lazy approach of organizations to solution-seeking. Argyris (1982) aggressively described the inability of groups working in organizations to break through the entrenched behavioral patterns that involve trying to deal with all issues in the same way, regardless of their underlying differences.

Conflict situations

The modern industry of 'conflict resolution' is characterized by an almost total lack of documented and peer-scrutinized empirical research. Even the philosophizing that is done or overdone is unashamedly metaphysical, such as Burton's (1987) unwavering restriction of analysis to an insistence that it is 'deeply-held, non-negotiable values' that prevent the resolution of conflicts. One must note that if this view is accurate it seems to preclude any resolution of any conflict. Consider these two incompatible arguments:

(a) V is the only cause of C. V cannot be changed. Nonetheless C can be eliminated.
(b) V is one of several contributing factors in causing C. V cannot be changed. But because *other contributing factors can be changed*, C can be eliminated.

Argument (a) appears to be the one that Burton has made, but it does not seem tenable. Argument (b) seems tenable and practical. The consequence of accepting argument (a), where V represents the deeply held, non-negotiable values and C represents conflict, seems to be that it is totally futile to try to eliminate conflict. On the other hand, if argument (b) is accepted, a strategy for eliminating conflict could be based on a consideration like the following.

While it is true that there are deeply held values, it is also true that there are a variety of stimuli involved in creating and sustaining the behavior that constitutes conflict. The route from stimuli to conflict behavior is mediated by those deeply held values. If additional stimuli can be brought into the situation (e.g., cognitive considerations that are appealing), the values can mediate in the aggregate both the older, conflict-producing stimuli and the newer, conflict-resolving stimuli. The result may be that the conflict may be resolved. While the focus on resolving the conflict may benefit considerably from insight into those deeply held values, it is the willingness to accept two beliefs that may enable the conflict resolution to succeed:

(a) there are more things causing the conflict than the deeply held values, and (b) a process that facilitates the capacity of those in conflict to allow their values to mediate the mix of old and new ideas will be very appropriate.

Summary
The lack of data relevant to work with complex, high-stakes issues leaves open issues of validation of any theories or beliefs concerning such issues. Shrewd observations or generalizations have been made based on much experience, but it still remains to validate these by high-quality experimental evidence. For these reasons, it is believed that the empirical results to be presented here are uniquely valuable in the history of research on groups. If they will be taken seriously by investigators who propose categories and hypotheses, and integrated into their frameworks, not only can new perspectives be gained on how to deal with groups when complex issues are involved; but new opportunities for additional data-gathering can be created that will help reinforce or amend the conclusions to be offered.

Objectives of group work

In this context, the objectives of group work are viewed as twofold, in the light of past experience. The first is that the *working group* should reach a *state of serenity* in regard to (a) their understanding of the issue, and (b) their consensus on how to deal with the issue. Such a state could arise out of a newly found confidence that, at last, the issue and its resolution can be understood, and that the proposed resolution can confidently be defended in forums against any alternative proposals coming from other sources. The second objective is that the *intervening agent will have previously made a commitment* to understand the products of the group work and to take one of two actions in a timely way. Either the agent will choose to embed the issue in a larger one, and feed the products into a new group that will incorporate the results in consideration of the next larger issue; or the agent will proceed immediately to work with the participants toward implementing the results of the group work. (An appropriate combination of these two possibilities may sometimes be indicated.)

Components of serenity

A state of serenity involves both individual and group *equilibrium.* As in the physical science situation involving equilibrium, the state of the object or objects involved has become impervious to small perturbations arising from the environment, and the state will persist indefinitely unless some major incursion arises that involves forces well beyond the norms of the existing situation. Individual equilibrium reflects the fact that an individual has reached a state of serenity relative to the particular issue. Group equilibrium reflects the fact that every member of the group has attained virtually the identical state of serenity. Consensus is the hallmark of this serenity. It can only be reached by extended, high-quality, thoughtful communication, accompanied by agreement on the key patterns relevant to the issue.

Serenity in the individual and the group involves two major components. These two components correspond to the conditions involved in the two hemispheres of the brain.

Cognitive equilibrium

One of these components is *cognitive equilibrium* (Zeleny, 1989a, b, c and 1991). This component refers to the patterns of knowledge of the issue that have been constructed by and accepted by group interaction. The building elements of these patterns reflect the separate and constructive contributions of the individual members; likewise they reflect, by their absence, those earlier individual contributions of individual members that have been discussed, clarified, and found wanting in the light of the patterns discovered by the group. Members of the group are both teachers and students. Cognitive equilibrium arises from a period of sharing of information and thought, including a period of development and sharing of patterns that define the issue and its proposed resolution.

Emotional Equilibrium

The other component of the state of serenity is emotional equilibrium. This condition grows from the elimination of doubt and the satisfaction of having finally reached a viable perspective on a complex issue. *Emotional equilibrium means that the proposed resolution of the issue is compatible with the individual value systems of each member of the group and with the set intersection of these value systems reflecting group shared values.* Such sharing is a consequence rather than a predecessor of the group activity.

Further insight into the meaning of cognitive and emotional equilibrium is gained by reviewing Bales's (1951) categories of 'task-oriented behavior' and 'emotional behavior'. The existence of emotional equilibrium can be assessed by noting the winding-down or absence of the kind of emotional behavior that Bales describes. Cognitive equilibrium can be assessed by noting the winding-down or lack of further need for the kind of 'task-oriented behavior' that Bales describes.

Necessary conditions for serenity

If serenity is a goal, what are the necessary conditions to attain it? *A state of serenity cannot be reached through emotional equilibrium alone.* In high-stakes issues involving many people it will not be possible to reach serenity in an environment of relative ignorance. Such an environment cannot provide any closure on the likelihood of resolution of the issue and cannot, therefore, bring about a state of emotional equilibrium. It must be appreciated that time scale is significant here. Research on groups shows that apparent consensus is reached when groupthink is involved (Janis, 1982). But this apparent consensus will disintegrate rapidly under the impact of bad outcomes, as Allison's study (1971) of the Bay of Pigs incident makes clear.

Cognitive equilibrium is a necessary condition for emotional equilibrium (though not a sufficient condition, as will be indicated). Even if everyone in the group attains a feeling of confidence in the group understanding of the issue and its prospective resolution, thereby attaining cognitive equilibrium, there is no assurance that the resolution will not require executive action on the part of individuals who may not wish to hear, study, accept, and implement the work of the group. That is why prior commitment by the intervening agent (or executive), as discussed previously, is important to attaining emotional equilibrium. But once again the time scale rears its head, and rapid disintegration of consensus is not compatible with equilibrium, as defined.

Issues, as originally defined, have a tendency to escalate beyond the initial bounds (Warfield, 1982b). Products of groups may deal with limited versions of issues that have to be integrated with larger issues. Therefore a state of serenity is finally attainable only when closure is reached. Empirical evidence to be discussed can only highlight the aspects of the group work that produce cognitive equilibrium. Emotional equilibrium cannot be highlighted by empirical results to date.

Data origins in methodology

To appreciate the data obtained, it is necessary first to understand the two principal methodologies that were involved in gathering the data. It should also be appreciated that no member of any of the groups involved in producing the data was advised that data were being taken on the group activity for purposes related to scientific ends. A principal reason for this is that the data gathered are *only those that are required by the methodologies as an integral part of the approach to defining and resolving the issue.* In other words, the data are mainstream requirements of issue-resolving, not determined by needs for empirical evidence. Given these circumstances, to have told the group members that the data were being collected for scientific reasons would not only have been misleading, but might even have affected adversely the members' decisions to participate. The lesson to be learned here is that methodology that is well designed for issue resolution and faithfully practiced can become the source of valuable data for assessing the benefits and shortcomings of the methodology itself. Focusing on data collection as though it could not be achieved by focusing on methodology for issue-resolution is not conducive to gathering needed scientific results.

The nominal group technique
The Nominal Group Technique (NGT) has been widely used since its intro-duction as a means of enhancing group work (Delbecq et al., 1975). The particular cases where this methodology was used, and from which data are drawn, were all conducted by the Center for Interactive Management under the leadership of Dr. Alexander N. Christakis, with support from Dr. David Keever and others. Reports on the cases are archived in the IASIS File, Fenwick Library, George Mason University, Fairfax, Virginia.

In applying NGT, members of the group work from a context statement about the issue to generate ideas about the issue silently. Then there is a round-robin recording of the ideas. Next there is a formal period of clarification of the ideas, aimed at assuring that everyone in the group has the opportunity to understand every idea. As used by the Center for Interactive Management, the last step in applying NGT is to ask each individual member of the group to vote anonymously on what that individual believes are the five 'most important' ideas in the set of ideas that remains after clarification. This voting record becomes part of the permanent data set on how members of the group share or do not share beliefs about relative importance of constituent factors in the complex issue under consideration. It allows a ranking pattern to be produced reflecting a group product at a certain point in time in con-sidering the issue. This ranking pattern will be referred to as Pattern One in the subsequent discussions.

Interpretive structural modeling
The second methodology always used in the cases being discussed is called Interpretive Structural Modeling (ISM) (Warfield, 1976, 1982a). It is a methodology for group construction of patterns that relate to the issue. It is also a powerful learning method, because it involves disciplined, detailed examination of relationships between factors involved in the complex issue, accompanied by discussion and further clarification.

The patterns produced by the use of this methodology can take any of a variety of forms. A very common form of pattern that is produced is called a 'problematique'. This particular pattern shows how a set of problems, each of which is involved in the issue, are interrelated in an influence pattern. Specifically, such a pattern shows how a given problem may cause some other problems in the set to become worse. Problematiques typically contain 'cycles': i.e., subsets of problems such that each problem in a subset makes every other problem in the subset worse. Cycles represent (i.e., model) escalating situations that may only be susceptible to corrective action by working with all members of the cycle as a group, rather than working individually and independently with problems uninformed by their interaction.

Another type of pattern that can be produced using ISM is called a 'priority structure'. Such a structure shows the sequence in which component problems of an issue should be addressed. These structures also typically contain cycles, meaning that some problems need to be addressed simultaneously.

The priority structure should be informed by the problematique. Otherwise, problems will be treated in a way that is uninformed by their mutual interaction. Such a piecemeal approach is responsible for many of the complex issues that persist through time, and for the failure of many ameliorative actions that are taken with good intentions.

Once a structure is produced, various data can be taken from the structure itself, without regard to the content. For example, it is possible to count the number of cycles that are present, and to count the number of members in each cycle. It is also possible to quantify the length of the complete structure, which is a measure of the complexity and difficulty of working holistically with the issue at hand. Such data are described as *structural features of the patterns*. It is notable that such data have been impossible for most group researchers to gain for the simple reason that ordinary discourse does not make visible the patterns, so that no structural information is available.

In addition, there will always be one pattern produced from the ISM work that can be compared meaningfully with Pattern One produced from the NGT work. This second pattern will be called Pattern Two.

Finally, it is possible to do studies correlating Pattern One with Pattern Two. These *correlation studies* are the only data that must be computed through analysis of data arising directly in the issue studies. The correlation studies involve well-known statistical techniques.

Since all the data originate in the application of the two methodologies in a group setting, other investigators who create the environmental conditions of the type applied in the Center for Interactive Management, and who apply these methodologies, will be able to generate additional data and to construct new correlation studies to verify, refute, or elaborate on what is reported here.

Three laws

The study of the various types of data discussed previously has been focused in the statement of three laws. This is to make very clear the central conclusions of the research, and to challenge other investigators to acknowledge them and take advantage of what they say or, alternatively, to carry out studies that challenge the laws.

The law of inherent conflict

The Law of Inherent Conflict is empirically realized by examining the nature of the voting that leads to Pattern One. Data from forty-three working group applications of NGT show the following:

■ Average number of ideas clarified: 64
■ Average number of ideas receiving at least one vote in the top five   33

The complete data are presented elsewhere (Warfield, 1990, Appendix 5). What appears here is a small excerpt from the total data array. Note that if there were unanimity among the members, out of the average number of 64 ideas that were clarified, only 5 would receive any votes in the top five. The actual number receiving votes is almost seven times that number. The average number, as well as the individual-case data, shows that there are always major differences between the group members concerning the relative importance of individual factors in the issue.

The Law of Inherent Conflict then reads as follows:

No matter what the complex issue, and no matter what the group involved in its study, there will be significant inherent conflict within the group stemming from different perceptions of the relative significance of the factors involved in the complex issue.

If one chose to assume that there is some correct answer to the question: 'what are the five most important factors in this issue?', the data indicate that at most one member of the group has the 'right answer' and the rest are wrong. A much more likely conclusion is that they are all wrong in some sense.

The question may arise as to whether the conflicts can be separated into cognitive and emotional differences. If they can, it is clear from the data that the differences are individualized rather than associated with blocs or groups. The common treatment of conflict, which assumes two parties to the conflict, is not at all consistent with the data. The data do not show blocs or groups. They show individuals expressing different beliefs. It is reasonable to assume that the majority of the differences stems from cognitive factors. Before such an assumption is allowed to take much credibility, it is important to look at what the other two laws have to say.

The law of structural underconceptualization

The Law of Structural Underconceptualization stems from data arising in 31 cases of application of ISM. These data show the following:

- Average number of ideas structured: 22
- Average length of the longest cycle appearing in the structural pattern: 7.1
- Average length of condensed hierarchy: 6.3
- Average walk-length along the longest cycle plus the condensed hierarchy: 13.4
- Percentage of structures with at least one cycle: 96.8

The complete data appear elsewhere (Warfield, 1990, Appendix 5). What is presented here consists of excerpts from the total array of data.

Structural underconceptualization means that the organization of the information about a given issue is insufficient to enable the important patterns to be inspected. Because the structuring of the information with the help of

ISM produces structures with cycles in almost 97 percent of the cases, and because cycles are almost never mentioned, much less identified, in the ordinary way of looking at complex issues, we can say as a first aspect of underconceptualization that ordinary processes omit recognition and interpretation of the cycles that are at work in a given issue. The second aspect of underconceptualization stems from the normal absence of any sense of length of logic, which in the above data is conservatively at least 13 units long (including that part of the logic walk that traverses the longest cycle). The third aspect of underconceptualization arises by ignoring in ordinary approaches to issues the human limitations on working mentally with information, which are well known from the work of Miller, Simon, and others; but which seem systematically to be ignored in systems analysis and design activity.

The formal statement of the Law of Structural Underconceptualization is as follows:

No matter what the complex issue, and no matter what the group involved in its study, the outcomes of ordinary group process (i.e., process in which computer support for developing the formal logical structure of the issue is lacking) will be structurally underconceptualized (as evidenced, for example, by the lack of delineation of the cycles and of any structural connections among them).

The law of uncorrelated extremes

The Law of Uncorrelated Extremes is a consequence of analysis and comparison of data arising from NGT and ISM sessions dealing with a common issue. It arises from a statistical comparison of Pattern One (seen as one extreme in the evolution of an adequate perception of a complex issue and its resolution, i.e., the initial synthesized group view); and Pattern Two (seen as the other extreme in the evolution, i.e., the view synthesized by the group during the ISM sessions).

If one presumed that the group had a satisfactory initial interpretation of the complex issue, and that only modest change in this view would appear as a consequence of the use of ISM, the result would be that there would be a strong correlation between Pattern One and Pattern Two. In fact, what was discovered (Kapelouzos, 1989) is that there is *no correlation* between Pattern One and Pattern Two! This startling result shows that there is major learning going on during the ISM exercise which results in patterns for interpreting the issue that were entirely absent in the initial thinking of the group.

It is probably impossible to overstate the implications of this finding for group work on complex issues. This finding alone explains to a large extent why so many complex issues continue unresolved year after year and, in some instances, decade after decade. This finding is, however, indicative of a necessary condition and far from conclusive in terms of a sufficient condition for resolving complex issues. The reason does not lie in the data or in the process. Instead it lies in the absence of adequate usage and adequate follow-up study. Why is there inadequate usage and follow-up? It is largely because of the lack of understanding on the part of authority figures, i.e., intervention agents or executives with implementation authority to understand, appreciate, and be guided by the findings given herein. Without this attention, it is not possible to tap the resources required to do what is needed, in spite of the fact that the financial and human burdens that arise from ignoring or neglecting this condition far exceed the costs of the resources required to take advantage of it.

The formal statement of the Law of Uncorrelated Extremes is as follows:

No matter what the complex issue, and no matter what the group involved in its study, the *initial* aggregate group opinion concerning the logical pattern of the factors involved in the issue and the *final* aggregate group opinion concerning the logical pattern of the factors involved in the issue (i.e., the views at the two extremes of the application of the Generic Design Science, before and after) will be uncorrelated; showing that significant learning takes place through the application of the generic design processes.

Compatibility With Prior Study

The research results described above have been compared with earlier research of such authors as Bales, Tuckman, Miller, Simon, Argyris, and Janis mentioned earlier. There do not appear to be any conflicts between these results and those reported by these authors in their referenced work. On the other hand, there is a major discrepancy between these results and the work on conflict resolution reported by Burton (1987). As mentioned earlier, Burton insists that conflicts involve deeply rooted values that are non-negotiable, and this is why so many conflicts are so difficult to work with. Burton does not integrate the work of the authors mentioned above, and does not discuss any ideas having to do with the cognitive component of group activity, but places all of the emphasis on the emotional. Such a posture applied to conflict resolution precludes any findings of a comprehensive nature, for it is equivalent to an assumption that knowledge plays no role in conflict resolution. In contrast, the research results reported above, while not conclusive with regard to their significance in conflict resolution, stress that in the absence of cognitive equilibrium, emotional equilibrium is not likely to be found. And in the absence of both emotional and cognitive equilibrium, conflict is not likely to be resolved.

The conceptual shortcomings discussed here may have prevented the introduction of the kinds of processes into conflict-resolution group work that help provide interpretive means to cognitive equilibrium; thereby precluding any study of the potentially beneficial impact of cognitive equilibrium in promoting emotional equilibrium. Also these shortcomings may have prevented the testing and use of processes that can be highly effective in resolving conflict.

Conclusions

New research results suggest strongly that effective group work on complex issues should begin with a facilitated approach to cognitive equilibrium, followed by efforts to achieve emotional equilibrium. The combination of these two components, if achieved, would produce a state of serenity based in human satisfaction at having discovered how to interpret and to resolve complex issues.

In spite of the potential benefits of applying these research results to all group work involving complexity, it will still be necessary to make significant inroads into the relevant community power structures before the true benefits of high-quality group work can be translated into human society.

References

Allison, G.T. (1971), *Essence of Decision: Explaining the Cuban Missile Crisis*, Little, Brown, Boston.

Argyris, C. (1982), *Reasoning, Learning, and Action*, Jossey-Bass, San Francisco.

Bales, R.F. (1951), *Interaction Process Analysis*, Addison-Wesley, Cambridge, Massachusetts.

Burton, J.W. (1987), *Resolving Deep-Rooted Conflict: A Handbook*, University Press of America, Lanham, Maryland.

Delbecq, A.L., Van de Ven, A.H., and Gustafson, D.H., (1975), *Group Techniques for Program Planning: A Guide to Nominal Group and DELPHI Processes*, Scott, Foresman, Glenview, Illinois.

Janis, I.L. (1982), *Stress, Attitudes, and Decisions*, Praeger, New York.

Kapelouzos, I.B. (1989), 'The impact of structural modeling on the creation of new perspectives in problem-solving situations', *Proceedings 1989 European Congress on Systems Science*, AFCET, Lausanne, pp. 915–932.

Miller, G.A. (1956), 'The magical number seven, plus or minus two: some limits on our capacity for processing information', *Psychology Review*, 63, pp. 81–97.

Perrow, C. (1984), *Normal Accidents: Living with High-Risk Technologies*, Basic Books, New York.

Salk, J. (1985), *Anatomy of Reality: Merging of Intuition and Reason*, Praeger, New York, (orig. publ. by Columbia U. Press).

Simon, H.A. (1974), 'How big is a chunk?', *Science,* 183, pp. 482–488.

Tuckman, B.W. (1965), 'Developmental sequences in small groups', *Psychology Bulletin*, 63, pp. 384–399.

Warfield, J.N. (1976), *Societal Systems: Planning, Policy, and Complexity*, Wiley, New York (reprinted, 1989, Intersystems, Salinas, California).

Warfield, J.N. (1982a), 'Interpretive structural modeling', in S.A. Olsen, ed., *Group Planning and Problem-Solving Methods in Engineering*, Wiley, New York, pp. 155–201.

Warfield, J.N. (1982b), 'Organizations and systems learning', *General Systems*, 27, pp. 5–74.

Warfield, J.N. (1988), 'The magical number three − plus or minus zero', *Cybernetics and Systems,* 19, pp. 339–358.

Warfield, J. N. (1990), *A Science of Generic Design: Managing Complexity through Systems Design*, Intersystems, Salinas, California (2 vols).

Zeleny, M. (1989a), Book Review: *Patterns, Thinking, and Cognition*, by H. Margolis, in *Human Systems Management,* 8, pp. 248–249.

Zeleny, M. (1989b), 'Stable patterns from decision-producing networks: New interfaces of DSS and MCDM', *MCDM WorldScan*, 3, pp. 6–7.

Zeleny, M. (1989c), 'Cognitive equilibrium: A new paradigm of decision making?', Editorial, *Human Systems Management*, 8, pp. 185–188.

Zeleny, M. with Kasanen, E. and Ostermark, R. (1991), 'Gestalt system of holistic graphics: New management support view of MCDM', *Computers and Operations Research*, 18.

Problem-solving exercises and theories of conflict resolution

The cluster of informal third-party intervention techniques known variously as 'problem-solving workshops' (Burton, 1969, 1987), 'inter-active problem solving' (Kelman, 1986), 'third party consultation' (Fisher, 1983), or 'collaborative, analytical problem solving' (Banks and Mitchell, 1991) have conventionally been regarded as the epitome of practicality within the field of conflict research. They are seen as processes through which informal, powerless, and – usually – academic third parties can affect the course of protracted and deep-rooted conflict, by providing parties to such conflicts with opportunities to interact in an analytical rather than coercive manner as well as giving scholarly insights into the parties' mutual predicament. The main thrust of the use of such innovative approaches has always tended to be the practical one of bringing about positive, conflict-reducing effects on conflictful relationships, which have resisted the efforts of those using more traditional means of reducing or resolving conflicts, such as formal negotiation, mediation or conciliation.

On the other hand, there is a less obvious aspect of the use of such informal approaches that emphasises less the practical impact that these exercises might have upon the ongoing conflict and more their effects upon the academic participants – the 'panel' as it is called in many such exercises. This aspect concerns the worth of such exercises in terms of the insights into conflicts in general gained from participating and, in certain cases, of their 'theory development' potential. John Burton, one of the pioneers of this school, has long argued that problem-solving exercises provide unique opportunities for the direct field-testing of general theories about protracted conflicts and their resolution, and that *only* such occasions provide the chance of unambiguously testing the appropriateness of particular conflict resolution initiatives and their associated theories (Burton, 1972).

In this chapter, I wish to take up this theme of the relationship of theory to practice in problem-solving exercises and consider how such exercises might be used to develop theories about conflict and its resolution.

That they do so is, in my experience, undeniable. Almost everyone involved in the use of such approaches has commented informally on the number of insights into the nature of conflict they have gained and the number of conventional and accepted views they have discarded, after participating in them. It may be that such exercises are equally powerful in *theory building* as in practical *conflict resolution*, but until they are systematically examined in this role, their theory-building potential may remain neglected.

Types of problem-solving exercise

The nature of problem-solving exercises has been fully described and criticised elsewhere, both by those practising and those attempting to analyse them. It would be pointless to repeat that work here. Those interested in the detailed analysis of such processes should consult a number of excellent surveys and analyses available (Burton, 1969; Yalem, 1971; Kelman, 1972; Fisher, 1972; Mitchell, 1973; Warfield, 1988). However, it seems necessary to provide an outline sketch of the processes involved and to make a number of distinctions between various types of exercise before proceeding to examine the manner in which such activities have been, or might be, used to fulfil any theory-building function.

Briefly, problem-solving exercises share a number of key characteristics, irrespective of how much they differ in details of structure, process, and purpose. Such exercises invariably involve informal, week-long meetings of the representatives of parties in protracted, deep-rooted, and frequently violent conflict in an informal, often academic, setting that permits the re-analysis of their conflict as a shared problem and the generation of some alternative courses of action to continued coercion, together with new options for a generally acceptable and self-sustaining resolution, involving agreement and a new relationship between erstwhile adversaries.

The first generally shared characteristic is that problem-solving exercises are *externally oriented*. By this I mean that the main focus of effort is on the conflict and the set of relationships outside the actual exercise itself, although both conflict and relationships are reflected in the structure and processes of the workshop itself – in the antagonisms of those who participate, their attitudes, goals and beliefs, and their interaction during the course of the exercise. Unlike some therapeutic group exercises, the principal objective of problem-solving workshops is not primarily to affect the individuals within the workshop itself, their feelings, perceptions, behaviour, or changing relationships, except insofar as such effects contribute to the analysis of the conflict. The principal objective is to affect the broader adversarial relationship.

Secondly, exercises are almost invariably *triangular in structure*, consisting of representatives of two (or more) parties or coalitions in conflict, together with a third party acting as convener, facilitator, moderator, and source of ideas for the adversaries. In most problem-solving exercises, *the 'third party' consists of a panel* rather than a single individual or pair of intermediaries, and this provides many of the strengths of the approach in (among other things) assisting participants to step out of the role of combative representative and, however temporarily, into that of an analyst of a shared, if intractable, problem. The presence of a third-party panel does, however, also introduce a complicating factor into third-party procedures, in that a further layer of interaction (intra-panel) is added to the already complex structure of more conventional forms of mediation or facilitation.

Finally, the nature of problem-solving exercises makes it clear that they are *small-group phenomena*, with the implication for research and theory building that many concepts and ideas from the literature on group dynamics or group decision-making are likely to be relevant to any theoretical understanding of problem-solving exercises.

It has been frequently argued that differences between various forms and examples of problem-solving exercise are more important than the similarities. Again, this point has been (inconclusively) debated in the literature on problem-solving and will be left on one side for the purposes of this chapter. However, in exploring the relationship between theory development and the practice of conflict resolution one familiar distinction seems to be helpful. This is the broad distinction, proposed by Foltz (1977) in his discussion of the various *purposes* of such exercises, between *problem-solving* and what he terms *process-promoting* workshops.

In Foltz's scheme, the former are deliberately designed and intended to have an immediate and direct impact on the course of the conflict, usually through their involvement as participants of individuals close to top decision-makers. As Foltz comments, such exercises can 'gradually take on the appearance of a negotiating session, but one characterised by considerably more openness and willingness to examine radical solutions than is usual'. They often produce an output that can be communicated back to others in the world outside the workshop 'who may then treat them as staff work for more traditional formal negotiations, if they wish' (Foltz, 1977, p. 203).

In contrast, the objectives of *process-promoting* workshops are to have a more indirect, longer-term, impact on the conflict, through the involvement of opinion leaders, or key members of the attentive public, whose experience at the exercise can be translated into ideas and actions that, at some stage in the future, may form an intra-party environment that permits and encourages conflict-reducing strategies on the part of the leaders. For Foltz, they 'seek to prepare participants to take back to their ordinary roles in the outside world new abilities and knowledge which will help them function more effectively', at the very least there will be 'a more nuanced view of themselves and their opponents', as well as 'greater effectiveness in working within organised groups' (Foltz, 1977, pp. 203–204).

Starkly put, the contrast between *problem-solving* and *process-promoting* exercises is thus between the former's function of having a *direct* effect on the conflict and the adversaries' relationship, and the latter's of having a direct effect on the participants, who will, at a later stage, have an *indirect* effect on the conflict through their understanding of it and ability to convince others about the benefits of conflict reduction moves or conflict-resolution strategies.

This distinction may be considerably overdrawn. For one thing, it is clear that, even in the most policy-oriented workshops, the conflict is affected initially by influencing the participants themselves. Only when this has been achieved can there be any hope of affecting the future course of the conflict 'outside' the workshop. For another, there has been a great deal of work which attempts to affect both decision-makers and opinion leaders, and to prepare the way for formal negotiations between the former by establishing agree-able formulae, building a necessary level of trust, or enabling parties jointly to consider how to help one another move from bargaining corners in which they have become separately entrapped.

With this in mind, it might be better to discuss the matter in terms of time span envisaged for the exercise to have an impact on the conflict. Problem-solving exercises may thus be intended and shaped to have a direct effect upon key decision-makers and the immediate course of the conflict; they may be set up to have a medium-term effect by developing new insights and visions of opportunity for key opinion-leaders and opinion-formers, and thus preparing a suitable intra-party environment for the successful launching of conflict-reduction procedures; they may be aimed at an even-longer-term, educational goal through the transferring of conflict-resolution skills, techniques and philosophies widely within one or two communities, so that very long term expectations and relationships can be transformed eventually into those not based upon conflict and coercion. (The link here with skills-training workshops needs no emphasis.)

Any discussion of the *effects* of a problem-solving exercise returns the argument directly to the issue of theory and its relationship to the use of such exercises, for the most obvious, broad-gauge theoretical linkage postulated by those who use such approaches is that between the problem-solving exercise itself and the effects it is alleged to have on those who attend (participants); on the entities involved in the dispute (parties), especially their leaders; and on the conflict itself. For the purposes of this chapter I suggest that a rough meaning of 'theory' is *any assertion about regular, causal relationships between phenomena in the natural or social world outside the observer*. This, like most definitions of 'theory', emphasises the central conception of *linkage* in any theoretical formulation. Hence, a simple starting point for any examination of problem-solving exercises and theory is this assumption of a linkage between the holding of the exercise itself and its effect on the conflict. This is often expressed by asking questions about the 'success' of the exercise.

'Theories' about success

At a basic, 'common-sense' level, writers about problem- solving exercises frequently imply, or state directly, that the vindication for a workshop and the validation of the theories underlying the process arise from the exercise's 'success' in having an impact on the conflict in question. In more extreme claims, 'success' is interpreted as playing an undeniable and major part in the final resolving of that conflict or, at least, in clearly preparing the ground for more formal negotiations that lead to a settlement of the conflict and some new, productive relationship between former adversaries. Claims about success vary, therefore, according to the practitioner in question and the objective of the particular exercise being conducted.

I would like to suggest that the literature on *international* problem-solving deals with the issue of 'success' at three complementary levels and that, while there are differences in emphasis among practitioners, all make the theoretical assumption that there is a regular causal connection between the holding of their particular type of exercise and one or all of these three possible levels of effect. (As I argue above, all practitioners aim at affecting the conflict; they merely differ in whether they propose to do so directly or indirectly and whether they do so in the short or long term.) Thus, a problem-solving workshop is expected to have:

(1) An *impact* on the actual participants in the exercise, in the sense that it alters the perceptions, images, and attitudes of those taking part; changes their expectations; produces new perceived options and opportunities; and, in some cases, wholly alters the manner in which they view the situation facing them their party.

(2) An *output* from the workshop, in the sense that some exercises, at least, end with participants taking specific ideas or proposals, agreed principles, or some type of report back with them to their leaders or to other key members of their party for consideration and future action. In my own experience, outputs from problem-solving exercises vary greatly, ranging from a set of notes on possible future moves (on one occasion left ostentatiously on the workshop table by departing participants) through a list of agreed principles for a future settlement (see Azar, 1986) to a detailed plan for a bi-community arts and crafts exhibition proposed as an initial confidence-building measure.

(3) An *outcome* from the exercise, in the sense of a longer-term effect on the actual conflict itself, by diminishing the level of violence and coercion operative prior to the exercise, by bringing about a clear change in the policies of the adversaries (or, at a more modest level, a change in the rhetoric of the leaders) or by initiating some more formal continuation of the dialogue started during the exercise.

Unfortunately, it is often difficult to regard much of the writing about problem-solving exercises as 'theoretical', even if this merely implies some clear connection with *prior* conditions, structures and processes and a noticeable *subsequent* change in attitudes, statements, or behaviour on the part of those involved in the protracted conflict. Much existing literature takes the form of handbooks or manuals that list rules or sets of instructions on how to conduct a successful exercise, rather in the manner of a simple cookbook (Fisher with Ury, 1968; Burton, 1987; Ury, 1991). One looks in vain for 'if–then' propositions or clearly delineated sequences of linked hypotheses involving dependent and independent variables. The most usual format for such works is to suggest a set of steps, stages, or procedures that will ensure a 'successful' exercise, together with warnings about what to avoid if the exercise is not to break down and have a malign impact on the participants and, hence, on the conflict.

Micro-level theorising

However, with all three categories of result, the notion of a 'successful' workshop does embody or imply a theoretical element in the central argument that a properly conducted exercise will produce the anticipated and desired effects. Indeed, in *process-promoting* exercises, emphasis is on *impact* on the participants, rather than *output* or *outcome*, and the initiation of the exercise becomes a test of the broad hypothesis that an exercise conducted in a particular fashion will produce a noticeable and predictable change in the perceptions of those taking part. The change can, methodologically speaking, be simply indicated by some 'before and after' sampling of participants' perceptions and attitudes (Fisher, 1980).

Within that broad hypothesis, theories are implied about the effects of (a) various group dynamics; (b) third-party roles and functions; (c) size of workshop 'teams'; (d) the nature, status, and commitment of participants; (e) the precise procedures employed during the exercise; and (f) their sequence, on participants' post-exercise perceptions and expectations. For example, some problem-solving exercises involve a highly structured sequence of planned activities, designed to minimise antagonisms between adversaries, break down barriers, and create a minimal sense of trust between participants before moving on to further exercises directly related to the conflict in question (Doob, 1970; Levi and Benjamin, 1977). In others, a highly unstructured format is used, with relationships being implied between the ambiguity of the process or participants' sense of 'process ownership' and the final *impact* on those who have taken part in the exercise (Burton, 1969; Kelman, 1972). The theories underlying these alternative practices are usually left unstated (and hence untested − at least in any formal sense) by those using them, but they are nonetheless present.

Similarly, theories about *impact* on participants are implied, at least, in the handbooks for the conduct of the various types of problem-solving exercises mentioned above. Advice in these about, for example, the optimum number of participants in problem-solving exercises is clearly informed by some theoretical presuppositions derived either from experience, or from parallel theories of group behaviour transferred to problem-solving 'groups'. Again, instructions about the best 'mix' of individuals for a third-party panel involve such variables as the (relative) size of the panel and the experience, nationality, background, discipline, and behaviour of its members. These clearly involve some unstated theories about the effects on the course of the workshop and the *impact* on participants some less-than-optimal mix of 'panel structure' variables will have. These sub-optimal consequences are usually expressed rather ambiguously, by implying simply that the exercise will *not* achieve the desired aim of altering participants' self-images and images of the adversary or the overall analysis of their conflict.

In spite of much general ambiguity, at least at the *micro* level of theorising there is beginning to develop a body of hypothesis-testing literature which investigates the relationship between *exercise structure and procedure* and *participant change*, beginning with de Reuck's pioneering efforts to describe the phases of problem-solving exercises (de Reuck, 1974) and continuing with Ronald Fisher's work on measuring changes in participants' views of themselves, their adversaries and the conflict once they have been through various forms of problem-solving exercise (Fisher, 1991). Clearly, in this work there is now less of a willingness to accept the straightforward observation that some practices work well while others work badly and a growing desire to develop more precise theories about what independent (but controllable) variables produce what effects on what dependent variables.

Macro-level theorising

It has to be admitted, however, that much of this *hypothesis-testing* work has been carried out: (1) only at the level of the *impact* on those participating in exercises and (2) mainly in exercises involving participants who are representative of the views and feelings of 'rank and file' members of parties in conflict. Thus, efforts to test theory tend to be most systematic and advanced at the *micro-theoretical* level of problem-solving processes. They are much sketchier as regards proposing or testing hypotheses about patterns of relationships between workshop structure and process and various types of *output* from an exercise. They are almost nonexistent regarding the *outcome* of problem-solving exercises, that is, at testing regular relationships between the exercise itself and recognisable changes in the ongoing conflict.

In a paradoxical way, however, some practitioners have argued in their writings that problem-solving exercises themselves provide an opportunity to test more general theories about the causes and nature of conflicts and that the whole point of conducting such exercises is twofold: (1) to have a practical and positive effect upon the course of the conflict and the search for a solution; but also (2) to enable theorists of the nature and dynamics of social conflicts to test out their hypotheses with those actually involved in and knowledgeable about a particular case.

This argument is implied in most of the existing literature on problem-solving, particularly that which embraces the principle that problem-solving exercises enable participants and parties to analyse and thus fully understand the nature of the conflict in which they are involved, before generating conflict-resolving options for the future. Its main tenet is that the major input from third parties facilitating or conducting an exercise consists of 'insights' (or general *theories*) which enable parties to understand more fully their own situation and hitherto unrecognised alternatives for achieving their goals and underlying interests. Thus, in the 'analytical' stages of any exercise, what might be called *macro theories* of the sources and dynamics of social conflict are advanced as a way of having an *impact* on participants and as a prelude to producing an appropriate *output* from the exercise that will enable it to have a productive *outcome* by altering the adversarial relationship.

Problem-solving exercises thus *use* ideas and hypotheses from such *macro*-level concepts and theories as malign interaction spirals (Holsti and North, 1965; Deutsch, 1973), self-fulfilling prophecies (Merton, 1957), group identity (Kelman, 1969), or protracted conflict (Azar, 1985), among many others. It has also been argued that exercises provide an unrivalled opportunity to *test* such ideas, in that their acceptability to the participants is a good indication of whether they have any relevance to the case of conflict under analysis. If there is any validity for the ideas and propositions advanced during a problem-solving exercise about (for example) protracted social conflict, then their relevance will be apparent through the acceptance or rejection of the applicability and analytical utility of these ideas by participants themselves intimately involved in and affected by one example of this type of conflict. If participants have found that they or their leaders are involved in a self-reinforcing malign spiral of coercive interaction, then this will be recognised and acknowledged should this particular theory be presented as part of a possible explanation of their mutual predicament. This type of confirmation or rebuttal of an idea or hypothesis might fall far short of the kind of experimental or statistical testing required by classical science, but it does seem to offer the kind of tentative confirmation or disconfirmation required for developing sound 'craft' knowledge in the manner outlined by Caspary in his discussion of the nature of social science theory (Caspary, 1991). This may be the best level at which theory-testing can be carried out as far as the current stage of development of conflict research is concerned.

Meso-level theorising

Whatever the nature and rigour demanded of the theory-testing process, the argument up to now indicates clearly that there are at least two levels of theory involved in the use of problem-solving exercises: micro- and macro-level theory. To these I would like to add a third, neglected level, somewhere between the other two. If micro-level theory concerns the relationship between the structure and dynamics of the exercise itself and its impact on the participants, and macro-level theory deals with broad, general theories of social conflict which are related to problem-solving exercises through their use in that exercise, it also seems to be the case that problem solving uses, either implicitly or explicitly, what might be called *meso-level theories*. These involve hypotheses about the anticipated *outcome* of the exercise, and focus on the dynamics of the conflict, particularly at the stage when the problem-solving exercise is initiated.

Again, many of the ideas and hypotheses of meso-level theory are implied in what problem-solving practitioners write and are at least implicitly tested by problem-solving activities. Meso-level theories deal with such issues as:

(1) The most effective level to pitch a problem-solving exercise when third parties confront a complex, multi-party, multi-issue conflict.
(2) The conditions and relationships in the conflict that make a problem-solving exercise most appropriate.
(3) The most appropriate objectives for a problem-solving exercise, given the existing conditions and relationships in the ongoing conflict.
(4) The most appropriate level of representation of the parties at the exercise.
(5) The appropriate strategy to pursue when confronted with adversaries themselves subject to divisive internal conflicts that might need to be dealt with before the central, and most obvious, conflict is tackled.
(6) The most appropriate mix of parties to be invited to participate in the exercise, given the situation that more than two clearly defined and coherently structured parties are involved in the conflict.
(7) The most influential and appropriate *output* to aim for at the end of the conflict, given both the existing relationship between the adversaries and the divisions and factions within each.
(8) The most appropriate follow-up activities to aim for in order to minimise the *re-entry problem* for participants.

From this exemplary list it can easily be seen that most *meso-* theoretical issues deal with questions of the dynamics of a conflict, the stages through which conflicts pass and the most appropriate set of conditions for:

(1) the organising and holding of a problem-solving exercise (When are the leaders of adversary parties least likely to welcome the proposal of a problem-solving exercise and when most likely to reject?); and

(2) the input of new insights regarding options and alternatives from a successfully conducted exercise (When will these have most and when least impact?).

It can also be seen that testing any hypotheses about appropriate times for proposing a problem-solving exercise involves a familiar process: review and compare the conditions that existed on past occasions when problem-solving initiatives occurred and were either accepted or rejected out of hand. This procedure should give some indication of propitious and unpropitious circumstances which can be used as guidelines and thus tested when new problem-solving initiatives are proposed or launched.

In passing it should be recognised that some theoretical work on this issue has recently been initiated in confronting the issue of when conflicts are 'ripe' for reduction or resolution initiatives, including problem-solving exercises (Zartman, 1985; Fisher and Keashly, 1988; Zartman and Aurik, 1991). Much of this theoretical work posits a sequence of stages through which protracted international and intranational conflicts pass, starting with a latent stage and passing to a stage of prosecution or 'confrontation'. From that point, should resolution efforts fail, some crisis will lead to the employment of increasing levels of coercion and violence between the adversaries, at which point efforts at conflict reduction or resolution become pointless until, through a variety of processes that protract the conflict, the adversaries come to face an impasse or both approach some imminent mutual catastrophe and become willing to consider resolution opportunities. Hence, the use of problem-solving exercises becomes possible once again.

This approach to theory development seems a fruitful one, although my own experience with the use of problem-solving exercises suggests that they have been usefully employed at the height of violent interactions and confrontation (the Indonesia–Malaysia–Singapore workshop in 1965–6; see Mitchell, 1981); in periods of impasse (the Cyprus workshop in 1966 and the Lebanon workshops in 1983); and in the period immediately following the short but violent 1982 war in the South Atlantic (the Maryland workshops, 1983–5; see Little and Mitchell, 1989). This suggests that, while it may be the case that there might be some stages in all conflicts when problem-solving exercises have no chance of having any impact or outcome (and this is by no means proved), protracted conflicts can pass through a wide variety of stages in their 'life cycle'. Moreover, this progression may not be linear, in the sense that some conflicts circle back to 'earlier' stages and might pass through both malign and benign cycles of interaction several times. I outline one possible model of such a 'dynamic protraction' in Figure 6.1 and include a number of cases of problem-solving initiatives at the appropriate stage.

A further implication of the conception that protracted conflicts can pass through a complex and iterative series of stages is that certain types of problem-solving or conflict-reducing activities may be more appropriate

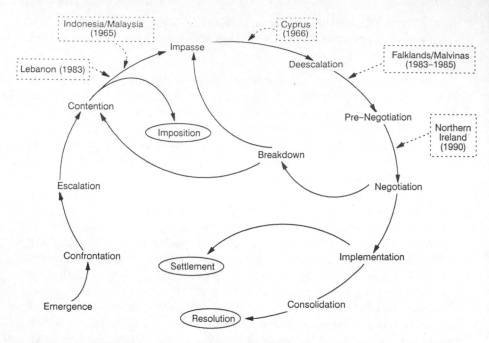

Figure 6.1 Dynamic protraction model of conflict

than others, depending upon the stage reached, or returned to, by the conflict under study. Again, this argument is simply an extension of that which holds that *no* third-party activity can have anything other than a detrimental effect at *certain stages* of a protracted conflict. If this is the case, then it is important for theory-building to delineate the characteristics of those stages, and also to delineate those circumstances in which third-party initiatives, including problem-solving exercises, *are* likely to have positively evaluated effects on the conflict, and which is the most appropriate form of such initiative or exercise to be used in particular circumstances. Fisher has already begun to tackle the development of this branch of meso-theory for conflict resolution with his *contingency model* approach and has used the set of exercises initiated since 1965 by third parties trying to bring about change in the Cyprus conflict as data to compare inputs and effects (see Fisher, 1991; Fisher and Keashly, 1991).

Fisher's work represents one area in which *meso-level* theories of conflict and its resolution are beginning to be formulated and tested in order better to inform the practice of problem-solving exercises. Similarly, testing of the effectiveness of exercise *outputs* simply involves, at least in principle, evaluation of past effects of exercises and a pragmatic noting of the circumstances in which problem-solving inputs had major, peripheral, or no effects. Kelman has already made a start on developing and pragmatically testing meso-level theories of problem-solving: (a) by hypothesising that outputs from problem-solving exercises that demand major change from existing policies will be rejected and have no effects on the course of the conflict (Kelman, 1972); and (b) by investigating the fragile dynamics of cross-adversary coalition building (Kelman, 1993). However, meso-level theory development and testing remains the most neglected theoretical aspect of the informed use of problem-solving exercises.

In summarising the above arguments, it seems important to emphasise that problem-solving exercises do appear to provide a variety of opportunities to examine and test theoretical ideas at a variety of levels, from micro-level hypotheses about 'within-exercise' relationships to macro-level propositions about the effects of the exercise output on the subsequent course of the conflict. I have tried to outline where such theory-testing opportunities arise in Figure 6.2, which employs a simple input–output model of problem-solving to show where theories necessarily become involved in such procedures and, hence, where opportunities for their testing arise.

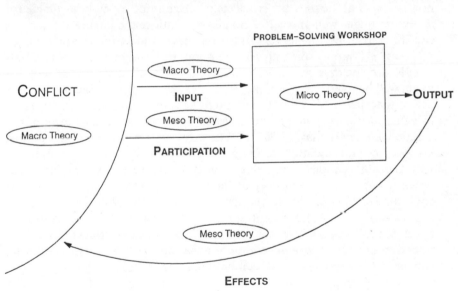

Figure 6.2   Theorising and problem-solving

Theory generation and problem-solving exercises

In spite of the work mentioned above, it has to be admitted that, while opportunities for *using* theories in problem-solving exercises have been seized upon by practitioners (either consciously or unconsciously), opportunities for systematically *testing* theories in such settings have been afforded a relatively low priority. This is understandable. For one thing, there is the ethical question of whether practitioners can ever justify using problem-solving exercises, which inevitably involve people locked in an adversarial relationship and a protracted, and usually destructively violent, conflict, for any purpose other than trying to seek a solution to that conflict. If the answer is that using problem-solving workshops for other purposes is not justified – a position taken by most practitioners – then theory testing becomes wholly subordinate (and occasionally utterly irrelevant) to the main purposes of the exercise. Again, such opportunities for testing theories in problem-solving exercises in any save Caspary's 'craft knowledge' sense are further limited by the small universe of such exercises carried out to date on protracted and deep-rooted conflicts. At some stage, it might be possible to increase the numbers available for comparative analysis and theory testing by developing quasi-experimental exercises, in the same manner as Lindskold and his colleagues in their examination of de-escalatory strategies such as Graduated and Reciprocal Initiatives in Tension reduction (GRIT) (Lindskold and Collins, 1978; Lindskold and Finch, 1981). At present, however, and at the most generous count, the number of cases available for analysis remains well under 100. Some systematic and comparative analysis can, of course, be further conducted on these, and in the final section of this chapter I outline some suggestions about how this might be carried out.

It is also the case that there exists a third way in which theory building might well be related to practical problem- solving exercises, apart from the *use* of theories in conducting such exercises and the *testing* of theories by using participant reaction and evaluation as a form of 'crucial test'. Many practitioners have remarked on how their own involvement in problem-solving exercises has, through the almost unique opportunity for direct involvement with and observation of participants interacting, generated new ideas and insights into (a) the psychology of 'being in conflict', (b) the dynamics of conflictual interaction, and (c) the opportunities for and obstacles to processes such as confidence building, entrapment, or de-commitment, to name only a few. Thus, it seems unarguable that problem-solving exercises offer unique opportunities for *theory generation* on the part of the practitioners who conduct and observe such procedures. That this is the case should occasion no surprise. Problem-solving exercises are frequently and justifiably described as unique learning experiences, although this argument usually concentrates upon the unique opportunities afforded parties in conflict to learn about their conflict and about one another. While this may be the key practical dynamic for affecting the course of the conflict and – hopefully – its resolution, the insights generated in the members of the third party – the practitioners, facilitators, or panel – are likely to form a major input into the development of theories of social conflict at macro-, meso-, and micro-levels. This is so, provided it is possible to approach the task of theory development at all three levels in some systematic manner, rather than – as has been the case until relatively recently – by treating each exercise as unique and unrepeatable, or simply as an opportunity to *apply* already well-understood and well-tested theory.

Future directions for theory development

I would, therefore, argue that the field of conflict research is approaching a point at which problem-solving exercises are no longer regarded simply as pioneering and unique efforts to *apply* some theoretical ideas about the effects of single inputs of new information into a conflict interaction in the hope of having some beneficial effect. Rather, there will be an attempt to develop some soundly based 'craft knowledge' about the generating, testing, and utilisation of relevant theories about social conflict and its resolution in problem-solving exercises. These will be systematically scrutinised and categorised so that the relationship between their structure and processes and their effects can be compared and examined. Thus, from a *theory development*, as opposed to a *practical effect*, viewpoint, problem-solving exercises will contribute in three ways and at three levels (see Fig. 6.3).

Theory Level

Theory Focus		Micro Level Exercise Dynamics	Meso Level Conflict Dynamics	Macro Level Conflict Causes, Origins and Solutions
	Generating			
	Testing			
	Applying			

Figure 6.3   Theoretical aspects of problem-solving exercises.

There is much evidence that the old approach to problem-solving exercises as unique and essentially practical — or, at most, merely *theory-using* — activities is beginning to change; and that both analysts and practitioners are beginning to try to develop a body of systematic and comparative information about the testing and generation as well as the use of theories relevant to problem-solving exercises. Initial efforts at systematically gathering descriptive and comparative data on problem-solving exercises on deep-rooted and protracted conflict have been going on for some time (Fisher, 1972; Mitchell, 1981; Hill, 1982; Fisher, 1983), as have efforts to develop plausible hypotheses from practical involvement in individual workshops (Kelman, 1972). There are increasing signs that these efforts are developing into systematic attempts to develop maps of micro- and meso-level theories about problem-solving exercises, particularly theories which deal with appropriate conditions for various types of problem-solving exercise to be used with the greatest prospect of bringing about the predicted and desired alteration in the subsequent course of the conflict (Fisher and Keashly, 1991; Fisher, 1992).

Allied to this is the development of systematic efforts to categorise the main types of problem-solving exercise and other third-party intervention processes currently employed by practitioners of 'multi-track diplomacy' (Diamond and McDonald, 1991). Finally, an interesting and relatively new development in the practice of third-party problem-solving has been the increasing use of a series of exercises involving the same participants, which affords greater opportunities of making *within-series* comparisons of exercise structure, process, impact, output, and outcome. Such series also enable the monitoring of the outcome of each of the exercises in the series, and the comparing of effects from different types of output on a changing conflict, rather than confining analysis to a single output from one exercise which becomes a single input to a complex conflict at one point of time (Little and Mitchell, 1989; Mitchell, forthcoming).

It may be that such series of exercises will offer greater opportunities for theory development in the threefold sense of hypothesis generation, theory testing, and theory use, than have previously been available to students of the 'art' of facilitated and collaborative problem-solving in protracted and deep-rooted conflicts. If this turns out to be the case, such opportunities will assist in moving our theoretical understanding of the nature and effects of problem-solving workshops away from its present level which resembles, in many ways, Pruitt's characterisation of mediation theory as being in the same condition as eighteenth-century medicine and surgery, in that it 'remains at a primitive level of development' and 'consists largely of aphorisms about appropriate actions' (Pruitt, 1986, p. 237). Such a movement in our theory of third-party problem-solving is long overdue.

References

Azar, E.E. (1985), 'Protracted social conflict: Ten propositions', *International Interactions*, 12, pp. 59–70.

Azar, E.E. (1986), 'The Lebanon case', in E.E. Azar and J.W. Burton, eds, *International Conflict Resolution: Theory and Practice*, Wheatsheaf Press, Brighton.

Azar, E.E. and Burton, J.W. (eds) (1986), *International Conflict Resolution: Theory and Practice*, Wheatsheaf Press, Brighton.

Banks, M.H. and Mitchell, C.R. (1991), *A Handbook of the Analytical Problem-Solving Approach*, Institute for Conflict Analysis and Resolution, Fairfax, Virginia.

Burton, J.W. (1969), *Conflict and Communication*, Macmillan, London.

Burton, J.W. (1972), 'The resolution of conflict', *International Studies Quarterly*, 16, pp. 5–29.

Burton, J. W. (1987), *Resolving Deep Rooted Conflict: A Handbook*, University Press of America, Lanham, Maryland.

Caspary, W. R. (1991), 'Craft knowledge and clinical inquiry: An approach to the philosophy of social science', Mimeo, Washington University, St Louis, Missouri.

de Reuck, A. V. S. (1974), 'Controlled communication: Rationale and dynamics', *The Human Context*, 6, pp. 64–80.

Deutsch, M. (1973), *The Resolution of Conflict: Constructive and Destructive Processes*, Yale University Press, New Haven, Connecticut.

Diamond, L. and McDonald, J. (1991), *Multi-Track Diplomacy: A Systems Guide and Analysis*, Iowa Peace Institute Occasional Paper 3, Iowa Peace Institute, Grinnell, Iowa.

Doob, L. W. (ed.) (1970), *Resolving Conflict in Africa: The Fermeda Workshop*, Yale University Press, New Haven, Connecticut.

Fisher, R. (with Ury, W.) (1978), *International Mediation: A Working Guide*, Harvard Negotiation Project, Cambridge, Massachusetts.

Fisher, R. J. (1972), 'Third party consultation; a method for the study and resolution of conflict', *Journal of Conflict Resolution*, 16, pp. 67–94.

Fisher, R. J. (1980), 'A third party consultation workshop on the India-Pakistan conflict', *Journal of Social Psychology*, 112, pp. 191–206.

Fisher, R. J. (1983), 'Third party consultation as a method of conflict resolution: A review of studies', *Journal of Conflict Resolution*, 27, pp. 301–334.

Fisher, R. J. (1989), 'Pre-negotiation problem-solving discussions: Enhancing the potential for successful negotiations', *International Journal*, 64, pp. 442–474.

Fisher, R. J. (1991), 'Conflict analysis workshop on Cyprus: Final workshop report', Canadian Institute for International Peace and Security, Ottawa.

Fisher, R. J. (1992), 'The potential of third party consultation as a method of international conflict resolution', Occasional Paper, Canadian Institute for International Peace and Security, Ottawa.

Fisher, R. J. and Keashly, L. (1988), 'Third party intervention in inter-group conflict: Consultation is *not* mediation', *Negotiation Journal*, 4, pp. 381–393.

Fisher, R. J. and Keashly, L. (1991), 'The potential complementarity of mediation and consultation within a contingency model of third party intervention', *Journal of Peace Research*, 28, pp. 29–42.

Foltz, W. J. (1977), 'Two forms of unofficial conflict intervention: The problem-solving and the process-promoting workshops', Chap. 11 in M. R. Berman and J. E. Johnson, eds, *Unofficial Diplomats*, Columbia University Press, New York.

Hill, B. J. (1982), 'An analysis of conflict resolution techniques: From problem solving to theory', *Journal of Conflict Resolution*, 26, pp. 109–138.

Holsti, O. R. and North, R. C. (1965), 'The history of human conflict', Chap. 8 in E. B. McNeil, ed., *The Nature of Human Conflict*, Prentice-Hall, Englewood Cliffs, New Jersey.

Kelman, H. C. (1969), 'Patterns of personal involvement in the national system; a social psychological analysis of political legitimacy', Chap. 26 in J. N. Rosenau, ed., *International Politics and Foreign Policy*, Free Press, New York.

Kelman, H. C. (1972), 'The problem-solving workshop in conflict resolution', in R. L. Merritt, ed., *Communication in International Politics*, University of Illinois Press, Urbana, Illinois.

Kelman, H.C. (1982), 'Creating the conditions for Israeli-Palestinian negotiations', *Journal of Conflict Resolution*, 26, pp. 39–75.

Kelman, H.C. (1986), 'Interactive problem-solving: A social-psychological approach to conflict resolution', in W. Klassen, ed., *Dialogue Toward Inter-Faith Understanding*, Tantur Ecumenical Institute for Theological Research, Jerusalem.

Kelman, H.C. (1993), 'Coalitions across conflict lines; The interplay of conflicts within and between the Israeli and Palestinian communities', in J. Simpson and S. Worchel, eds, *Conflict between People and Peoples*, Nelson Hall, Chicago.

Levi, A.M. and Benjamin, A. (1977), 'Focus and flexibility in a model of conflict resolution', *Journal of Conflict Resolution*, 21, pp. 405–425.

Lindskold, S. and Collins, M.G. (1978), 'Inducing co-operation by groups and individuals', *Journal of Conflict Resolution*, 22, pp. 679–690.

Lindskold, S. and Finch, M.L. (1981), 'Styles of announcing conciliation', *Journal of Conflict Resolution*, 25, pp. 145–154.

Little, W. and Mitchell, C.R. (1989), *In the Aftermath: Anglo-Argentine Relations after the War for the Falklands/Malvinas*, University of Maryland, College Park, Maryland.

Merton, R.K. (1957), *Social Theory and Social Structure*, Free Press, Glencoe, Illinois.

Mitchell, C.R. (1973), 'Conflict resolution and controlled communication; some further comments', *Journal of Peace Research*, 10, pp. 123–132.

Mitchell, C.R. (1981), *Peacemaking and the Consultant's Role*, Gower Press, Basingstoke.

Mitchell, C.R. (1992), 'The Falklands/Malvinas workshop series: Light on the re-entry problem and on cross-adversary coalitions', Institute for Conflict Analysis and Resolution, George Mason University.

Pruitt, D.G. (1986), 'Trends in the scientific study of negotiation and mediation', *Negotiation Journal*, 2, pp. 237–244.

Ury, W. (1991), *Getting Past 'No': Negotiating with Difficult People*, New York, Bantam Books.

Warfield, J. (1988), 'Do as I say: A review essay of John W. Burton, *Resolving Deep-Rooted Conflict: A Handbook*', *International Journal of Group Tensions*, 18, pp. 228–238.

Yalem, R.J. (1971), 'Controlled communication and conflict resolution', *Journal of Peace Research*, 8, pp. 263–272.

Zartman, I.W. (1985), *Ripe for Resolution: Conflict and Intervention in Africa*, Oxford University Press, New York.

Zartman, I.W. and Aurik, J. (1991), 'Power strategies in de-escalation', Chap. 6 in L. Kriesberg and S.J. Thorson, eds, *Timing the De-Escalation of International Conflicts*, Syracuse University Press, Syracuse, New York.

Part II

Concepts and aspects of the resolution process

Managing differences in conflict resolution: The role of relational empathy[1]

Perhaps the fundamental characteristic of interpersonal conflict is the existence of *differences* between the participants. While the presence of differences does not necessarily lead to conflict, almost all conflicts revolve around dissimilarity in attitudes, perceptions, cultural values, communication style, needs, or goals. In order to promote successful conflict resolution, these differences must be dealt with productively by the participants. At the same time, it is precisely this dissimilarity that makes it difficult to resolve conflict. This chapter proposes that the concept of *relational empathy* can provide a means for understanding how to effectively manage differences in conflict situations.

In the *communication* literature communication behaviors are usually seen as influenced by communicators' attempts (or lack thereof) to consider the perspective of the other person. Empathy is associated with many important aspects of communication behavior, including *formulating communicative intentions* and goals, *devising strategies* to accomplish communicative purposes, and *constructing messages* consistent with communicative strategies (Arnett and Nakagawa, 1983; Barnlund and Nomura, 1985; Bennett, 1979; Berlo, 1960; Bochner and Kelly, 1974; Dance and Larson, 1976; Howell, 1982, 1983; Stewart, 1983). In the fields of *psychology, counseling, and psychotherapy*, empathy has been defined as a personality characteristic (Hogan, 1969; Truax and Mitchell, 1971), as *accuracy* in predicting another's internal state (Gompertz, 1960), as *emotional identification* with another individual (Feshbach, 1978; Stotland, 1969), as the process of *cognitive role-taking* (McCall and Simmons, 1978), and as *communicating a sense of understanding* to another (Rogers, 1975).[2]

In spite of the attention empathy has received in the communication and psychology literature, there has been relatively little conceptual development of empathy in the theory of conflict resolution. For example, influential books by Burton (1987), Cross, Names and Beck (1979), Filley (1975), Fisher (1980), Fisher and Ury (1981), Folger and Poole (1984), and McDonald (1984) do not address the concept. Other books, such as Borisoff and Victor (1989) and Hocker and Wilmot (1991), often used as texts in communication courses on conflict, only mention the term in passing. Perhaps this is due to the commonly held belief that empathy is made more difficult, and perhaps even rendered impossible, by major differences between communicators in values, attitudes, beliefs, and experiences. As Katz (1963, pp. 6−7) writes: 'It is a matter of common experience that we find it more difficult to establish empathy with those who are different from us.' Howell (1982, p. 108) makes a similar point: 'Empathy does not transcend the limits imposed by culture and knowledge and has no magic power to overcome differences in personality and background. *What has not been experienced cannot be perceived*' (emphasis in original). Such a conceptualization of empathy limits its usefulness for the study of conflict interaction. It is the purpose of this essay to describe the implications of a relational view of empathy for conflict resolution. While differences may indeed increase the difficulty of interaction, it is proposed that relational empathy is the key to managing such differences.

A relational view of empathy

Prevailing conceptualizations of empathy suffer from a *psychological view of understanding*, in which the emphasis is upon the re-creation in the listener of the meaning originally created by the speaker. A relational view of understanding, such as that outlined by Arnett and Nakagawa (1983), Stewart (1983), and Stewart and Thomas (1986) overcomes many of the limitations associated with the traditional notions of empathy. Based on the hermeneutic phenomenology of Heidegger and Gadamer, their view of what this paper refers to as relational empathy emphasizes a *productive* rather than a *reproductive* approach to understanding.

A relational approach goes beyond individual psychology and focuses on the creation of *shared meaning* during the interpersonal encounter. Understanding is not viewed as a 'product', but as a 'tensional event' occurring between the communicators. Because conflict interaction usually revolves around differences between the individuals, the traditional psychological view of empathy offers little basis for understanding. A relational view of empathy, on the other hand, provides a basis for building shared meaning between communicators.

Understanding is dynamic and provisional
Accuracy in inferring another's thoughts is an important characteristic of empathy in many conceptualizations (Dymond, 1949; Hill, 1983; Hobart and Fahlberg, 1965; Rogers, 1957, 1959, 1975, 1980; Taft, 1955; Truax, 1967). For example, Carl Rogers (1959, p. 210), one of the most influential writers on the concept of empathy, wrote in one of his earlier pieces that the state of empathy 'is to perceive the internal frame of reference of another with

accuracy and with the emotional components and meanings which pertain thereto as if one were the person, but without ever losing the "as if" condition'. Later he described empathy as 'entering the private perceptual world of the other and becoming thoroughly at home in it' (1980, p. 142). This emphasis on accuracy decreases the usefulness of empathy for conflict resolution since the differences in perspectives that characterize conflicts make it less likely that participants will be able to successfully predict each other's thinking processes.

Reviews by Cook (1971), Hastorf, Schneider, and Polefka (1970), Tagiuri (1969), and Warr and Knapper (1968) show that understanding others can be influenced by variables such as context, cognitive and affective characteristics of the perceiver, the relationship between the perceiver and the perceived, and developmental and cultural factors. Schutz (1967, pp. 106–107) points out that we always fall far short of grasping the totality of another's lived experiences. While it can be said that one's own stream of consciousness is given 'continuously and in all its fullness', the other's experience is given to the perceiver 'in discontinuous segments, never in its fullness, and only in interpretive perspectives'. Not only is understanding discontinuous and incomplete, but the inferences upon which understanding hinges are based upon the prior understandings and prejudices of the interpreter. As Buie (1981) shows, we make inferences about others by comparing cues we perceive about the other to our own past and present experiences.

Understanding is not an all-or-nothing phenomenon, something that does or does not occur. We can have no direct knowledge about the cognitive processes of another person. As Kelly (1963) proposes, individuals look at the world through transparent patterns or templates that they create and attempt to fit over the realities of which the world is composed. We come to understand our world through an infinite series of successive approximations. We formulate a construct, test it for its usefulness, and either maintain it or reformulate the construct. It is, of course, then retested time and again. Stewart (1983) emphasizes that the process of developing understanding is necessarily open. Meanings are not 'given' in language or even in the person; instead, the interpreter participates in the development of understanding as he or she encounters the discourse. In viewing empathy as a series of successive approximations to the other's point of view during social interaction, there is not as much concern with 'accuracy' as in many conceptualizations of empathy. More importantly, it negates the view that empathy can be 'achieved' in any kind of absolute sense. As Schutz (1967, p. 106) points out:

When I become aware of a segment of your lived experience, I arrange what I see within my own meaning-context. But meanwhile you have arranged it in yours. Thus I am always interpreting your lived experiences from my own standpoint. ... everything I know about your conscious life is really based on my knowledge of my own lived experience.

While one can never become another person, it is possible to erect a structure within the framework of which the other's interpretation of the world or of us takes shape or assumes meaning. This is a continuous process and these constructions must be continually adjusted during interaction through feedback. The other's feedback, both conscious and unconscious, both verbal and nonverbal, allows individuals to determine how well they have construed each other's perspective. Perceptions and messages are continually adjusted and corrected, allowing dyadic partners to seek some degree of integration.

Human understanding is always provisional, open to present and future change. Stewart and Thomas (1986) emphasize that relational understanding requires 'playfulness'. Rather than seeking 'certainty, closure and control' in the conversation, we must be tentative and experimental. If conversational partners can display a sense of open-endedness, they will find themselves 'literally playing with the ideas' they are discussing (Stewart and Thomas, 1986, p.198). They will 'enter a dynamic over which they do not have complete control, and the outcome of their talk can be a surprise to both of them, a creation of their meeting' (Stewart, 1983, p.387). Empathy, as defined in this essay, is part of an ongoing, corrective process that is dynamic and circular. In this way, it reflects the interdependence of participants and the transactional nature of communication. Thus, relational empathy allows two individuals to move toward varying degrees of understanding.

Understanding requires integration of affect and cognition

According to the counseling literature, it is the therapist's job to sense the other's 'confusion or his timidity or his anger or his feelings of being treated unfairly' (Rogers, 1967, p.92). The counselor's job is viewed as 'an active experiencing with the client of the feelings to which he gives expression' (Rogers, 1951, p.29). Havens (1979, p.41) discusses the need in psychotherapy for 'appreciating, sometimes verbalizing, the complexity of the other's emotions; hence the need for complex empathic speech'. In the communication literature it is sometimes advocated that the term empathy 'should be reserved for the process of feeling what another feels' (Burleson and Bingham, 1983, p.12). As Basch (1983) points out, some writers argue that an attempt to be rational may interfere with empathy, preventing one from experiencing the other's feelings.

Focus on affective responses has often led to empathy being confused with sympathy, or with a feeling of identification or commonality in feelings with the other. Wispe (1986) discusses the confusion between sympathy and empathy, showing the blurring of distinctions that exist between the two. Sympathy, which has a long history in social and developmental psychology, comes from the Greek *sympatheia*, which means literally 'with' (*syn*) 'feeling' or 'suffering' (*pathos*). Sympathy leads to increased sensitivity to the emotions of the other person and intensifies both the representation and the internal reaction to the other person's predicament (Wispe, 1986). Feelings of compassion and emotional identification often result. The pain (or other emotions) that one feels with the other arises from imagining how such a situation would be experienced by the self. The sympathizer looks to the past for similar experiences and thus draws from memory emotions thought appropriate for the situation.

Sympathy is based on projection and depends on similarity, making it inappropriate for most encounters involving conflict. Bennett (1979) warns against the use of the 'Golden Rule', which is based on sympathy, and advocates use of what he calls the 'Platinum Rule', which involves empathy. Reliance on sympathy, which is based on one's own standard of appropriate behavior, is usually misleading, can be disruptive, and leads to little progress in developing shared understanding in dealing with conflicts.

It is suggested here that the 'classical threefold division of psychology into cognition, affection, and conation' (Kelly, 1963, p. 130) is not useful in studying conflict interaction. This is not to argue that feelings do not exist or that they need not be understood, but it is to agree with Piaget (1974), who said that cognitive and affective aspects of behavior are inseparable and complementary. As pointed out by Reardon (1983, p. 4): 'Since empathy is neither a purely cognitive nor purely emotional activity, it requires concurrent usage of those areas of the brain which allow reasoning and emotion'. Seeking to create an understanding with another, an individual can certainly experience feelings similar to the other's, but the focus of empathy is the process of arriving at mutual integrative understandings of each other's perceptual field by an affective *and* cognitive assimilation of the other's values, meanings, symbols, intentions, etc. As understanding begins to take place between communicators, they come to know the organization of each other's world- or self-view, and this includes feelings and emotions.

Understanding is embedded in context

Understanding involves the process by which participants 'collectively determine the contextual values which structure their conversation' (Ricoeur, 1981, p. 107). These contextual values are of two types. Participants must seek to understand (a) the context underlying the other's expressions, and (b) the context in which the encounter itself is embedded.

The role of contextualizing the other's expression is addressed by Schutz (1967), who contends that understanding another person involves both 'objective' understanding and 'subjective' understanding. Establishing objective meaning involves placing the symbols and actions of the other into an interpretive scheme that one has established based on one's own life experiences. Thus, objective meaning is part of perceivers' interpretation of their own experience to themselves. However, establishing objective meaning of another's actions is not the same as understanding the subjective experience of the person performing these actions or using these symbols. Understanding subjective experience involves learning something about the communicator's own meaning-context.

In understanding the meaning-context of the other, the perceiver interprets not only the individual words or actions and their 'objective' meaning, but the 'total articulated sequence of syntactically connected words' (Schutz, 1967, p. 125). While every word or action retains its individual meaning, it is necessary to grasp the whole meaning of the action sequence or word statement. This synthesis is built up in steps as the encounter unfolds. In this way, unconnected words and actions 'constitute meaningful wholes and become discourse' (ibid.).

Moreover, the subjective meaning that a perceiver establishes can be based either on one's own meaning-context or on the other's meaning-context. In the first case, the perceiver can search her or his own past for experiences related to the other's action, in which case the subjective meaning is completely dependent on her or his own interpretive scheme. In the second case, the perceiver can look for clues to subjective meanings held by the other. Schutz explains that 'to know the subjective meaning of the product means that we are able to run over in our own minds in simultaneity or quasi-simultaneity the polythetic Acts which constituted the experience of the producer' (1967, p. 133). In other words, when we seek to understand the subjective meaning of another person, we are asking about the unique experiences that are occurring or have occurred for the other. However, as Schutz reminds us, 'no other person, not even he himself at another moment, can stand in his shoes at this moment' (1967, p. 135). Thus, while we are seeking to understand the other, this understanding will necessarily be imperfect; however, it will allow a deeper level of understanding than that obtained either through 'objective meaning' or through 'subjective meaning' based on one's own meaning-context.

Of course, comprehension of the other's meanings, including the context in which the other has produced these meanings, is not sufficient for the development of relational understanding. Meanings are constantly sifted and determined by the situation, and all interpretation depends to a large extent on the setting and the circumstances of the encounter. Research shows that efforts to seek the other's point of view may be more persistent in some situations than in others. Studies by Broome (1981, 1983) suggest that responses to others that take into account the other's perspective can be facilitated by the verbal messages used by the other person. Redmond (1983) suggests that empathy depends on particular dimensions of (a) the situational context, (b) the nature of the empathee's feeling-state, including certain appraisals about that context, and (c) the manner in which those feelings are expressed. Buie (1981) discusses the transactional nature of empathy when he notes that people are able to prevent being understood empathically. He cites Greenson (1960, p. 422), who says: 'One's capacity for empathy can be influenced by the other person's resistance or readiness for empathic understanding. There are patients who consciously or unconsciously want to remain ununderstood; they dread being understood'. Katz (1963, p. 40) suggests that interpersonal climate could exert a major influence on empathy, when he points out that empathy 'emerges when certain conditions are ripe'.

A relational approach to empathy suggests that mediators, negotiators, facilitators, and other interveners must pay a great deal of attention to variables in the communication process that might influence the development of understanding. Relational empathy is co-directional, involving all parties in an interpersonal encounter, together seeking to create common meanings for purposes of moving toward understanding. While persons possessing certain characteristics may be more adept at this than others, it is also important to consider characteristics of the encounter itself. As Hornblow (1980) points out, the stability of behavior has been comprehensively reviewed, and the conclusions from these reviews are that behavior is often perceived to be more stable than it really is. Interactions between situational and personal variables account for more variance than either situational or personal variables alone. A relational approach to empathy shifts the focus to the context in which conflict interaction takes place. By anchoring one's perspective of the conflict in such a framework, participants can explore the conditions that help to create empathic understanding. In order for empathy to have validity in the study of conflict resolution, it must be seen as part of the communication process itself, and thus it may be influenced by the variables in that process.

Stewart (1983) and Stewart and Thomas (1986) believe that the primary task is not to simply reproduce the other's meaning but to be open to the meanings that are being developed *between* oneself and one's partner. These meanings, Stewart (1983, p. 384) says, are 'open-fluid, and continuously context-dependent'. An empathic encounter results in more than each individual developing a deeper understanding of the other; rather, it leads to the genesis of a unique whole that reflects a merging of each individual's construction of the other.

Creation of a 'third culture'

The process of understanding another does not mean disregarding oneself in order to stand in the place of the other. Rather, understanding is better viewed as 'a move *from* the separate, to some degree "thesis" and "antithesis" positions of the individual interlocutors *to* a synthesizing position that subsumes relevant aspects of each' (Stewart, 1983, p. 388). Stewart quotes Gadamer (1975, p. 272), who emphasizes that the process of understanding 'is not the empathy of one individual for another, nor is it the application to another person of our own criteria, but it always involves the attainment of a higher universality that overcomes, not only your own particularity, but also that of the other'.

Meanings, then, are not simply brought to the conversation; rather, they are a product of the meeting between individuals. Interculturalists often use the phrase 'third culture' to describe the outcome of a long-term relationship, such as marriage or deep friendship, between individuals from different societies. Because two individuals may not be able to operate competently or comfortably according to the norms of either culture represented in the dyad, together they create a somewhat new and different 'culture' in which they are both able to operate. This third culture is characterized by unique values and norms that may not have existed prior to the dyadic relationship. Originally proposed by Useem, Donoghue and Useem (1963), this concept has been more fully developed by Casmir (1978), Gudykunst, Wiseman, and Hammer (1977) and others as a way of clarifying the dynamics of communication in an intercultural setting. Casmir and Asunción-Lande (1989, p. 294) describe the third culture concept in the following manner:

> Though beginning with contrasting perceptions and behaviors, two individuals, through their interaction, create a unique setting for their interaction. In the conjoining of their separate cultures, a third culture, more inclusive than the original ones, is created, which both of them now share. Within that third culture, the two can communicate with each other more effectively. Thus a third culture is not merely the result of the fusion of two or more separate entities, but also the product of the 'harmonization' of composite parts into a coherent whole.

This third culture can only develop through interaction in which participants are willing to open themselves to new meanings, to engage in genuine dialogue, and to constantly respond to the new demands emanating from the situation. The emergence of this third culture is the essence of relational empathy and is essential for successful conflict resolution.

Implications for management of conflict interaction

Adopting a relational view of empathy has direct implications for managing discourse in conflict situations. First, it suggests that *participants must go beyond similarity in order to develop understanding.* Although similarity of constructs may aid in understanding, similarity is not essential in order for empathy to characterize the communication encounter. In Stewart's (1983) relational view of the creation of meaning, understanding comes from a 'fusion' of horizons, implying that individual horizons expand to include the horizon of the other. He is careful to point out, however, that this fusion does not mean that the horizons are reconciled. Rather, a 'critical aspect of hermeneutic consciousness is acceptance and even celebration of the *tension* between irreconcilable horizons' (p. 388).

As Kelly (1963) points out, even if a person has experienced the same events as another, the two will not necessarily construe them in the same way, and two people can have similar constructions of reality even if they have each been exposed to quite different stimuli. Rather than resting on the assumption of similarity, empathy instead makes possible the bridging of differences. Every person construes reality in different ways, and individuals cannot always create a sense of understanding by referring to a common experience in the past. By assuming similarity, individuals turn their attention back on themselves, and this preoccupation with their own feelings blunts sensitivity to others.

Relational empathy is particularly important when there are significant differences between the subjective worlds of two participants in a communication event. As long as two individuals who have developed relatively similar constructs for viewing the world are in communication, they can engage in satisfactory communication on the basis of projection. However, communicators of different viewpoints often lack significant overlapping of interpretations and understandings.

Without these overlaps, it is impossible to move toward understanding solely on the basis of projection; accuracy may be an unattainable goal. Empathy reduces the tendency to use ourselves as lightning rods, to judge others by our own feelings, choices, and preferences (Stewart, 1976). When two participants are each seeking the other's point of view, they communicate on a deeper level and apprehend the other person more completely. While differences may make it more difficult to understand another, participants can create through decentering what Howell (1983, p. 7) calls 'on-the-spot homogeneity' that can provide the information necessary for understanding.

Second, *participants must rely on more than individual abilities and skills* in managing conflict situations. Many discussions of empathy portray it as an inborn capacity or personality characteristic (Buie, 1981; Lipps, in Gladstein, 1984; Truax and Mitchell, 1971). Others focus on characteristics of the empathic individual (Grief and Hogan, 1973; Hogan, 1969; Katz, 1963). While empathy might involve some form of ability or skill of the individual, to restrict empathy in this manner reflects a unidirectional view of the process, since the focus is on the skill of one person empathizing *with* another. Developing understanding does not rely merely on the characteristics or skills of the communicator. It may be very difficult, despite one's best efforts, to decenter and seek the other's perspective when the other's communication discourages the attempt by being evaluative and closed-minded. As discussed earlier, empathy can be encouraged by such variables as verbal messages that indicate a willingness to be open. It is also important to take into account cultural differences in how empathy is expressed. Any ability or skill is situation-specific and must be tied to interaction in a specific cultural setting, since many of the skills that might lead to better understanding in one society could communicate disrespect and lead to rejection in other cultural contexts.

Third, *participants must shift away from a preoccupation with self and similarity* as they work at resolving differences. Egocentrism, which stands as a major barrier to conflict resolution, must give way to relational understandings. Arnett and Nakagawa (1983) suggest that a shift to a relational view of understanding might be analogous to the Copernican Revolution. The self, like the earth, would no longer be viewed as the center of one's world.

Instead, persons might come to see themselves as 'situated in relationship with the ecological system or relational systems between persons' (p. 375). Previous definitions of empathy may have actually encouraged egocentrism by asking individuals to perform an impossible task, i.e., to lay aside self and to become the other. Discouraged by their inability to attain this goal, participants had no alternative but to remain caught in their own perspectives. With an emphasis on developing relational empathy, the task is more realistic and should be perceived by participants as more attainable.

Fourth, *participants must understand how their own prejudices influence the development of understanding* in the encounter. Rather than being told to completely abandon their own perspectives, which is an impossible directive, participants must learn to work at merging their views with those of the other in order to form common understandings. Previous approaches to empathy implied that participants needed to 'overcome' their prejudices, or set them aside, whereas a relational approach suggests they learn to recognize the influence of prior understandings and seek to integrate them with those of the other in developing empathic understandings. Stewart (1983, p. 388) says that a relational approach to understanding leads one to 'emphasize the global breadth of prejudices that always affect one's interpreting, to highlight the open, fluid nature of those prejudices, and to underscore the fact that understanding is not a static state but a tensional event, a *stasis* defined by the contact of two lifeworlds'.

Fifth, *participants must focus on building understandings rather than exclusively trying to determine 'where a person is coming from'*. In conflict situations, it is often impossible to 'see behind' the verbal and nonverbal expressions of the other because of blinders produced by the different perspectives brought to the situation. The reservoir of meanings available to the perceiver may not be adequate for interpreting the other's actions. While relational empathy calls for and values attempts to continuously place the other's actions in the appropriate context, the focus of the conversational partners is on developing new meanings that will provide the basis for continued dialogue and relational growth. Stewart and Thomas (1986) refer to this process as 'sculpting mutual meanings', where the focus is on the communication and not the psychology. Such a focus brings greater hope for success and perhaps more stimulation to the conflict interaction.

Finally, *participants must adopt a set of 'dialogic attitudes' for use in conflict interaction* in which 'truth' is seen as a product of the encounter. In order to develop understanding, participants learn they must: (a) be willing to put forth the *effort* necessary to work through differences, (b) demonstrate *commitment* to the encounter necessary to overcome likely 'breaking points', (c) be able to explore and negotiate *alternative meanings* for ideas and events, and (d) be willing to participate in the *mutually creative* exploration that occurs in the development of their 'third culture'. These attitudes represent what Stewart (1984) calls a 'coherence perspective', which recognizes the inherent openness of any quest for understanding. Instead of trying to understand the other as a separate objective entity, the focus is on co-creating with the other a shared reality.

Conclusion

Previous definitions of empathy have offered more confusion than inspiration and more discouragement than motivation when dealing with differences. A relational view of empathy helps to promote the potential creative aspects of differences in conflict communication and points to the importance of establishing the appropriate environment for moving toward understanding. The apprehension, anxiety, and stress often associated with conflict can result in new meanings and development of stronger ties when an open, tentative approach is taken to the development of understandings and when the focus is upon the fostering of shared meanings.

When significant differences exist and must be confronted, relational empathy can play a key role in managing conflict. While not all of our interpersonal encounters require the development of empathic understandings, it is increasingly important to deal with conflict situations by engaging in the process of developing shared meaning rather than by simply attempting to play the role of 'counselor' in interaction with the other. By developing an empathic attitude towards communication and by seeking to co-create relational meaning in conflict situations, we increase the prospect for mutual engagement in effective and productive resolution of differences.

Notes

1. Portions of this paper were previously published in *Communication Education*, Volume 40, No. 3, 1991, pp. 235–249.
2. Discussions of empathy have not been limited to the psychology literature. Mead (1934) believed that empathy was essential to cognitive role-taking. Parrella (1971) and others have discussed the role of empathy in drama and literature. Cooley (1930, p. 290) and others in sociology have written about 'empathic knowledge' by which we can understand the behavior of human beings by sharing their 'state of mind'. Discussions of *Verstehen* by Theodore Abel, Richard Rudner, Talcott Parsons, Alfred Schutz, and Max Weber (see Dallmayr and McCarthy, 1977) examine the use of empathy in methodology for understanding and social inquiry. Philosophers such as Martin Buber (1965) discuss 'genuine dialogue' as requiring the turning of one's attention away from one's 'I' and toward the other as a 'partner'.

References

Arnett, R. C. and Nakagawa, G. (1983), 'The assumptive roots of empathic listening: A critique', *Communication Education*, 32, pp. 308–377.

Barnlund, D. C. and Nomura, N. (1985), 'Decentering, convergence, and cross-cultural understanding', in L. A. Samovar and R. E. Porter, eds, *Intercultural Communication: A Reader*, Wadsworth, Belmont, California, pp. 347–366.

Basch, M. F. (1983), 'Empathic understanding: A review of the concept and some theoretical considerations', *American Psychoanalytic Association Journal*, 31, pp. 101–126.

Bennett M. J. (1979), 'Overcoming the golden rule: Sympathy and empathy', in D. Nimmo, ed., *Communication Yearbook 3*, Sage, Beverly Hills, California, pp. 407–422.

Berlo, D. K. (1960), *The Process of Communication: An Introduction to Theory and Practice*, Holt, Rinehart and Winston, New York.

Bochner, A. P. and Kelly, C. W. (1974), 'Interpersonal communication instruction: Theory and practice', *Speech Teacher*, 23, pp. 279–301.

Borisoff, D. and Victor, D. A. (1989), *Conflict Management: A Communication Skills Approach*, Prentice-Hall, Englewood Cliffs, New Jersey.

Broome, B. J. (1981), 'Facilitating attitudes and message characteristics in the expression of differences in intercultural encounters', *International Journal of Intercultural Relations*, 5, pp. 215–237.

Broome, B. J. (1983), 'The attraction paradigm revisited: Response to dissimilar others.' *Human Communication Research*, 10, pp. 137–151.

Buber, M. (1965), 'Elements of the interhuman', in M. Friedman, ed., *The Knowledge of Man: Selected Essays* (M. Friedman and R. Gregor, trans.), Harper and Row, New York.

Buie, D. H. (1981), 'Empathy: Its nature and limitations', *American Psychoanalytic Association Journal*, 29, pp. 281–307.

Burleson, B. R. (1984), 'Role-taking and communication skills in childhood: Why they are related and what can be done about it', *Western Journal of Speech Communication*, 48, pp. 155–170.

Burleson, B. R. and Bingham, S. (1983), *Centration, Egocentrism, Role-taking, and Empathy: Some Distinctions and Clarifications*. Paper presented at the meeting of the Speech Communication Association, Washington, D.C., November.

Burton, J. W. (1987), *Resolving Deep-Rooted Conflict: A Handbook*, University Press of America, New York.

Casmir, F. L. (1978), *Intercultural and International Communication*, University Press of America, Washington, D.C.

Casmir, F. L. and Asunción-Lande, N. C. (1989), 'Intercultural communication revisited: Conceptualization, paradigm building, and methodological approaches', in J. A. Anderson, ed., *Communication Yearbook 12*, Sage, Newbury Park, California, pp. 278–309.

Cook, M. (1971), *Interpersonal Perception*, Penguin, Harmondsworth.

Cooley, H. E. (1930), *Sociological Theory and Social Research*. Scribner's, New York.

Cross, G. P., Names, J. H. and Beck, D. (eds) (1979), *Conflict and Human Interaction*, Kendall/Hunt, Dubuque, Iowa.

Dallmayr, F. R. and McCarthy, T. A. (eds) (1977), *Understanding and Social Inquiry*. University of Notre Dame Press, Notre Dame, Indiana.

Dance, F. E. X. and Larson, C. E. (1976), *The Functions of Human Communication: A Theoretical Approach*, Holt, Rinehart and Winston, New York.

Dymond, R. P. (1949), 'A scale for the measurement of empathic ability', *Journal of Consulting Psychology*, 13, pp. 127–133.

Feshbach, N. D. (1978), 'Studies of empathic behavior in children', in B. A. Maher, ed., *Progress in Experimental Personality Research*, Vol. 8, Academic Press, New York, pp. 1–47.

Filley, A. C. (1975), *Interpersonal Conflict Resolution*, Scott, Foresman, Glenview, Illinois.

Fisher, G. (1980), *International Negotiation: A Cross-Cultural Perspective*, Intercultural Press, Chicago.

Fisher, R. and Ury, W. (1981), *Getting to Yes: Negotiating Agreement Without Giving In*, Penguin, New York.

Folger, J. P. and Poole, M. S. (1984), *Working through Conflict: A Communication Perspective*, Scott, Foresman, Glenview, Illinois.

Gadamer, H. (1975), *Truth and Method*, The Seabury Press, New York.

Gladstein, G. A. (1984), 'The historical roots of contemporary empathy research', *Journal of the History of the Behavioral Sciences*, 20, pp. 38–59.

Gompertz, K. (1960), 'The relation of empathy to effective communication', *Journalism Quarterly*, 37, pp. 533–546.

Greenson, R. R. (1960), 'Empathy and its vicissitudes', *International Journal of Psychoanalysis*, 41, pp. 277–280.

Grief, E. B. and Hogan, R. (1973), 'The theory and measurement of empathy', *Journal of Counseling Psychology*, 20, pp. 280–284.

Gudykunst, W. B., Wiseman, R., and Hammer, M. (1977), 'Determinants of a sojourner's attitudinal satisfaction', in B. Ruben, ed., *Communication Yearbook 1*, Transaction, New Brunswick, New Jersey, pp. 415–425.

Hammer, M. R. and Wiseman, R. L. (1987, November), *The Situational Dynamics of Intercultural Communication Competence: A Research Proposal*. Paper presented at the meeting of the Speech Communication Association, Boston, November.

Hastorf, A. H., Schneider, D. J., and Polefka, J. (1970), *Person Perception*, Addison-Wesley, Menlo Park, California.

Havens, L. (1979), 'Explorations in the uses of language in psychotherapy: Complex empathic statements', *Psychiatry*, 42, pp. 40–48.

Hill, S. E. K. (1983), *Empathy Stages and Communication*. Paper presented at the meeting of the Speech Communication Association, Washington, D.C., November.

Hobart, C. and Fahlberg, N. (1965), 'The measurement of empathy', *American Journal of Sociology*, 70, pp. 595–603.

Hocker, J. L. and Wilmot, W. W. (1991), *Interpersonal Conflict*, W. C. Brown, Dubuque, Iowa.

Hogan, R. (1969), 'Development of an empathy scale', *Journal of Consulting and Clinical Psychology*, 33, pp. 307–316.

Hornblow, A. R. (1980), 'The study of empathy', *New Zealand Psychologist*, 9, pp. 19–28.

Howell, W. S. (1982), *The Empathic Communicator*, Wadsworth, Belmont, California.

Howell, W. S. (1983), *Toward an Ecologically Valid Conceptualization of Empathy*. Paper presented at the meeting of the Speech Communication Association, Washington, D.C., November.

Katz, R. L. (1963), *Empathy: Its Nature and Uses*, Free Press, London.

Kelly, G. A. (1963), *A Theory of Personality*, W. W. Norton, New York.

Martin, J. N. and Hammer, M. R. (1987), *Conceptualizing Intercultural Communication Competence: An Analysis of the Perceptions of Everyday Language Users*. Paper presented at the meeting of the Speech Communication Association, Boston, November.

McCall, G. J. and Simmons, J. L. (1978), *Identities and Interactions: An Examination of Human Associations in Everyday Life*. Free Press, New York.

McDonald, Jr., J. W. (1984), *How to Be a Delegate*, Foreign Service Institute, U.S. Department of State, Washington, D.C.

Mead, G. H. (1934), *Mind, Self, and Society*, University of Chicago Press, Chicago.

Parrella, G. C. (1971), 'Projection and adoption: Toward a clarification of the concept of empathy', *Quarterly Journal of Speech*, 57, pp. 204–213.

Piaget, J. (1974), *The Language and Thought of the Child*, New American Library, New York.

Reardon, K. K. (1983), *The Roles of Reason and Emotion in Empathic Communication: A Position Paper*. Paper presented at the meeting of the Speech Communication Association, Washington, D.C., November.

Redmond, M. V. (1983), *Towards Resolution of the Confusion among the Concepts Empathy, Role-taking, Perspective Taking, and Decentering*. Paper presented at the meeting of the Speech Communication Association, Washington, D.C., November.

Redmond, M. V. (1984), *Exploring the Meaning and Relationships of Empathy, Role-Taking, Perspective Taking and Decentering*. Paper presented at the meeting of the Speech Communication Association, Chicago, November.

Redmond, M. V. (1986), *An Inclusive Conceptualization of Empathy*. Paper presented at the meeting of the Speech Communication Association, Chicago, November.

Ricoeur, P. (1981), 'Phenomenology and hermeneutics', in J. B. Thompson, ed. and trans., *Hermeneutics and the Human Sciences*, Cambridge University Press, Cambridge, pp. 101–128.

Rogers, C. R. (1951), *Client-Centered Therapy: Its Current Practice, Implications, and Theory*. Houghton Mifflin, Boston.

Rogers, C. R. (1957), 'The necessary and sufficient conditions of therapeutic personality change', *Journal of Counseling Psychology*, 21, pp. 95–103.

Rogers, C. R. (1959), 'A theory of therapy, personality and interpersonal relationships as developed in the client-centered framework', in S. Koch, ed., *Psychology: A Study of a Science*, Vol. 3, McGraw-Hill, New York, pp. 184–256.

Rogers, C. R. (1967), 'The interpersonal relationship: The core of guidance', in C. Rogers and B. Stevens, eds, *Person to Person*, Real People Press, Lafayette, California, pp. 89–103.

Rogers, C. R. (1975), 'Empathic: An unappreciated way of being', *Counseling Psychologist*, 33, pp. 307–316.

Rogers, C. R. (1980), *A Way of Being*, Houghton Mifflin, Boston.

Schutz, A. (1967), *The Phenomenology of the Social World*, Northwestern University Press, Evanston, Illinois.

Stewart, E. C. (1976), 'Cultural sensitivities in counseling', in P. Pedersen, W. J. Lonner, and J. G. Draguns, eds, *Counseling across Cultures*, University Press of Hawaii, Honolulu, Hawaii, pp. 98–122.

Stewart, J. (1983), 'Interpretive listening: An alternative to empathy', *Communication Education*, 32, 379–391.

Stewart, J. (1984), *Empathy and Logos*. Paper presented at the meeting of the Speech Communication Association, Chicago, November.

Stewart, J. and Thomas, M. (1986), 'Dialogic listening: Sculpting mutual meanings', in J. Stewart, ed., *Bridges Not Walls: A Book about Interpersonal Communication*, McGraw-Hill, New York, pp. 192–210.

Stotland, E. (1969), 'Exploratory investigations of empathy', in L. Berkowitz, ed., *Advances in Experimental Social Psychology*, Vol. 4, Academic Press, New York, pp. 271–314.

Taft, R. (1955), 'The ability to judge people', *Psychological Bulletin*, 52, pp. 1–23.

Tagiuri, R. (1969), 'Person perception', in G. Lindzey and E. Aronson, eds., *Handbook of Social Psychology*, 2nd edition, Vol. 3, Addison Wesley, Reading, Massachusetts, pp. 395–449.

Truax, C. (1967), 'A scale for the rating of accurate empathy', in C. Rogers, E. Gendlin, D. Kiesler, and C. Truax, eds, *The Therapeutic Relationship and its Impact*, University of Wisconsin Press, Madison, Wisconsin, pp. 555–568.

Truax, C. B. and Mitchell, K. M. (1971), 'Research on certain therapeutic interpersonal skills in relation to process and outcome', in A. E. Pergin and S. L. Garfield, eds, *Handbook of Psychotherapy and Behavioral Change*, Wiley, New York, pp. 299–344.

Useem, J., Donoghue, J. D., and Useem, R. H. (1963), 'Men in the middle of the third culture', *Human Organization*, 22, pp. 169–194.

Warr, P. B. and Knapper, C. (1968), *The Perception of People and Events*. Wiley, London.

Weaver, R. L., II (1990), *Understanding Interpersonal Communication*, 5th edition, Scott, Foresman, Glenview, Illinois.

Wispe, L. (1986), 'The distinction between sympathy and empathy: To call forth a concept, a word is needed', *Journal of Personality and Social Psychology*, 50, pp. 314–321.

The healing function in political conflict resolution

This chapter deals with ethnic and religious conflicts, which are consistently the most resistant to traditional techniques of diplomatic or political mediation and negotiation. Because the losses from these conflicts are so painful in terms of lives, sometimes territory, and always a sense of safety and justice, even the more psychologically sensitive approaches to conflict resolution described in this volume have had only limited success in starting a healing process between the nations or peoples in conflict.

After well over a decade as practitioner and theorist in political conflict resolution, the author is convinced that healing and reconciliation in violent ethnic and religious conflicts depend on a process of transactional contrition and forgiveness between aggressors and victims which is indispensable to the establishment of a new relationship based on mutual acceptance and reasonable trust. This process depends on joint analysis of the history of the conflict, recognition of injustices and resulting historic wounds, and acceptance of moral responsibility where due.

Coming from a career in traditional diplomacy in which superpowers and lesser states have relied on economic and military coercive power as the ultimate 'conflict resolvers', the author has no illusions about the ease with which governments, including his own, can accept the idea that forgiveness is a key element in peacemaking. He believes, nevertheless, that both theory and real-world political experience provide persuasive evidence for the thesis.

Victimhood and the persistence of conflict

In a conference at the Foreign Service Institute in June, 1991, James Mace, a political scientist at the University of Illinois, described the relationship between the Ukraine and Soviet Russia as a 'gaping, unhealed wound'. He was referring, of course, to the heritage of Stalin's forced collectivization in the early 1930s in which millions of Ukrainians died. The metaphor of a gaping, unhealed wound could not be more apt for understanding the depth of pain, fear, and hatred a history of unatoned violence creates in a *victim*ized people.

The three main components of victimhood (Montville, 1989) are a history of violent, traumatic aggression and loss; a conviction that the aggression was unjustified by any standard; and an often unuttered fear on the part of the victim group that the aggressor will strike again at some feasible time in the future. To complicate matters, many nations and groups in conflict have competing, if not entirely symmetrical, psychologies of victimhood.

At this writing, Serbs and Croats in Yugoslavia, each outraged at the assertions of historic victimhood of the other, face off for an armed clash of potentially genocidal proportions. Not far behind in this category of fear and loathing are Arabs and Israelis, Armenians and Turks (in Azerbaijan), with low-level violence continuing in the historic dispute between Catholics and Protestants in Northern Ireland. How, indeed, can even the most experienced and psychologically sensitive specialists in conflict resolution approach confrontation so laden with passion and current or potential violence?

From victimhood to healing: The beginning of a process

It must be acknowledged at the outset that the methodology of third-party facilitation of communication between groups or nations in conflict is probably least effective on the eve of or in the midst of violent combat. In such a case, a process of gradual confidence-building between representatives of the groups in conflict would most likely be swamped by the passions of the moment. Far more appropriate would be third-party states or international organizations — the European Community or UN Security Council — arranging a cease-fire or separation of combatants and backing this up with a neutral peacekeeping force. When emotions had cooled down and parties were ready to proceed, a conflict resolution process could get under way. All other long-standing or protracted ethnic and sectarian conflicts are appropriate for third-party facilitation provided valid representatives of the adversary groups request help or agree to participate.

The social-science theoretical description of the early tasks in arranging and then facilitating constructive communication between representatives of groups in conflict revolves around the issue of changing political attitudes (Smith, 1973), or political beliefs (Lane, 1973), or belief systems (Seliktar, 1986). Almost always deeply rooted in the belief systems of ethnic and religious groups with a history of violent conflict are dehumanized images of the other side. Common beliefs are that the enemy is deceitful, aggressive, heartless, often sexually licentious, with unclean personal habits, and incapable of change for the better. One way to define the goal of facilitated communication is to *delegitimize* stereotyped beliefs about the enemy by introducing new information which is cognitively dissonant, i.e., which challenges the negative stereotype.

For example, in 1980, in the first five-day problem-solving workshop organized by the American Psychiatric Association for Egyptians and Israelis (discussed further below), an Egyptian intellectual and journalist said that the newest and most important thing he learned in the meetings was that Israelis could be afraid. Before the meeting, his image of Israelis had been one of fighter-bombers attacking the Nile Valley at will, in callous, contemptuous disregard for Egyptian dignity and life. The knowledge he acquired directly from Israelis in a safe, facilitated exchange in Washington, D.C., produced a much more complex and ultimately hopeful image of the adversary.

In social-psychological terms, the Egyptian had undergone a transvaluation in which new beliefs, more consonant with a new reality he had experienced, had been generated. As will be discussed further on, the big challenge is to delegitimize the negative stereotypes of the enemy in enough people so that a group or nation as a whole will discard old beliefs and values and undergo a transvaluation in an evolving collective belief system. Such a transformation is, however, especially difficult in societies whose perceptions of morality tend to be absolutist. All societies moralize their behavior codes to strengthen commitment to laws and customs as well as group cohesion (Seliktar, 1986, p. 339) and to inhibit defectors and deviants. Absolutist moralities of the sort found in aggravated ethnic conflicts are least likely to consider positive change in the enemy even scientifically possible. In extreme cases of enmity, the dehumanized characteristics can be seen as basically genetic and simply incurable.

The problem-solving workshop

To confront the bleak scene of aggressive antagonism in protracted ethnic and sectarian conflict, practitioners of conflict resolution have made effective use of problem-solving workshops. Pioneered by John W. Burton, former senior Australian diplomat and later professor at London, Kent, and George Mason Universities, the four-to-five-day workshop has become a basic tool in conflict resolution strategies. Opinions vary, but the ideal delegation of representatives of groups in conflict will range from three to seven, while the third-party team or panel of facilitators can range from two to five. Variations and elaborations of this formula are found elsewhere in this volume and in the works of Herbert Kelman (1991), a master in the field, as well as Vamik Volkan (1991), Demetrios Julius (1991), and the author (1991).

In simplest terms, the workshops make possible a process of undermining negative stereotypes held by the participants and rehumanizing their relationships. By dealing with each other at close quarters over a period of days, representatives of the groups in conflict learn that they can act openly and honestly with each other assuming the individuals selected for the workshops pass the minimum standards of character and emotional maturity for such a process.

One useful way of describing the interactive psychological process of trust-building in a problem-solving workshop has been suggested by Maurice Friedman (1983) in the concept of 'confirming'. In general dictionary definition to confirm is to remove doubt. In a dialogue between adversaries, confirmation implies acceptance of the other person's fundamental values and the worth of the person him- or herself.

Human beings crave confirmation throughout life, but it is gained only in relationships. The best form of confirmation is in love, but absent that a conflictual relationship may suffice at least to attest to one's significance as a person. It is said that the opposite of love is not hate but indifference. Facing the latter, people feel meaningless and empty. Dialogue, the engine of relationship, promotes mutual confirmation and thereby serves a fundamental need of parties to a conflict to be recognized as individuals with values and unique (and valued) identities. The goal is to establish working trust, in Kelman's phrase (1991), and the role of a third party, like that of a therapist, is to involve and confirm individuals representing groups in conflict who for a variety of reasons find it very difficult to reach out directly to their adversaries.

The conflict resolution strategy: Taking a history

Reconciliation is to understand both sides, to go to one side and describe the suffering being endured by the other side, and then to the other side, and describe the suffering being endured by the first side.
(Thich Nhat Hanh, Vietnamese Zen master)

The first substantive stage of the workshop is taking a history of the conflict. Whether this is initiated by the third party or begins spontaneously between the adversary sides should be determined on a case-by-case basis. The purpose of the walk through history is to elicit specific grievances and wounds of the groups or nations in conflict which have not been acknowledged by the side responsible for inflicting them. Only the victims know for certain which historic events sustain the sense of victimhood and these become cumulatively the agenda for healing. Published histories and official government versions of violent events initiated by aggressors very rarely convey the unvarnished truth. The almost universal tendency is not to discuss or to gloss or mythologize an event or military conquest as a justified defense if not heroic advance for the nation or perhaps civilization itself.

That nations have used the traditional psychological devices of denial and avoidance to exempt themselves from the moral consequences of their behavior has long been known. And the need for revising and cleaning up the published historical record of a conflicted intergroup or international relationship has become widely accepted as an essential part of a reconciliation process.

The extent of historical detail to be sought will depend on how much important information has been ignored. The Israeli–Palestinian case is recent enough that relatively less education for the parties is necessary, although Arabs can benefit from knowledge of Christian historical abuse of Jews in Europe. For the cases of Northern Ireland, South Africa, Armenia and Turkey, or Cambodia and Vietnam, the historical record takes on much more of a central role.

Attempts at rigorous analysis of historic grievances need not depend entirely on the existence of a problem-solving workshop. Unilateral efforts at balanced, psychologically attuned review might prove useful in drawing the attention of certain publics to the previously unknown or ignored critical history of aggression and abuse.

The author (1982) tried to do this in an (unclassified) internal U.S. government document analyzing the psychological roots of violence and terrorism in Northern Ireland. A portion of the paper which otherwise focused on current events drew a line between modern Irish violence and the degradation of the Catholic Gaels in Ireland from the landing of Henry II in 1171 to the 'heritage of hate', in the phrase of a modern Irish historian, spawned under Elizabeth I and James I (1588–1625), and irredeemably hammered home by the violent mass repression of Oliver Cromwell. After his military victory in 1649, Cromwell ordered the exile of all suspected Irish subversives, massive Catholic depopulation, and devolution of the Roman Catholic Church.

Winston Churchill has written, 'The consequences of Cromwell's rule in Ireland have distressed and at times distracted English politics down to the present day. To heal them baffled the skill and loyalties of successive generations ... Upon all of us there still lies "the curse of Cromwell"' (Lester, 1991, p. 6). The author's goal in the State Department study was to put today's ethnic and sectarian terror in historic perspective, something neither the U.S. in this case nor (especially) the United Kingdom government has done even with the benefit of Churchillian insight.

Providing an opportunity for articulating grievances in a meeting of ethnic adversaries, even if not organized as a problem-solving workshop, has some benefit. This was the case in a weekend seminar held in 1988 by the University of Maryland's Center for International Development and Conflict Management for Sinhalese and Tamil leaders. There was little problem-solving progress (nor had much been anticipated), but representatives of the Tamil minority had and took the opportunity to present their grievances in historic context in a way which would be imprinted on the minds of the Sinhalese for well into the future.

A comparable event was a two-day didactic seminar on track-two diplomacy for a mixed, high-level Northern Ireland delegation at the University of Virginia's Center for the Study of Mind and Human Interaction in 1989. In the meeting, a brief and only illustrative walk through history led by the third-party facilitators resulted in an (unplanned) deeply moving analysis of the hurt and losses on both sides of the conflict. The visitors left with a sense of new insight and common destiny which they said they had never experienced before.

116

In an example of a sequence of two planned, actively facilitated problem-solving workshops organized by the American Psychiatric Association in 1980 (Washington) and 1981 (Vevey, Switzerland), Israelis and Egyptians exchanged views, accusations, and lessons from their mutual sense of history. (Four more workshops with Palestinian leaders participating followed through 1984. The author participated in the design of and in the third-party team in five of the six.) The following is excerpted from reports on the first two meetings which totaled more than eighty hours:

In their often profound and emotional exchanges, the Egyptians and Israelis revealed the significant cultural gaps between the European-oriented Israeli elite and Arabs in general. But the Israelis especially reflected the deep sense of victimization Jews had suffered before 1948 and the establishment of Israel and since in the face of Arab hostility. It became clear that the major psychological means of facilitating negotiations would be through highly developed sensitivity to the Israeli suspicion of Gentiles that is based on the Jewish historical experience. The underlying political assumption of most Israelis is that Gentiles, at best, are indifferent to Israel's survival and, at worst, actively conspire to destroy the state. This is why unconditional, public acceptance of Israel's right to exist — which Egypt conveyed — must be seen as *the* minimum Arab and Palestinian move necessary, for non-negotiable *psychological* reasons, to begin negotiations toward a political settlement.

Accepting responsibility, contrition, and forgiveness

To recapitulate the assertion of the importance of historical analysis in a political conflict resolution process, it might be useful to examine one incident in the postwar German–Soviet relationship which does that and simultaneously introduces the themes of subsequent and interactive contrition and forgiveness. The event was described by Helmut Schmidt in his memoir, *Menschen und Mächte* (1987).

In 1972 Brezhnev went to Bonn on the first visit of a Soviet leader to West Germany. Willy Brandt, a trusted friend of Schmidt and Brezhnev, hosted an informal evening at his home for the two leaders. Schmidt reports that Brezhnev suddenly began to pour out one story after another of German Army atrocities in Russia during the war. When he finished, Schmidt spoke of his personal experiences as a young soldier on the Russian front and his anxieties and guilty feelings about the invasion. It seems clear from this account that Brezhnev's presentation of historic grievances was explicit, as was Schmidt's admission of responsibility and contrition as a German. While there is no suggestion that Brezhnev openly expressed forgiveness to Schmidt, the latter writes (p. 187), 'Probably it was this exchange of bitter war memories that significantly contributed to the mutual respect which has characterized our relationship between 1972 and up to his death'.[1]

A psychological parsing of this account in political conflict resolution theory would state that representatives of two nations with a history of violent conflict met in a safe, confidential environment (Brandt's home), in the presence of a trusted third-party facilitator (Brandt). They took a history of their conflict with the victim (Brezhnev) presenting his grievances in depth. The aggressor, or his symbolic representative (Schmidt), acknowledged the injustices of the act, accepted responsibility and expressed contrition. The victim accepted the contrition as genuine and thereby was drawn out of his victimhood psychology, at least with Schmidt, with whom he developed a trusting personal relationship. This transformation came, after time, to be generally reflected (with numerous other subsequent contrition/forgiveness transactions and rituals) in the relationship between the two nations.[2]

The role of contrition and forgiveness in the resolution of conflict has not been discussed widely in the scholarly literature of clinical psychology, psychiatry, and psychoanalysis. Indeed, when the author (1989) introduced the subject in his plenary address to the American Psychoanalytic Association (December 1986) which was then refereed and published in the *Journal of the American Psychoanalytic Association* as 'Psychoanalytic Enlightenment and the Greening of Diplomacy', one very supportive, anonymous reviewer defied his colleagues to identify any significant reference to forgiveness in depth psychology scholarship.

There are, however, some useful scientific references to the potentially profound effect of contrition and forgiveness which provide empirical support for the thesis of this chapter. One is found in the psychoanalytically oriented *Austen Riggs Center Review*, in an essay by the senior Israeli psychoanalyst, Rafael Moses (1990), entitled 'Acknowledgement – The Balm of Narcissistic Hurts'. Citing the pioneering work of the late Heinz Kohut in self psychology, Moses notes the predictability of the repetitiveness in the cycle of narcissistic blow, narcissistic injury, and narcissistic counter-blow. The resultant rage from a wound to the sense of self (individual or collective) requires acknowledgement if the destructive cycle is to be broken.

The interactive exchange of hurts is most familiar to clinicians in the family – between parents and children or husband and wife. Most interestingly, Moses also points out the occurrence of inadvertent offenses by therapists toward their clients or analysands. In the old days, he notes, analysts never openly admitted errors – their minds wandering, failure to point out something important, perhaps even falling asleep. Today therapists find that apologizing for mistakes invariably evokes an emotionally powerful and pleasing reaction in the patient.

Moses is also conversant and experienced in dealing with group political wounds. He is a veteran of the American Psychiatric Association Arab–Israeli workshops described previously and he reports from his personal experience the keen disappointment of Palestinians in a small workshop when their strong need for Israeli acknowledgement for the hurts inflicted on the Palestinians was not recognized (1990, p. 1).

The tension in the air grew palpably. The third party tried to encourage more direct and mutual interchanges ... The most articulate and vociferous spokesman of the Palestinian group made the following statement: 'If you Israelis would only acknowledge that you have wronged us, that you have taken away our homes and our land – if you did that, we would be able to proceed without insisting, without needing to get them back.' This was said somewhat wistfully. It sounded in the main honest, real, genuine. No such acknowledgment was made. The Israelis were frightened of the consequences, of what it might imply to make such an acknowledgment.

In separate essays focused specifically on therapeutic forgiveness in the journal *Psychotherapy*, Donald Hope and Richard Fitzgibbons provide clinical evidence for its effectiveness with clients. Greatest success was with adults who have suffered mental and physical abuse as children, which among other things, severely undermines their sense of self-worth. In what could be taken as a metaphor for the political history of the world as we know it, Hope (1987, p. 241) says, 'All therapists are confronted in their work with the facts of injustice, the abuse of the weak by the strong, betrayals of trust, loyalty and innocence'. He points out that after a therapist has helped a client explore the past and experience repressed feelings of anger and loss, the clinical literature offers little guidance about the potential cathartic effect of forgiveness as a component of a mourning process on the way to completion.

The question is how does a person let go of her past of humiliation and injustice, her victimhood? By suggesting forgiveness as an answer, Hope realizes that he is effecting a conjunction of religious tradition and scientific psychology, which may account for the scarcity of clinical references to forgiveness. He notes that in modern cases the therapist often substitutes for the spiritual confessor. He listens to all the client wishes to say, suspends moral judgement and exhibits tolerance and acceptance, thereby freeing the client to let go of past hatreds, including elements of self-hatred. What is clear in Hope's theory and a case study he presents is that the act of forgiving is unilateral, a fact which is helpful in individual therapy where the 'aggressor' mother or father may be dead, but unilateralism is rarely helpful in political conflict resolution.

Richard P. Fitzgibbons (1986) explains his cathartic use of forgiveness as initially a cognitive or intellectual process after the clinician analyzes the sources of the client's pain. The examination also includes efforts to understand the motives of the aggressor. In fact, 'Forgiveness is possible through a process of attempting to understand the emotional development of those who have inflicted pain' (p. 630). And while the cognitive process of forgiveness invariably precedes the affective or emotional release of hatred and desire for revenge, the author admits that obstacles to forgiveness can be quite serious. Individuals might be loath to give up their anger because they use it as an unconscious defense against further betrayal.

Striking much closer to the political parallel, Fitzgibbons notes that anger for some clients makes them feel alive and wards off the threat of possible emptiness in their lives. Further, many individuals see revenge as a sign of strength and forgiveness as weakness. Similarly to Hope, Fitzgibbons deals basically with therapeutic strategies of unilateral forgiveness, which begs many questions in ethnic conflict resolution which can only be based on a relationship with the adversary. Transforming a victimhood psychology into a normal relationship in political conflict resolution requires interaction — essentially the negotiation of a new political and social contract between previous enemies.

A vivid example of how unilateral forgiveness in a political conflict can fail is conveyed in Frost's (1991, p. 123) account of a generous — some say foolhardy — act of forgiveness by the then Sandinista Interior Minister Thomas Borge. In 1979, members of the Nicaraguan National Guard imprisoned and tortured Borge and raped and murdered his wife. After the revolution Borge went to see imprisoned guardsmen and recognized two of them. Borge addressed them:

Don't you know me? ... I am Borge whom you tortured — and whose wife your colleagues killed ... Now you are going to discover the full weight of this Revolution ... I forgive you ... Go on. Out through the door. You are free.

This was not a transaction. The gesture fell flat. Borge released over 5000 national guardsmen at that time, most of whom fled to Honduras and joined the U.S.-backed Contra movement which, of course, worked to overthrow the Sandinista regime.

Yet again from Central America comes evidence of genuine, if somewhat flawed, transactional contrition and forgiveness which gives strong support for the healing thesis in political conflict resolution. In March 1991, the author was part of a small Freedom House mission to El Salvador which among other activities visited Gregorio Rosa Chavez, Auxiliary Bishop of San Salvador. Rosa Chavez had been very active in pursuing charges of human rights abuses by the Salvadorean military and police. At the time of the visit, negotiations toward a settlement between the government of President Alfredo Christiani and the guerrilla FMLN were on the verge of success. Rosa Chavez said he was concerned about Salvadorean reconciliation at the grass-roots level. He thought that it was extremely important for the durability of a future peace that the families of disappeared victims of military repression be able to retrieve the bodies of their loved ones and mourn their losses properly. This could help the healing.

In this regard, Rosa Chavez also said that Salvadorean priests were beginning to adopt the method the Chilean church had been using which was to act as go-between in contrition/forgiveness transactions. Priests were making it known that they would take and protect the confessions of soldiers who had 'disappeared' and killed civilians and who were ready to let the victims' families know where the bodies could be found. The families seemed to accept this form of imperfect, one might say filtered, contrition as the best available since the soldiers feared extreme punishment if they revealed their identity. Yet the soldiers genuinely wished to communicate their remorse – the confessions were voluntary – and to shed their personal burdens of guilt.

The author did little to conceal his excitement and gratitude for this information and briefly described to Rosa Chavez the empirical research which supported his instinct. The Bishop responded with a warm smile and a single word, 'Precioso'.

Public rituals of contrition and forgiveness

One of the ironies of the contrition/forgiveness theory is that while scholarly literature supporting it is scant, daily events constantly occur which affirm it. The author has reported examples of healing interaction between previous enemies – French–German, Japanese–American, English–Irish – in an article first published by the Foreign Service Institute (Montville, 1987).

Perhaps the most noteworthy of these cases was the formation of a Franco–German commission of historians after World War II, whose task was to review existing French and German texts and revise them in light of available information, regardless of how painful or embarrassing it might be (Willis, 1965). The commission's work was critical to the postwar healing process which laid the psychological foundation for later establishment of the European Community, of which France and Germany are the core. This commission can probably also be taken as the model for all subsequent, similar analytical processes or efforts to resolve outstanding political conflicts. A random review of the press since 1986 reveals truly heartening evidence that many national groups and, most importantly, governmental leaders understand and accept the necessity of accepting responsibility for past transgressions as part of a reconciliation and peacemaking process.

In 1986, for example, the *Christian Science Monitor* reported (29 December, p. 10), that the German Protestant organization, *Aktion Suhnezeichen* (Action Reconciliation/Service for Peace), which had for ten years been working in the Holocaust memorials in Israel and Auschwitz, had built a youth center in Auschwitz and given it to the Polish people. Planned for the ensuing year were meetings of church congregations, schools, trade unions, and other independent youth organizations which would bring together West Germans, Poles, Dutch, Israelis, and Americans. Programs at the center would include reading the history of the Nazi extermination camps, viewing documentary films, meeting with survivors, and holding seminars on lessons of the past for the future. It is noteworthy that *Aktion* conceived of the plan in 1970, but Poles, who proportionally suffered more dead than any other country in the war, were reluctant to meet with Germans then.

An excellent case of institutionalized contrition and forgiveness was reported in the *New York Times* on March 7, 1990, in a story entitled 'Where Nazis Took Fierce Revenge, French Hatred for Germans Recedes' (p. A12).

Tulle, a city in southwestern France, was the site of a Nazi atrocity on June 9, 1944. In reprisal for the killing of 40 Germans by the French Resistance, the Nazis hanged 99 village men. Each year on the June date, the town of 20,000 remembers the 99, 18 others shot 'savagely', and 101 others deported to Dachau who never returned. But a 'healing process' got under way when Tulle was twinned with a German town, Schorndorf, in the mid-1960s. Since then hundreds of war veterans and students have exchanged visits, staying in each other's homes. While memories for the older French generation can be quite tender, the youth face their history openly, pay homage to its bitter lessons, and strengthen the sense of Franco–German community to assure that it can never happen again.

Mikhail Gorbachev's first visit to Warsaw in June 1988 brought to the surface one of the most painful incidents in the long-running story of Poland's victimization by the Russians. Powerfully illustrating the critical need for admission of past crimes before a new relationship can be established, Poles of all strata demanded Soviet confession of Stalin's murder of the 15,000 Polish reserve officers taken by the Red Army to Katyn in Byelorussia in 1939. One leader of Solidarity told the *Christian Science Monitor*, 'Katyn, it's to Poles what Auschwitz is to Jews'. Another said, 'It is the pure symbol of the Polish tragedy'. Yet another said, 'For Poles, Katyn dug the roots of the present Communist system. That is why, if confidence is to be restored between our two peoples, it must be treated' (12 June 1988, p. 7). In 1990, after a joint Polish/Soviet commission of historians completed an investigation of Soviet state archives, Moscow formally acknowledged Soviet responsibility and apologized to the Polish people.

On January 30, 1990, the *Los Angeles Times* reported that Jewish and Catholic leaders in southern California had issued a joint statement suggesting that the Roman Catholic Church inadvertently helped Hitler rise to power before World War II. A priest–rabbi committee had decided to launch its historical inquiry after the controversial reception by Pope John Paul II of Austrian President Kurt Waldheim in 1987. Jewish leaders expressed gratitude for the document which they said was an open and honest acceptance of responsibility. The report will be made available for incorporation into Catholic school curricula.

Two major acts of contrition made big headlines in 1991. On 20 May, Poland's President Lech Walesa, speaking in the Israeli Knesset said, 'Here in Israel, the land of your culture and revival, I ask for your forgiveness'. The *New York Times* story (21 May 1991, p. A5) noted that the chamber, filled with Israeli leaders, also held many survivors of Auschwitz and other Nazi death camps built in Poland. Many have blamed Poles for not having done more to protect the Jews. Significantly, the *Times*, which takes responsibility for reporting news of special interest to American Jews, ran a large front-page photo of Walesa and Israeli Prime Minister Shamir.

On 7 July, 1991, the *Washington Post* reported that Austria, for the first time since World War II, admitted its role in the Holocaust. The historic event came in a speech by Chancellor Franz Vranitsky, broadcast live on state television, in which he apologized for atrocities committed by Austrians. He said, 'Austrian politicians have always put off making this confession. I would like to do this explicitly, also in the name of the Austrian government, as a measure of the relationship we must have to our history, as a standard for the political culture of our country' (p. A14).

Transforming public consciousness

The foregoing stories are moving and very encouraging as evidence of political maturity in Eastern and Western Europe. In fact, these examples of highest leadership stand as continuing challenges to those who claim to be leaders in other countries and who have not been able to come to terms with their own histories. But as noted previously, deeply ingrained political belief systems are extremely resistant to attempts to change them by political leaders, especially if they are reinforced by an intense victimhood psychology. One need look only at Croatian attitudes toward Serbians and vice versa, or Armenian attitudes toward Turks. Yet there is empirical evidence that thoughtfully designed initiatives in providing cognitive data – new information from credible sources – even if dissonant with existing beliefs, can effect constructive change.

Without suggesting that ethnic stereotyping in a conflicted relationship is neurotic behavior, one might be encouraged by the use of cognitive therapy in the treatment of depression or low self-concept for example (Beck, 1976). There is abundant evidence that even individuals with serious behavior disorders can be influenced by a reasoning process.

The basic assumption of the therapy is that harmful feelings and actions are linked to distorted or maladaptive thinking and that such thinking must be changed. In the process, therapist and client examine erroneous assumptions together, identify illogical thinking, and then, hopefully, the client abandons the cognitive errors thus exposed.

But how can maladaptive or destructive stereotypical thinking in mass opinion be addressed cognitively with any efficiency? There is a body of research which suggests some answers. Adams (1987) affirms that systematic study of persuasive mass communication shows that it is most likely to strengthen already held views rather than change them. In particular, when it is a question of public attitudes toward disliked or distrusted groups or nations, both sociological factors – from social networks, value systems, and influential leaders – and psychological factors – family, peer, ethnic biases – act as barriers to the receipt of new, favorable information. Yet even these barriers are vulnerable if the dissonant, 'good' news, conveyed by mass media, comes from a credible source; and is repeated with variation, is disseminated via multimedia, reinforced by personal contact, and presented in balanced, 'two-sided' accounts.

Everett M. Rogers (1988), a professor of communications at the University of Southern California, agrees that mass-media channels are effective in creating knowledge of new ideas, but less so in persuading people to adopt them. Change of attitude depends, instead, on interpersonal communications networks in which respected opinion leaders and then near peers accept the new information as valid and thus change their attitudes. He reports consistent empirical findings that once an innovative idea is accepted by 15 to 20 percent of the population, it takes on a diffusion rate that cannot be stopped.

Experimental strategies for changing negative belief systems in Northern Ireland and the Middle East

To draw this chapter to a conclusion, I will describe two projects which address specific activities in conflict resolution strategies for Northern Ireland and the Middle East applying theory previously discussed. Both projects aim at influencing deeply rooted belief systems among adversaries in each region in order to help create an environment in public opinion which would promote other conflict resolution efforts.

The first project is an exploration of the feasibility of a Bill of Rights for Northern Ireland. To date it has brought together in a small workshop in Des Moines, Iowa, representatives of Northern Ireland political parties, Commonwealth specialists on human and civil rights, and American facilitators. Because the political atmosphere in Northern Ireland is highly charged, there was no intention to make the four-day meeting a problem-solving workshop devoted to finding a solution to the Catholic/Protestant conflict. Had this been the purpose, party representatives would most likely have refused to participate.

The purpose of the meeting, rather, was to discuss a draft Bill of Rights for Northern Ireland already drawn up by the respected Belfast-based Committee on the Administration of Justice. The CAJ, made up of Protestant and Catholic lawyers, academics, and others interested in civil liberties and equal treatment under the law, consulted for three years with various political and other interest groups before producing its draft.

The rationale for the meeting in conflict resolution theory was to provide a venue removed from daily distractions for interested parties from Northern Ireland to discuss principles of law and custom based on concepts of human-needs-based human rights and civil liberties. Protection of minority interests, including cultural identity, was to be part of the agenda. While the project may have seemed legalistic and academic, the subject matter was the essence of values guiding the negotiation of a new political and social contract for Northern Ireland. As consensus develops over these values then political negotiations in Belfast will, in theory, have a much better chance of success.

Participants agreed that the Des Moines meeting provided a good opportunity for learning and analysis on the Bill of Rights concept especially in light of the experience of other Commonwealth countries. They also said they had never given the question so thorough an examination in Northern Ireland. The next steps in the project, which could last three years, would be a series of public meetings at the town and city level throughout Northern Ireland, led by experts in the Bill of Rights concept. This would be primarily a facilitative activity. It would be the responsibility of political leaders and parties to take whatever legislative initiatives they believed to be appropriate.

The second project addresses the antagonistic belief systems of Christians, Muslims and Jews in the Middle East, which are popularly thought to rest on religious doctrine and tradition. Called 'Pathways to Peace for the People of the Book: The Values of Tolerance in Judaism, Christianity and Islam', the project will convene highly respected scholars and theologians from each religion who practice their religion and are committed to an ecumenical view of interreligious brotherhood. The small group, not to exceed twenty, will have three four-day meetings at six-month intervals in which they will evolve studies and commentary on sacred writing which support the concept of diversity in community and tolerance of all religions, tribes and nations, or simply, all God's children.

The work in progress will be discussed in another Middle East project with which the author is connected and which aims to develop consensus on human rights concepts in the region through political and intellectual working groups in Cairo, Amman, and Jerusalem. The final product of People of the Book will be a book published simultaneously in English, Arabic, Persian, and Hebrew, with regional and international media attention via CNN and the United States Information Agency's WORLDNET satellite television facility.

As in the Northern Ireland project, the goal of People of the Book is not to resolve the conflict. It aims to create an environment which might promote peace negotiations by undermining the belief systems, particularly of Muslims and Jews, which support the conviction that the two peoples have no spiritual and human values in common. It is these belief systems which are exploited by religious extremists on both sides who work to sabotage peace negotiations. The project hopes to take religion away from these extremists and provide moderate politicians with room for maneuver in public opinion.

In sum, the two projects rely on the credibility of the sources of new information on common values which could support the concept of community for heretofore antagonistic ethnic and sectarian groups. Mass media will be used to create public awareness of the new information, but the strategy relies on the involvement of respected leaders of the various religions, groups, and countries to acquire the new information and then to diffuse it within their constituencies. With luck and perseverance, 15 to 20 percent of the communities will adopt the innovative thinking and the possibilities for success of full-scale, direct conflict resolution processes, including the healing component of contrition and forgiveness, will be enhanced.

125

Joseph V. Montville

Notes

1. This event is reported by Geiko Muller-Fahrenholz (1989).
2. Brian Frost (1991, pp. 16–17) records two incidents in *The Politics of Peace*. One was cited by Yevgeny Yevtushenko (1963), who recalls visiting Moscow with his mother in 1941 and seeing a march of some 20,000 German war prisoners. The sidewalks were lined with women, worn with work, 'Everyone of them must have had a father or a husband, a brother or a son killed by the Germans'. As the prisoners approached, the women saw 'soldiers, thin, unshaven, wearing dirty bloodstained bandages, hobbling on crutches or leaning on the shoulders of their comrades; the soldiers walked with their heads down'. Yevtushenko (p. 245) goes on:

Then I saw an elderly woman in broken-down boots push herself forward ... She went up to the column, took from inside her coat something wrapped in a coloured handkerchief and unfolded it. It was a crust of black bread. She pushed it awkwardly into the pocket of a soldier, so exhausted that he was tottering on his feet. And now suddenly from every side women were running toward the soldiers pushing into their hands bread, cigarettes, whatever they had ... The soldiers were no longer enemies. They were people.

Frost's second example is of a German, Klaus Krance (1984), who visited the Soviet Union and wrote in a Northern Ireland magazine that he was:

deeply moved by an old woman we met while travelling along a country road ... As soon as she heard that we were German, on our way to the memorial at Katyn, where German soldiers had locked the inhabitants of a whole village, 149 people in all, 76 of them children, the youngest only few weeks old, in a barn and set it on fire, she started giving us flowers and apples as gifts, having tears in her eyes.

References

Adams, W.C. (1987), 'Mass media and public opinion about foreign affairs: A typology of news dynamics', *Political Communication and Persuasion*, 4, pp. 263–278.

Beck, A.T. (1976), *Cognitive Therapy and the Emotional Disorders*, International Universities Press, New York.

Fitzgibbons, R.P. (1986), 'The cognitive and emotive uses of forgiveness in the treatment of anger', *Psychotherapy*, 23, pp. 629–633.

Friedman, M. (1983), *The Confirmation of Otherness: In Family, Community and Society*, The Pilgrim Press, New York.

Frost, B. (1991), *The Politics of Peace*, Darton, Longman and Todd, London.

Hope, D. (1987), 'The healing paradox of forgiveness,' *Psychotherapy*, 24, pp. 240–244.

Julius, D.A. (1991), 'The practice of track two diplomacy in the Arab-Israeli conferences', in V. Volkan *et al.*, eds, *The Psychodynamics of International Relationships, Vol. II, Unofficial Diplomacy at Work*, Lexington Books, Lexington, Massachusetts.

Kelman, H.C. (1991), 'Interactive problem solving: The uses and limits of a therapeutic model for the resolution of international conflicts', in Volkan, *Psychodynamics*.

Krance, K. (1984), untitled article, *Peace by Peace*, 10 November, pp. 4–8.

Lane, R.E. (1973), 'Patterns of political belief', in J. Knutson, ed., 1973, *Handbook of Political Psychology*, Jossey-Bass, San Francisco.

Lester, J. (1991), 'Ireland and the English Question', *For a Change*, 4.

Montville, J.V. (1982), 'The psychological roots of violence and terrorism in Northern Ireland', (unpublished internal memorandum).

Montville, J.V. (1987, 1991), 'The arrow and the olive branch: A case for track two diplomacy', in J. McDonald and D. Bendahmane, eds, *Conflict Resolution: Track Two Diplomacy*, Foreign Service Institute, Washington, D.C., reprinted in Volkan, *Psychodynamics*.

Montville, J.V. (1989), 'Psychoanalytic enlightenment and the greening of diplomacy', *Journal of the American Psychoanalytic Association*, 37, reprinted in Volkan, *Psychodynamics*.

Moses, R. (1990), 'Acknowledgement: The balm of narcissistic hurts', *The Austin Riggs Center Review*, 3.

Muller-Fahrenholz, G. (1989), 'On shame and hurt in the life of nations – a German perspective', *Studies: An Irish Quarterly Review*, 78, pp. 127–135.

Rogers, E.M. (1988), 'Diffusion of the idea of Beyond War', in A. Gromyko and M. Hellman, eds, *Breakthrough: Emerging New Thinking*, Walker, New York.

Schmidt, H. (1990), *Men and Power*, Random House, New York.

Seliktar, O. (1986), 'Identifying a society's belief system', in M. Hermann, ed., *Political Psychology*, Jossey-Bass, San Francisco.

Smith, B. (1973), 'Political attitudes', in J. Knutson, ed., *Handbook of Political Psychology*, Jossey-Bass, San Francisco.

Volkan, V.D. (1991), 'Psychological processes in unofficial diplomacy meetings', in Volkan, *Psychodynamics*.

Willis, F.R. (1965), *France, Germany, and the New Europe, 1945–1963*, Stanford University Press, Palo Alto, California.

Yevtushenko, Y. (1963), *A Precocious Autobiography*, Collins, London.

Part III

Theory and practice at different levels

Conflict resolution in intercultural settings: Problems and prospects

Introduction

The purpose of this chapter is to alert students and practitioners of conflict resolution to some of the special considerations that arise when conflict theory and practice are applied to intercultural situations. The chapter explicates the dimensions of a cultural approach to conflict resolution, and touches explicitly on 'problem-solving' as a conflict resolution technique. It closes by considering some issues that a third-party intervenor may face in different intercultural settings.[1]

Several years ago we became interested in the relation of culture to conflict resolution. Exploring the work of theorists and practitioners in the emerging field of Conflict and Peace Studies (CAPS), it seemed to us that those attempting the admirable goal of a universally valid set of conflict resolution techniques were in danger of running into serious conceptual and methodological difficulties. These difficulties stemmed from relegating culture to the background and taking it to be, in effect, an obstacle to be set aside by theory- or process-builders because it merely masks underlying common genetic, or at least generic, human nature (Burton and Sandole, 1986, but see also Sandole, 1984). A good part of the reason for assigning culture to the background is the notion that since culture highlights *differences* between groups, if it were to be foregrounded there could be no possibility of developing conflict resolution practices of universal applicability. Unfortunately, dismissing culture results in theory or processes which, in one way or another, demand that participants in situations of conflict resolution fit themselves into the process-designer's structure, even if this means ignoring or suppressing much of what may be most meaningful to them. This is true, as we shall argue later, even when the process − analytical 'problem-solving' − is held to be, *a priori*, culture-free or culture-transcendent.[2]

To be fair, when one examines the concept of culture used by many theorists and practitioners in conflict resolution, one sees why it is so often relegated to a secondary place. In brief, 'culture' in this view stands for rather superficial group differences. It is generally associated with descriptions of traditional, stereotypical modes of behavior, characteristic of some group of 'others'. Hence, such discussions of culture largely focus on questions of etiquette and tolerance. Culture is spoken of as though it were a thing, as if it were evenly distributed across members of the group of which it is an attribute, as though it were synonymous with 'custom' and 'tradition' and, finally, as if it were impervious to change through time. Such discussions also seem bedeviled by an intractable confusion between statements about cultural matters (those having to do, that is, with features of human consciousness) and statements about the actual behavior of individuals or groups of individuals. The point here is that culture is not reducible to behavior; to 'know' a culture is not to be able to predict each and every act of each and every member of a group. In this vein, culture is sometimes treated merely as a label for group differences – as a way of naming the groups. This is especially true in intercultural conflict situations, where 'culture' and 'ethnicity' (or ethnic identity) are used synonymously. That these terms are unselfconsciously used this way by the parties to the conflict themselves – as well as by analysts or third-party intervenors – is what makes the confusion intractable.[3]

In contrast, our perspective on the role of culture in conflict arises from a conception of social life in which culture is seen to be a fundamental feature of human consciousness, the *sine qua non* of being human (Black and Avruch, 1989). It is held to be constitutive of human reality, including such behavioral manifestations of that reality as 'conflict'. Metaphorically speaking, culture is a perception-shaping lens or (still metaphorically) a grammar for the production and structuring of meaningful action. Therefore, an understanding of the behavior of parties to a conflict depends upon understanding the 'grammar' they are using to render that behavior meaningful.

If one wishes to understand conflict behavior it is particularly useful to attend to the indigenous understandings of being and action which people use in the production and interpretation of social action. These understandings, like all cultural knowledge acquired through social learning, are, like much cultural knowledge, organized into sets of propositions and prescriptions of various levels of complexity and generality. Providing one bears in mind their often inchoate, contradictory, and symbolic rather than logical organization, it makes sense to call such understandings 'theories'. The sets of understandings about conflict held *by the people involved* in a dispute are crucially important. We have called such cultural knowledge 'ethnoconflict theories'. These theories undergird the techniques or processes of conflict resolution used indigenously, which we have called 'ethnopraxis' (Avruch and Black, 1991). It is useful to consider theories and practices put forth by academics and practitioners in conflict resolution from the perspective of ethnotheory and ethnopraxis (Avruch, 1991). All theory and practice – be they 'scientific' or 'folk' – rest on implicit assumptions about such culturally constituted beliefs as the nature of human nature (Avruch and Black, 1990). And, in its turn, every theory of conflict (whether an academic theory or an ethnoconflict theory) is but a piece of some general theory of action.

When the parties to a conflict come from different cultures – when the conflict is 'intercultural' – one cannot presume that all crucial understandings are shared among them.[4] Their respective ethnotheories, the notions of the root causes of conflict, and ethnopraxes, the local acceptable techniques for resolving conflicts, may differ one from another in significant ways. The first task of a third-party intervenor in intercultural conflict situations, is to pay serious analytical attention to these cultural dimensions. The third party must assay a *cultural analysis* of the situation.

Cultural analysis

Conflict resolution in intercultural settings requires, perhaps on the part of the parties to the conflict and most certainly on the part of the third-party intervenor, an analysis of the conflict that is also a cultural analysis. This cultural analysis is preliminary to other aspects of third-party intervention, although it may well continue throughout the intervention. What does such an analysis consist of, and what are its entailments?

In the terms and analogies we have used, one's own culture provides the 'lens' through which we view and bring into focus our world; the 'logic' (known as common sense) by which we order it; the 'grammar' by which it makes sense. Above all, our culture provides ways of seeing, thinking, and feeling about the world which in essence define normality for us – the ways things are and the way things ought to be. In intercultural encounters it is precisely one's sense of normality that may be put at risk. But in most people, a sense of normality is fairly well-established and pretty well-defended. So rather than question our own normality, we tend to assert the relative abnormality, the strangeness and bizarreness of the other: 'the French are arrogant'; 'the English are cold'; 'Moroccans are untrustworthy'. In most intercultural encounters, in fact, moments of noncomprehension and un-intelligibility are deflected and dismissed by being glossed over by terms laden with value-judgments. Not only do the French think about this differently than we do, but they are 'wrong' (arrogant, rude, etc.) to do so. Thus, inter-cultural encounters present us with situations (other peoples' behaviors and understandings) that appear strange and bizarre; our common sense labels them as such and our moral sense evaluates them as good or (more likely) bad. To revert to the lens metaphor, our own culture seems to us transparent, and the world seen through it seems to us veridical, simply the way things are. A glimpse of the world *through* another culture (one possible result of an intercultural encounter) presents us with areas of opacity, things we cannot see through clearly. We demarcate these; then we set about dismissing them.

A cultural analysis demands first that one *stops* at moments of noncom-prehension and unintelligibility; that one resists deflecting them dismissively (and pleasurably) in moral terms; that one makes them – the seemingly opaque and unintelligible – the objects of scrutiny. In short, the analyst is well advised to remain reflexively attuned to the disconcerting moment. To turn to one's advantage the sensation of surprise is not an easy thing to do, however, because it demands that one resists such dismissive reflexes when being faced with the strange and bizarre. Secondly, a cultural analysis is a scrutiny with a peculiar sort of goal. 'Cultural analysis', writes Raymonde Carroll (1988, p.2), in a study of French–American cultural misunderstandings, is 'a means of perceiving as 'normal' things which initially seem 'bizarre' or 'strange' among people of a culture different from one's own'. It is a way of making transparent that which first appeared as opaque. 'To manage this', Carroll continues, 'I must imagine a universe in which the 'shocking' act can take place and seem normal, can take on meaning without even being noticed.'

The key word here is 'meaning', of course.[5] Since our culture provides us with systems of symbols by which meaning is asserted (or, as often as not, negotiated) and established in the world, a cultural analysis at root is the searching out of meaning in these systems of symbols. When directed towards a culture different from our own, such an analysis orients us to different meanings – other lenses, other logics, other grammars. Notice that in principle one can attempt a cultural analysis of one's own culture, and in practice as well, although many anthropologists deem this to be a much harder analysis – because one is usually not 'stopped' by moments of noncomprehension and unintelligibility in dealings with one's own culture. This is exactly what one's own culture allows one to avoid. It takes a subtler mind and a more perverse sensibility (not to mention perhaps a case of chronic and clinical alienation), to allow oneself to be struck by, and stop at, the utterly familiar and veridical. And of course, conceptually, one result of a cultural analysis of one's own culture produces an effect opposite to that done on another culture. Aimed at one's own culture, such an analysis can have the eerie effect of rendering the previously 'normal' both strange and bizarre. It can make opaque that which was transparent. It is almost always unsettling, very often critical, and so usually taken by others to be subversive – or surreal (Clifford, 1988).

So much for what a cultural analysis is; how does one do it? Carroll uses the word 'imagine' as a kind of shorthand answer to this question. Is this a methodology? Clearly any sort of analysis introduced with reference to subtle minds, perverse sensibilities, and clinical alienation – not to mention shameless recourse to metaphors like opacity and its opposite – is likely to seem problematic to social or behavioral scientists used to the comforting rigors of formal techniques for testing operationalized hypotheses.[6] Nevertheless, there is a method for pursuing cultural analysis. Although it may take a certain sensibility to do it easily or well (and what methodology doesn't?), it certainly does not demand a mystical or occult one.

Here we follow (part of the way, at least) the now classic account found in Geertz (1973, pp. 3–30), and its very lucid précis by Carroll (1988, pp. 5–9). For Geertz, the essence of a cultural analysis is that it consists of 'thick description', an ethnographic presentation of an event (a conversation, a person, a practice, a dispute, a belief ... etc.) that stresses the placement of the event (... etc.), for the social persons who enact it, within deeper and deeper, richer and richer, more and more layered contexts of meaning ('structures of signification,' in Geertz's words). Carroll's interest lies in using cultural analysis to explore specific intercultural (French–American) misunderstandings; thus she emphasizes how one would go about describing something 'thickly'.

First, if one is trying to analyze the culture of another, be on the lookout for the bizarre; recognize the opacities. Be prepared to stop and avoid the social scientist's tendency to immediately explain (and explain *away*) the phenomenon by reference to causal theories – psychodynamic, materialist, ecological, or biological, to name a few (Black, 1991). Because culture does not 'cause' behavior – neither aggression, nor the business cycle, nor the grand flow of history – cultural analysis is not causal analysis. Precisely where causal analysis and cultural analysis come together, if they do, has been a matter of some considerable intramural debate between those committed to 'interpretive' (Geertz, 1973) and 'explanatory' (Wolf, 1990) anthropology. Simplifying the debate, one camp allows cultural analysis in as part of the ethnographic, descriptive stage – as a data-base-provider for the powerful Science (the theories of underlying causality) to come. The other camp asserts that cultural analysis *is* the science to come. When it comes to the understanding of human social action, these partisans maintain, the inscription and specification of meaning is the terminus (and an asymptotic one, at that) of our enquiry. For the first camp, ethnography serves Science; for the second, the science consists of Ethnography.

Our own position in this debate lies at neither extreme, but is rather more respectful of the search for causes (cybernetically construed, at any rate) than not. In fact, it is our respect for the power of causal theories – which tend to be indiscriminately omnivorous of data-bases in the hands of the naive or scientistic – that makes us place such a high premium on the avoidance of explaining away before one has the chance to explain. In this more limited sense, then, we agree with Geertz and Carroll that in cultural analysis one is not operating in the same conceptual domain as in causal analysis.

The second thing to be on the lookout for is the glossing of the strange with value-judgments ('the English are cold', 'the French are rude', and so forth). These propositions are not so dissimilar in fact to the first set we advised avoiding: value- judgments are, after all, causal explanations put in the modality of a moral discourse; they are the 'science' of our own culture's common sense. For most of us most of the time, the value- judgment, the moral accounting, is entirely sufficient as explanation. Too many social scientists, however, use value- judgments as a way-station to a fully causal

135

explanation: 'Why did your colleague say that to you at the departmental meeting? He is French, you know; they are rude ... And why are they rude, you ask? Didn't you know they are all weaned with vinegar?' (Psychodynamic); '... the red wine they drink to excess inhibits endorphin production' (Biological); and so on.

Next, having been struck (stopped) by the opaque or the strange and having avoided moralizing, psychologizing, biologizing, ecologizing, or economicizing it away, one gets down to its proper, thick, description. This involves recording it ('inscribing' it, in the text-oriented work of these analysts) and, text now before you, contextualizing it. Simply put, this key procedure (or act of imagination in Carroll's term) requires that the 'text' be put into different, deeper, and more widely ramifying frames of meaningful reference. As the frames of reference ramify, the initial strangeness should begin to ease; within the deepening and widening contexts of the cultural analysis, at least, the bizarre should begin to make sense, the opaque reveal the shadow of what lies behind it. One begins to translate. It is during this inscription/contextualization process that the true, the *interpretive*, nature of the enterprise emerges.

To call any analysis 'interpretive' immediately raises questions of validity and verification. Such questions are justified. All interpretations – at least in our world – are not equal. An interpretation should be judged by how well it accounts for and explains – in the sense of makes meaningful – other aspects of the culture that appear bizarre, or the same aspect as it appears in the culture in other 'texts'. This is not, of course, 'prediction' in the sense promised by covering-law, causal theories. It is closer to the 'retrodiction' of a grammatical analysis: tell us the sentence just now uttered; we will tell you if it is grammatically appropriate in that language.

Finally, since one is always and necessarily doing this from the standpoint of one's own cultural presuppositions, the entire process is iterative. One is always in effect tacking back and forth in cultural analysis: between an interpretation that makes sense in the other culture and a translation – for every translation is also an interpretation – that makes sense in your own. (This is a simple gloss on the 'hermeneutical circle' formed between interpreter and text.) In this sense we would argue that a cultural analysis is in fact the paradigmatic form of an enlightened intercultural encounter – one that is now ready for problem-solving.

Intercultural encounters

Consider an American tourist in a foreign land. She does not speak the language (needless to say). She asks an old man, a native of the country, for directions to the train station. The old man does not speak English. He looks at the tourist quizzically. The tourist repeats her question, this time in a louder voice. From the old man another quizzical look, perhaps a nod of the head or shrug of the shoulders. The tourist speaks yet more loudly, and, looking around, tries to imitate (pulling an imaginary cord to train whistle: 'choo, choo') the sound of a train. Now the quizzical look becomes open amusement, but still without comprehension. The tourist looks around again and sees a young boy approaching them. 'Do you speak English?' 'A little.' 'Do you know where the train station is?' 'I do not, but I will ask this old man.' And he does, and the tourist will make her train.

What makes this little scenario the very model of an opaque intercultural encounter is, of course, the fact that neither party speaks the language of the other. Our tourist tries to get around this first by raising her voice (a reflexive, but not a bad, first option: in a monolingual setting, it probably is the case that noncomprehension is linked to not hearing the message, perhaps because of noise). Then she tries to bypass speech and use an alternative channel of communication, gesture, and mimicry. The first option, raising the voice, consists of simply repeating the original message in the original code and medium, but varying physical parameter (amplitude). The second option is of a different order entirely and consists of a transformation of the original message and code. Here, the tourist is attempting a translation of her question into a (gestural) code she believes is more universal than (even) English. Alas, she is wrong, for in this native's land the gesture of pulling on a cord signifies a bad attack of dysentery, while the sound, 'choo, choo' conventionally signifies a male's appreciation of an attractive female. Not surprisingly (but nevertheless fortunately), the old man is amused. Luckily, a third party comes along – a native himself – who shares enough of the tourist's linguistic code to be able to interpret and translate the question.

A 'cultural analysis' of this encounter could be rudimentary, indeed. The opacity, the noncomprehension was simply the result of mutual nonsharing of linguistic codes, and the third party was an interpreter in the weakest sense of that term. Moreover, the problem that needed solution – directions to the train station – was simple enough and straightforward enough that the third party's admitted limitations as an interpreter (he spoke 'a little' English) were not fatal. Moreover, in this scenario the older native was merely amused by the tourist's gestures – rather than offended, angered, insulted, and moved to retaliate in kind. If he had been, then we might imagine the third party as having a more substantial and difficult role to play. Correspondingly, our cultural analysis of the encounter (anger and passion have colored the opacity: why?) grows more complex. The tourist's recourse to a code – gesture and body language – that she thought was more generic or universal turned out to be neither, although it was definitely full of meaning. The third party, *even if he understood what the tourist meant*, might find it harder to translate the gestures and placate his countryman. 'Translation' implies that the third party attempts a cultural analysis of the tourist's gestures (what Americans *mean* by 'choo, choo') and 'placation' implies that he communicates the results of his analysis to his countryman. (And that such communication is feasible or likely: can a young boy mollify an old man, appropriately, in this culture? Maybe not, if the old man seems to get angrier and angrier.) And now, the third party's limitations – intellectual, temperamental, or social-structural – as an interpreter (a cultural analyst) and problem-solver might well prove fatal.

This scenario – the revised one, in which the older native becomes angry – is a model intercultural encounter in another sense. For here we have an instance of a conflict that we can say with assurance is caused by 'culture'. To be more precise, the conflict is a result of cultural *differences* in the interpretation of meaning, by the parties, of the same events: the initial noncomprehension (what are you trying to say?) compounded subsequently by misapprehension (just who the hell are you accusing of diarrheal lechery?). Such intercultural conflicts 'caused' by culture do occasionally occur, of course, and they are the ones most amenable to thin cultural analysis on the level of explaining to the parties involved the differential etiquettes at play. They are the ones where problem-solving can be reduced to simply correcting 'a failure to communicate'. But while such conflicts do occur, they should not be taken as representative of most conflictual intercultural encounters and certainly not of conflicts of the deeply rooted sort.

This is so for two reasons. First, many intercultural encounters take place in shared linguistic settings, for instance nation-state diplomacy (where diplomats use English or French) or intranational interethnic disputes. In these cases, the shared language (the presumed mutual comprehension) can actually mask paralinguistic or other deeper cultural differences. Shared language can fool the parties into thinking much else, or all else, is shared as well. Secondly, and more profoundly, although it is only sometimes the case that cultural differences can themselves be said to account for *all* of the noncomprehension, and thus *all* of the reasons for the conflict, it is always the case that culture molds the ways in which the parties understand what the conflict is about, how to carry on through it, and what possible resolutions look like. In the rather homely and synthetic scenarios we have been spinning thus far, we can imagine the distinction in this way: If two parties, speaking different languages (cultures), think they are both vying for the same *pie*, but it turns out that one is really after the bottle of *lye*, then the dispute was about their noncomprehension, and a simple translation ought to solve the problem in a positive-sum (win–win) manner. But, if it turns out that both parties really do want the same pie (and each wants all of it), then translation only serves to clarify what the conflict is about (an important step, to be sure); but it does not represent its solution. The conflict is about control of valued resources; it is *about* the pie. Here we have encapsulated the core of the 'realist' position in international relations and much of the 'materialist' position in the other social sciences. But the conflict also is very much about why certain resources – things like pies – are valued, about how one ought to fight over them (and how to fight to win), about how fights end, and about the costs, bearable and unbearable, involved. And these parts of the conflict, always present, are culturally constituted; they comprise ethnotheory.

So much for synthetic scenarios. They have the virtue of allowing us to introduce wrinkles and manipulate variables at will — now we have insulted the old man. We can also find the same processes at work in the 'real world'. At the level of nation-state diplomacy, for example, Raymond Cohen has written extensively of the cultural factors which have complicated recent Egyptian–Israeli relations. Preferring an auditory metaphor to the visual one (lenses and opacity) used here, he has characterized the Egyptian–Israeli case as a sort of 'dialogue of the deaf', marked by the 'symmetrical autism' of mutual and costly noncomprehension (1990, p. 7). Writing about the 1979–1981 Iranian hostage crisis, William Beeman (1986) has focused on the key cultural understandings ('beliefs') that marked the Americans' perception of how foreign policy ought to be pursued, and how these perceptions contributed to the American mishandling of the crisis and the new revolutionary regime.

On the intranational interethnic front, where language is shared, Thomas Kochman (1981) has written incisively of the many cultural differences that bedevil interactions between African-American and white in the U.S. These differences include the differential valences in both cultures between argument and confrontation; the appropriate role that emotionality should play in discussions and negotiations; how male–female interactions ought to play out; how to know when a 'fight' has really begun; whether information about a person is akin to private property; what constitutes valid 'truths' or evidence, or guilt or responsibility — in other words, matters of fundamental importance. In a real sense, the sharing of a common language only serves here to cover up profound differences in perception, style, and moral evaluations of conflictual behaviors.

Again on the interethnic front, a similar situation is described by Edward Hall (a pioneer in the exploration of intercultural encounters), for Anglo- and Spanish-Americans in New Mexico. We quote at length to give some flavor of the process (1977, p. 157):

In Anglo-American disputes, one progresses by steps and stages — from subtle innuendo and coolness (one must be polite) to messages via a third-party, to verbal confrontation, then legal action, and finally force — if nothing has worked and the law is on your side. For the Spanish-American, another system is used. First there is brooding ... and, since verbal confrontation is to be avoided, the 'If I could have found my tongue, I would not have struck him' law is applied. The first inkling that something is wrong is a show of force. Force or action is to the Spanish-American not a step in a chain but a communication in itself. It is designed to get attention. Later, much later in the process, they resort to the courts.[7]

Each of these examples, alluded to briefly here, is much richer — thicker and more complex — than the simple and made-up scenario of the old man, the young man, and the monolingual tourist. Each invites — demands — a cultural analysis as a key component of intercultural conflict resolution or problem-solving.

Problem-solving and conflict resolution in intercultural settings

As we pointed out in the beginning of this essay, neither conflict resolution nor problem-solving in the usual sense of these terms, has dealt adequately with culture. When reduced to mere custom, it is felt that the culture question can be handled as part of etiquette or protocol. Reduced (in a different way) to ethnicity, it is felt that culture is just the label, a name, given to a people or, alternatively, a strategic site for their bargaining over resources. In the first case — custom — a competent and unharried interpreter (a 'translator' in the simplest sense possible) is all that is necessary to see one through. In the second case — ethnicity — a hardheaded, pragmatic, even slightly cynical orientation steeped in political 'realism', combined with the patience to wait out the posturing and rhetoric — to wait for the conflict's 'ripening' — will prove sufficient.

We think not. Culture is more than custom; it is lens, not label. And to adopt the notion that culture is just ethnicity, or that the conflict is 'really' always about utilities that can be maximized in the same way everywhere, is to end up in the position of our monolingual tourist, whose first assumption is that everyone of course speaks English, and one must therefore only repeat the question yet more LOUDLY, and a response will be forthcoming. (Recall Raymond Cohen's metaphor for the Egyptian—Israeli case: a dialogue of the deaf.)

Proponents and partisans of, specifically, problem-solving for the resolution of conflicts have another reason for discounting culture. They say that problem-solving is special, that it goes beyond negotiating or bargaining, processes that are perhaps culture-sensitive. They contend that problem-solving depends on analytical techniques that — on the assumption that people every-where *reason* the same way — render cultural differences ultimately trivial. These are deep and not completely charted waters. Nevertheless, there are two points that must be stressed. First, we need to look carefully at the problem-solving techniques that are declared culture-transcendent and generic. John W. Burton (1990), for example, writes extensively of the 'costing' of conflicts as one such technique. It may well be that 'costing' is a generic human trait, though it certainly looks best suited to a *Homo sapiens* who is mostly a *Homo economicus*. Often, in an unreflexive way, our own ideas about the nature of persons, or the nature of human nature, end up deter-mining the assumed 'universals' of our theories. But of course, such ideas are themselves culturally constituted (see Avruch and Black, 1990).

Secondly, we must look carefully at what is meant by the presumed cultural transcendency of human reasoning — this is where the waters get deep and are unsatisfactorily mapped. Earlier, along with lenses and grammars, we depicted culture as the 'logic' by which we reason our way through the world. And we asserted other lenses, other grammars, and other logics. But if we assume that people everywhere reason the same way, then is there not but one logic — and cannot analytical problem-solving utilize that one Logic? (This begs the question of whether or not 'costing' is part of the universal logic.)

The cross-cultural study of cognition and the anthropology of human reasoning (for these are the waters we have tramped into) are far from united in giving us simple answers to these questions. But some recent work (Hamill, 1990) on 'ethno-logic' suggests a possible outline of those answers. Hamill compared syllogistic (categorical) logical reasoning and propositional-calculus logical reasoning in a number of cultural settings. In brief, categorical reasoning appears to look the same (though nowhere quite like the Aristotelian version of our logic textbooks) across cultures, but propositional reasoning does not. So if one takes the ability to 'do' a syllogism as the *sine qua non* of reasoning, then language and culture seem not to matter so much. The vistas for analytical problem-solving seem endless — or at least acultural!

But propositional reasoning (the logic that Whitehead and Russell introduced in 1910 in their revolutionary *Principia Mathematica*), which uses premises and operators from a semantic domain to compose arguments, is different. 'Propositional patterns vary with language and culture because the semantic elements of the arguments mean different things in different settings. Those semantic differences can have both linguistic and cultural sources' (Hamill, 1990, p. 104). Moreover, all logics, even categorical ones, involve ultimately the interaction of *meaning* with logical structure, to define validity — or 'truth'. Hamill (ibid.) writes:

Meaning not only structures validity in human thought patterns but also defines truth. Thus syllogisms are structured in the same way from culture to culture. Yet the inventory of true categorical statements varies from culture to culture. Therefore it is possible for a valid conclusion to follow from a syllogism in one culture but to be false in another. Premises are a variable of culture in the same way as attributed causes.

Once we are thrown back to meaning, of course, then culture is inescapable. Whatever else this augurs for analytical problem-solving, it does not seem to us to suggest a process that is either self-evident or uncomplicatedly 'generic' and 'culture-free'.[8]

Third parties and intercultural conflict resolution: Some cautions and prospects

There are several possible scenarios for third parties in intercultural encounters, and the dynamics of each is different:

(1) The parties to the conflict come from different cultures, and the third party is from yet a different culture.
(2) The parties to the conflict share the same culture, but the third party is an outsider.
(3) The parties to the conflict come from different cultures, but the third party shares a culture with one of them.

Let us begin by immediately noting the limitations of this scheme: culture is not in fact a unitary or boolean variable that a person 'has' or 'hasn't'; we 'share' culture more or less perfectly with others; we all control (in the sense of speaking a language or dialect) multiple cultures with varying degrees of competence. Moreover, nowhere does this scheme take account of such real-world complications as power or resource differences among the parties. Keeping these limitations in mind, the scheme provides a useful starting-point for conceptualizing the different roles of third parties in intercultural conflict resolution. In a way, each scenario demands a different commitment to cultural analysis on the part of the third party as a prerequisite to whatever sorts of conflict resolution techniques are utilized. What follows, and concludes this chapter, is a preliminary discussion of this point.

In the first case, where all the parties and the third party come from different cultures, the 'inter'-cultural dimensions are maximized. Here the third party must function as an interpreter in the fullest sense of the term – translating first to his or her culture, then to the relevant party's, then back again. Opacities abound, and they might appear in surprising places: for example, some issues may be more quickly interpretable as between the contesting parties, and less so for the third party (here one of the contestants may have to pause to educate the third party). Sometimes (as Raymond Cohen points out for the Egyptians and Israelis) the contestants may share very little outside the notion that third parties are valuable and relevant resources in the resolution of conflicts. Here, in any event, cultural analysis will be going at full throttle.

In the second case, where the contesting parties share a culture but the third party is an outsider, one must wonder what role the third party should be prepared to play – perhaps a facilitating one, or a role that provides 'good offices', or a neutral venue. Perhaps the third party is chosen because it is seen by the contestants as being willing and able to guarantee or enforce their compliance to negotiated settlements. Here, the third party should be careful not to get in the way, to complicate matters by imposing his or her own cultural views on the parties. And here, for what it is worth, the third party must be especially careful not to be hoodwinked, snookered, gulled, or otherwise used by the parties – for example on such an issue as enforcing compliance – at least not without knowing something about it.

In the final case, where the third party shares a culture with one of the contesting parties, questions of power differentials (is the third party coming from the stronger or the weaker of the contestants?) and neutrality come to the fore. The third party must worry especially about underinterpreting (accepting as translucent too easily or too soon) the views of his or her own group, while perhaps overinterpreting the views of the other.

Each of these cases presents different problems for third-party interventions. Each invites a different set of cautions and, perhaps, a different sense of hesitancy. In the second case we have come very near to saying that the optimal role of a third party who is a cultural outsider may well be to help the contestants find a third party who is an insider. In the first case, where all the parties are 'Others' to one another, we assert that a thorough (and probably continuing) analysis by the intervenor of the contestants' ethnotheories of conflict and their respective ethnopraxes, are in order. These involve commitments to translations (where caution is due because mistakes are probable and possibly costly) and interpretations (where hesitancy is called for as part of a wholly appropriate humility).

Nevertheless, in a world where intercultural conflict often means violence, bloodshed, and suffering, perhaps it is equally important to say that caution and hesitancy are not to be taken as excuses for inaction. Cultural analysis in conflict resolution does not aim – as in some academic cultural studies – to produce texts merely for aesthetic contemplation. On the contrary, cultural analysis is necessary, and due caution and hesitancy are called for, precisely because in the real world the stakes are so high.

Summary

This chapter was in response to some of the extant, reductionist assumptions for intercultural practice that seem presently to predominate in the field. We have called the most inadequate of these assumptions 'the notion of culture as differential etiquette' (Avruch and Black, 1991). Working from a more complex ('thick') conception of culture, we argued that intercultural conflict resolution requires, on the part of the parties to the conflict and especially the third-party intervenor, an analysis of the dispute that is essentially a cultural analysis. In setting forth its parameters, we paid particular attention to what such an analysis can and cannot promise. A set of metaphors (including especially those of *translation* and *interpretation*) were offered to link up cultural analysis to activist or intervenor contexts. We closed with a set of cautions for the overcommitted or overzealous conflict resolver: a sense of limits intended to frame the natural optimism and horizonless possibilities that characterize this young field.

Notes

1. Earlier drafts of this chapter benefited from the comments of S. K. Avruch, Dennis Sandole, and B. D. Webster. Both Avruch and Black have worked through

most of these ideas in classes each has taught in the Institute for Conflict Analysis and Resolution. We thank our students collectively.

2. The assumption that cultural differences are superficial differences has already proven disastrous in psychology – especially when mixed up with race. One need only think of the damage wrought by those imposing 'culture-free' or 'culture-fair' IQ tests (Gould, 1981). And the so-called Third World is littered with the wreckage of development projects whose designers ignored local culture (see Kottak, 1990).

3. The relationship between culture and ethnicity is very complex. For a beginning see Hobsbawm and Ranger, 1983.

4. See Avruch and Black (1991, pp. 34–40) for an extended discussion of the term 'intercultural'.

5. At least in this context. Later, as we show how to carry out such an analysis, Carroll's use of the word 'imagine' will be key.

6. See George Devereux's aptly named (and spectacularly ignored) *From Anxiety to Method in the Behavioral Sciences* (1967) for a provocative discussion of the uses and abuses of formal methods in social research.

7. This quote by Edward Hall, marked by his characteristic lucidity and sense of prescriptiveness, is a good place to repeat the caution we noted earlier in our discussion of culture and behavior. A cultural model for conflict (or anything else) is not a prediction for a given individual's behavior in a given situation. (One should not mistake the map for the territory.)

8. Richard Shweder (1991) has made a similar point with respect to moral and ethical judgments.

References

Avruch, K. (1991), 'Culture and conflict resolution', in K. Avruch, P.W. Black and J.A. Scimecca, eds, *Conflict Resolution: Cross-Cultural Perspectives*, Greenwood Press, Westport, Connecticut.

Avruch, K. and Black, P. (1987), 'A generic theory of conflict resolution: A critique', *Negotiation Journal*, 3, pp. 87–96, 99–100.

Avruch, K. and Black, P. (1990), 'Ideas of human nature in contemporary conflict resolution theory', *Negotiation Journal*, 5, pp. 221–228.

Avruch, K. and Black, P. (1991), 'The culture question and conflict resolution', *Peace and Change*, 16, pp. 22–45.

Beeman, W. (1986), 'Conflict and belief in American foreign policy', in M.L. Foster and R.A. Rubinstein, eds, *Peace and War: Cross-Cultural Perspectives*, Transaction Books, New Brunswick, New Jersey.

Black, P.W. (1991), 'Surprised by common sense: Local understandings and the management of conflict on Tobi, Republic of Belau', in K. Avruch, P.W. Black and J.A. Scimecca, eds, *Conflict Resolution: Cross-Cultural Perspectives*, Greenwood Press, Westport, Connecticut.

Black, P.W. and Avruch K. (1989), 'Some issues in thinking about culture and the resolution of conflict', *Humanity and Society*, 13, pp. 187–194.

Burton, J.W. (1990), *Conflict: Resolution and Provention*, St. Martin's Press, New York.

Burton, J.W. and Sandole, D.J.D. (1986), 'Generic theory: The basis of conflict resolution', *Negotiation Journal*, 2, pp. 333–344.

Carroll, R. (1988), *Cultural Misunderstandings: The French-American Experience*, University of Chicago Press, Chicago.

Clifford, J. (1988), *The Predicament of Culture: Twentieth-Century Ethnography, Literature and Art*, Harvard University Press, Cambridge, Massachusetts.

Cohen, R. (1990), *Culture and Conflict in Egyptian–Israeli Relations*, Indiana University Press, Bloomington.

Devereux, G. (1967), *From Anxiety to Method in the Behavioral Sciences*, Mouton, The Hague.

Geertz, C. (1973), *The Interpretation of Culture*, Basic Books, New York.

Gould, S. J. (1981), *The Mismeasure of Man*, Norton, New York.

Hall, E. T. (1977), *Beyond Culture*, Anchor Books/Doubleday, New York.

Hamill, J. F. (1990), *Ethno-Logic: The Anthropology of Human Reasoning*, University of Illinois Press, Urbana.

Hobsbawm, E. and Ranger, T. (eds) (1983), *The Invention of Tradition*, Cambridge University Press, Cambridge.

Kochman, T. (1981), *Black and White Styles in Conflict*, University of Chicago Press, Chicago.

Kottak, C.P. (1990), 'Culture and "economic development"', American Anthropologist, 92, pp. 723–731.

Sandole, D. J. D. (1984), 'The subjectivity of theories and actions in world society', in M. Banks, ed., *Conflict in World Society: A New Perspective on International Relations*, St. Martin's Press, New York.

Shweder, R. (1991), *Thinking through Cultures*, Harvard University Press, Cambridge, Massachusetts.

Wolf, E. (1990), 'Facing power – old insights, new questions', American Anthropologist, 92, pp. 586–596.

Analyzing and resolving class conflict

Conflict resolution and dispute settlement

The emergence of conflict analysis and resolution as an autonomous field of study has required serious reevaluation of the field's origins in labor–management relations, international diplomacy, and processes of individual, organizational, and intergroup dispute resolution. Many scholars are now agreed that the proper province of this new discipline is the study of profoundly alienated social relationships and the processes that may be used to reconstruct them. Its primary focus, in other words, is not on disputes that may be settled by deriving solutions to particular cases from commonly accepted legal, political, or cultural norms, but on conflicts between parties that do not participate in or have access to a legitimized system of norms and institutions. According to this understanding, the practical aim of conflict resolution is not to 'settle' or to 'manage' disputes in such a way as to preserve existing normative or power-based systems. It is to resolve conflicts – or avert them before they have escalated to destructive levels – by assisting parties to identify and eliminate their systemic causes (Burton, 1990a).

Accordingly, effective conflict resolution processes generate new norms and decision-making systems capable of satisfying the conflicting parties' basic human needs (Burton, 1990b). For this reason, they do not focus so much on negotiation, bargaining, and reconciliation of competing interests as on the analysis of the conflict's root causes, the generation of new systemic models, and the 'costing out' of these models by the conflicting parties. By implication, then, conflict analysis and resolution may be distinguished both from 'alternative dispute resolution' (ADR) and from coercive methods of conflict management (Burton and Dukes, 1990). ADR concerns itself with processes that may be used to settle consensual disputes when legal or political mechanisms are ineffective or unavailable. Conflict management relies on power-based instrumentalities (e.g., legal systems) that seldom address the causes of conflict at their systemic level. *A fortiori*, conflict resolution is also to be distinguished from 'negotiation', which is either a form of ADR (in the case of consensual disputes) or a method of

146

wielding coercive power within or without a system of shared norms (e.g., see Raiffa, 1982).

Labor–management disputes in most industrialized nations, for example, are virtually never *resolved*. If they arise under collective bargaining agreements, they are generally *settled* by ADR processes, in particular, by arbitration. If they involve creating or amending such agreements or ending strikes and lock-outs, they are settled by power-based negotiation. And if they are about the right to organize labor unions, or about the fundamental powers and obligations of parties to labor–management disputes, they are settled by conflict management techniques, e.g., by legislated labor codes, interpreted by administrators and judges, that were originally enacted as a result of power-based negotiation (see, e.g., Dunlop, 1984). At first glance, at least, conflict resolution seems irrelevant to labor–management disputes. A wage dispute is a disagreement about the price of labor. Like other disputes about price in a capitalist society, it is to be settled by negotiation between buyer and seller. Such negotiations, to be sure, are frequently conducted within the framework of some legislated conflict management scheme. Still (runs the argument), both the principles of commercial negotiation and the fact of labor legislation reveal the existence of consensual norms that permit such disputes to be settled by bargaining, by litigation, or by ADR.

From this dispute-settlement perspective, the collective terms 'labor' and 'management' refer to groups whose interests are in some cases naturally opposed and in others naturally coincident. Where they are coincident – for example, where the economic viability of the industry that employs labor is put in question – disputes are mitigated or tend to disappear. Thus, in the United States, trade unions in threatened or declining domestic industries customarily accept attrition of the labor force as a necessary price to be paid for keeping the industry alive. Labor may also join with management in favor of restrictions on foreign competition. Where labor and management interests are opposed, on the other hand – most typically, in connection with claims involving wages, benefits, and working conditions – disputes arise, but since they involve only immediate, conscious 'interests', they exist to be settled or managed rather than resolved (Burton and Dukes, 1990). In the United States, for example, federal and state labor codes generally establish mandatory duties to negotiate such matters, as well as creating supplemental mediation and conciliation services to help settle them. The employee's right to strike and the employer's right to lock out striking workers are legally guaranteed, but these rights are strictly limited both by statute (e.g., 'political' strikes, secondary boycotts, and other militant labor tactics are either unprotected or illegal) and by contract (e.g., 'no-strike' clauses in existing collective-bargaining agreements are strictly enforced) (Klare, 1990).

At least since the 1930s, conflicts between social classes in most modern capitalist states have been dealt with as negotiable interest-based disputes. It is doubtless for this reason that those who study or practice resolving

147

'intractable', 'deep-rooted', non-consensual conflicts have had relatively little to say about class conflict (see, e.g., Kriesberg, Northrup, and Thorson, 1989). The struggles that attract their attention are primarily those between ethnic, racial, national, religious, or ideological groups – 'qualitative' conflicts, as it were, between collectivities whose members are driven by unsatisfied intangible needs, e.g., for identity, recognition, and personal development. That many of these conflicts also present 'quantitative' questions is not denied; who would think of attempting to help resolve the ethnic conflicts in Northern Ireland, Eastern Europe, Russia, or South Africa without taking cognizance of economic issues? But to consider these issues as merely quantitative is to frame them as ordinary conflicts of interest – 'bargainable' differences that may be settled by the methods already mentioned in connection with labor–management disputes.

Suppose, however, that one or both of the parties to a conflict presents itself as representative of an entire class claiming the right to reorganize the politico-economic system. This 'class struggle' situation characterizes a number of conflicts of recent concern, including the violent struggles in Nicaragua, El Salvador, Peru, and the Phillipines. Or suppose that a prior 'social contract' regulating the labor–management relationship has broken down, and that no legitimized system has yet replaced it. This seems roughly to describe the state of affairs in the former Soviet Union and many nations in Eastern Europe. Finally, suppose that the issue posed by a particularly hard-fought strike is the continued existence of the labor union and the future (if any) of collective bargaining in the industry affected – a situation that now recurs with increasing frequency in a number of advanced industrial states, including the U.S. The issues raised by such conflicts are not 'bargainable' in the sense in which disputes over wages or working conditions are ordinarily negotiated. Since they are not 'consensual conflicts' (Coser, 1956), involving immediate interests, they lie outside the normal limits of dispute settlement. But since they are not the sort of 'identity group' conflicts with which conflict resolvers ordinarily concern themselves either (see, e.g., Montville, 1990), they represent unexplored territory for conflict resolution as well.

Labor and management as interest groups

At the heart of the argument that labor–management disputes are proper subjects for dispute settlement, not conflict resolution, lies a tautological and often quite partisan assumption – that the parties to conflict are *interest groups* rather than representatives of social classes (Greenstone, 1977, pp. 360ff). Now, interest groups are aggregations of individuals organized to operate *within* a consensual normative and institutional framework. Originally, the term was used to describe groups established to promote some common and limited economic interest; for example, bondholders, milk producers, tenants, independent accountants, welfare recipients, buyers of new automobiles, railroad engineers. The concept was both more diffuse and shallower than that of social class; more diffuse, because 'interest' included specific commonalities far more varied than a group's collective relationship to the means of production; shallower, because these commonalities were generally defined in terms of their members' immediate and conscious dollars-and-cents wants rather than their long-term human needs. In time, the concept was extended to include groups sharing a wide variety of noneconomic interests; e.g., gun owners, parents of children in parochial schools, advocates of civil liberties, music lovers. But even here, group members tended to treat their common concerns as if they were immediate economic interests that could be secured by bargaining or negotiating with similar groups or with state agencies (see McConnell, 1967, pp.119ff).

Economic or noneconomic, what interest groups share is a commitment to negotiate with other groups or with the state within a commonly held normative framework. It is assumed that these negotiations can proceed without raising fatally disruptive normative issues because these issues have been previously settled; i.e., there is an accepted 'social contract' already in existence. But to assert the existence of a legitimate social contract implies, first, that the fundamental distribution of power, property, and prestige in society is generally accepted as inevitable, merited, or just; second, that social values and institutions ratifying and maintaining these arrangements are accepted as natural or sacred; and third, that basic human needs and vital interests are perceived, on the whole, to be satisfied (or at least, *in principle*, 'satisfiable'). It is not the province of interest groups to challenge or to reconstruct the existing system of power, norms, and need-satisfiers. Their role, as defined by the system, is to represent their members' interests within the framework established by this social contract.

Putting this somewhat differently, one may say that interest groups do not seek to represent the whole individual in his or her quest to satisfy basic human needs, nor do they represent entire social classes seeking fundamental change in the system of power and social norms. In modern capitalist societies, both the 'whole individual' and the 'whole class' are irrelevant abstractions. The individual is conceived of and treated as a bundle of specialized, conscious, transient wants, each of which requires representation by a different group or groups. Similarly, the class is conceived of and treated as a congeries of interest groups, many of which, in fact, are organized *across* social-class lines. These groups may sometimes coalesce, but their general rule is neither to contract permanent alliances nor to make permanent enemies. Thus, in negotiations with an employer over wages, a worker may be represented by a labor union. In negotiations with other groups over public-policy issues affecting workers, she may be represented by a multi-class political party. Where women's rights issues are concerned, a more specialized cross-class organization will represent her; where religious issues are relevant, a church or 'moral issues' group; and so forth.

149

The history of most labor organizations in the capitalist world is the story of their transformation from class-conscious workers' organizations into interest groups. Seeking at first to represent the entire working class and to fulfill the basic needs of its members, they end by seeking temporary economic advantages for their members within the framework of an accepted 'free market' system. In the United States, this transformation took place as a result of the New Deal, which (*inter alia*) federalized labor relations in inter-state industries, guaranteed workers the right to organize labor unions, made labor–management negotiations over wages and working conditions issues mandatory, protected (while limiting) the right to strike, and created national systems of unemployment compensation and social security (Leuchtenburg, 1963).

Prior to this restructuring of the American social contract, leading labor unions in major industries saw their mission as representation of the working class as a whole. Indeed, many organizers hoped to topple the business class from power and replace the capitalist market with a planned economy under workers' control. In 1934, for example, the most significant strikes under-taken by labor organizations were the West Coast Longshoremen's strike, led by members of the Communist Party; the Minneapolis Teamsters' strike, led by members of the Socialist Workers Party; and the Toledo Auto-Lite strike, led by members of the American Workers Party (Goldfield, 1989a). These militant unions consciously rejected the limited interest-group role traditionally played by the craft unions affiliated with the American Federation of Labor (AFL). Unlike the 'bread and butter' unions, they solidarized with workers in other industries by attempting to make their strikes general and by boycotting or 'hot-cargoing' products produced by struck companies. They refused to separate their members' economic interests, narrowly defined, from the more general political goals expounded by socialist, communist, and syndicalist organizations. And they considered it their task to assist workers to satisfy basic human needs for identity, recognition, solidarity, and personal development (e.g., see Dobbs, 1972).

At the high point of the New Deal (1936–1938), most militant labor unionists were drawn into the 'popular front' created by Franklin Roosevelt's Democratic Party in alliance with more conservative labor leaders, urban political machines and ethnic associations, organizations of small businessmen and farmers, white Southern political organizations, and a number of leading business corporations. The principal labor representative of this coalition was the Congress of Industrial Organizations (CIO), later merged with the American Federation of Labor. The CIO began prior to World War II by purging anti-Stalinist radicals from the labor movement, and ended after the war by purging the pro-Moscow Communists (Preis, 1964). In general, the terms of the bargain struck by organized workers with representatives of capital were these: in exchange for recognition of the right to organize unions, to compel large companies to negotiate wages, benefits, and working conditions, and to strike, organized labor would surrender its claim to represent the working class as a whole and to represent union members in their capacities other than that of 'employees' of particular companies or industries. Essential to this bargain was labor's agreement to recognize the legitimacy of management (i.e., of capitalist ownership, the profit-driven market, and 'management rights' in the conduct of business) and the state's legitimacy as a neutral third party capable of settling labor–management disputes (Goldfield, 1989b).

For a time, at least for workers and owners of large interstate industries, the results of this bargain seemed wholly advantageous. So long as major U.S. corporations faced no serious competition from foreign sources, they were able to meet the demands of the labor unions, to raise the standard of living of American industrial workers far above the industrialized-world average, and to reap the profits of virtually unfettered global expansion. But the revival of German and Japanese industry two decades after World War II, as well as competition from other sources, increasing raw-material costs, and the expenses of maintaining a global empire, seriously altered this picture. Beginning in 1973, the wages of American workers entered a long-term period (not yet ended!) of stagnation and decline. Family income levels were maintained only by an unprecedented entry of women into the workforce and a vast increase in hours worked per family. Deindustrialization severely depressed primary industrial production in the United States, creating a 'rust belt' of impoverished industrial areas. Workers were driven into unorganized white-collar or service occupations or into the ranks of the underclass, gravely weakening the labor unions. By 1991, only 17 percent of American workers were represented by unions – organizations that, for the most part, had neither the will nor the power to oppose plant relocations and closings, 'give back' contracts, and the continued attrition of their own memberships.

It is important to note that the obsolescence of the American labor movement was not only the result of economic forces; it was inherent in the organizational dynamics of interest groups seeking only to represent the immediate, partial, and transient interests of individuals rather than their long-term needs and interests. One can state this as a 'law': whatever the specific form of human bonding or solidarity that originally spawns interest groups, change in the socioeconomic environment is almost certain to dissolve these bonds by redefining group members' immediate interests, hence, by redefining the group itself. This is also true of business interest groups, for example, trade associations and cartels, but class solidarity is less germane to the maintenance of capitalist power, which rests in the hands of the owners of concentrated capital. Working-class 'interests', on the other hand, are dispersed and finally annihilated as such by interest groups whose identity depends upon the play of market forces. Thus, it was foreseeable that, under economic pressure, workers in automobile production would come to view their interests as counterposed to those of workers in competitive industries;

that American auto workers would come to view foreign auto workers as economic enemies; that 'pattern bargaining' in the U.S. auto industry would come under attack; and finally, that auto workers with seniority would sanction the elimination of less senior workers' jobs.

From a dispute resolution perspective, there might seem to be an easy answer to this dilemma: end the economic pressure. Terminate the 'zero-sum game' by increasing the total amount of resources available for distribution to all workers. But *so long as interest-group consciousness is primary*, this solution remains utopian. In a universe of interest groups, where the 'working class' has become little more than a sentimental fiction, relatively privileged groups of workers lack any incentive to struggle to increase the resources available to the class as a whole. Moreover, at the point that these workers find their own interests threatened, they also discover that the absence of class-wide, class-conscious organization has rendered them defenseless – incapable of challenging the system that ties the output of goods and services to immediate profitability. How can a protean interest group unrepresentative of the working class as a whole challenge the business cycle or other 'iron laws' of the market? How, indeed, can it act politically at all, other than in coalition with antagonistic class forces? The product of this vulnerability, we are beginning to understand, is not only the decline of labor organizations but the obsolescence of dispute resolution as a method of settling labor disputes. For as the interest groups purporting to represent workers weaken or disappear, the social contract allocating rights and duties to unions and companies – the consensual framework for dispute resolution – comes undone.

The interest group, in short, is the form *par excellence* of *capitalist* organization. Transferring the psychology and sociology of capitalist economics to the political sphere, it operates to subject all forms of group identity to perpetual redefinition in accordance with the dictates of the market. For this reason, the use of dispute-settlement and conflict-management techniques in the labor–management arena is not a 'neutral' practice – at least not where the social contract is obsolescent or defunct. By accepting the definition of the parties in conflict as interest groups rather than as social classes, the third-party intervenor acts indirectly to *preserve* the market system that inevitably, over time, favors the interests of capital over those of labor. Moreover, if the social contract originally constituting labor as a collection of interest groups has decayed or collapsed, dispute settlement practices become unusable, at least in their original form. Thus, what is sometimes called 'dispute resolution' in the labor–management field today frequently turns out to be a form of management consultancy in which third-party experts advise companies or governments how to minimize conflict with workers in the *absence* of an effective labor representative.

Assuming that this trend continues, one of two alternatives is foreseeable. Either the workers in each company or industry will reconstitute themselves as members of an interest group *including* that company's or industry's owners, or they will reconstitute themselves across company and industry (and perhaps national) lines as a politically conscious social class. In the former case, we will have replaced the social contract of the 1930s with some form of 'corporatism' or state capitalism; in the latter, we may well witness a resurgence of open class struggle. At present, the trend towards corporatism (absorption of labor into economic 'blocs' dominated by capital and heavily managed by the state) is marked, especially in Japan and Germany, but the historic association of this socioeconomic model with ruthless exploitation of labor and bellicose imperialism does not bode well for conflict resolution (see, e.g., Sweezy, 1970, pp. 307ff). Any system, I would argue, that fails to satisfy working people's basic human needs and long-term interests will generate increasing instability, political repression, and violence. In this emerging crisis, although dispute settlement techniques are unavailing, conflict-resolvers may have a constructive role to play.

Class conflict and conflict resolution

The goals of conflict resolution are to assist severely alienated parties in conflict to analyze the causes of their conflict, to imagine methods of reconstructing or replacing the system that is generating it, to 'cost out' various conflict-resolving options, and to implement the options agreed upon. In a situation involving serious class conflict, this means, in effect, that the third-party facilitator will function as a consultant to the parties on the redesign of a malfunctioning or collapsed socioeconomic system. Unlike the practitioner of dispute settlement, who assists parties to function within an accepted framework of social norms and institutions, the conflict-resolver will assume the task of helping them to create a new social contract capable of satisfying long-term human needs and class interests. The aim of this practice, therefore, is to facilitate the carrying out – with a minimum of violence – of an agreed-upon social transformation.

To many, this goal may seem wildly unrealistic. Conventional wisdom suggests that, since ruling classes seldom consent to limit their own power, significant changes in the social constitution must always be the result of mass violence. But it is clear that where the level of civil violence accompanying demands for revolutionary change is high enough, the changes eventually adopted may be deformed or even undone by the consequent damage to social relationships and to the economic infrastructure (see, e.g., Deutscher, 1959). For his part, Karl Marx *denied* any invariable connection between violence and radical change in class relationships; both in England and perhaps in the United States, he thought, a peaceful transition to socialism was possible (McLellan, 1973, p. 444). No doubt, as in other cases of deep-rooted social conflict, violence or the threat of it will continue to accompany class-based struggles. Still, recent events give us reason to question

153

the old equation of radical sociopolitical change with mass violence and state terror.

Significant normative and institutional changes have taken place during the past few years in the former Soviet Union, the Eastern European states, and in South Africa with a level of violence falling far short, to date, of that ordinarily associated with serious social restructuring. If only because the threat of massive violence in an age of nuclear and high-technology weapons raises prospects of total annihilation, it is now possible to envision a role for conflict resolution in the analysis and resolution (and provention) of serious class-based conflicts. Suppose, for example, that a wave of violent strikes were to strike Russia, where no social contract with broad acceptance has yet replaced the discredited Stalinist system, or that disorders were to erupt in a major American industry in which an obsolescent union had been replaced by a militant, class-conscious workers' leadership. In broad outline, a conflict resolution process designed to deal with such conflicts might operate as follows.

Stage one: Convening the parties
Initially, the third-party facilitator's role would be to identify the relevant parties and to inform them of the advantages and disadvantages of participating in a conflict resolution process. The first step − the identification of relevant parties − is crucial. It requires a preliminary conflict analysis adequate to ensure that those appearing as representatives are not, in fact, representing temporary interest groups whose identity will be altered or annihilated by foreseeable changes in the socioeconomic environment. It also requires the participation, at some stage in the process, of all parties whose consent is necessary to the construction of a satisfactory and durable agreement. The temptation to make peace between 'moderates' on both sides, when they are likely to be replaced in fairly short order by 'extremists', is to be resisted. The third party's efforts may then be directed to assist the representatives so identified to reckon the costs and likely outcomes of their continuing to dispute *without* making use of conflict resolution processes. As in all other phases of the process, the decision to proceed or not to do so will rest with the parties themselves.

Stage two: Constructing the forum
Assuming that an agreement to proceed is reached, what form will the process take? As the conflict resolution literature suggests, there are numerous possibilities, but it is likely that the *analytical problem-solving workshop* (APSW) will play a key role, perhaps followed by a public forum in the nature of a constitutional convention. The advantages of the APSW are that it is private, enabling the parties' representatives to participate in analysis outside the glare of publicity; it focuses their attention on problem-solving to satisfy basic needs rather than on bargaining to satisfy immediate interests; it

facilitates the envisioning of alternative systems; and that panels of facilitators have developed some expertise in using the process in other cases of serious and violent social conflict (Burton, 1987). Such a forum might be convened periodically over a period of several months or, if necessary, several years, giving representatives the opportunity to consult frequently with their constituencies. It is important to note that current governments do not function as sponsors of APSW forums, although they may appear as parties. The third-party facilitators are independent actors whose first priority is to assist in collective problem-solving, not to reestablish a temporary social peace.

Stage three: Conducting the workshop

The APSW itself would very likely be conducted in four phases aimed, respectively, at (a) defining the problems causing system breakdown; (b) envisioning alternative models of a new or restructured socioeconomic system; (c) assessing the costs and benefits of alternative models; and (d) arriving at a consensus supporting some model of a transformed system. Obviously, one cannot guarantee that the last stage will be reached, nor should the facilitator attempt to promote an agreement that unconvinced parties will subsequently reject. Nevertheless, the greatest challenge of the process may well be to assist the participants to envision methods of organizing industrial production that transcend the current limitations of current capitalist, social-democratic, and Stalinist models, and that promise to satisfy the parties' basic human needs and long-term interests. For this purpose, it is essential that no alternative be ruled out *ab initio*. Just as participants in, say, ethnic conflict workshops are invited to consider and discuss alternative forms of political constitution, the participants here should be free to consider the advantages and disadvantages of corporatist and 'pure free-market' systems, as well as of systems featuring publicly distributed capital, the 'mixed economy', democratically controlled state planning, worker self-management, decentralized communitarianism, and so forth. What may seem at first a purely 'academic' exercise has the capacity to generate new understandings of how basic needs may be satisfied. For this reason, the results of the APSW are frequently surprising to all parties concerned.

Stage four: Implementation

In this crucial stage — the least analyzed in current conflict resolution literature — understandings arrived at in the workshop (assuming that they have been reached) are either translated into public policy or fail to gain public acceptance. The analytical problem-solving process, in other words, becomes a political process in which public consent is sought to a new or reconstructed social contract. Here, prior workshops and other processes intended to secure the agreement of national or group leaders to make peace among themselves may be less relevant than processes designed to seek ratification of new constitutions or passage of major legislative reform programs. To describe

155

these processes is outside the scope of this chapter, but one can envision a series of constitutional and legislative initiatives that would involve the public actively in debating, amending, and adopting a new system designed, for the first time, to satisfy all parties' basic human needs. As in the case of constitutional amendments, the aim of such processes would be to test a proposal's ability to command consensual support, not just majority approval. Popular democracy, which functions so poorly in a universe of interest groups, might at this point become a living reality.

Signs of things to come

I have argued here that the analysis and resolution of class-based conflict, along with theories and practices designed to facilitate the resolution of racial, ethnic, and religious struggles, constitute the next frontier for conflict resolution. For if class conflicts are left to be settled by the methods of power politics and dispute resolution, the incapacity (or so it seems to me) of all current industrial systems to satisfy basic human needs will generate both structural and political violence at increasingly intense and destructive levels. It seems astounding – does it not? – that so few commentators in the U.S. have linked the growing anarchy in American cities, where death by gunfire has become a principal cause of youthful mortality, to serious problems rooted in that nation's system of production. This anarchy, I want to predict, will not long remain limited to large cities or to impoverished minority communities in the U.S. Indeed, signs of increasing alienation and violence are increasing everywhere where working people's interests are trampled underfoot, from America's ravaged cities and impoverished farming areas to the rapidly growing communities of 'near poor' workers, marginalized laborers, ethnic pariah groups, and children without a future inhabiting virtually every industrial nation. Sooner or later – one hopes, sooner – conflict-resolvers will have the opportunity to make a contribution toward solving this difficult problem.

References

Burton, J. W. (1987), *Resolving Deep-Rooted Conflict: A Handbook*, University Press of America, Lanham, Maryland.

Burton, J. W. (1990a), *Conflict: Resolution and Provention*, St. Martin's Press, New York and Macmillan, London.

Burton, J. W. (ed.) (1990b), *Conflict: Human Needs Theory*, St. Martin's Press, New York and Macmillan, London.

Burton, J. W. and Dukes, F. (1990), *Conflict: Practices in Management, Settlement and Resolution*, St. Martin's Press, New York and Macmillan, London.

Coser, L. (1956), *The Functions of Social Conflict*, Free Press, Glencoe, Illinois.

Deutscher, I. (1959), *The Prophet Armed, Trotsky: 1879–1921*, Oxford University Press, Oxford.

Dobbs, F. (1972), *Teamster Rebellion*, Monad Press, New York.

Dunlop, J. T. (1984), *Dispute Resolution, Negotiation, and Consensus Building*, Auburn House, Dover, Massachusetts.

Goldfield, M. (1989a), 'Worker insurgency, radical organization, and New Deal labor legislation', *American Political Science Review*, 83, pp. 1257–1282.

Goldfield, M. (1989b), *The Decline of Organized Labor in the United States*, University of Chicago Press, Chicago.

Greenstone, J. D. (1977), *Labor in American Politics*, University of Chicago Press, Chicago.

Klare, K. E. (1990), 'Critical theory and labor relations law', in D. Kairys, ed., *The Politics of Law: A Progressive Critique*, Pantheon Books, New York.

Kriesberg, L., Northrup, T. A., and Thorson, S. J. (1989), *Intractable Conflicts and Their Transformation*, Syracuse University Press, Syracuse, New York.

Leuchtenburg, W. E. (1963), *Franklin D. Roosevelt and the New Deal, 1932–1940*, Harper and Row, New York.

McConnell, G. (1967), *Private Power and American Democracy*, Alfred A. Knopf, New York.

McLellan, D. (1973), *Karl Marx: His Life and Thought*, Harper and Row, New York.

Montville, J. (ed.) (1990), *Conflict Resolution and Peacemaking in Multi-Ethnic Societies*, Westview Press, Boulder, Colorado.

Preis, A. (1964), *Labor's Giant Step: Twenty Years of the CIO*, Pioneer Press, New York.

Raiffa, H. (1982), *The Art and Science of Negotiation*, Harvard University Press, Cambridge, Massachusetts.

Sweezy, P. (1970), *The Theory of Capitalist Development*, Modern Reader, New York and London.

Public organizations and policies in conflict: Notes on theory and practice

Disciplinary dialogues

Conflict theory and professional conflict specialization arose out of the common concern in several disciplines with two practical questions. First, are there patterns in and generic explanations for the genesis, maturation, and alternative outcomes of conflict of all kinds? Second, are there principles, if properly understood, which permit constructive interventions in chronic, costly, deep-rooted, sometimes violent, kinds of conflict, thus preventing violence and encouraging cooperation in social intercourse. This is an over-simplified account, but it will permit us to see certain connections between the conflict field and various social sciences with overlapping concerns.

Another set of theories, these concerned with subjects in public management, organizational behavior, and public policy, arose to address situations where enduring, effective cooperation was needed to exploit social opportunities and overcome social differences. They had in common an interest in understanding and applying principles related to the establishment, operation, direction, and change of social structures under conditions of individual, group, and social differences. In general, we can say their concerns were with governance — *both* self-governance and enforcement of orderly, peaceful, productive community relationships. Conflict theories and these other theories have faced great challenges in relating theory to practice, and, as we shall see, in relating their theories to one another. One objective of this chapter is to explain why these theories remain so separated and indicate how and why they are and should be coming closer together.

Often theories developed in distinctive disciplines are targeted on what seem to be the same social phenomena, but, like the blind men feeling the elephant, the parts often do not appear to be related or integrated. One wise group goes off to dialogue about the nature of pillars and the other group about legs. Each discipline chooses its fundamental categories and seeks its own unique perspective on social problems and possibilities. Furthermore the reward systems and traditions of the separate disciplines have a momentum that supports prized language and specialized perspectives. All these forces, and more, make integration between and even within disciplines difficult.

Conflict theory, or for some, the conflict 'discipline' (Sandole, 1987b, p. 298) is one of the youngest fields in the social sciences. Here, the words discipline, field, study, and theory will be used interchangeably, despite useful distinctions. The management, organization, and policy fields mentioned above are hard to combine under one label, although they have an acknowledged close relationship. The emphasis will be on organization studies, but public management and policy studies will often be implied, and at times mentioned. I will, perhaps paradoxically, claim that all of the above studies, including conflict, have a common focus on human cooperation.

People in the conflict field have tried hard to integrate theories, but so far it is a field that mainly incorporates useful and presumably related principles from other fields. Adherents are a motley company, most based in anthropology, international relations, law, psychotherapy, social work, sociology, and political science. One motivation for banding together has been the common conviction that there are anomalies in the normal science of their parent disciplines which require a new set of explanations – a new paradigm – to account for the dynamics of non-cooperation, damaging confrontations, and the remedies for them. The most ardent among them believe there are ideas and practices that may convert or provide the grounds for converting even the most negative and serious forms of conflict into collaborative, joint problem-solving which will expand social justice, human-needs satisfaction, and peaceful, productive social relations at every level (Burton, 1990).

The field is more open than most others to insights from other fields. Yet when those of us in the administration and policy field read or listen to the dialogue between people centrally identified with the conflict field, two disjunctive impressions emerge. On the one hand we see they have helped develop powerful insights and tools for constructive analysis and intervention in many conflict situations. The skills of conflict consultants, facilitators, and mediators are in growing demand. However, when it comes to the myriad important disputes in the arenas of American public policy and government organization, students of conflict have been very selective and have severely limited their zone of attention.

In their quest for efficacy, recognition, and separateness, the family of concerns called dispute, conflict, and peace studies inevitably display a certain disdain and distancing from what they see as more tradition-bound, resistant disciplines, especially those dealing with politics and established authority. From the conflict viewpoint other disciplines are wedded to competitive, power-politics outlooks which prevent them from seeing the enormous opportunities for cooperation hidden in the proper understanding of conflict. There is enough truth to this perception, not to mention the rising costs of conflict, to fuel growing recruitment of scholars and practitioners to the conflict camp.

There are other reasons why conflict people have not been more attentive to administrative, organizational, and policy matters. To some extent there is a bias that organizations, more particularly bureaucracies, are hostile to the interests of individuals and groups in their embrace of the power-politics paradigm. This position, however, is also common even among writers who specialize in the study of bureaucracy; big organizations, some writers believe, are part of the problem, not the solution (Thayer, 1981). One recent writer, although advocating cooperation and human development in public organizations, described bureaucracies as follows (Williams, 1980, p. 168):

At the personal and sometimes petty level, one ... may get the feeling that the woods are full of enemies. The struggle to hold on to your job, the campaign to win a promotion, and the hunger for a little personal glory are but a few commonplace occurrences in the realpolitik of the civil servant at whatever level. Beyond that, regrettably, realpolitik seems to be the name of the administrative game everywhere, in both public and private enterprise.

Another related reason for the distancing is the belief that formal authority structures and norms of bureaus often discourage conflict in order to avoid radical change in the organization or preserve the advantages and comforts of office holders. Conflict suppression, or quick settlement, at least in the short run, conserves the energy and order of the organization even at the risk of deepening alienation and opposition. Two notable but largely ignored works in the administration and policy fields that analyze this behavior and would be useful to conflict specialists are Weinstein's *Bureaucratic Opposition* (1979) and Levi's *Bureaucratic Insurgency* (1977).

The neglect of governmental organizations could also be partly an accident of the conflict field's preoccupation in its infancy with individuals and groups (or states in international conflict) as the units of analysis. The field simply has not been at work long enough, some might argue, to get around to the variety of conflict situations worthy of study and action. In its early stages, conflict specialists were attracted to the grand clashes of states, ethnic rebellions, and the drama of personal and group confrontations as found in divorce, labor unrest, race relations, environmental battles, and the like. These subjects, along with the spectacular and deadly conflicts in the international arena, might be all the field can bite off and chew for some time to come.

My response to this last point is that a half-conscious slighting of organizational-level conflict is even reflected in the social typologies drawn up by conflict writers to guide their investigations. The usual references are to individual, group, social, and international levels of conflict, skipping organizations as though they were not significant social constructs (Laue, 1987, p. 17; Burton, 1990). Much of what follows is intended to show that the purview of conflict theory must be extended more affirmingly to organizations if either theory or practice is to be fully realized. In many cases current research and applications are disadvantaged by inattention to the organizational dimensions of conflict.

Disregard from the other side

The sharing of ideas and practices between disciplines depends on forces of push and pull. Conflict specialists do not carry the whole onus for failing to consider or exploit germane experience and theory of other disciplines. To an even greater degree the fields mentioned above have been negligent in recognizing the discoveries and successes generated by work on conflict. As I will soon show, after some scattered early efforts, regular work on conflict is only now beginning to appear in the administration, organization, and policy literatures. It is still hard to tell how much of the work is spontaneous within these disciplines, and how much derived or directly inspired by conflict studies.

But first, to parallel the critique of neglect by conflict specialists, let us look at some possible reasons for the neglecting *of* conflict studies by these disciplines. First, to turn a reason given above on its head, the relative newness of the conflict field in the eyes of the more established disciplines could account for the failure to see its relevance (or accept its standing) in social analysis. Second, the traditional approaches to organization and policy studies do tend to take disputes and even serious conflict for granted. Employment of power politics, the building of competitive coalitions, and the utilization of hierarchical authority are *part* of the reality assumptions of these fields. Newcomers who question these assumptions or profess uncommon insights about taken-for-granted processes are viewed with some suspicion.

Third, and related to the second point, conflict theorists may be looked upon as reinventing the wheel. Organization and policy specialists have had an ongoing concern with improving the efficiency, effectiveness, and productivity of public enterprises. They have already accepted and incorporated contributions from the fields of human relations, organizational development (OD), decision-making, systems theory, and many others. The aim in many cases has been to understand how to enhance adaptiveness, co-operation, openness, responsiveness, and public approval. The self-identified conflict field has those same aims, but has no monopoly on ideas for achieving those results. Besides, negotiation and mediation strategies, problem-solving techniques, and change strategies have to some extent already been in the mainstream of organization theory and consulting before the conflict-oriented 'shops' entered the picture.

This short review of reasons that may explain why organization and conflict studies have passed one another by like ships in the night is not the whole story. Rendezvous and flirtations have occurred and have laid a base for considerably more cooperation and communication than in the past. Before dealing with the extent to which management, organization, and policy studies

161

have been or are becoming interested in conflict, however, a discussion of the salient features of public organizations would be useful to dispel some stereotypes, remind ourselves of some relevant history, and set the stage for what follows.

The salience of public organizations

This section discusses aspects of public organizations and the policy process that should be of special interest to conflict specialists. Though some of it might be familiar, the discussion in part recommends to the conflict community that it examine organizational and policy factors in conflict more closely. 'Public organizations' here refers to any offices, agencies, bureaus, departments, and institutions, staffed by appointed, full-time officials, publicly funded, lawfully created and restrained and whose main purpose is to create, maintain, and distribute public profit (benefits) rather than private profit or personal enjoyment. A typical formal definition of organizations found in the public administration literature identifies organizations as 'enduring collections of people conducting specialized and interdependent activities related to a common purpose' (Barton and Chappell, 1985). Excluded from the discussion, mainly for purposes of simplicity, are legislatures and courts. This discussion of organizations will underscore conflict dimensions frequently.

It has been a long hard road to create democratic forms of polities in a world where historically and presently they are not the dominant form. However imperfect they remain, they should be distinguished as major departures, at least many degrees removed from systems where management, organization, and policy are essentially dictated by more or less whimsical, arbitrary, self-appointed elites or conquerors. Conflict processes *usually* follow a different course in democratic systems than they do in the others and that is a significant fact.

However, even in the absence of democratic systems many polities of the past have *produced* in some admirable measure community, identity, security, order, and opportunity within their societies. Public authority can be a force for creative and effective relationships in society. We do not know exactly what the alternatives may have been, but it would be churlish to examine history only in reference to the brutality that the older managements, organizations, and policies of generals, kings, priests, and war-lords visited on people. Past nations also produced highly valued social products unlikely to have resulted from private, voluntary, or scattered effort.

Modern democratic, humane, orderly society, such as we know it, is in large part made possible through the governmental processes and structures. Bureaucracies build roads, maintain sewers, inspect food and drugs, light our streets, educate children, enforce law and order, regulate commerce, and do much else that is essential to civic life. Dwight Waldo, a leading public administration theorist, has long accentuated the positive qualities of public institutions, arguing that, 'Public administration is a powerful creative force ... that has helped create and maintain civilization and provide for the well-being and even survival of societies' (1980, pp. 17–18).

Organizations are not locked into a rigid or inevitable pattern of operating or responding to conflicts. According to Baveles, 'Organizations are not biological organisms; they are social inventions' (1960, p. 498). They are intentionally created constructs within which planned, specific, and recurring forms of human actions take place. It is this intentionality of design as well as the many alternative ways of planning and specifying functions and tasks that make them malleable and adaptable to human purposes. *Every* type of large organization – churches, businesses, unions, and governments – has abused power, but every type has also permitted communities of needs to be expressed and forwarded.

The conduct of modern life itself increasingly turns on organizational activity. Arnold Tannenbaum captures the essence of this when he notes (1978, p. 267):

Man's life in contemporary society can be characterized largely as one of organizational memberships. Man commits a major portion of his working life to participating in one – and more and often several – social organizations. His motivations, aspirations, his general way of life, are tied inextricably to the organizations of which he is part – and even to some of which he is not.

The 'members' of public organizations (modern democratic ones) are people who act or try to act mainly as organizational representatives and agents of the public, rather than on their own behalf. The extent and desirability of this bifurcation of self-interest and interest-as-member is one of the enduring arguments in management and organization theory. Downs (1967, pp. 50–51) has provided a notable discussion of personal and organizational differentiation and some implications for conflict *within* public bureaus. In discussing hierarchy he notes:

Conflicts of interest spring from differences in explicit goals officials pursue, and in their modes of perceiving reality. In any organization, no two members have exactly the same explicit goals and, as a result, may disagree about what the organization ought to be doing, even if they possess the same information and face no uncertainty ...

If all the inconsistencies arising from the above sources were allowed to flourish unchecked, the overall impact of any large organization's efforts would be seriously diminished – if not destroyed – because the actions of some members would offset those of others. To avoid this outcome some mechanism must be created for settling conflicts; that is, adjusting inconsistent behavior patterns among the organization's members to an acceptable level of complementarity.

The views expressed by Downs are mirrored by Blake and Mouton (1964, pp. 162–163) who are among the rare organization theorists widely accepted in the conflict field. They write:

Relations of [organizational] members to one another are dealt with as of core significance since all are embedded in a situation of common stakes where success for one and all comes from accomplishing the mission of the organization in the fullest way possible. *In a real sense, people and work are interconnected.*

In the course of managing operations, tensions often arise among people in their interactions with one another, in deciding what should be done, how to do it, and in the actual execution of it. ...

From a practical point of view, then, conflict might as well be accepted as inevitable. But this is far from saying that it is not resolvable. In areas where there is conflict, it must be dealt with in some way. ... The issue, then is not in whether conflict is present. It will be present. *The key is in how conflict is managed.*

Boulding (1990, pp. 176–177) has also tackled the issue of how conflicts arise in organizations and between them and others on the outside. His immediate context was religious organizations, but the application can be extended:

Those who share a common view of the world and common rituals and beliefs tend to form a community to practice the rituals [read: organizational procedures] and to propagate and persuade people of these common beliefs. These communities can develop great integrative power, as do the organizations that build up around them. ...

Each believer sees the non-believer as a threat to the validity of the believer's own beliefs. If somebody does not agree with me, then either I must be wrong or they must be wrong, and ... change in beliefs is a rather painful and rare event. ... The answer that we might both be crazy or both be wrong is seen on both sides as a threat to existing integrative structures.

Boulding further argues that dialectical thinking (thesis, antithesis, then synthesis) is much less common than generally believed. More common is that the parties with different theses withdraw from one another. In *all* the cases just cited, organizational members tend to protect or are encouraged to protect *the organization*. Members who differ with other members or organizational policy or processes only come into conflict, or see it escalate, *if* resolution mechanisms do not work. It is for these kinds of reasons that I argue that the organizational factor, not just individual needs or general appeals to social justice, must be considered in approaches to the analysis and resolution of conflict.

Public organizations are durable, evolving, self-conscious managers (and makers) of conflict by design. They incorporate a wide variety of approaches to handling conflict from compulsion to genuine collaborative problem-solving. The approaches are built-in and, although often taken for granted, new approaches are from time to time adopted. Administrative organizations are an *integral* part of the political system that determines to a great degree — in Lasswell's (1936) famous definition of politics — who gets what, when, and how.

Political scientists have often ignored the bureaucratic part of government in their treatment of political systems. Major qualifications to the splitting apart of politics and administration have been introduced by the field of public administration. Robert Denhardt (1984, p. iv), for example, describes the very important role of bureaucracy as follows:

Though perhaps intended as an instrument for carrying out the will of the executive and the legislature, the public bureaucracy in modern society – simply by virtue of its immense presence and complexity – impacts the political system in many ways. Not only are important issues decided within the bureaucracy; public organizations direct the attention of the public, play a significant role in setting the national agenda, and help establish the values of society.

When we move the discussion of organization to the level of political systems we confront the question of the legitimacy of their authority. This theme has been extensively discussed and roundly criticized by Burton (1990, Ch. 8), where he sees most state use of authority as illegitimate and based on inflexible, and therefore, oppressive law. His argument is based on a theory of conflict stressing the existence of deep-rooted, universal individual needs. While I do not deny the existence and importance of such needs, this discussion of the role of organizations in our lives tries to make it clear that associational or organizational life *also* is an expression of deep-rooted human needs. Human beings are cooperators, and the need to establish, use, or modify structures of cooperation has always vied with individual needs as such. From this vantage point, Burton is probably wrong when he says, 'Twentieth century experience has persuaded writers that the individual may be an independent variable, that there may be no institutional devices, rule-governed norms or organizational influences that can contain the ontological propensities of the individual' (ibid., p. 94).

Nation-states and a nation's bureaucracy

Modern nation-states were born in violence. They arose from the devastation of the Thirty Years' War in Germany which culminated in the Peace of Westphalia in 1648. That agreement established the concept of independent, sovereign nation-states with absolute power over their subjects and a right to be free of interference by other states when exercising such power (Ray, 1990, pp. 185–190). With the American and French revolutions the idea took hold that the state belonged to the people. In the American case sovereignty extended to individuals, whose approval was necessary for the form of government the state employed. (But in most systems it was the state alone that remained sovereign.)

The principles of state sovereignty and a state's monopoly of legitimate power within a nation were soon challenged by the need for states to establish agreements about how people would relate to one another and to the state. Ideas from the Enlightenment, classical democracy, and colonial experience led to the establishment of such devices as bills of rights, federalism, frequent elections, and separation of powers. Over time, powers in the system were further fragmented and shared with an independent commercial sector, citizens' associations, formal interest groups, new local jurisdictions, and an increasingly professionalized bureaucracy. All this was accompanied by increasing heterogeneity of the population (class, ethnicity, race, religion, etc.) which increased the interfaces across which conflict could occur.

There are kinds of conflict over which bureaus do have and use coercive powers. Among them are the powers of arrest, eviction, incarceration, and execution, the taking of property, seizure of assets, removal of licenses, detention and deportation of illegal residents, and more. When these things are done properly they are visible and lawful and can be appealed. But they can still be contentious as were deportation orders for South Americans who were being protected in the 1980s by the Sanctuary Movement. Bureaus also have the power to give or withhold information, services, and resources. If citizens or organizational members believe any of these powers are being abused or exercised unjustly, serious conflict arises, most of which is legally settled rather than resolved collaboratively.

Even though many citizens are distrustful about government's powers, when disputes break out in general society participants frequently turn *to* government, seeking alliances, coalitions, endorsements, resources, or protection, that strengthen their claims and views of justice. For example, when the citizens of Mono County, California thought Los Angeles was unfairly depleting their underground water supplies, a decades-long struggle ensued with each party attempting to get the state and federal government agencies to intercede in their favor. While nation-state *theory* provided for a great deal of coercion, *practice* has been mixed.

Disciplinary awakenings: organizations in conflict, conflicts in organizations

If the many governments established in the U.S. had been in the main incompetent and grossly poor managers of conflict, fragmentation would have riven the country apart long before now. It almost did during the Civil War. But not until the 1960s did the incidence and range of conflicts again rise to intensities that required self-conscious attention to new alternatives for their reduction in academia, business, government, and elsewhere. Some of the reactions are captured in an article by A. J. Auerbach in the *Public Administration Review* (1969, p.639) at the time:

Conflict and confrontation in forms and dimensions never experienced before seem to have become a normal element of the life of our public institutions. Organizations and agencies which have in the past been able to resolve difference — mostly of an internal character — through negotiation, accommodation, and compromise, have had to face militant and seemingly unreasonable demands often accompanied by violence. The usual techniques for resolving difference of opinion in social institutions do not appear adequate to resolve the current crisis. ...

Auerbach was not alone in seeing the sixties as a watershed. It was a decade marked by confrontational bipolarism, the dismantling of colonialism, and the anti-war, civil rights, environmental, student, and women's movements.

In large part reacting to the events described, students of conflict and those who dealt with public organizations and policies looked for new insights to explain and mechanisms to facilitate social change. Emery and Trist introduced a new paradigm to explain how environments themselves evolved and were becoming connected (1978). Conflict, change, and organizational development began to be seen as interrelated activities. L. David Brown (1983, p. v) captured the relationship in one of the very few book-length analyses of these subjects:

Change is often closely tied to conflict. Sometimes change breeds conflict; sometimes conflict breeds change. Effective conflict management is often critical to constructive change processes. Change is important if inequitable and unacceptable conditions exist for some party, but so too there is a need for order, consensus, and common goals *within and between organizations and between organizations and the publics they serve* in an open society.

Brown recognizes that organizational debate and cooperative efforts are hampered both by too much as well as by too little conflict and he recommends 'strategies and tactics for promoting constructive conflicts as well as interventions for reducing destructive fighting' (ibid., p. vi).

One of the first public administration books that substantially wove conflict dynamics into the fabric of organizational analysis was Anthony Downs's *Inside Bureaucracy* (1967). He not only explained the reasons conflict is integral to organizational growth and maintenance, but how it was typically reduced and settled. Before Downs there were very few case studies in that literature focused on conflict, a notable exception being two cases included in the very popular *Reader in Bureaucracy* (Merton *et al.*, 1952, p. 282). In introducing the cases Merton wrote:

bureaus may engage in acute conflict as a result of overlapping jurisdictions, competing loyalties, and incompatible objectives. [Marshall] Dimock provides a case study of bureaucratic infighting which illustrates a tactic utilized by a newly-created division to maintain itself against the opposition of rival agencies in a larger bureaucracy. The selection from the Hoover Commission presents another case study analyzing the sources and consequences of continued conflict between two Federal agencies operating in the same sphere.

A few other early efforts to explore relationships between the fields stand out. One was a management journal article, 'Organizational conflict: Concepts and models', by L. R. Pondy (1967). Another by Walton and Dutton presented a general model of interdepartmental conflict and its management, together with a review of the literature (1989, originally 1969, p. 201), but concentrating on higher executive responses to these conflicts. Boulding, one of the founding fathers of conflict studies, also devoted attention to the issue in 'The

167

organization as a party to conflict' (1972). A literature search results in only a meager handful of other works before the late 1970s.

Contemporary effort to join conflict and organizational studies

Most of the management and organization people continue to view organizations primarily in terms of their economy, efficiency, performance, and productivity. Learning how to gain control (via measurement) over these parameters of organization is their preeminent concern. Researchers and practitioners with this classic bent are the ones Mason Haire (1989, p. 461) criticizes for treating conflict as 'error' — as a deviation in organizational routines that must be controlled:

Classic organization theory puts special emphasis on error and particularly the detection of error and its correction after it happens. The standard organization is set up so that everyone has something he ought to do, and as soon as he does not do it, we find out about it and give him hell.

The classic perspective has been one of command-and-control which emphasizes conventional solutions to problems by altering various features (usually incrementally) such as assignments, discipline, incentives, structures, and technology. Opposition or competition are treated as anomalies — signals that authority and program logic may be threatened. The preferred strategy is to block or eliminate the conflict signals. This proclivity to avoid or defend against, rather than confront, conflict is such a common response that it constitutes one of the reasons conflict specialists often see organizations as part of the problem and not the solution. Their response then is to recommend channeling conflict outside the organization into so-called neutral settings using third-party facilitators or intervenors, implying that insiders cannot be trusted to seek resolution on their own.

While the classical school remains preeminent, some of those who have always been attracted to the social dimensions of organizational and policy questions have begun to pay a great deal of attention to conflict research and intervention. Works focused on arbitration, mediation, dispute resolution, and mutual problem-solving increasingly make an appearance in the main journals of the field. They have recognized that most of the traditional management, organization, and policy process theories are very inadequate when it comes to conflicts which are intense or intractable. Moreover, the increasing number and kinds of disputes with which government organizations have become engaged have strained conventional wisdom and theories. In this sense Burton (1990, p. 71) is correct when he says our legacies, and traditions are not working right. Thus researchers and practitioners in the several social sciences have either invented or borrowed ideas about conflict resolution from wherever they could. The crystallization of a distinct field of dispute and conflict studies has provided help just when it was needed.

In commenting on the increasing inclusion of a separate concept of conflict by those studying the public sector, the term 'conflict management' is often used. In most of this work the term is used in the broad sense presented by Sandole when he commented:

'Conflict management' as expressed here is synonymous with 'conflict regulation', more comprehensive than 'conflict intervention' which focuses on third party activities, and more comprehensive than 'conflict resolution', which may or may not be the end result of the conflict management processes (1987a, p. 4).

Parenthetically, it should be noted that Burton's condemnation of authority and public organizations confines him to using 'management' only in the sense of containment: our history, he insists, is one of authoritarianism and protection of immediate interests (1990, pp. 71–72). This reservation, however, gives few organization theorists pause.

One of the most ambitious recent efforts to incorporate conflict theory into the body of organizational practice is found in Mastenbroek's *Conflict Management and Organization Development* (1987). Here he blends theories of conflict, organizational development, and systems to produce a synthesis which he calls 'network intervention theory'. One of its major characteristics is 'its unusual combination of organizational development, conflict handling and principles of organizational success' (ibid., p. 1). His objective is to specify the organizational structures and cultures that successfully combine self-interest and organization interests. Some conflict theorists may find the book disheartening because it does not challenge the legitimacy of existing power relationships and because it ignores the larger environmental, moral, and ethical considerations. Trust and openness to Mastenbrock are rhetorical terms that simply act as a 'coverup' for power relationships (ibid., p. 162). A second work of bridge-building is Stevenson and Pops's article, 'Conflict resolution methods and the policy process' (1989). They claim to present 'a descriptive model intended to grasp the realities of how conflicts are resolved in the policy process. The approach is one of juxtaposing environmental factors, policy stages, and other variables that produce a specific range of resolution methods.' In their view such an approach 'is essential to improve both theory and practice of policy-related conflict resolution' (ibid., p. 463). The authors are highly critical of conflict researchers and practitioners, 'who design a conflict resolution method and employ it ad hoc in varying situations to test whether it works' (ibid., p. 471), which they see as inefficient experimentation. They scold, 'For too long, those interested in conflict resolution have all but ignored the impact of the policy process on the selection of conflict resolution technique' and they advise conflict researchers to 'expand their models to incorporate insights from the literature of both conflict resolution and public policy making' (ibid.). Again, conflict specialists may be upset with the authors' focus on the substantive outcomes of policy rather than processes of conflict prevention, reduction, or resolution, but there is a very ambitious attempt to intermix the disciplines.

Public administration writers are also applying conflict theory to contentious intergovernmental problems. Buntz and Radin bill their study, 'Managing intergovernmental conflict: The case of human services' (1983), as one of the very few public organization or policy studies to apply conflict theory to practice. Their focus is on tensions 'between the federal government's responsibility to hold [state and local] governments' grant recipients accountable to national goals and priorities and the state and local governments' drive to meet self-determined needs and priorities' (ibid., p.403).

While the authors employ a robust definition of conflict and make extensive use of L.D. Brown's (1983) conflict interface model, they reveal little about the impact of strong ideological pressures of Reaganomics on the lower governments or the implications of the conflict for the clients who bear most of the costs in the process. Nevertheless, they are very self-conscious about the need for dialogue across the disciplines, noting, 'Attention needs to be directed to conflict and conflict management at this time because it appears that conflict is highly misunderstood by both practitioners and students of public management, and, as a result, systematic attention to conflict management is lacking' (ibid.).

In a wide-ranging book of readings on dispute resolution, Miriam Mills, in *Conflict Resolution and Public Policy* (1990), raises some fundamental questions about conflict in public settings. She notes that when particular interests of particular parties become linked to interpretations of society's highest goals it often makes relationships more adversarial and strained. The reason, she says, are linkage complexities (ibid., p.x):

One aims very much at the idea of a speedy resolution of conflict. Yet some disputes are so complex and so intricately interwoven with other resolutions that they perhaps will never receive ultimate settlement. Some disputes are likely to continue only until the parties become exhausted. While the values of speed, cost, and efficiency are frequently stressed, they may not always be desirable. What constitutes satisfaction for the parties may, in the final analysis be deleterious to society as a whole.

Of course, a public agency as a party is more likely to have the resources for survival and continue to operate even if another party 'becomes exhausted'. Still the stress on public-interest factors is an important counter to an exclusive focus on individual-needs satisfaction. The relationship requires much more extensive argumentation than it has so far received.

The organization and policy people are moving as well into more applied conflict resolution areas. One of the most heralded recent applications of conflict theory to public-sector problems has been in the area of negotiated rule-making by federal agencies that operate in such areas as environmental protection, food and drugs, and transportation. A chapter by Daniel Fiorino

(1990, p. 140) in Mills, cited above, concentrates on the theory and practice of the new procedures:

One of the more interesting applications of alternative dispute resolution (ADR) technique in recent years has been administrative rule making. In theory and practice, [it] differs fundamentally from more typical uses of ADR techniques, including site-specific mediation, minitrials, or arbitration. Its purpose is less to resolve [existing] conflict then to formulate policy that is prospective and general in its application.

A burgeoning literature on the technique indicates the enthusiasm with which it is being embraced. West (1988), for example, sees rule-making as establishing a pattern of internal conflict resolution that replaces a long tradition of rules being the product of the regulatory bureaus alone. Formal recognition of the value of this approach was achieved under the Negotiated Rulemaking Act of 1990, Public Law no. 101–648 which was signed by the President in November 1990. It clarified the authority of federal agencies to establish negotiating committees to draft proposed regulations and encourages them to do so, seeking to develop a process of rule-making that will not create a battleground for interest groups.

Richman (1985) has documented the introduction of formal mediation into municipal annexation negotiations in Virginia. He also reports on how the technique is spreading to deal with more kinds of public disputes (e.g., hazardous-waste siting) and lists more than a dozen states which 'had established or were considering funding alternative settlement programs, including mediation as a complement to traditional state regulatory and adjudicatory processes' (ibid., p. 517).

In a related development, the Administrative Conference of the United States (ACUS), an independent federal advisory agency, approved a recommendation 'encouraging every [federal] department and agency with significant interaction with the public to establish an ombudsman service for receipt of and inquiry into complaints from members of the public', because, as Commissioner Breger (1990) noted, '[e]xperience shows that it can increase cooperation with government and reduce occasions for litigation. Equally important, the ombudsman can provide high-ranking decision makers with the information needed to identify and treat systemic problems before they get out of hand.'

The ACUS has also carved out a role in developing other dispute-resolving mechanisms for government use, especially in the management of what Wallace Warfield calls the Balkanized management of government contract disputes. In commenting on the relevance of conflict resolution to administrative practices, Warfield (1989, p. S93) observes:

Unlike community disputes, where there are no set rules of procedure and parties have no formal ... relationship, administrative disputes usually arise from a base of formal rules and procedures affecting agencies with functional lines of authority. Moreover, these agencies' relationships with individuals and private organizations

171

that utilize or are affected by their activities are usually defined in great detail. There-fore, in crafting alternative techniques to resolve administrative disputes, one must be mindful of this formal structure and the reality of its institutional limitations.

The ACUS has actively sponsored legislation that would have wide impact on more consensual decision-making in federal government programs. One of its biggest recent successes has been getting Congressional and Presidential approval for the Administrative Dispute Resolution Act of 1990, Public Law No. 101−552 (the ADR Act). It calls on every federal agency to explicitly consider potential ADR uses, encourages judicial officers to take greater advantage of mediation and other ADR techniques, requires efforts to train government personnel to be better negotiators, and to appoint senior agency officials as dispute resolution specialists. The ADR Act amends the Admin-istrative Procedures Act, the Federal Torts Claims Act, and the Contract Disputes Act. The ACUS has been given specific roles in training and other support for the Act and is directed to report to Congress periodically on agencies' implementation of the Act.

These new applications of conflict theory and practice in public organization and policy arenas join with well-established efforts of earlier federal programs such as the Federal Mediation and Conciliation Service (FMCS) which has long been active in age-discrimination and labor−management disputes. The genuine needs of bureau managers for better alternatives to deal with the increasing pace and variety of conflict reflects what Sandole and others (Banks, Wedge, Sandole; all 1987) point out as signs of a new paradigm, with the best evidence to date being recent repetitions by the Bush administration that new conflict resolution approaches should be substituted for litigation wherever possible (*Washington Post*, 1991 p. 2).

Conclusion: Disciplinary dividends and dangers

There is considerable evidence of a rapid institutionalization of conflict prac-tices fed by increasing experience and learning from corporations, general society, public experiments, and academic research. There will, according to Singer (1990), also be commercialization and, in my view, fads. In the near future classes, conferences, and workshops, throughout government will be set up to signify the embrace of conflict resolution as a major emphasis. This has happened before in government with human relations, organizational development, participative management, and total quality management. A goodly share of hucksterism will ensue, but research opportunities will also be opened up and important basic ideas legitimized. To Burton this could all seem a palliative to protect existing interests and improve the image of basically authoritarian systems, but to many organization and policy theorists it will come as a revelation. There may, however, be dangers that even Burton has not anticipated.

The rise of demands for new conflict research and services has been traced to the fact that conflicts are increasing in number, complexity, and severity. So too, I expect, will new branches of conflict resolution proliferate to meet the 'market' demand being created. Unless the fraternity of specialists interested in conflict and its resolution anticipate and plan for their professional future, they may be coopted into creating large, formal professional and trade associations that are in competition with one another. If there are not enough of the right kinds of conflicts around they may try to stir them up, replicating the competitive behavior they so much abhor in traditional settings. The competition would, if this scenario unfolds, be organizational in the classic sense. Agencies and jurisdictions will vie with one another to select (by contract or incorporation) the best, and most popular gurus and brands of conflict resolution services. Conflict will become commoditized!

Even with Singer's vague warnings about the dangers of commercialization of the conflict resolution field, we have hardly begun to appreciate that successful *institutionalization*, commercial or not, can have a negative impact on the development, integrity, and mission of the field. Contributions to the improvement of public organization and policy processes might then only be marginal rather than substantial. If the temptations to treat conflict as fad or merely a market opportunity can be resisted, the conflict field will have vast new theoretical horizons in the study of the domestic public sector. Then management, organizational, and policy theorists will be positioned to render more powerful insights and assistance to the beleaguered public services − to those who serve in them and those served by them.

References

Amstutz, M. K. (1982), *An Introduction to Political Science: The Management of Conflict*, Scott, Foresman, New York.

Auerbach, A. J. (1969), 'Confrontation and administrative response', *Public Administration Review*, 5, pp. 639−646.

Banks, M. (1987), 'Four conceptions of peace', in D. J. D. Sandole and I. Sandole-Staroste, *Conflict Management and Problem Solving: Interpersonal to International Applications*, New York University Press, New York, pp. 259−274.

Barton, R. and Chappell, W. L. Jr. (1985), *Public Administration: The Work of Government*, Scott, Foresman, Glenview, Illinois.

Bavales, A. (1960), 'Leadership: Man and function', *Administrative Science Quarterly*, 4, pp. 491−498.

Blake, R. R. and Mouton, J. S. (1964), *The Managerial Grid*, Gulf Publ., Houston, Texas.

Boulding, K. E. (1972), 'The organization as a party to conflict', in J. M. Thomas and W. G. Bennis, *Management of Change and Conflict*, Penguin, Harmondsworth, Middlesex.

Boulding, K. E. (1990), *The Three Faces of Power*, Sage Publications, Newbury Park, California.

Breger, M. (1990), Memorandum from the Chairman. To: Persons interested in dispute resolution and the ombudsman. Administrative Council of the United States, Washington, D.C.

Brown, L.D. (1983), *Managing Conflict at Organizational Interfaces*, Addison-Wesley, Reading, Massachusetts.

Buntz, G.C. and Radin, B.A. (1983), 'Managing intergovernmental conflict: The case of human services', *Public Administration Review*, 43, p. 403.

Burton, J. (1990), *Conflict: Resolution and Provention*, St. Martin's Press, New York.

Denhardt, R.B. (1984), *Theories of Public Organization*, Brooks/Cole, Monterey, California.

Downs, A. (1967), *Inside Bureaucracy*, Little, Brown, Boston.

Emery, E.F. and Trist, E.L. (1978), 'The causal texture of organizational environments', in J.M. Shafritz and P.H. Whitbeck, eds, *Classics of Organization Theory*, Moore, Oak Park, Illinois.

Fiorino, D.J. (1990), 'Dimensions of negotiated rule-making: Practical constraints and Theoretical implications', Chapter 8 in M. Mills, ed., *Conflict Resolution and Public Policy*, Greenwood Press, New York.

Gerston, L.N. (1983), *Making Public Policy: From Conflict to Resolution*, Scott, Foresman, New York.

Haire, M. (1989), 'The concept of power and the concept of man', in J.S. Ott, *Classic Readings in Organizational Behavior*, Brooks/Cole, Pacific Grove, Calilfornia, pp. 454–469.

Kingdon, J. (1983), *Agendas, Alternatives, and Public Policies*, Little, Brown, Boston, Massachusetts.

Lasswell, H. (1936), *Politics: Who Gets What, When, and How*, Whittlesey, New York.

Laue, J. (1987), 'The emergence and institutionalization of third party roles in conflict', in D.J.D. Sandole and I. Sandole-Staroste, *Conflict Management and Problem Solving: Interpersonal to International Applications*, New York University Press, New York, pp. 17–29.

Levi, M. (1977), *Bureaucratic Insurgency*, Lexington Books, Lexington, Massachusetts.

Mastenbroek, W.F.G. (1987), *Conflict Management and Organization Development*, Wiley, New York.

Merton, R.K., Gray, S.P., Hockey. B., and Selvin, H. C. (1952), *Reader in Bureaucracy*, The Free Press, New York.

Mills, M.K. (ed.) (1990), *Conflict Resolution and Public Policy*, Greenwood, New York.

Pondy, L.R. (1967), 'Organizational conflict: Concepts and models', *Administrative Science Quarterly*, 12, pp. 296–320.

Ray, J.L. (1990), *Global Politics*, 4th edition, Houghton Mifflin, Boston, Massachusetts.

Richman, R. (1985), 'Formal mediation in intergovernmental disputes: Municipal annexation negotiations in Virginia', *Public Administration Review*, 45, pp. 510–517.

Sandole, D.J.D. (1987a), 'Introduction', to D.J.D. Sandole and I. Sandole-Staroste, *Conflict Management and Problem Solving: Interpersonal to International Applications*, New York University Press, New York.

Sandole, D. J. D. (1987b), 'Bibliographical epilogue: For further reading and beyond', in ibid.

Singer, L. R. (1990), *Settling Disputes*, Westview, Boulder, Colorado.

Stevenson, M. O. Jr., and Pops, G. M. (1989), 'Conflict resolution methods and the policy process', *Public Administration Review*, 49, pp. 463–473.

Tannenbaum, A. S. (1987), 'Control in organizations: Individual adjustment and organizational performance', in W. E. Natmeyer, *Classics of Organization Behavior*, Moore, Oak Park, Illinois.

Thayer, F. C. (1981), *An End to Hierarchy and Competition*, Franklin Watts, New York.

Waldo, D. (1980), *The Enterprise of Public Administration*, Chandler and Sharp, Novato, California.

Walton, R. E. and Dutton, J. M. (1989), 'The management of interdepartmental conflict: A model and review', in J. S. Ott, *Classic Readings in Organizational Behavior*, Brooks/Cole, Pacific Grove, California (original article published 1969).

Warfield, W. (1989), 'The implication of alternative dispute resolution processes to decision making in administrative disputes', *Pepperdine Law Review*, 16, pp. S93–S104.

The Washington Post, 7 September 1991, p. 2.

Wedge, B. (1987), 'Conflict management: The state of the art', in D. J. D. Sandole and I. Sandole-Staroste, *Conflict Management and Problem Solving: Interpersonal to International Applications*, New York University Press, New York, pp. 279–288.

Weinstein M. (1979), *Bureaucratic Opposition: Challenging Abuses at the Work Place*, Pergamon Press, New York.

West, W. (1988), 'The growth of internal conflict in administrative regulations', *Public Administration Review*, 20, pp. 773–782.

Williams, J. D. (1990), *Public Administration: The People's Business*, Little, Brown, Boston, Massachusetts.

Public-policy conflict resolution:
The nexus between culture and process

Various efforts have been made to describe the manifestations of conflict when public policy runs counter to some element of the public interest (e.g., Susskind and Cruikshank, 1987; Carpenter and Kennedy, 1988). But not a lot has been said about the organizations which initiate the policy. What do we know, for instance, about the culture of these organizations and how it contributes to the generation and perpetuation of policy conflict? Are organizational client groups who function as stakeholders in policy conflict responding to the policy decision or the culture-driven process behind the decision?

These questions are made more complex because different client groups and affected classes have their own cultural perspectives of the policy conflict. Culture provides an interpretational lens for the origins of conflict, shapes the contours of how conflict will be processed and the expectations concerning outcomes. As will be noted later in this chapter, culture,[1] as a determinant of conflict resolution, confounds popular notions concerning the roles of parties in conflict, the role of the so-called neutral, and the concept of neutrality.

There are, of course, many definitions of *organizational culture* (e.g., Schein, 1985, p. 9). For the sake of simplicity, I describe it as *the paradigm of behavior, knowledge, shared experiences, and decision-making styles of an organization.* This chapter will examine how organizational culture frequently 'conflicts' with the culture(s) of the organization's clients and affected classes as that organization creates and attempts to implement policy. What I try to do is to create an awareness for practitioners that conflict interactions between public organizations and traditional low-power cultural groups (at least in the U.S.) have elements of complexity that are not found in disputes of the same kind where these factors are not present. While I realize that practitioners may not have the time or inclination to study the nuances of all the cultures of an increasingly diverse society or the web of interactions that form the network of organizational relationships, they need to move beyond the cookbook processes of intervention to 'thicker'[2] understandings of the conflict dynamics.

Demographic Influences on Public Policy

The influx of new immigrants into the United States is not only transforming the socioeconomic environment, but is beginning to impact the map of public-policy disputing as well. Consider the following changes: From 1930 to 1960, roughly 80 percent of the country's immigrants came from Europe or Canada. But from 1977 to 1979, this proportion fell to 16 percent and Asia and Latin America accounted for about 40 percent each. In 1979, the nine leading 'source' countries for legal migration were Mexico, the Philippines, Korea, China and Taiwan, Vietnam, India, Jamaica, the Dominican Republic, and Cuba. The United Kingdom fell to 3 percent of the total (DeVita, 1989). It is now a statistical 'given' that by the year 2000 or shortly thereafter, California will become the first so-called 'Third World' state in the nation.

In many instances, this demographic transformation has brought about formal increases in power through a greater diversity in political representation, particularly at the local level. There are now twenty cities with populations over 100,000 that are headed up by African-Americans (Joint Center for Political Studies, 1990). As a parallel to this racial and ethnic diversity, the growth of an environmental consciousness and the women's movement have added to the mosaic of policy respondents. Changing demographics, coupled with the awakening of new special-interest groups, have transformed the landscape of policy conflict from one in which relatively homogeneous stakeholder groups operated in parochially defined issue arenas, to one which is increasingly heterogeneous, encroaching upon sacred policy cows.

For example, policy protestations around the discretionary use of police force and police–community relations, long the domain of African-American and Hispanic groups, has seen new stakeholders come onto the scene. In cities such as Oakland, California, Houston, Texas, and Portland, Maine, Southeast Asian immigrant groups have become the newest entrants onto the negotiating plain. In communities afflicted by the now-commonplace scarce resources, the effect has been increased competition and sometimes conflict between native minority groups and new immigrants, each jockeying for negotiating advantage with police officials and other decision-making bodies.

Some historical background on stakeholder roles in policy conflict

As alluded to earlier, there are innumerable special-interest groups which function as stakeholders in public-policy conflict. One need only look at some of the regulatory negotiations engaged in by the Environmental Protection Agency (EPA) and the Nuclear Regulatory Commission (NRC) to get a sense of proliferating stakeholder groups that can emerge to protest a new rule.[3]

But inclusive policy negotiations of this sort, designed to bring about consensual agreements (usually with the aid of third parties), are a relatively new and still not widely used process. Traditional paths to policy inclusion by U.S. racial and ethnic minorities, women, and those of nontraditional sexual preference (hereafter referred to as 'low-power cultural groups'), have tended to be narrowly defined and despite the Gandhian leanings of the civil rights movement, conflict-generating (Branch, 1988, pp. 195, 475). When settlement *was* reached, it was more often the result of hard-fought litigation.

The civil rights movement, having struck down much of *de jure* segregation against racial minorities, moved on to *de facto* issues in housing, employment, welfare entitlement, and education. Prior to the civil rights movement and the 1964 Civil Rights Act itself, low-power cultural groups, to the extent they were clients of public-service organizations, had little visibility or impact. Moreover, these groups were not amply represented in these organizations, particularly in the street-level bureaucracies that most impacted their lives. Organizational polities such as police departments, welfare bureaus, and local departments of education were dominated by whites. Where minorities were employed, they were most often seen as low-level functionaries.

President Johnson's Great Society programs were the logical extension of the civil rights movement and were designed to transform political and legal events into long-term programs. These efforts, better known as anti-poverty programs, were designed to bring about 'maximum feasible participation'[4] of those who were usually excluded from the policy formulation and implementation of traditional public organizations. Racial and ethnic minorities engaged in seminal efforts to develop and implement policy in areas such as fair housing, community control of schools, welfare rights reform, and job training. Anti-poverty activities became an early training ground in negotiations in that policy clients — frequently in competition for limited resources — learned interest-based techniques for negotiating desired outcomes. Moreover, it was not unusual for groups to form coalitions to increase bargaining power with impacting public agencies.

There are a few reasons why the anti-poverty program as an experiment in public-policy negotiations, was not as successful as it could have been:

(1) Although, here and there, efforts at interest-based negotiations could be noted, essentially these efforts were strong on protest and confrontation but weak on effective negotiations. Coming out of the civil rights movement, low-power cultural groups had ample experience with various forms of protest such as demonstrations and sit-ins, but little experience with knowing how to get to the table in negotiations and once there, sustain negotiations for desired outcomes.

(2) Many of the groups lacked the technical resources to negotiate effectively and reached agreements that were not broadly interest-based. Agreements often unraveled in a short period of time.

(3) Negotiations to reach decisions on projects were often compressed into artificially short time-frames without adequate studies or evaluative mechanisms (Pressman and Wildavsky, 1975, p.126).
(4) Attempts at coalition building were fragile and internal group dissention often undercut negotiating leverage.
(5) As pluralistic systems designed to make inroads into traditional public-policy forums, they had limited impact.[5]
(6) Alternative conflict-resolution systems had not reached the comparative level of sophistication that exists today. The notion of professional dispute-resolution neutrals did not exist much beyond the labor field and the then-parochial conflict-resolution efforts of the Justice Department's Community Relations Service. Forms of joint problem-solving under the guidance of a third-party neutral could have made a qualitative difference in many of the outcomes.

Despite these drawbacks, the anti-poverty programs provided valuable learning experiences in negotiations, opened up heretofore closed policy positions to low-power cultural groups, and created the first opportunities for formal community dispute-resolution programs.

Comparative roles in policy conflict: A contemporary perspective

The momentum provided by the anti-poverty programs emerged most forcefully in the policy areas of education and law enforcement. Along with housing and welfare, education and law enforcement were the street-level bureaucracies that most often permeated the lives of low-power cultural groups.

The civil disturbances of the mid-to-late 1960s and early 1970s, with their triggering incidents imbedded in instances of police use of excessive force, provided the catalyst for community groups (mainly African-American and Hispanic) to confront law-enforcement agencies with demands for policy change in the areas of recruitment, service, and professional behavior. Vocal and organized groups have had fragmentary success in negotiating incremental change in some areas of police service such as increases in beat patrolling and faster response times to calls for assistance. In education, the proliferation of school desegregation lawsuits in the 1970s emphasized the rights-and-standards approach to resolving major inequities. Because the remedial orders were court-issued, they contained no consensual negotiating clauses that anticipated difficulties in implementation and governance, which is where court orders frequently broke down.

A theory of community conflict

A useful device for examining roles in policy conflict is the Continuum of Community Relations (my term) first introduced by Laue and Cormick (1978) and later expanded by the author (1985). As shown in Figure 12.1, most communities exist somewhere along this continuum. But this is not a static

Cooperation	Competition	Heightened Tension	Conflict	Crisis
Interest groups engage in:	*Interest groups:*	*Interest groups engage in:*	*Interest groups:*	*Interest groups:*
Resource trade-offs	Challenge the status quo	Angry exchanges in the media and other public forums	View the status quo as not representative	Attack the status quo
Creating values	Disagree over allocation of resources			Disrupt public order
		Boisterous public meetings	Engage in: demonstrations and lawsuits	
Agreement on process	Test and stretch existing processes	Positional, claiming stances		Provoke incidents and arrests
Mutual respect			Regard public processes as unfair	
		Challenging public processes		Traumatize policy
				Regard public processes as illegitimate

Communities are always moving along this continuum.

⟵――――――――――――――――――――――――――――――⟶

Figure 12.1   A continuum of community relationships

situation; communities frequently move back and forth along the continuum, particularly between the positions of cooperation and competition, as they bargain for aggregative solutions to problems of resource distribution (Lax and Sebenius, 1986, pp. 118–120). Indeed, in larger jurisdictions, the likelihood is that several positions can be occupied simultaneously by different communities within that jurisdiction. Thus, marginal communities containing low-power cultural groups may find themselves in protracted states of heightened tension and conflict, whereas more economically and socially stable communities may exist most often in a state of cooperation or, at worse, competition.

The continuum can be viewed descriptively when posed against the backdrop of Miami, Florida and the events leading up to the massive civil disturbance in May 1980. Tensions had been building in the African-American communities of Overton and Liberty City for a number of months due to a confluence of events. The second exodus of Cuban exiles began with 10,000 'Marielistas'[6] who joined an earlier immigration that came to the United States in the early 1960s after the fall of Batista. Resentment began to build in the African-American community when it was perceived that a new low-power group was draining away the few available public resources. Around the same time, a high-ranking African-American school official and an African-American judge were indicted on separate charges, fueling resentment and a belief that African-American leaders were being singled out for persecution.

If competition with Cuban émigrés and the seemingly methodical destruction of African-American role-models were the tap roots of underlying tension, police–community relations provided the ammunition for the triggering incidents. Using the African-American community's relationship with city and county police as an example of positions along the continuum, it can be said that there was rarely a time when relationships between these two entities existed in a state of cooperation. Years of provocative behavior by police towards African-Americans and 'war-zone' antagonisms conducted by members of inner-city neighborhoods against police, coupled with the absence of effective dialogue, destroyed any sense of mutual respect. The fact that the African-American community had virtually no political power meant that its leaders had very little clout to bring police and other city officials to the table to negotiate using resource trade-offs or a creating-values approach (Lax and Sebenius, 1986). A series of publicized incidents of police use of excessive force culminating in the beating to death of Arthur MacDuffie, an African-American businessman, were the events that sparked the May 1980 civil disturbance in Liberty City resulting in several deaths, numerous injuries, and hundreds of millions of dollars in damages.

We can assume that within the framework of the continuum, various forms of relations between stakeholders may be going on simultaneously. Thus, the African-American community found itself in a state of political competition with a burgeoning Cuban community on the one hand and social-service resource competition with newly arrived Haitian boat people on the other (U.S. Commission on Civil Rights, 1982). In a landscape of resource disputes, these newer low-power cultural groups challenged the African-American community's historical legitimacy to distributional justice (see Susskind and Cruikshank, 1987, pp. 16–20 for a discussion of distributional disputes). What made this scenario particularly complex in Miami was that the African-American community's grievance with local officials dealt not only with issues of fairness in the distribution of resources, but also with perceptions of guaranteed rights. Objectively, the former could be viewed as issues of competition within the social realm of ongoing relationships. On this basis, resource distribution should be resolvable by engaging in equitable

181

trade-offs using some form of consensual negotiations. The latter moves it from an informal venue to one more formally structured around legal precedents for rights and standards. For African-American groups, the distinction is often blurred since the contours of the disputing paradigm are shaped by memories of *de jure* segregation and persistent *de facto* discrimination where the courts, not consensual processes, have been the savior.

As a result, the African-American community had very little experience with consensus-building forms of negotiations at the cooperative stage, or even positional bargaining at the competition stage that could have been transformed into more desirable outcomes (Morin, 1980). Instead, repeated acts of police use of excessive force against African-American citizens in Liberty City and other African-American neighborhoods drove the state of relations to one of heightened tensions, then conflict,[7] and finally crisis.

How a city and its policy units respond to conflict is really a study in organizational decision-making. Communities that exist in a state of cooperation have public organizations that engage in a process of shared decision-making with stakeholder groups. They use 'we decide' inclusive styles ranging from a pre-decisional advisory role, to post-decision feedback, to various forms of inclusion in implementation. In communities where relationships between governmental units and citizens are in a state of competition or at the more deteriorated points of the continuum, public organizations engage in correspondingly 'I decide' exclusive styles of decision-making. Thus, in the state of competition, those organizations that find their status quo challenged by low-power stakeholder groups tend to marginalize pre-decisional input, retaining exclusivity over substantive and procedural decisions. As relationships deteriorate down through the various stages to crisis, decision-making becomes increasingly exclusive.

In Miami, the mayor and the county manager largely delegated procedural decisions involving police–community relations to the respective law-enforcement heads. In turn, these individuals and their immediate commanders used highly exclusive styles of decision-making that limited low-power stakeholder groups to mainly post-decisional reactive roles. Despite warning signs that the situation was rapidly escalating towards large-scale violence, no meaningful attempts were made to use more inclusive forms of decision-making with representatives of the African-American community.

Susskind and Cruikshank (1987, p. 11) tell us that consensual processes should be considered supplemental to authoritative decision-making of government as opposed to coopting normative roles of local polities. Ideally, constitutionally delegated authority to manage the affairs of government should not be usurped by situationally oriented informal procedures. But this presupposes that government's trustee role within the social contract is viewed as legitimate by affected stakeholder groups.

In the cooperative stage of the continuum, there is harmony between the executive and legislative branches of government, the decision making-delegated to public agencies, and how decisions get implemented. The organizational cultures of the instrumental agencies accept and work within this framework. In the competition through crisis stages of the continuum, government's trustee role, or at least, the interpretation of that role by the implementing agencies is seen as increasingly illegitimate. Correspondingly, stakeholder groups demand increasingly intrusive levels of involvement in decision-making.

March and Olsen (1979) suggest that organizational cultures produce styles of decision-making that run counter to processes described by Mitchell (1978). For example, in the 'garbage can' style of decision-making, any organization has a closed universe of problems, choices, and solutions that are continually matched (or mismatched) to make decisions. Regardless of the problem, the organization seldom goes beyond defined boundaries to develop innovative ways of resolving problems. In paramilitary organizations like law-enforcement agencies, shared values create a paradigm that is isolationist by nature; that emphasizes a high-task, low-relationship style, making decisions that fit within the contours of the paradigm rather than the needs of stakeholders' interests. As the situation in Miami deteriorated towards crisis, African-American spokesperson demands for an increasing involvement in decision-making in *substantive* (more African-American police officers represented throughout the ranks of the police department) and *procedural* (changes in excessive force policies, methods of patrolling) issues were met with increasing resistance.

Even if it were possible for negotiated resolutions to emerge from a highly conflictual state of affairs, conventional decision-making styles in public organizations will have to be recalibrated to a more consensual form if they are to satisfy the needs of culturally diverse stakeholders in the governance of an agreement. Thus, the ultimate goal of a joint problem-solving process that involves representatives of low-power stakeholder groups with public officials is not merely to arrive at a substantive agreement, but to change the decision-making *process* for purposes of governance and the conduct of future relationships.

While it is agreed that those vested with the authority to preserve the public trust cannot and should not redelegate this authority to stakeholder groups, it will mean that the way those decisions necessary to execute that policy are made will be more inclusive. Looking at this from the perspective of degrees of participation in decision-making, more decisions will shift from 'I decide' to 'we decide', altering the balance of power between street-level bureaucracies and community stakeholders. Negotiating procedural power through enhanced roles in decision-making can result in a more equitable distribution of resources.

Community-based public-policy disputes tend not to reflect negotiations in the classic dispute model (Moore, 1984; Murray, 1986). In highly conflictual situations, interaction between community stakeholders and policy officials seldom takes the form of face-to-face negotiations except in spontaneous circumstances.[8] Nonetheless, dialogue, fractious as it might be in deteriorating stages of the continuum, represents a form of negotiation.

A model for determining effectiveness of policy negotiations

As the events in Miami demonstrate, there is a positive correlation between the status of relationships between public officials and stakeholders, degree of stakeholder inclusiveness in policy formulation, and negotiations posture. Figure 12.2 attempts to depict the status of organization–stakeholder relationships by comparing that to the degree of stakeholder inclusiveness in policy implementation. The model assumes that the degree of effectiveness of negotiations along the axis has a correspondingly positive impact on policy inclusiveness, which in turn improves the relationship of stakeholders to policy officials. Therefore, the opposite would hold in that less effective negotiations tend to be positional, which means less inclusiveness in policy implementation and a deteriorated state of relationships.

It is important to recognize that there are many stakeholders in conflicts such as the one being described in Miami who would have varying status of relationships with relevant organizations. The model attempts to reflect only

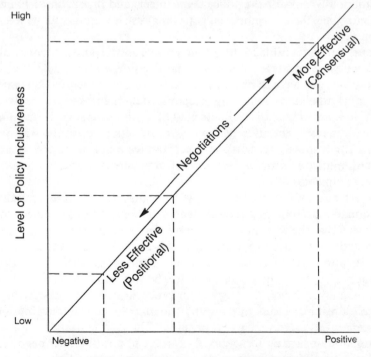

Figure 12.2 Government–stakeholder relationships

those low-power cultural groups who occupy negative status roles with public-policy officials.

The civil rights movement effectively bypassed Miami. Consequently, a cadre of African-Americans, schooled in the experience of transforming confrontational tactics into policy negotiations for a greater degree of distributional justice, never materialized as it did in cities like Atlanta, Georgia and Durham, North Carolina. Absent a history of negotiations with white officials, relationships never really matured beyond event-focused strategies, attempting to influence fragmented policy. When face-to-face negotiations took place, they tended to be positional and antagonistic.

Many observers would be quick to point out that civil rights lawsuits, as a product of positional negotiations, have achieved policy inclusion. I argue that public-policy lawsuits may have changed policy orientation to some degree and enhanced inclusiveness, but the absence of a consensually facilitated process that takes into consideration the interests of all stakeholders, has generated frequent challenges and counter-suits. Rights-and-standards awards or remedies based on decisional rulings tend to be weak on implementation and governance. Conflict over school desegregation, bilingual education, affirmative action, and the establishment of civilian review boards for police actions are dramatic examples of where decisional standards fail to take into consideration how agreements will be maintained and implemented. Of course, constitutionally derived rights and standards, based on universal principles of human dignity, are rightfully non-negotiable, but not all value-based conflict necessarily falls into this category.

The model in Figure 12.2 is not meant to imply a graph-like precisional correlation between negotiations effectiveness and policy inclusion, but rather approximate relationships. Secondly, intervening variables, such as changes in political administrations, can impact policy inclusiveness even where negotiations have been successful (Henton *et al.*, 1981, p. 28). Thirdly, in the history of most public-organization—stakeholder relationships, policy negotiations are ongoing and incremental. Degrees of inclusiveness vary from one set of negotiations to another, depending on how vested the organizational culture is in maintaining the status quo or the level of interest of stakeholder groups. Thus, the U.S. military, which for a number of years maintained a discriminatory position against racial minorities, gays, and women in combat roles, remains resistant to women and gays fulfilling tasks that have traditionally reflected the male norm of virility and dominance.

Cultural influences on negotiations

Susskind and Cruikshank (1987, p. 80) discuss the importance of understanding parties' interests beyond positions. But that concept, drawn from empirical studies and observations of culture-bound Western negotiations (see, for example, Fisher and Ury, 1981) can be misleading. Low-power

185

stakeholder groups in public-policy disputes bring powerful cultural–historical frames of reference to conflict which confound rationalistic approaches to reaching agreements. Using the layered model of conflict (Laue, 1986; Avruch and Black, 1991) depicted in Figure 12.3, values lie at an even deeper level

The many orientations to conflict resolution may be categorized into a few basic approaches:

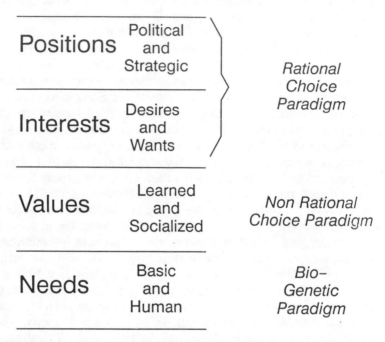

Figure 12.3   A theory of conflict

of conflict manifestation than interests, with human needs such as identity (Gudykunst and Ting-Toomey, 1988) and security representing the foundation of deep-rooted conflict. In this depiction of responses to conflict, reactions by parties at the *positional* and *interest* levels are inclined to be rational in that parties can use cognitive methods to sort out strategies and tactics. When conflict is perceived through the lens of cultural values, responses tend to be nonrational (Babbie, 1992, p. 28). Individuals or groups are guided by affective histories that largely determine reactions to conflict. Actors tend not to engage in rational-choice forms of decision-making that attempt to weigh and objectify bargaining alternatives to arrive at optimal solutions (Mitchell, 1978). At the biogenetically driven level of human needs, one responds intuitively.

It might be worthwhile explaining more carefully what is meant by 'values'.

There are really two types of values. There are 'outer core' values that can be described as universal values. That is, no matter what our attributes (race, ethnicity, gender, sexual preference, and so on), most of us would share a common value response to the rescue of a baby from a burning building. According to Boulding (1962), however, there are what he calls 'inner core' values: unique epistemologies shaped by experiences of *who* we are, how we identify ourselves in the social universe, and how others have responded to us in that universe. It is the latter that complicate understanding of conflict and its potential for resolution.

Disputants who use value-based conflict-framings tend to be nonrational and 'spiral' in their perception of the origins, processes, and outcomes of conflict; they loop back to include tangential history to inform their views of real-time events and future behavior of opposing parties. For low-power cultural groups such as racial or ethnic minorities, women, and persons of alternative sexual preference, the history of how others have dealt with them and their group is as much a part of the context of a policy conflict that impacts their personhood as are the conflict-specific issues. Dominant-culture public-policy managers who rely on an interest-based approach to negotiate with disputants from the aforementioned groups, may find their overtures spurned when confronted with deeply held values and culturally defined human needs. For, in essence, you have opposing parties attempting the dialogue of negotiations, who are speaking different languages.

Triggering incidents such as the one that took place in Miami, tend to elicit parochial, interest-based solutions from high-power policy actors such as suspending the police officers involved for a limited time or taking them off the streets and placing them on desk duty should they be found in violation of departmental regulations. Low-power stakeholder groups respond with demands that seek to transform the habitat in ways that will provide more security for their identity and the well-being of the group. This would be articulated in demands for hiring more police officers representative of the low-power group and means for controlling policy, including dismissal of the offending officers involved and frequently the law-enforcement chief him/herself.

The role of third parties in culturally influenced policy conflict

The 1980 civil disturbance in Miami and its sequel in 1982 can be described as a deep-rooted conflict (Burton, 1988) in that the issues, as dramatized by the triggering incident and its underlying causes, were seen as nonresolvable using traditional means of dispute resolution. When low-power groups perceive that culturally understood norms of justice have been explicitly or implicitly violated by dominant power-individuals or groups, deep-rooted conflict is likely to be involved. In communities existing in the state of intense and sustained conflict and crisis, classic 'table' mediation (see, for example,

187

Goldberg, Green, and Sander, 1985; Kressel and Pruitt, 1989), with its presumptions of power equity and rational, interest-based equations for resolution, has no logical foundation.

The intervention process starts from where the parties are, not where the intervenor would like them to be. In situations of intense conflict or crisis, trust-building mechanisms need to be put in place. This will allow conflict participants to test forms of risk-taking that will minimize loss of face within their respective habitats should they fail. For example, the intervenor may want to encourage officially recognized self-policing arrangements by community representatives in exchange for withdrawal of law enforcement to less intrusive boundaries. The understanding is that if violence escalates or specific emergencies have to be responded to, the police can carry out the necessary functions. This is important because in homogeneous, paramilitary organizations such as police departments, group norms of identity and ethos must be recognized and carefully negotiated. From the community perspective, in violent civil disturbances where police behavior is perceived to be causal, low-power-community combatants often demand the removal of police from the impacted area. Controlling police behavior is essential for establishing the credibility of low-power actors within their communities if they intend to play negotiating roles at some later date.

In the Miami May 1980 disturbance, police withdrew to a predetermined perimeter in Liberty City, but without negotiating a contingency role with community activists. The prevailing wisdom seemed to be to keep the violence from spreading to other parts of the city and essentially let it burn itself out in the impacted area. This strategy alienated rank-and-file officers as well as community residents. Police officers felt they had 'given up the streets to the criminals' and were being told to abandon sworn duties. Morale was seriously affected. Within the impacted area, mothers could not safely go to the store to get milk for infants and fires burned unchecked, further endangering lives.

Yet at this stage of intervention the task has only begun. The challenge is to connect these experiments in risk-taking to transformational change at the causal level. But this cannot be accomplished by merely building sequential blocks of greater risk-taking. The result will likely be a series of disaggregated agreements supporting a veneer of tranquility that will dissipate with the next incident. Parties to the conflict must jointly arrive at a vision of what a just relationship will look like. What principles must be in place? What substantive, procedural, and relational criteria have to be acknowledged? The role of the intervenor at this stage is to help parties to the conflict build a contextual map of how the various and several agreements lend themselves to the vision.

In this construct, how the intervenor views his or her role philosophically is critical to the success of the intervention. Foremost, is the need to deal with illusions of 'neutrality'. The neutrality of the mediator's role is frequently cited as the foundational canon upon which rests the raison d'être of the mediation process. It is as though the mediator were some clear vessel, a hovering *deus ex machina*, waiting to be called upon to lay an impartial hand on the fevered brow of the disputants.

In the origins of labor-dispute resolution in the U.S. (particularly after World War II) where labor and management held rough parity in power and shared similar majoritarian cultural backgrounds, this concept of neutrality had more validity. Moreover, most labor mediators were from the same cultural background as the disputants, creating a triadic compatibility of roles where presentations of neutrality were more easily accepted. In reality, this was rarely as clear-cut as it is stated here. All mediators bring something of themselves to a dispute and have a sense of the contours of the resolution they would like parties to achieve. But compared to community-based public-policy disputes where power imbalances are more common, this concept of neutrality in labor—management disputes tends to be the rule rather than the exception.

Outside of the labor field, practitioners and social scientists have begun to question the validity of the classic third-party neutral role. In public-policy conflicts which have broad ramifications for social outcomes and a disequilibrium of power, pronouncements of neutrality would be suspect. Imagine an African-American mediator presenting him- or herself as a neutral to either side in the Miami scenario. In conflicts of this kind, parties have acknowledged and accepted that the mediator has values that may contribute to the outcome of the conflict (Gulliver, 1979, pp. 215–216). For example, during the Camp David peace talks between Egypt and Israel mediated by President Carter, Anwar Sadat knew that the U.S. was not neutral in its view of the role of Israel in the Middle East. This did not preclude the U.S. from being accepted as a mediator by Sadat because the Egyptians knew that the U.S. had a vital interest in a peaceful settlement.

Even in the absence of a formal third party, mediative opportunities arise in dyadic negotiations where a member of a negotiating team will step out of his or her role as negotiator to act spontaneously as a mediator between disputing parties (see Colosi, 1987, on 'quasi-mediators'). For public-policy conflicts that are culturally shaped, passive neutrality is a fiction best reserved for Pollyannaish treatises on alternative dispute resolution. The intervenor is an activist and is as much a part of the social change as are parties to the conflict.

Using the layered conflict model, issue formulation by policy officials is likely to emerge from the positional or at best, the interest level. Negotiating strategies will be rational and incremental. Low-power cultural protagonists responding from a primarily values/human-needs perspective, will use negotiation strategies that appear nonrational and holistic in scope. They appear nonrational because they seem not to be based on calculated measures of distributive trades, but on historical expectations of just outcomes. There can be no effective dialogue where parties are operating on different levels of response.

In this form of conflict, in the prenegotiations stage, the intervenor has to be the cultural role interpreter for the more rational positional/interest-oriented policy official. This is a form of reframing where the intervenor takes the cultural response and tries to find a context that retains its essence and at the same time can be understood by the responding policy officials. One way this can be accomplished is by identifying outer-core values that both sides hold in common. What the intervenor is attempting to do is to remove the demonizing images both sides tend to have of each other. By humanizing the responses of the parties to a conflict, the intervenor provides rational perspectives for behaviors that can move the dialogue in a more positive direction. This should be considered a transitional role since it is assumed that relationships are badly strained or nonexistent and communications are traumatized. The intervenor has to know when it is time to transfer the responsibility for role articulation to representatives of the groups themselves. Bringing the policy official(s) into the loop of awareness of a particular culture's response to conflict is an early step in moving the negotiations from agreements in principle to the ultimate distributional agreement which *will* be interest-based and rational.

There is greater risk in this form of third-party intervention because the intervenor—activist gives voice to visions of a just society that identify him or her as a stakeholder in the outcome of the conflict, even though he or she may not live in the community in which the conflict is occurring. Thus perceived, policy officials may 'invite you out' of the conflict-resolver role for reasons of bias. Alternatively, the intervenor may overextend the role of interpreter and find that he or she has slipped into the role of negotiator. Once down this slippery slope of cooptation, it will be difficult to back out. Eventually, the intervenor will lose his or her credibility and can do irreparable damage to the resolution of the conflict. On the other hand, there is a sense of reward in placing one's hand in the stream of social change, knowing that the currents will never flow quite the same way again.

What I have tried to do in this chapter is to develop an appreciation for the complexity of roles in public-policy conflict. Low-power cultural groups, who have traditionally been kept away from the negotiating table, see the origins, processes, and outcomes of conflict through the lens of values that have historically shaped their relationships with the dominant culture. They bring different voices to the negotiating process that often do not fit the protocols of interest-based bargaining. At the same time, public organizations are complex entities that have cultures of a different kind, as was noted earlier in the chapter. When these forces are joined in conflict, the third-party intervenor must find a way to bridge the cultural gap. Frequently, this means playing an interpreter role for one side or both, in a way that provides a context for the actions and language of the opposing side.

Traditional concepts of third-party neutrality are often inapplicable in these kinds of conflicts because of power imbalances between parties. Moreover, the techniques that emerge from this role tend to result in reductionist outcomes that will lead to further conflict and a discrediting of the alternative conflict resolution approach. Clearly, there is greater risk in the intervenor–activist approach, but there is also greater opportunity for agreements that work towards the transformation to a more just society.

Notes

1. For the purposes of this chapter, I am limiting my definition of client culture to those attributes that pertain to race, ethnicity, and gender.
2. I borrow the term 'thicker' from Clifford Geertz, who in *Interpretation of Cultures* (1973) calls for thick descriptions of culture where the observer goes beyond casual understandings of what is happening to a deeper interpretation of events.
3. EPA adopted a rule setting performance standards for residential woodburning stoves which limit emissions of particulate matter from newly manufactured units. The rule emerged from a consensus reached by a negotiating committee that included representatives of the wood heater industry, the environmental community, consumer groups, state air pollution control and energy agencies, and EPA.
4. The term 'maximum feasible participation' was built into the enabling legislation to underscore the expectation that low-power cultural groups would be given every opportunity to be included in the decision-making process for the development and implementation of programs. I was on the staff of an organization that had a higher percentage of residents voting for board members than participated in the local Democratic primary.
5. Frustrated with the resistance and immobility of street-level bureaucracies, many anti-poverty agencies attempted to duplicate client services that were supposed to be provided by these agencies. For example, centers provided services for such things as tenant and welfare rights and even educational instruction at the secondary level. Ultimately, because these services operated outside the traditional policy milieu and were inadequately funded, they made little impact in changing fundamental policy.
6. So named because they departed from the Cuban port of Mariel.
7. Of course, there is conflict whenever any physical act of force is used by one person against another. The term is used in this context to describe a community-wide state of mind as much as a single act or series of acts of violence.
8. Leaders of a street demonstration negotiating protocols with a police commander would be an example of spontaneous face-to-face negotiations.

References

Avruch, K. and Black, P. (1991), 'The culture question and conflict resolution', *Peace and Change*, 16, pp. 22–45.

Babbie, E. (1992), *The Practice of Social Research*, Wadsworth Publishing Co., Belmont, California.

Boulding, K. E. (1962), *Conflict and Defense: A General Theory*, Harper and Row, New York and London.

Branch, T. (1988), *Parting the Waters*, Simon and Schuster, New York.

Burton, J.W. (1988), *Conflict Resolution as a Political System*, Working Paper 1, Center for Conflict Analysis and Resolution, George Mason University, Fairfax, Virginia.

Carpenter, S.L. and Kennedy, J.W.D. (1988), *Managing Public Disputes*, Jossey-Bass, Inc., San Francisco, California.

Colosi, T.R. (1987), 'A model for negotiation and mediation', in D.J.D. Sandole and I. Sandole-Staroste, eds, *Conflict Management and Problem Solving: Interpersonal to International Applications*, New York University Press, New York.

DeVita, C.J. (1989), 'America in the 21st century', Population Reference Bureau, Washington, D.C.

Fisher, R. and Ury, W. (1981), *Getting to Yes*, Houghton Mifflin, Boston, Massachusetts.

Geertz, C. (1973), 'Thick description: Toward an interpretive theory of culture', in C. Geertz, ed., *The Interpretation of Cultures*, Basic Books, Inc., New York.

Goldberg, S.B., Green, E.D. and Sander, F.E.A. (1985), *Dispute Resolution*, Little, Brown, Boston, Massachusetts.

Gudykunst, W.B. and Ting-Toomey, S. (1988), *Culture and Interpersonal Communication*, Sage Publications, Inc., Newbury Park, California.

Gulliver, P.H. (1979), *Disputes and Negotiations: A Cross-Cultural Perspective*, Academic Press, New York.

Henton, D.C. *et al.* (1981), 'Rethinking urban governance: An assessment of the negotiated investment strategy', Center for Policy Analysis, SRI International, Menlo Park, California.

Joint Center for Political Studies (1990), 'Black elected officials national roster, 1990', JCPS, Washington, D.C.

Kressel, K. and Pruitt, D.G. (1989), *Mediation Research*, Jossey-Bass, Inc., San Francisco, California.

Laue, J. (1986), 'Levels of conflict content', remarks delivered at a conference on Guidelines for Newcomers to Track II, Washington, D.C.

Laue, J.H. and Cormick, G. (1978), 'The ethics of intervention in community disputes', in G. Bermant, H. Kelman, and D. Warwick, eds, *Ethics of Social Intervention*, Halsted Press, New York.

Lax, D.A. and Sebenius, J.K. (1986), *The Manager as Negotiator*, The Free Press, New York.

March, J.G. and Olsen, J.P. (1979), *Ambiguity and Choice in Organizations*, Bergen University Press, Bergen, Norway.

Mitchell, T.R. (1978), *People in Organizations: Understanding Their Behavior*, McGraw-Hill, Inc., New York.

Moore, C. (1984), *Interest-Based Bargaining*, Center for Dispute Resolution, Boulder, Colorado.

Morin, R. (1980), 'Miami rioters don't feel justice exists', *The Washington Post*, 8 May.

Murray, J.S. (1986), 'Understanding competing theories of negotiations', *Negotiation Journal*, 2, pp.179–186.

Pressman, J.L. and Wildavsky, A. (1975), *Implementation*, University of California Press, Berkeley, California.

Schein, E. (1985), *Organizational Culture and Leadership*, Jossey-Bass Inc., San Francisco.

Susskind, L. and Cruikshank, J. (1987), *Breaking the Impasse: Consensual Approaches to Resolving Public Disputes*, Basic Books, Inc., New York.

U.S. Commission on Civil Rights (1982), *Special Report: Confronting Racial Isolationism in Miami*, Washington, D.C.

Warfield, W. (1985), 'Triggering incidents for racial conflict: Miami, Florida riots of 1980 and 1982', *Proceedings of the Thirteenth International Conference of the Society of Professionals in Dispute Resolution*, SPIDR, Washington, D.C.

States, boundaries, and environmental security[1]

Traditional definitions of security are bound up with concepts of the state as defender of boundaries within which its citizenry is safe from threats to survival, whether those threats are military, economic, or involve environmental-resource deprivation. Boundaries, however, are becoming increasingly irrelevant to security, since contemporary threat technologies can cross all boundaries.

Security from threat, then, has become an inherently transboundary phenomenon. Hence the concept 'common security' elaborated in the Palme (1983) and Brundtland (1987) Commission reports. These reports are, however, primarily directed to governments. This paper will explore the limitations of the state as a provider of security, and the characteristics of other entities that contribute to security. The possibility of greater interfacing between state structures and non-state structures in the management of the more complex security problems of the next century will be examined.

The state as defender

Very substantial amounts of the world's resources are allocated to boundary maintenance by nation-states. In the West, military research and development (R & D) alone absorbs more than half of all publicly supported research funds, dwarfing research expenditures for the entire range of needs for which governments have responsibility, including health, education, the environment, and energy sources (Sivard, 1989).

In the states of the Two-Thirds World,[2] total military expenditures swallow resources required to meet basic human needs, in some countries rising as high as 20 to 30 percent of the GNP (UNDP, 1991). This preoccupation with military threat creates a forcing system that distorts every other part of a society's structure and resource allocation systems; further, there is the cultural distortion that is required to legitimate the curtailing of other types of economic and social productivity in the name of defense.[3] This forcing system feeds on itself, helping create the wars it is intended to prevent. In 1989 there were 32 major armed conflicts resulting in 1000 or more battle deaths, and 75 armed conflicts involving less than 1000 deaths, for a total of 107 conflicts (Lindgren *et al.*, 1990). Most of them were fought in the Two-Thirds World with arms largely produced in the First World. Since most of these wars are being fought over boundary and resource issues, the state's preoccupation with territory and boundaries would seem to make it peculiarly vulnerable to military action.

Not only does military action damage environments incidentally, as is most obvious in the case of devastated battlefields, but making war on the environment is a key aspect of military strategy. Damage targets for environmental warfare include space, the atmosphere, the lithosphere, the hydrosphere, and the biosphere, leaving no part of the earth's environment sacrosanct. (Traditional injunctions as found in the Hebrew Bible and the Koran to spare fruit orchards in wartime have long since gone by the board.) The Environmental Modification Convention of 1977 has had little effect on preparations for and actual practice of such warfare, and today most refugees from war-torn areas are fleeing environmental devastation, not war itself (Holst, 1989). Refugee flows, environmental devastation, and resource exhaustion generate new causes for military action as nations seek access by force to new resources for increasing populations. Each military response worsens the conditions it was meant to alleviate. This is today nowhere more evident than in the Gulf states, where environmental destruction was used by both sides in the conflict as a tool of combat.

If security against military threat is a state's first priority, providing social and economic security to its citizenry is very much a secondary priority, as government social-welfare budgets indicate. When economic issues do come to the fore, this often results in government protection of environmentally exploitative commercial and industrial practices in the name of economic efficiency and profit. State regulation of environmentally harmful industrial activity is about as ineffectual as international regulation of environmental warfare.

Among government priorities, protection of the environment for its citizenry comes in a poor third. It is a matter of record that every state treats certain parts of its territory as 'sacrifice zones' where military exercises are carried out that are deadly for the environment, and lethal for the human beings exposed to the subsequent air, water, and soil contamination. I do not know what percentage of the land area of most nations is under military control but it happens that in the United States the Department of Defense is the third largest landowner in the country (*Environment*, 1990, p. 22). While some of this stewardship is benign, involving conservation practices, a significant part is not. Going beyond home territories, the practice of making sacrifice areas of trusteeship islands in the south Pacific, as most notably carried out by France and the United States, has long and ineffectually been deplored. It now appears that some of the nations bordering on the Arctic could make the Arctic a sacrifice zone by default, with incalculable consequences for the global environment (Young, 1989, p.106).

All this suggests that state perceptions of security have very little to do with awareness of human dependence on vulnerable environments. It might be said that state perceptions have very little to do with any kind of security. Given bureaucratic inertia, slowness of the political process in arriving at changes in policy priorities even after social learning has taken place, and the sheer complexity of the international system, states alone cannot be counted on to meet the new challenges to security arising from rapidly increasing environmental deterioration within and across their borders. Nor can they be counted on to recognize the need for limitation of their sovereignty in competing with other states for scarce environmental resources.

The systems complexity issue is a serious one, since decision-makers have come to operate with increasingly meager empirical clues about the systems for which they have responsibility. If reliable feedback systems had been working to help societies understand the empirical consequences of their military, economic, and resource-development strategies over the past 200 years, the chances are that the international community would not be in the crisis situation in which we now find ourselves.

In the following pages other types of social units in addition to states will be explored, from communal groups and transnational voluntary associations to intergovernmental and United Nations structures, to see what other feedback systems might be available, and what their contributions to environmental security might be.

Bioregions and the 10,000 Societies

During the aeons of prehistory in which the human species lived by toolmaking, hunting and gathering, and simple soil cultivation in small movable settlements, humans learned to read a great number of cues and signals in their natural and social environment and to understand the relationship between these cues in ways that resulted in highly diverse and adaptive cultures under different kinds of environmental conditions. Today one school of ecologists has identified these kinds of feedback-providing biosocial clusters as bioregions. A bioregion is a community of interdependent life, biological and social, in a well-defined physical space. Bioregions are generally watersheds, though these are not always easily defined. Additional criteria include biotic shift, a percentage change in plant/animal species composition from one place to another; distinctive landforms (coastal range, plateaus, etc.); and, less precisely definable, culture regions identified as such by the people who live there.[4]

Needless to say, bioregions do not have firm boundaries, but zones of interaction with other bioregions. A Swiss canton, a small state, or a tribal society might qualify as defining a bioregion. The key attribute is a kind of biosocial coherence, a recognizable ecosystem defined by more than one criterion. Cities play a special role in bioregions, and the pattern of city/ surrounding town/village/countryside interaction may be as defining of the bioregion as a watershed.

There is as yet no world map of bioregions, although bioregionalists are working on this. Neither is there a world map of the 10,000 societies[5] – ethnically, racially, or linguistically based identity groups that inhabit these bioregions, spread over the 168 states of the contemporary world. Although modernization theory assumes ethnic groups will be assimilated into the modern nation-state, supposedly extinct ethnicities are reappearing at a rapid rate, and new ones are created as migrant streams from the Two-Thirds World settle in First World societies and create hybrid new cultural identities distinct from the society in which they have settled (Boulding, 1990). Generally, these identity groups have a keen awareness of the bioregions they inhabit.

The resurgence of these identity groups may in fact be a response to the failure of the modern state to meet the needs of its diverse populations – not only the need for physical protection and the equitable distribution of social and environmental resources, but the need for meaning and a sense of self-worth, which are also part of security. It is a possibility worth exploring that these identity groups may contribute in important ways to solving the multidimensional security problems that state structures cannot effectively cope with. These include: (1) the problem of scale, with the center unable to manage its peripheries effectively; (2) the problem of adequate knowledge of local terrains, where the environmental damage and many of the resources for environmental problem-solving are located; and (3) the problem of relevant skills for the issues at hand.

Identity groups are to varying degrees storehouses of folk wisdom and technical problem-solving skills relating to the environment, and traditional negotiation skills for dealing with serious conflicts of interest. On the one hand, that wisdom/skill complex may undergo distortion and even degeneration in interaction with an indifferent or hostile state. On the other hand, there are intense and continuing efforts to evolve new constitutional formats based on a recognition of identity groups in countries with strong and diverse ethnic communities, like Canada, Switzerland, Belgium, Spain, Italy, the (former) Soviet Union, and other Eastern European countries (as well as in a number of countries in the South including Ethiopia, Nigeria, Sudan, Malaysia, and India). A creative reformulation of the relationship between identity groups and the states they inhabit may in the long run produce a new, more environmentally and bioregionally aware and more peaceful, constitutive order in the twenty-first century.[6]

It is true that ethnic groups at this moment in history seem to be more conflict-generating than conflict-resolving. This situation represents a massive failure in the exercise of political imagination since World War I. There was a clear need at that time to deal with the human needs of highly articulate identity groups that did not fit into the 'new order' defined by treaty at the close of that war. Now the needs of those groups are back on the political agenda, facing unprepared decision-makers. As a result, catch-up political innovation is everywhere demanded.

The task of innovation may not be as impossible as it seems because people and societies have always been capable of imagining the other and different. It is an interesting fact that the image of the peaceable garden − a localist world in which people live harmoniously with each other and with their environment, with warriors laying aside weapons has persisted in every major cultural tradition throughout the centuries. For the Greeks it was the Elysian fields; for the Hebrews the Holy Mountain where none shall hurt nor destroy; for the Arab Moslems it was the garden in the desert; for the Norse Vikings it was the Plains of Ida.

Workshops[7] held during the past decade to imagine a future without armies have revealed that this imagery of a differently arranged and peaceful social order is still alive and well today. In response to instructions to spell out what institutions and behaviors would sustain a world with a high degree of diversity without means of military defense, workshop participants first describe local communities focused on nurturance of the environment and each other, the growing of food, the skills of conflict resolution, and high-tech capabilities related entirely to human development. The word 'bio-regional' is rarely used, but the concept keeps appearing. When participants move in imagination to the larger world, computers become important, providing linkage to other communities, to regional and global bodies representing the totality of local communities. Nation-states rarely appear in these images, only people-linkage systems. Travel from community to community, by people of all ages, supplements computers in binding the communities together. This pattern for the future appears repeatedly in widely different geographic and cultural settings. The basic concept of people-linkage is not just a workshop fantasy. It also has an empirical reality in the 1990s. This reality will be explored next.

Transnational networks: the 18,000 peoples' associations

Transnational voluntary associations, or nongovernmental organizations (NGOs) (to distinguish them from governmental structures) are boundary-crossing by definition. Acting in the human interest, on a human scale, they offer in their areas of concern − be it sports, science, culture, religion, social welfare, or trade − both horizontal and vertical linkages within and between countries independently of the action of the states they span. Having multiplied from 200 at the beginning of the century to 18,000 today, they act on local, regional and global concerns missed by state structures.[8]

Most of the new environmental awareness, really only three decades old, comes from these NGOs. On the scientific side, it is the international associations of the physical and social sciences that have developed most of our knowledge about the environment, and the understanding of the linkages between development policies and environmental and national security policies. Notable examples are the work done by the International Council of Scientific Unions (ICSU) on the International Geosphere–Biosphere Programme (IGBP, 1988) and by the International Social Science Council (ISSC) on the Human Dimensions of Global Change Project (HDGC, 1989). Perhaps about fifty new environmentally focused transnational networks have come into being in this same three-decade period, working through community education, dialogue, and political negotiation to create a new understanding of security as living at peace with the environment and other humans.[9] One interesting evidence of the growth in environmental awareness is that the 1976 edition of the *Encyclopedia of World Problems and Human Potential* (Union of International Associations, 1976) listed about 200 environment-related problems, whereas the 1986 edition (Union of International Associations, 1986) has about 700 entries for environmental problems.

The 'old' Western peace movement is increasingly a peace–development–environment movement, with a growing North–South emphasis. Having taken on new complexity, time will be required for this new peace movement to develop a fuller social and political impact.

Precisely because NGOs are transnational, they provide important inputs to national decision-makers in each country where a given NGO has a national branch. They provide the necessary interpretation of how national interest must take account of world interest in the fields of military and environmental security. They are the reshapers of national cultures in the context of world culture, preserving difference, valuing diversity, yet seeing the vision of a planet-nurturing world society.

The major recent challenge to NGOs has been the 1992 UN Conference on the Environment. Governments respond very differently to environmental threat depending on their size and level of industrialization. This is not a simple North–South divide, since nations of the North differ among themselves, as do nations of the South. The major actors who hold the global environment as primary and are pushing for governments to change environment-endangering practices are the environmental NGOs and those smaller states that they have been able to persuade to adopt a strong environmentally conserving national policy. Even the increasingly well-documented though still somewhat controversial threat of global climate warming has not substantially changed the posture of at least one major Western government: that it is safe to ignore that threat within its own borders. The tremendous changes in cultural attitudes to the environment required for global environmental well-being will take all the energy that NGOs can muster for several decades to come.

Intergovernmental organizations: The 2000

IGOs have grown over this century right along with NGOs, although at a much slower pace, from a handful to the present 2000.[10] The more states entered the international community, the more boundaries there were, and the more transboundary problems presented themselves. Possibly the first attempt at global environmental governance goes back to Theodore Roosevelt's (unsuccessful) initiative to convene a world conference on natural-resource conservation at The Hague in 1901. Given the general lack of interest on the part of nation-states in domestic environmental protection, and the slowness of states to perceive environmental security as a bona fide security issue, it is somewhat surprising that over 100 multilateral environmental treaties currently exist. Since threats to environmental security are very differently felt from one state to another, and richer nations of the West have been protected from awareness of those threats longer than poorer states, it is a tribute to the diplomatic skills of poorer and smaller states that so many agreements have been concluded, poorly enforced though they are.

Global treaties are the hardest to arrive at, and suffer from the lowest-common-denominator problem. Regional groupings of states have been more inventive in setting up flexible agreements that meet needs of individual states while still providing some environmental protection for all. IGOs, like NGOs, yet in a different way, can act as interpreters to individual nation-states of the world-interest context for national interest. Creative diplomacy has produced 'soft law' as compared to 'hard law' (Sand, 1990), with an emphasis on declarations that become norms, evolving into regimes voluntarily adhered to (Keohane and Nye, 1985), and with the setting of technical standards that by reason of scientific legitimacy are able to bypass ratification procedures.

A significant part of the technical work as well as the educational and advocacy activities that help bring the intergovernmental environmental agreements into being is done by scientific, educational, and legal professional NGOs, as in the case already mentioned of the work of ICSU and ISSC on environmental change. Thus NGOs and IGOs often have a strong symbiotic relationship in working for environmental security. At the same time, the NGO/IGO activities have trust- and confidence-building dimensions, lessening threat levels among nations working to achieve specific environmental agreements.

One important concept and set of potential future structures that has evolved over the years through IGO/NGO collaboration is the concept of regional zones of peace. Currently there are five nuclear-free-zone treaties, a more limited form of the zone-of-peace concept: Antarctic (1959), Outer Space (1967) Latin American Treaty of Tlatelolco (1967), International Seabed (1971), and South Pacific (1985).[11] These nuclear-free agreements are more honored in the breach than the observance, but represent an emergent norm for the behavior of states. Every region has some initiative ranging from nuclear-free-zone proposals or actual treaties to more comprehensive zone-of-peace proposals barring all forms of arms. More recently, the establishment of ecological security zones has been proposed (Katamakhin, 1989), a proposal that could be merged logically with the zone-of-peace efforts. Symbolically these initiatives represent a commitment to a nonmilitary, environment-sustaining security.

One significant aspect of zones of peace is that they provide conceptual action spaces for creative initiatives in peace building. Furthermore, governments, NGOs, and IGOs can and do interact in these spaces. Every zone-of-peace treaty has come about through such interaction, and all further realization of the potential in such treaties depends on continued interaction. Latin America is a striking example of a region where an initial treaty (Tlatelolco), through a combination of NGO and regional IGO activity, has grown steadily in its functional capabilities and degree of intergovernmental cooperation. One particular NGO, the South American Peace Commission, has been able to create substantial opportunities for cooperation of nongovernmental and governmental individuals and bodies. The Commission's work has led to recent breakthrough agreements to abide by nuclear-disarmament provisions of the Tlatelolco Treaty on the part of the largest states of the region. The effectiveness of the Latin American zone-of-peace movement has been the fruit of over two decades of grassroots education and political dialogue among peoples and governments.

United Nations system

The United Nations with its six principal organs, 35 agencies, programs, and specialized units, and 50 information systems represents what the world has achieved so far in terms of a global nonmilitary, environment-sustaining security system.[12] Every country in the world has some kind of UN office and information system within its borders, and every region has all the specialized services of the UN present in some form. The UN works with the 10,000 societies, with the 18,000 NGOs, with the 2000 IGOs, and of course with the 168 member states. For all its bureaucratic complexity and organizational inadequacies, it is the most effective global instrument the world has, and it has roots in every region.

The Plan of Action drawn up in 1972, when the UN Environmental Program was established, is still far from being implemented, but it is in process. The World Meteorological Organization monitors world climate and water resources at strategically located stations around the world. The International Seabed Authority moves steadily along with the very limited regulatory powers available to it. Of the over 24,000 UN treaties and agreements in existence in the 1980s, a substantial number bear on the environment. What is evolving is what Jessica Mathews has described as 'a rolling process of intermediate or self-adjusting agreement that responds quickly to growing scientific understanding' (cited in Sand, 1990, p. 36). The feedback loop that humans have depended on for millennia to understand and survive in their environment, and that has been missing for so long during the industrial era, may finally be getting back into working order.

The UN recognizes even more than its member states the importance of NGOs in facilitating its work: (1) through contributions of know-how, (2) through creating a climate of public opinion in which the UN can work, and (3) as advocates of UN agendas with national governments. This is why NGOs have special status in the UN system, and can contribute in specified ways via consultative roles, to decision-making processes within UN bodies including the General Assembly.

The transboundary nature of the environment and state security

In nature, everything flows. Water flows, air flows, soil flows, ice flows, and molecules dance in and out of stones. People flow too; they are continually on the move. Walls have never stopped flows of anything – not in ancient China and not in modern Europe. All boundaries are permeable, including temporal ones. Past, present, and future flow together in us, heightening our awareness of what is happening to the earth. Unilaterally formulated national-security policies have little meaning in this context.

One particular kind of flow, a possible 5-meter rise in the level of the seas, has captured human attention in a new way. Such a sea-level rise is one of several possible global climate change scenarios, one which would remove one-third of global cropland and remove the existing dwelling space of one billion of the earth's people (Jacobsen, 1990). Some coastal ecosystems are already suffering with locally rising sea-levels. The symptoms of global change are different in each region, and the actual nature and direction of the change is still not understood. The enormous fact of change itself, however, of a magnitude that dwarfs our dreams of managing the earth, is beginning to be understood. The state becomes something different and less powerful with this new understanding. At the same time it may become more threatening, if military action is contemplated to gain control over dwindling resources.

The term *common security* was invented to give meaning to a world where national sovereignty has come to have very limited usefulness. The permeability of all national borders does not, however, mean their disappearance. The 168 (or more) nation-states are likely to remain, but their security strategies will be changing. When national borders are thought of as interfaces and zones of interaction instead of as walls, then states can begin to make fuller use of their interfaces with their internal bioregions and the identity groups that know those bioregions best, with the NGO networks that crisscross their territories, and with the IGO and UN networks that crisscross the planet. These interfaces permit the kind of collaborative problem-solving and resource-sharing that lead to common security. What kind of behavior does this call for on the part of states?

Changing the traditional diplomatic/military balance
First of all, it calls for a shift from military to diplomatic preparedness. The military security system of the nation-state consists of: (1) weaponry, personnel, training, procurement, deployment, and C_3 (command, communication, and control) systems; (2) research and development; (3) military alliance systems; and (4) overseas bases. The nonmilitary security system consists of a government's foreign office, its diplomatic corps, information and espionage systems, and treaty systems. The high rate of military expenditures by the major Western powers and Middle East countries has been well documented elsewhere (Sivard, 1990, pp.46–55). Reducing military expenditures and increasing diplomatic capability would seem to be called for in the interests of common security. The treaty process can be considered a major aspect of the diplomatic capability of a state. Treaty-making is by definition a consensual process in which the interests of all parties must be considered. Of the two types of treaties, multilateral and bilateral, the multilateral requires the greater skill since the interests of a larger number of parties must be considered.

The world treaty system as a whole moved away from multilateralism after 1945, with the Nordic countries and the United Kingdom as exceptions to the trend. Nevertheless, for most countries, between 40 and 80 percent of the treaties are multilateral. The superpowers have the fewest multilateral treaties. The trend away from multilateralism is somewhat mitigated by the developments in soft law and regimes mentioned above. However, there clearly needs to be an attitude change on the part of the states with large military establishments, toward increasing diplomatic capability and decreasing threat capability, with accompanying attentiveness to the importance of environmental conservation for human security.

The September 1988 speech to the UN by Soviet Foreign Minister Shevardnadze linking environmental and security concerns and calling for a series of three international environmental meetings under UN auspices, along with the Soviet sponsorship of the concept of International Environmental Security Regimes, to be applied initially to the Arctic (Nikitina, 1989, pp. 123–132), are indicators of such an attitude shift. Concerns for the environment remain alive in the maelstrom of reorganization that the republics of the (former) Soviet Union are now experiencing, and new channels for those concerns will be developing in this decade. The Brundtland Commission Report itself, and the Bergen Declaration from the May 1990 meeting in Bergen, Norway of the thirty-four countries of the Economic Commission for Europe (including Canada and the U.S.) on 'Action for a Common Future', also show signs, albeit hard-won, of attitude change (Lesh, 1990).

Culture change

Diplomatic skills do not come out of the blue. They emerge from the values, religious beliefs, and behavioral practices of a society – in short, from its culture.[13] Every culture has contradictory components, including usually an idealization of both the warrior and the peacemaker. The state draws more heavily on the warrior culture for its self-image, leaving peaceableness to women and children. History, preserved as a record of wars won or lost, reenforces the image of the warrior-state. Yet the core human experience is one of nurturance and social bonding alternating/clashing with individualization and conflicting wants. The fact of human difference guarantees this clash, which can be creative rather than destructive. Society, in fact, as it goes about its daily business, resorts far more frequently to negotiation than threat as it deals with these differences. While the culture of negotiation exists in every society, it goes largely unrecorded.

In the modern world the state is ill-served by the warrior image, with its complex of threat power, dominance values, and aggressive behaviors. It spills over into all sectors of society, nourishing a legacy of violent behavior in family and community that is mirrored in and exacerbated by violence in the media, sports, and elsewhere. The secondary status of women everywhere deprives every society of the skills, wisdom, and insight of half the population.[14] Their peacemaking and problem-solving experience remains unavailable in every sector. As a result, it is easy to arouse people to violent conflict, as events in Eastern Europe, Africa, and the Middle East indicate.

Within the civil society men and women work together for culture change. One important example is the Earth Covenant, 'A Citizen's Treaty for Ecological Security' (Mische, 1989). Asserting that governments alone cannot secure the environment, it sets forth principles and commitments for individual citizens to follow in accepting responsibility for protecting the integrity of the Earth. Begun as a joint Soviet–American initiative, it quickly became worldwide, and the Register of Signatories was presented to the World Conference on the Environment in 1992. The Covenant project will be strongly reenforced by the hundreds of transnational networks of NGOs, religious and secular, that engage in education and political advocacy to create the conditions for peace with humans and peace with the earth.

Modifying local political and economic structures in every state so they can take account of bioregions and thereby work with what nature has to offer instead of against it – structures that can work with ethnic groups and their special knowledge instead of against them – is a necessary part of the long-term culture change process. Feedback loops have to be reinserted into local communities. Solutions to environmental problems must be developed locally where the first-hand knowledge is and where the problems are, not by distant bureaucrats.

States as presently organized are not well-suited to the protection of the environment and its inhabitants. Only as states begin to acknowledge and work with the interfaces available to them – the internal interfaces with community structures and microsocieties, the interfaces with the transnational citizens' associations that crisscross each nation, the interfaces with the intergovernmental and UN structures that crisscross the planet itself – will they become effective contributors to a newly conceived multidimensional kind of security.

Since no one can work for a future that cannot even be imagined, it is important to imagine types of supporting institutional infrastructures, local, regional and global, both citizen-based and of intergovernmental and UN devising, that can make the twenty-first-century world secure for all living things. Imagining will not make it so, but imagining is the first step in the never-ending task of constructing the world social order.

Conclusion

It has been suggested that the gradual evolution of new attitudes toward the earth and its peoples may shift nation-states away from territorial obsession and displays of military strength to problem-solving, resource-sharing, and nonviolent conflict resolution. Evidence for this shift has been indicated by: (1) the growth of awareness that security is a different problem than traditionally conceived of, and one that cannot be handled by individual nation-states unilaterally or bilaterally; (2) the linking of peace and environmental movements worldwide, and the acceptance of responsibility for the planet by individual citizens (the Earth Covenant); (3) the growth of zone-of-peace concepts and zone-of-peace experiments, governmental and non-governmental; and (4) the development of global regulatory systems, inter-governmental and UN-administered (formal and informal, 'soft' and 'hard') in the context of acceptance of new norms of resource-sharing and coopera-tion. None of these developments can be taken for granted, however, and much hard work lies ahead if future generations are to enjoy a secure earth.

Notes

1. An earlier treatment of this subject was presented at the International Conference on Environmental Security held by the Research Center on Environmental Politics, University of Laval at Manior Montmorency, Quebec, 28–30 September, 1990.
2. The Two-Thirds World is a more graphic way of describing the Third World, since two-thirds of the world's population lives in the Third World.
3. See the *International Social Science Journal* issue on Reconciling the Sociosphere and the Biosphere: Global Change, Industrial Metabolism, Sustainable Develop-ment, Vulnerability; No. 121, August 1989, for an in-depth analysis of the system-wide effects of strong forcing functions on the ecosphere. See also Michael Renner (1989).
4. I am drawing in part on Dodge (1981) for this set of definitions.

5. The '10,000 societies' is a term loosely used by some anthropologists. According to Nietschman, quoted in Gurr and Scarritt (1989, p. 375), there are '5000 distinct communities in the contemporary world [that] might claim that they are national peoples on grounds that they share common ancestry, institutions, beliefs, language and territory'. In a 1979 study, I identified 6276 significant ethnic groups in 159 countries (Boulding, 1979, p. 276). How many groups you find obviously depends on how you count them.

    Some material in this section is taken from my 'Ethnicity and new constitutive orders: An approach to peace in the twenty-first century', 1990.

6. Note Boulding (1979), Brown (1989), Clay (1989), Ra'anan (1989).
7. For a description of Imagery Workshops, see Chapter 6 and Appendix 2 of E. Boulding, *Building a Global Civic Culture*, 1990.
8. For further discussion of NGOs, see E. Boulding, 1990, op. cit.
9. See *The World Directory of Environmental Organizations*, 1989, cited in *Breakthrough*, Summer/Fall 1989.
10. See the *Yearbook of International Organizations*, 3 Vols., 1986, or a more recent edition.
11. For data on local, national, and regional nuclear-free zones see the *New Abolitionist*, March 1990, or a more recent edition.
12. See *Everyone's UN*, 10th (1986) or more recent edition, and *Directory of UN Information Systems*, 1980, or a more recent edition.
13. For an excellent series of essays on this subject see Arthur Westing, Ed., *Cultural Norms, War and the Environment*, 1988. For a discussion of the warrior culture versus the peace culture, see E. Boulding, 'The two cultures of religion as obstacles to peace', 1986.
14. See, for example, Virginia Held, 'Gender as an influence on cultural norms relating to war and the environment', pp. 44–52, and Birgit Brock-Utne, 'Formal education as a force in shaping cultural norms relating to war and the environment', pp. 83–100, in Westing, 1988.

References

Boulding, E. (1979), 'Ethnic separatism and world development', in Louis Kriesberg, ed., *Research in Social Movements, Conflict and Change*, 2, JAI Press, Greenwich, Connecticut.

Boulding, E. (1984), 'From locality to the planet: An approach to grounded planning', in *Festschrift for Chihiro Hosoya*, Hitotsubashi University Press, Tokyo.

Boulding, E. (1986), 'The two cultures of religion as obstacles to peace', *Zygon*, 21, pp. 501–518.

Boulding, E. (1988, 1990), *Building a Global Civic Culture: Education for an Interdependent World*, Teachers College Press, New York; Syracuse University Press, Syracuse, New York.

Boulding, E. (1990), 'Ethnicity and new constitutive orders: An approach to peace in the twenty-first century', in H. Usui and T. Uchida, eds, *From Chaos to Order, Vol. 1: Crisis and Renaissance of the World Society* (in Japanese), Yushindo, Tokyo.

Brock-Utne, B. (1988), 'Formal education as a force in shaping cultural norms relating to war and the environment', in Arthur Westing, ed., *Cultural Norms, War and the Environment*, Oxford University Press, Oxford.

Brown, D. (1989), 'Ethnic revival: Perspectives on state security', *Third World Quarterly*, 2, pp. 1–17.

Brundtland Report (1987), World Commission on Environment and Development, *Our Common Future*, Oxford University Press, Oxford.

Clay, J. (1989), 'Epilogue: The ethnic future of nations', *Third World Quarterly*, 2, pp. 223–233.

Dodge, D. (1981), 'Living by life: Some bioregional theory and practice', *Coevolution Quarterly* special issue on Bioregions, No. 32, pp. 6–12.

Environment (1990), 'Secure ecological niches', 32, pp. 22–23. (Quoted from *The Nature Conservancy Magazine*, July/August 1989).

Gurr, T. R. and Scarritt, J. R. (1989), 'Minorities' rights at risk: A global survey', *Human Rights Quarterly*, 11, pp. 375–404.

Held, V. (1988), 'Gender as an influence on cultural norms relating to war and the environment' in Arthur Westing, ed., *Cultural Norms, War and the Environment*, Oxford University Press, Oxford.

Holst, J. J. (1989), 'Security and the environment: A preliminary exploration', *Bulletin of Peace Proposals*, 20, pp. 123–128.

Human Dimensions of Global Change Programme (1988), 'Tokyo International Symposium on the Human Dimensions of Global Change, 11–22 September 1988', HDGC Secretariat, Toronto.

International Geosphere-Biosphere Programme (1988), 'Report No. 4: A plan for action', IGBP Secretariat, Stockholm.

International Social Science Journal Symposium Issue (1989), Reconciling the Socio-sphere and the Biosphere: Global Change, Industrial Metabolism, Sustainable Development, Vulnerability, No. 121.

Jacobson, J. L. (1990), 'Holding back the sea', *The Futurist*, 24, pp. 20–27.

Katamakhin, A. (1989), *Ecology and the Twenty-First Century*, Moscow, USSR. Excerpt translated by Andrew Bromfield in, *Breakthrough*, Ecological Security Issue, Summer/Fall 1989, p. 72.

Keohane, R. and Nye, J. (1985), 'Two cheers for multilateralism', *Foreign Policy*, No. 60, pp. 148–167.

Lesh, D. (1990), 'Bergen outcome', *Interaction*, 9, pp. 1, 2, 4.

Lindgren, K., Wilson, G. K., Wallensteen, P. and Nordquist, K. (1990), 'Major armed conflicts in 1989', Chapter 10 in *SIPRI Yearbook 1990, World Armaments and Disarmament*, Oxford University Press, Oxford.

Mathews, J. (1989), 'Redefining security', *Foreign Affairs*, 68, p. 176.

Mische, P. (1989), 'Earth Covenant: The evolution of a citizen's treaty for common ecological security', *Breakthrough*, pp. 31–33.

The New Abolitionist (1990), 8, No. 1. (Baltimore: Newsletter of Nuclear Free America.)

Nikitina, E. N. (1989), 'International mechanisms and arctic environmental research', *Current Research on Peace and Violence*, Tampere Peace Research Institute, 3, pp. 123–132.

Palme Report (1983), Independent Commission for Disarmament and Security Issues, *Common Security: A Blueprint for Survival*, Simon and Schuster, New York.

Ra'anan, U. (1989), 'The nation state fallacy', in Joseph Montville, ed., *Conflict and Peacemaking in Multi-Ethnic Societies*, D. C. Heath and Co., Lexington, Massachusetts.

Renner, M. (1989), *National Security, The Economic and Environmental Dimensions*, Worldwatch Paper 89, Worldwatch Institute, Washington D.C.

Sand, P. H. (1990), *Lessons Learned in Global Governance*, World Resources Institute, Washington D.C.

Sivard, R. (1989), *World Military and Social Expenditures 1989*, 13th edition, World Priorities, Washington D.C.

Union of International Associations (1976), *Encyclopedia of World Problems and Human Potential 1976*, Union of International Associations, Brussels.

Union of International Associations (1986), *Encyclopedia of World Problems and Human Potential 1986*, K.G. Saur, Munich.

United Nations (1980), *Directory of the United Nations Information Systems*, I and II, United Nations, New York.

United Nations (1986), *Everyone's United Nations*, United Nations, New York.

United Nations Development Program (UNDP) (1991), *Human Development Report 1991*, Oxford University Press, Oxford.

Westing, A. (1988), *Cultural Norms, War and the Environment*, Oxford University Press, Oxford.

Young, O. (1989), 'Arctic environmental issues: Prospects for international co-operation', *Current Research on Peace and Violence*, Tampere Peace Research Institute, 3, pp. 105–110.

Part IV

Relevance of theory to the practitioner

Theory and alternative dispute resolution: A contradiction in terms?

Alternative Dispute Resolution (ADR), sometimes called 'Delegalization', represents a movement, away from formal adversarial proceedings on the part of the courts, toward informal processes. As such it is one of the fastest, if not the fastest, growing area in the overall field of conflict resolution. Indeed, ADR had become so commonplace that even the conservative Bush administration has pushed for a wider acceptance of this practice, advocating ADR as part of an attempt to reform the administration of justice in the United States.

In other works (Scimecca, 1987, 1991a, 1991b) I have presented the major criticisms of ADR, expressing the view that those who practice ADR will not become true professionals until ADR incorporates a theoretical base to undergird its practice and, until it has such a base, it will remain an instrument of social control. At present, I remain convinced that practitioners do little more than pay lip service to theory.

Having said this, I am reminded of something the late Bryant Wedge, a co-founder of the Center (now Institute) for Conflict Analysis and Resolution at George Mason University and himself a leading practitioner, once told me. His words, which I am paraphrasing were: 'It is easy to criticize. But what are you offering to help solve the problem?' With this challenge in mind, I will present a theory of conflict that hopefully can be used to offset the criticisms that have been raised about ADR, and show that theory and ADR do not have to be contradictions in terms, as I believe they have been. In the interests of clarity,[1] before presenting this theoretical framework – one that is grounded in the classical social science of Max Weber – I will briefly define what I mean when I use the term ADR.

What exactly is ADR?

The beginnings of ADR are usually traced to the 1970s (Adler, 1987). A major impetus for ADR's rapid growth was a 1976 American Bar Association sponsored National Conference on the Causes of Popular Dissatisfaction with the Administration of Justice. The Conference concluded that alternative forms of dispute resolution, in particular mediation and arbitration, would ease congested courts, reduce settlement time, and minimize costs. The development of neighborhood justice centers (which practice mediation) and multi-door courthouse programs (which direct disputants to the most appropriate dispute-resolving mechanism: facilitation, mediation, or arbitration) were encouraged. Today there are hundreds of alternative dispute resolution centers in the United States. These ADR centers roughly fall into three categories: (1) those attached to, run by, or closely connected to the courts; (2) those connected to prosecutors' offices; and (3) those that are community- or church-based.

ADR, like other terms in conflict resolution, has been very broadly and loosely defined. For example, the National Institute for Dispute Resolution, under the sponsorship of the U.S. Department of Justice, convened an Ad Hoc Panel on Dispute Resolution and Public Policy in 1983, and defined its scope of inquiry as 'all methods, practices, and techniques, formal and informal, within and outside the courts, that are used to resolve disputes' (Administrative Conference of the U.S., 1987, p. 12). In short, ADR was officially seen as encompassing all of the major processes which are now being used to deal with disputes (ibid., pp. 44–46). The following were listed: arbitration, court-annexed arbitration, conciliation, facilitation, fact-finding, med-arb, mediation, mini-trial, multi-door center (or multi-door courthouse), negotiated investment strategy, negotiation, neighborhood justice centers (NJC), ombudsman, public policy dialogue and negotiations, and rent-a-judge.

If the Ad Hoc Panel's definition of what constitutes ADR is accepted there can be no 'alternative dispute resolution' because every conceivable dispute resolution technique is encompassed by the Panel's definition. Therefore, in order to sharpen the amorphous definition of ADR, I will define ADR as *those* non-coercive processes which are alternatives to the formal *legal or court system, in particular, multi-door courthouse programs, neighborhood justice centers (NJCs), or community justice centers (CJCs).*

Is there any theory in the practice of ADR?

As stated previously, my position is that there is little, if any, theory in the field of ADR. What is called theory is basically the idiosyncratic use of various processes, what is usually referred to by practitioners as 'seat-of-the-pants theory'. What little actual theory there is, is derived from the overall field of conflict resolution. However, as I have stated elsewhere: 'although there are many comprehensive theories of conflict, theories of conflict resolution are few and far between' (Scimecca, 1991b, p. 33). Since 'seat-of-the-pants theory' is a misnomer, I will address the use of what little actual theory there is in the field of conflict resolution.

Theory as presently defined in the field of conflict resolution can be divided into two categories: game-theoretical frameworks and human-needs theory.[2] Both, unfortunately, are, at present, quite flawed.

Game theory uses assumptions of perfect information (that is, every party perfectly understands everyone else's possible actions), and therein lies its most basic weakness as a theory. Conditions of perfect information rarely if ever exist. Game theory also assumes that the parties or players, in the end, cooperate – their actions are in accordance with some agreed-upon plan. This, in turn, assumes communication between them, and also a mechanism for enforcing the agreements they reach. Players may jockey for relative position, but they end up working together toward a rational and mutually efficient goal (Schellenberg, 1982, p. 188). Such assumptions do not take into consideration that deep-seated conflicts are often irrational, nor does the assumption of an essential social vacuum consider the role that culture, social structure, and, I would argue most importantly, power, play in conflicts.

Human-needs theory fares no better than game theory. Although this approach has been a part of social science for some time, indeed has provided the foundation for the 'Goals, Processes, and the Indicators of Development' (GPID) project of the United Nations University, which resulted in a major edited publication, *Human Needs* (Lederer, 1980), it is John Burton who is most often associated with human-needs theory when one speaks of conflict resolution theory.

Burton's human-needs theory of conflict resolution has been criticized for its emphasis upon genetic determinism and its subsequent failure to take culture and social institutions into consideration (Scimecca, 1990). Avruch and Black (1987, p. 91) ask: 'Where do these needs come from? And why these and not others?' And Mitchell (1990) raises the question of whether some needs are more important than others. Although Burton originally saw what he refers to as basic human needs, as genetically based, in a response to Avruch and Black (Burton and Sandole, 1987, p. 97), he modifies his position somewhat by accepting the thesis of Boyd and Richerson (1986) that humans have a 'dual inheritance system', one part cultural and the other genetic. What is important 'is that universal patterns of behavior exist' (Burton and Sandole, 1987, p. 97). Although this represents a movement away from a pure genetically determined position, it still places Burton in the sociobiologists' camp and still does not answer the question of where needs come from, or whether some are more important than others; nor does it resolve the dilemma of ascertaining just how much culture influences human needs, dual inheritance system notwithstanding. Perhaps, though, the most telling criticism of Burton is that he sees power as irrelevant, claiming that it has no role in problem-solving or conflict resolution processes (Burton, 1987, 1990a, 1990b). Conflict resolution as envisioned by Burton is a purely analytical process. Power becomes a 'non-variable' when the parties to a conflict, with the help of a facilitation team, engage in analytical problem-solving.

Although Burton, to his credit, has been one of the few scholars in the field of conflict resolution to call for a conflict resolution process that is derived from a theoretical base, to formulate a theory of conflict or conflict resolution without a theory of power is simply naive.

Thus, given the, at best, flawed nature of conflict resolution theory, in particular, the failure of both game theory and human-needs theory to take power into consideration, the whole field of conflict resolution, not just ADR, is left with a number of processes which are dependent upon the idiosyncratic expertise of the individual practitioner. Can a theory of conflict be used to offset this state of affairs? It is to this question that I now turn.

Conflict theory

The origins of conflict theory are usually traced to the works of Karl Marx (1818–1883). However, conflict scholars (Collins, 1975; Duke, 1979; Scimecca, 1981) have recently rediscovered the relevance of the work of the great German social scientist Max Weber (1864–1920), seeing Weber as offering a much more comprehensive and accurate description of the nature of conflict in society than did Marx.

Because he based his views solely on experiences deriving from a capitalist economy, Marx (1964) provides a limited conflict analysis. For example, to Marx, capitalism is essentially the product of two interrelated and antagonistic groups: the *bourgeoisie* (those who own the means of production) and the *proletariat* (those who work for the owners). Eventually, the antagonism becomes so intense that a revolution occurs, resulting in the overthrow of the owning class by the working class. A communist society is then at hand, with the interests of all being reconciled. Here Marx's horror of capitalism clearly got in the way of his analysis, pushing him into a deterministic view of human behavior. Marx began with the assumption that human nature was basically creative and cooperative, but was faced with the reality that capitalist society was in constant conflict. How did the cooperative individuals come to engage in a competitive struggle with their fellows? Marx's answer was the idea of an externally determining economic system of relationships between human beings. Capitalism's structure determined human behavior. Marx has also been criticized for placing too much emphasis on conflict and economically based power. Conflict, instead, can often be seen as integrative. Consensus and cooperation are more frequently evident than is conflict (Coser, 1956; Simmel, 1955). This, along with the failure of many of Marx's predictions, in particular his failure to correctly identify the conditions necessary to produce a revolution, and the growth of the middle class, led students of conflict to turn to Max Weber (Duke, 1979).

Max Weber

Seeking to round off Marx's thought, a major concern of Weber's (1948) was how power led to social order and integration. Power must always be considered if society is to be understood, for both conflict and social order are differentially derived from social power. The distribution of power constitutes a continuing problem for society. Because power based solely on coercion is ineffective, society cannot remain stable unless the people see the power structure as legitimate and those who occupy positions of power as deserving to hold those position. Legitimate power, which, to Weber, is synonymous with authority, holds the society together.

Weber's views on legitimacy differ markedly from Marx's. Whereas Marx constantly emphasized the increasing tendency on the part of the lower classes to view the government as illegitimate, in Weber's formulation, the government constantly seeks to enhance its legitimacy, and loses it only when a powerful and charismatic leader capable of leading the people in a revolution comes on the scene – a rare historical phenomenon. Therefore, the power structure is able to convince or coerce members to accept the social order as legitimate even though it favors the interests of the more powerful.

Weber's contribution to conflict theory is an explanation of how power is legitimized and stabilized in society. Order rather than conflict prevails, but this order is achieved through the use of power to suppress or coopt the underlying conflict. Conflicts occur, in Weber's (1948) view, whenever an individual's action is oriented intentionally toward carrying out his or her own will against the resistance of the other party or parties. This shows the close association of conflict and power. Conflict results when there is a scarcity of resources and one individual gains at the expense of another. The ability to achieve one's own will in a situation of scarcity is what makes one powerful (Duke, 1979, p. 42).

Social life is a competitive struggle among individuals for social rewards and economic rewards, for the power over others. Societies differ in how power is institutionalized, and this institutionalization demarcates social stratification or the system of inequality in a given society. Conflict and the struggle to achieve and maintain power eventually lead to a hierarchical ordering of individuals. Like Marx, Weber recognized that conflict provides the basis upon which each society erects a stratification system. However, unlike Marx, Weber recognized that society or groups or individuals are not constantly in a state of conflict, that power becomes legitimized and it is this legitimacy that holds the society together. Numerous stable relationships contain conflict but the conflict is masked; it is under the surface because of the role of legitimacy.

Weber also did not fall into the determinism trap of Marx. For Weber, freedom and non-determinism are present in that individuals chose to embrace power – it does not determine them. They act in their own self-interest and use resources at their disposal to gain their self-interests. How much and how well resources can be marshaled, how much legitimacy is present, how much freedom of choice is available in a society, are questions that are to be investigated.

Sociologist James Duke (1979, pp. 69–70) has summarized, quite nicely, the essential elements of Weber's conflict theory:

(1) Conflicts are endemic in social life.
(2) Power is differentially distributed among groups and individuals in society.
(3) Social order is achieved in any society through rules and commands issued by more powerful persons to less powerful persons and enforced through sanctions.
(4) Both the social structure and the normative system of a society are more extensively influenced by powerful persons than by weaker persons (true by definition), and come to represent the interests of these more powerful persons.
(5) Social changes are often more disruptive to powerful persons than to less powerful persons. Powerful persons therefore generally support the status quo and oppose changes that would reduce their power.
(6) However, changes in a society occur as the result of actions by persons who stand to benefit from these changes and who accumulate power to bring them to pass. Powerful people see that they can benefit from a particular change (e.g., industrialization of a 'backward' society), and they will usually not hesitate to foster such things.

In short, Weber was interested in how order was established and showed how the effective use of power resulted in a legitimate order. The basis of social order lies in the process of legitimacy.

Weber's conflict theory, then, has four major components: (1) the role of power, (2) the emphasis upon organized systems, (3) legitimacy, and (4) the individual who acts in his or her self-interest and marshals resources to achieve his or her own ends.

Can Weber's theory of conflict be used to address the major criticisms leveled against ADR? Let us see.

ADR: The major criticisms

A search of the literature reveals that there are six major criticisms of ADR. These are:

(1) ADR lacks a reasoned justification that arises out of any broad concept of conflict (Burton, 1990b). ADR is simply a number of different processes used by NJCs and CJCs. Indeed, this is why 'dispute' as a term is employed rather than 'conflict'. The justification for using ADR and the processes employed is based more in the legal tradition and in the

experience of the individual practitioner than in any theoretical framework. As a consequence there is an overemphasis on process, unsupported by articulated insights into the generic nature of different disputes. ADR emphasizes how to settle disputes without regard to power disparities and the advantage such inequities give to the more powerful party. In most instances there is no real theoretical justification for when and why to use conflict intervention techniques. This blind faith in the how of the processes, without any understanding of the when and why, makes it particularly vulnerable to the criticism that ADR is primarily just another mechanism of social control.

Weberian conflict theory clearly addresses this criticism by offering a comprehensive framework for understanding conflict. The root cause of conflict is seen in 'the unequal power distributions in a given situation'. The amount of legitimation in a situation, group, or society shapes the amount of conflict that is manifested. ADR, if it is to be more than another mechanism of social control, must take the unequal distribution of power into consideration and try to resolve the dispute without assuming that the parties are equal and thereby, by default, coming out on the side of the more powerful.

(2) ADR, like formal law, is embedded in individualism. As such, the fundamental principle of individual responsibility is seen as the cause of the conflict (Able, 1982). This focus enhances social control by not looking to structured inequalities in the society as a reason for conflict. Grievances are trivialized and the basic social structure is rarely, if ever, questioned. The assumption is that rational individuals should be able to resolve their conflicts, and if they cannot, then the problem lies with them.

Weberian conflict theory focuses upon the society because it is primarily a structural theory. The roots of power, inequality, and conflict are seen in the struggle to establish order, via legitimacy, in a society where there is an unequal amount of resources and access to these resources.

(3) ADR has concentrated on particular types of disputes – organizational, industrial, matrimonial, communal, environmental, and others – which do not involve widespread violence, confrontations with authorities or defiance of legal norms. These conflicts limit the role of the third party to helping conduct discussion and to pointing out the misunderstandings in communication that arise. The underlying assumption is that the parties themselves have sufficient insight into the nature of their conflict, and of possible options to find an agreed outcome that will be lasting. All that is required and provided is a process which helps communication between disputants. However, as U.S. Court of Appeals Judge, Harry Edwards (1986, p.668) reminds us: 'It is a fact of political life that many disputes reflect sharply contrasting views about fundamental public values

that can never be eliminated by techniques that encourage disputants to "understand" each other. Indeed, many disputants understand their opponents all too well.'

Political disputes are over power. The legal system is based on legitimacy. Again, I reiterate that, from the perspective of Weberian conflict theory, the role of power must be assessed, before the parties can begin to deal with misunderstandings and any lack of communication.

(4) The supposed neutrality of the third party favors compromise and conceals the fact that values which confirm the existing advantages between unequals are necessarily biased (Laue, 1982). Very few, if any, practitioners of ADR challenge the neutrality position; for them it is an unexamined assumption. As such, their neutrality supports the status quo, no matter how unequal it may be.

Again, power and its unequal distribution, not neutrality or rationality, are the keys to understanding conflict and to eventually resolving conflict. From the perspective of Weberian conflict theory, the third party would always consider the role of power along with possessing an obligation to point out where and when the unequal distribution of power might force the weaker party to settle.

(5) ADR has lost sight of its original purpose: its concern for the poor, for all those who did not have access to the law (Harrington and Merry, 1988). The prime focus of ADR is seen as organizational expansion, and the carving out of profitable jobs for new professionals. Along these lines it has been argued that the American Bar Association's interest in ADR has less to do with providing alternatives to the law than with opening up new sources of revenue for lawyers (Nader, 1980).

By focusing upon power and, by extension, empowerment, Weberian conflict theory enables the practitioner to help the poor, to help those who do not have access to the law. In particular, it would follow that if unequal power leads to conflict, then empowerment of the less powerful person or group would facilitate resolution.

(6) ADR represents an alternative to politics and community organizing which lacks any organic connection to communities. Originally conceived to offer justice in communities by those who make up the community, it has let itself become the province of professionals from other fields (Tomasic and Feeley, 1982).

By proposing a theory based on power and empowerment, the locus for resolution is shifted to justice, whether it be for the individual or for the community. It would follow, too, that the implementation of justice would enhance community solidarity, and provide opportunities for members of the community to engage in the distribution of justice.

Summary and Conclusions

As it now stands, ADR lacks a comprehensive theory of conflict. In so far as practitioners provide any satisfaction with the services they have to sell to clients at one social level or another, it is because ADR may very well be adequate for a limited number of superficial disputes. Furthermore, failures, when seemingly superficial problems turn out to have more deep-rooted sources, are usually not recorded. When this becomes apparent, as when a strike is not resolved, or when a communal or international conflict escalates into violence and persists, failure is attributed, not to any inadequacy in theory or practice, but to the alleged inherent complexities of the situation or to the irrational preferences that the individual disputants bring to the conflict.

If ADR is to be anything more than a process which deals with superficial disputes, it must have a comprehensive theoretical framework that can undergird its practice. I have summarized the major criticisms raised against ADR, and have pointed to the possibility of using Weberian conflict theory as a means of overcoming these criticisms. Up to now the practice of ADR and the use of theory have been, for all intents and purposes, contradictions in terms. Hopefully, through the use of Weberian conflict theory, ADR may achieve some of the noble purposes its early advocates saw for it. Via an emphasis upon power as the staple of a theory of conflict and empowerment as the basis of conflict resolution, ADR could do what it was originally designed to do − help the poor, the downtrodden, those with no access to the expensive legal system. If not, ADR will continue to remain an instrument of social control, a process to keep the have-nots in their place.

Notes

1. The field of conflict resolution has been characterized by a lack of clarity of definitions.
2. I am making the distinction between conflict theory and theories of conflict resolution. The former, for example, includes the work of Marx, Simmel, Weber, and Coser among others. The latter is a much narrower body of work which includes only those theoretical frameworks which have been related to specific practices of conflict intervention.

References

Able, R. (1982), 'The contradictions of informal justice', in R. Able, ed., *The Politics of Informal Justice*, Academic Press, New York.

Adler, P. S. (1987), 'Is ADR a social movement?', *Negotiation Journal*, 3, pp. 59−71.

Administrative Conference of the United States (1987), *Sourcebook: Federal Agency Use of Alternative Means of Dispute Resolution*, ACUS (Office of the Chairman), Washington, D.C.

Avruch, K. and Black, P. W. (1987), 'A "generic" theory of conflict resolution: A critique', *Negotiation Journal*, 3, pp. 87–96, 99–100.

Boyd, R. and Richerson, P. J. (1986), *Culture and the Evolutionary Process*, University of Chicago Press, Chicago.

Burton, J. W. (1987), *Resolving Deep-Rooted Conflict: A Handbook*, University Press of America, Lanham, Maryland.

Burton, J. W. (1990a), 'The need for human needs theory', in J. W. Burton, ed., *Conflict: Human Needs Theory*, Macmillan, London.

Burton, J. W. (1990b), *Conflict: Resolution and Provention*, Macmillan, London.

Burton, J. W. and Sandole, D. J. D. (1987), 'Expanding the debate on generic theory of conflict resolution: A response to a critique', *Negotiation Journal*, 3, pp. 97–99.

Collins, R. (1975), *Conflict Sociology*, Academic Press, New York.

Coser, L. (1956), *The Functions of Social Conflict*, Free Press, New York.

Duke, J. (1979), *Conflict and Power in Social Life*, Brigham Young University Press, Provo, Utah.

Edwards, H. T. (1986), 'Alternative dispute resolution', *Harvard Law Review*, 99, pp. 668–684.

Harrington, C. and Merry, S. E. (1988), 'Ideological production: The making of community mediation', *Law and Society Review*, 22, pp. 501–527.

Hofrichter, R. (1987), *Neighborhood Justice In Capitalist Society*, Greenwood Press, Westport, Connecticut.

Laue, J. H. (1982), 'Ethical considerations in choosing intervention roles', *Peace and Change*, 7, pp. 29–41.

Lederer, K. (ed.) (1980), *Human Needs*, Oelgeschlager, Gunn and Hain, Cambridge, Massachusetts.

Marx, K. (1964), *Selected Writings in Sociology and Social Philosophy*, T. B. Bottomore (trans.), McGraw-Hill, New York.

Mitchell, C. (1990), 'Necessitous man and conflict resolution: More basic questions about basic human needs theory', in J. W. Burton, ed., *Human Needs and Conflict Resolution*, Macmillan, London.

Nader, L. (ed.) (1980), *No Access to Law – Alternatives to American Judicial System*, Academic Press, New York.

Sandole, D. J. D. (1985), 'Training and teaching in a field whose "time has come": A postgraduate program in conflict management', in C. Cutrona, ed., *The Elements of Good Practice in Dispute Resolution*, Society of Professionals in Dispute Resolution (SPIDR), Washington, D.C.

Schellenberg, T. (1982), *The Science of Conflict*, Oxford University Press, New York.

Scimecca, J. A. (1981), *Society and Freedom: An Introduction to Humanist Sociology*, St. Martin's Press, New York.

Scimecca, J. A. (1987), 'Conflict resolution: The basis for social control or social change?', in D. J. D. Sandole and I. Sandole-Staroste, eds, *Conflict Management and Problem Solving: Interpersonal to International Applications*, Frances Pinter, London and New York University Press, New York.

Scimecca, J. A. (1990), 'Freedom and self-reflexivity as basic human needs', in J. W. Burton, ed., *Human Needs and Conflict Resolution*, Macmillan, London.

Scimecca, J. A. (1991a), 'Conflict resolution and a critique of "alternative dispute resolution" ', in H. E. Pepinski and R. Quinney, eds, *Criminology as Peacemaking*, University of Indiana Press, Bloomington, Indiana.

Scimecca, J. A. (1991b), 'Conflict resolution in the United States: The emergence of a profession?', in K. Avruch, P. Black and J. A. Scimecca, eds, *Conflict Resolution: Cross Cultural Perspectives*, Greenwood Press, Westport, Connecticut.

Simmel, G. (1955), *Conflict and the Web of Group Affiliations*, K. Wolff and R. Bendix (trans.), Free Press, New York.

Tomasic, R. and Feeley, M. M. (eds.) (1982), *Neighborhood Justice: Assessment of an Emerging Idea*, Longman, New York.

Weber, M. (1948), *The Theory of Social and Economic Organization*, The Free Press, Glencoe, Illinois.

15 *John S. Murray*

Using theory in conflict resolution practice

Introduction

Conflict resolution theorists and practitioners operate within two independent cultures; yet, they both understand and appreciate their interdependence. Theory without grounding in practice generates increasingly distant and ethereal critiques that few can or want to understand. Practice without grounding in theory creates a confusing and unfocused profession with high risks for the public. Fortunately, most theory is generated from, founded on, and evaluated by a review of practical experience, and most practitioners use theory extensively to guide and support effective mediation and intervention work.

This chapter looks closely at the practitioner's use of theory. The goal is to trace the patterns of conflict resolution theory in the advice and activities of mediators and facilitators. Theory in this volume is found primarily in the writings of academics, although it should be remembered that many academics also conduct an active, albeit part-time, conflict resolution practice. For their part, practitioners do not often accept theoretical models without question, nor do they apply those theories without shaping them to fit specific conditions.

The chapter does not address how the lessons of practical experience are used in building and improving theory. The task for theorists is to use the work of practitioners to shape and reshape their theories, much like astronomers and physicists are now using the results of space travel and satellite technology to restructure their views of the universe. The obstacles facing conflict resolution theorists in handling this task are many: the demand for confidentiality by parties; the difficulty in creating control groups or laboratory conditions; lengthy gestation periods for most conflicts; complexity in the personalities, strategies, and motivations involved; and the different skills necessary for a practitioner, to name only a few. Tracing the use of practice in the work of theorists is a valuable and necessary effort, and the subject for a separate chapter (e.g., that of Christopher Mitchell, Chapter 6).

To illustrate the use of theory in conflict resolution practice, I am selecting a single case handled by the staff of the Conflict Clinic, Inc., during nine months from late 1989 to mid – 1990. My objective is to describe the case in as much detail as confidentiality and limited space will allow, and then trace specific applications of different theories as they appear in that account. The case-study method creates an opportunity for the reader to agree with, delete, add to, or amend the conclusions and lessons given in this chapter, based on his or her own experience.

The case: Designing and managing policy development in a large school district

Suburban County is a relatively large geographic area on the border of a major metropolitan area on the East Coast of the United States. Its population has more than doubled during the past thirty years, and the ethnic and racial mix in the eastern third of the county has changed recently to reflect the increasing diversity of the state's population. Hispanics, blacks, Asians, Africans, and Arabs combine to make up at least 40 percent of the neighborhoods close to the city.

Suburban County has one school district organization. A ten-member School Board oversees public education for over 65,000 students, with more than 4500 teachers and 2000 administrators and other staff.

Initial conditions

Board members are divided into three equally powerful factions, with no single leadership strong enough to bring them together. Two Board members had recently had a bitter dispute with the superintendent over sensitivity to minority student and parent concerns, so tension existed over internal decision-making roles already.

Within the prior two months, the Board had deleted from the school budget a promised pay increase for principals. It also reaffirmed a two-tier pay-scale for administrators: a lower scale for school-based principals and a higher one for area and central-office administrators. As could be anticipated, these actions promoted competition and antagonism within the administrative structure.

Teachers within the district belong to two different professional organizations, the National Education Association affiliate attracting the bigger share (80 percent). Although the state does not have any collective bargaining process for management – labor discussions in the public sector, the local administration has had an established, informal, yet structured procedure to negotiate working conditions with union representatives. Heavy competition and negative personal relations exist between the leaders of the two teachers' groups. Of course, the groups themselves vie strenuously for the allegiance of local teachers.

223

Parent and citizen activists have long been vocal on certain school staff-proposed projects, including adoption of new textbooks, the placement and use of computers, elementary school hours, and budget allocations. The central and area administrators believe that a few 'obnoxious' parents are obstructing good educational programs for the majority of the population.

The traditional way the Board and administrative staff has handled policy development issues is to convene a large committee (about forty-five members), most members being selected as organizational representatives by the different interest groups within the district, including the School Board, central-office administrative leadership team, elementary and secondary principals' organizations, the two teachers' groups, and the parent—teacher organization (PTO). This committee, staffed by the central office, usually meets for six-to-eight months and then submits a written final report (multiple volumes of conclusions, recommendations, and supplementary materials) to the administration and the School Board.

The problem

In October 1989, a central administrator for Suburban County School District asked the Conflict Clinic for assistance in defining the way the district might implement a site-based management system (SBM). SBM had been a priority goal of the Board for three years, but Board members had not been able to provide clear direction about how they wanted it to be interpreted in the district.

Five months earlier, Board members had demanded that the superintendent provide a detailed plan for implementation of SBM by the following May. The superintendent delegated the responsibility to his associate superintendent, who by October was feeling overwhelmed by internal pressure to produce a detailed plan in the face of a complete lack of consensus among district leadership. She understood that SBM affected power and identity relationships within the system, which made this issue a highly volatile subject for the school community to handle.

At their first meeting, the associate superintendent described the problem to the Conflict Clinic staff member. The resulting discussion focused on various ways to analyze conflict within communities and design consensus-building processes. The Clinic had just designed and conducted a successful process for policy development in a neighboring county, where a land-use planning problem had generated an equally volatile debate among county residents.

Consistent with this discussion, the Clinic recommended that an outside third party help the school community develop a responsive process, first, to define what the community means by SBM, and then determine how it wants to move forward with the concept. The goal was to include all major interests and stakeholders during both tasks.

Clinic staff recommended that the first two-and-a-half months (mid-November through early February) focus on building consensus on the process by which the community would define SBM. The associate superintendent expressed concern with the delay in working directly on a substantive policy. May, the deadline set by the School Board, was only six months away, and it was already too late to engage the traditional process to solve this problem. Yet, the risk of coming up without any policy, the sense of urgency in making a decision, and the high political visibility surrounding this issue combined to make this new consensus-building process attractive. The decision was made in mid-November to proceed with Phase I. A contract between the district and the Conflict Clinic was negotiated immediately and approved under a state law authorizing expedited procedures in special cases.

Consensus building: phase I

The system-design phase began in early December. Clinic staff interviewed over 125 teachers, administrators, Board members, non-instructional personnel, parents, and community representatives. Through individual interviews and focus-group discussions, the staff identified the school community's perceptions and expectations of the district's management system. There were multiple visions of how SBM might fit in Suburban County schools, ranging from giving local schools liberal autonomy on almost all issues to retaining almost all decision-making responsibility at the central or area administrative levels. The bitter antagonism and mistrust between groups and individuals could be seen in their positions on this SBM continuum.

Clinic staff distilled the interview data into a single-text draft and circulated it to all interviewees for review and comment. The Clinic convened additional focus groups, bringing together individuals from different interest groups in order to generate healthy criticism of the draft. After these discussions, an improved draft report was prepared for presentation to the district's administration and Board.

The report recommended, among other things, that an inclusive and collaborative working-group process (Phase II) be established to develop consensus among the divergent interests within the district. Job position and organizational allegiance were the traditional appointing criteria for policy planning in the district. Phase II, however, called for selection of working-group members based on their perspectives on SBM. This change in the way participants were chosen was perhaps the most controversial recommendation in the design and required consultation and reshaping before all groups were in support.

The superintendent and School Board approved the report and its recommendations quickly, partly because they had other, more urgent and controversial matters clamoring for attention, and partly because approval did not commit them to any particular result on SBM.

Consensus building: phase II

As recommended, Phase II included selection of working-group members based on their perspectives on site-based management, rather than on job position and organizational allegiance. Clinic staff were responsible for interviewing applicants for the working group and, with assistance from an advisory committee selected by position and organizational allegiance, for selecting the twenty-five members. Clinic staff worked closely with the associate superintendent to assure meaningful participation by all interests.

The working group had two preliminary get-acquainted meetings prior to a two-day retreat in late March. A two-member Clinic team facilitated the meetings and the retreat. The task at the retreat was to develop an initial draft definition of site-based management. The facilitators prepared an agenda that helped build a common understanding and consensus of governance issues among the twenty-five participants. An important product was an approved set of beliefs and values that any SBM system would need to support.

The Clinic team captured the retreat's work product in a draft document, which was distributed to working-group members one week after the retreat. The working group then held two follow-up sessions, with Clinic facilitation, to edit and improve the document. Consensus among all interests was the goal. Working-group members and the Clinic team jointly conducted focus-group discussions to allow the many school constituencies to comment on, and suggest improvements to, the single-text document. These discussions concluded with two meetings with the district's leadership team, a twenty-member group composed of the top area and central-office administrators.

Finally, the working group met as a group one last time, reviewed all comments and suggestions, and achieved consensus among themselves on a final draft report. The report defined SBM as the Suburban County school community desired, and recommended next steps for implementing the new model.

Seven working-group members, representing the major competing interests in the school community, participated in a Board session where the report was presented, explained, promoted, and defended. Board members noted with surprise the unanimity among the various school constituencies, something that most had never seen before on any issue of this size. Nevertheless, the members were quite divided over the way they would handle this issue at the Board level.

Consensus building: phase III

The administration and School Board had not established before the presentation a process for handling the working-group report on SBM. Board factions were particularly divided in mid-May, and therefore the residual hope among a majority of Board members was that the issue would just fade from view. Three weeks after the presentation, the Board held its annual retreat to review the past year's priorities and set directions for the coming year. The SBM issue came up, and the Board chair scheduled a working session in July to determine district policy on the issue. In an unusual step, the chair requested that a Clinic staff member facilitate the session.

Clinic staff interviewed four people to prepare for the Board meeting: the Board chair, the chair of the Board committee responsible for handling the SBM report, the superintendent, and the associate superintendent. These interviews focused on the working-group report, its recommendations, the different expectations of Board members, and possible expected outcomes. No one considered consensus likely.

Board members worked for two hours at the July session, analyzing the aims of the SBM report, discussing the primary issues for the district, identifying the existing decision-making process in the district, and developing possible options for implementing SBM. At the end of the meeting, to the surprise of most members and observers, the Board arrived at a consensus definition of what SBM meant and the procedures for implementing the policy during the coming year. Although the Board did not endorse the specific recommendations of the working group, the agreement that was reached could never have been achieved without the consensus-building efforts of the prior eight months.

The underlying theory

The Clinic practitioners appear to have applied theory throughout their intervention in this case, from the initial interview with the associate superintendent to the facilitation of the July Board session. Identifying that application, however, is made more difficult by the existence of a number of obstacles. First, the conflict resolution field itself is multidisciplinary, its theory woven with the threads of many other fields, including psychology, sociology, anthropology, political science, international affairs, law, economics, business, and organizational behavior. Second, practitioners often think or plan on a more-or-less intuitive basis, responding to the pressure of circumstances rather than directly applying theory at every step. Therefore, a practitioner's personal comments and written notes may not point toward the theory used.

Third, the most interesting casework may produce little documentary evidence of the complex web of parties, issues, relationships, and interactions that have been the practitioner's daily agenda. The only records of what happened are in the memories of the parties and the practitioner, and each has a separate and equally legitimate perspective on the events that occurred. Finally, confidentiality is a fundamental principle for practitioner involvement in most cases, and the release of factual information, opinions, motivations, and responses, even for research purposes, may not be in the best interests of the parties to the controversy.

An attempt to counter these limiting conditions is reflected in several assumptions underlying this effort to trace theory in the Suburban County schools SBM case. The Conflict Clinic is an organization whose affiliation with George Mason University supports policies that encourage its staff to document decisions and events with an eye to graduate student and faculty research. In addition, I was a member of the practitioner team on this case and therefore bring a more complete understanding of the process than recorded in the documents.

Moreover, confidentiality and protection for the parties is provided by using a pseudonym for the school system and altering several key descriptors that camouflage the situation while not skewing the analysis or evaluation. Finally, I refer below only to the primary conflict resolution theories, rather than try to be fully comprehensive in all relevant fields. The theorists cited here give credit to ideas gathered from many different disciplines. I rely on the reader's review of the bibliographic materials of their works to lead him or her to basic principles in other disciplines.

Joint analysis of the conflict

Complete analysis of the conflict is a fundamental building-block of conflict resolution. Theory here requires a mapping of the conflict, including a complete picture of the dynamics of the parties, their relationships and issues, and the processes being used to maintain or resolve their conflict. Most theorists discuss the importance of defining the problem before trying to find a solution, emphasizing the activities before negotiation actually begins in the problem-solving process (see Carpenter and Kennedy, 1988, pp. 54–60; Fisher with Ury, 1978, pp. 8–11).

Analysis alone, however, is insufficient in conflict-resolving situations. The parties themselves must play an important role in the process if the benefits are to be realized. The conflict resolution practitioner works closely with the parties throughout this early period so that parties can consider the analysis as their own, not the work of an outside consultant. In the school SBM case, Clinic staff not only interviewed community members, but also returned to them to shape and reshape the analysis before the final draft was complete. Because they participated fully in the analysis, community members were engaged in the process of working on the SBM problem, interested in the analytical findings, and eager to pursue the recommended process.

Joint design of the problem-solving process

Forums and processes are usually biased to some degree toward the interests of those who create them. Therefore, conflict resolution theory underscores the need to include all interested parties in designing the process by which they will try to settle their differences. This effort accomplishes many objectives: it encourages 'ownership' and greater participation by parties in the process of resolving the problem, models the kind of behavior that parties will use later in the problem-solving process, builds the positive working relationships that help to create elegant options and implement the chosen solution effectively, and permits outside facilitators to build sufficient credibility to serve in an impartial role (see Laue, Burde, Potapchuk, and Salkoff, 1988, pp. 7–21; Potapchuk, Laue, and Murray, 1990, pp. 22–23).

As is often done, Clinic practitioners combined analysis of the existing problem with design of the process for resolving that problem. Both tasks involved extensive contacts with community members. Even though the selection procedures for the working group were nontraditional and perhaps threatening to the status quo, the community accepted them because community members had already built 'ownership' in the process and confidence in the facilitating team.

Consensus in public policy

In fights over public policy, parties need to work jointly to clarify the problems which have caused controversy and develop agreements on the broad public issues involved. The working group needs to be large enough to reflect the major interests within the community and yet small enough to ensure adequate participation by each representative. Sufficient time must be provided for every working-group member not only to participate in the focused discussions, but also to coordinate at each step with his or her interest constituency. A 'policy dialogue', as it is called by some, brings together many different parties representing multiple interests involved in the conflict, and introduces outside facilitators to encourage constructive discussions about policy issues. Decision-making within the dialogue is by consensus, not by majority vote, status, or position (see Ehrmann and Lesnick, 1988, pp. 93–99).

Besides the two-day retreat, SBM working-group members met another five times over an eight-week period. In between these meetings, Clinic staff encouraged members to meet with their representative groups to receive feedback on the progress of the working group and input on what to do next. A policy dialogue requires time to digest as well as to draft new language, and it includes extensive off-stage as well as on-stage activity.

Facilitated communication

Open, effective communication is essential in developing and maintaining good relationships between parties who are working through important differences. Each needs to assert his or her own perspective clearly and fully, while listening actively to the perspectives of others. In complex public-policy disputes, a skilled facilitator plays a key role in structuring the communication between parties in the most constructive way (see Fisher and Brown, 1988, pp. 84–106; Bolton, 1979, pp. 205–231).

Through two pre-retreat sessions, the Clinic team prepared the retreat agenda closely with the full working-group membership. That agenda was carefully planned to encourage both active listening and clear speaking. During those early sessions, the facilitators modeled the communication behavior that would be the most positive for the group. These skills had also been used during the earlier analysis and design tasks. By its consistent behavior, the Clinic team showed that good communication is the foundation for problem-solving, not a means for manipulation of the issues or domination of the process.

Governance and conflict resolution

Conflict resolution serves as a governance mechanism to respond to changes in political, social, and economic variables within a community. To the extent that the process drives parties to consider the deepest levels of individual and group interests, values and needs, it suggests important institutional changes required to satisfy those needs. The informal process set up to handle particular issues must therefore be linked closely with the traditional decision-making process in the community.

At some point, the community will need to make a decision on what level to accept the results of the informal conflict resolution process. The deeper the level, the more change in the governance structure of the community, and the more difficult that acceptance will become for those holding positions of leadership in the establishment. Decisions about how much to accept are for the community and its decision-makers to make, after full recognition and consideration of the elements of the problem and their impact (see Burton, 1988, pp. 12–23).

In its deliberations and report, the SBM working group raised serious questions about the school district's authoritarian, top-down management structure. The final report recommended a radical change to a more consensus-based philosophy for decision-making at the school, area, and central administrative levels. Although the School Board did not adopt this significant departure from existing practice at its July session, it did accept the legitimacy of the process that raised it. Community members had been able to discuss and propose solutions to seriously threatening issues without destroying the relationships or good programs already in place.

Why theory in practice?

Practitioners have many reasons for placing a high value on having theory to guide their activity. Theories provide the tools with which practitioners attract the parties' acceptance of a nontraditional process. Parties in conflict will turn to someone outside the conflict only if they believe that that person has the capacity to understand the conflict and a contribution to make. An organized and structured approach, an obvious result of theory application, can provide these characteristics.

Practitioners also use theories to build personal credibility and a reputation for competence, both of which are important to performing as an effective third party. Theories provide the patterns that help practitioners: (1) understand the nature of the problems the parties face, (2) educate parties about other ways of seeing their own conflict, (3) motivate parties toward resolving their problems, and (4) establish standards to guide parties through the inevitable stormy waters as the process evolves.

In addition, theories provide a framework for measuring success in process terms when the conflict is concluded and the parties are implementing the resolution. Finally, theory can be easily transferred from practitioner to party, so that those who are faced with systems that generate continuous conflict can develop the knowledge, skills, and confidence necessary to handle problems without seeking outside help.

Using theory in practice, however, does have a potential down-side risk for the intervening third party. Consistent with a 'yin-and-yang' quality of much in conflict resolution, the weakness lies where its message is strongest, in bringing structure to an otherwise unstructured and chaotic factual situation. The presence of relevant theory can lull a practitioner into relying too heavily on the theoretical framework, thereby encouraging one to shape the parties and their conflict to fit the process, rather than the process to the parties and their conflict. Nevertheless, this risk can be lowered or eliminated altogether by a full awareness of the appropriate uses of theory, adequate preparation before any intervention, and acceptance of parties as partners in the design of process. In the final analysis, theory remains the practitioner's best friend.

References

Bolton, R. (1979), *People Skills: How to Assert Yourself, Listen to Others and Resolve Conflicts*, Simon and Shuster, New York.

Burton, J. W. (1988), *Conflict Resolution as a Political System*, Working Paper 1, Center for Conflict Analysis and Resolution, George Mason University, Fairfax, Virginia.

Carpenter, S. L. and Kennedy, W. J. D. (1988), *Managing Public Disputes: A Practical Guide to Handling Conflict and Reaching Agreements*, Jossey-Bass, San Francisco.

Ehrmann, J. R. and Lesnick, M. T. (1988), 'The policy dialogue: Applying mediation to the policy-making process', *Mediation Quarterly*, 20, pp. 93–99.

Fisher, R. and Brown, S. (1988), *Getting Together: Building Relationships as We Negotiate*, Houghton Mifflin, Boston.

Fisher, R. with Ury, W. (1978), *International Mediation: A Working Guide for Practitioners*, Harvard Negotiation Project, Cambridge, Massachusetts.

Laue, J. H., Burde, S., Potapchuk, W., and Salkoff, M. (1988), 'Getting to the table: Three paths', *Mediation Quarterly*, 20, pp. 7–21.

Potapchuk, W. R., Laue, J. H., and Murray, J. S. (1990), *Getting to the Table: A Guide for Senior Managers*, IWR Working Paper, 90-ADR-WP-3, U.S. Army Corps of Engineers.

From theory to practice in environmental dispute resolution: negotiating the transition

It is of great professional pleasure to me to observe the proliferation of writing on conflict analysis and resolution in the last five to ten years.[1] This literature offers an invaluable foundation upon which academicians and practitioners in the field can further develop their conceptual understanding of conflict and their skills in facilitating its durable resolution.

To date, however, there has been insufficient integration between this evolving body of theory and the intervention decisions practitioners are making in the field.[2] I attribute this problem to three impediments: (a) the still nascent state of market development for conflict analysis and resolution services; (b) related differences in the organizational cultures of academic institutions and entrepreneurial practitioner organizations; and (c) the lagtime in developing appropriate methods of training graduate students for careers in this rapidly evolving profession.

While all three of these impediments warrant concerted attention, for purposes of this chapter I wish to focus on ways of addressing only the third — how to integrate theory and practical skills in training new conflict resolution professionals. Even more specifically, I have addressed my remarks to those wishing to focus on environmental dispute resolution because that is the specialty in which I have most experience. Moreover, my professional experience has been primarily on a fee-for-services basis, and therefore my remarks will have most relevance to individuals planning careers as practitioners working in a market-driven financial context (as distinct from positions in the government or academia in the United States or work in non-capitalist countries). I also wish to acknowledge at the outset of this chapter that most of my professional experience has been in the United States, although I have participated in dispute resolution projects involving citizens of seven former Soviet republics as well as Lebanon. I will defer to readers of other nations, cultures, and professional specialties to determine which, if any, portions of my advice apply more broadly, and I would welcome comments in this regard.

In formulating my thoughts on what students of dispute resolution need to know to make a living in the environmental dispute resolution niche in the United States, I draw primarily from the experience I gained in hiring, training, and supervising twenty-five graduate students of conflict analysis and resolution to assist me in conducting various dispute resolution projects over the year and a half that I was an Associate with the Conflict Clinic, Inc. at George Mason University. In addition, I draw from my own academic training under Dr. Patricia Bidol, then of the University of Michigan's School of Natural Resources, and seven years of professional experience as an environmental dispute resolution practitioner. However, for purposes of this chapter, I will use the term 'student' to apply to any individual seeking to develop a career in environmental dispute resolution, whether or not he or she is formally enrolled in an academic institution.

Based on my experience, I suggest that individuals serious about becoming practicing environmental dispute resolution specialists should develop:

(a) some familiarity with the substantive issues that arise in environmental disputes;
(b) an understanding of the function of conflict in society, and when collaborative dispute resolution approaches are appropriate and when they are not;[3]
(c) familiarity with the range of dispute resolution techniques available for addressing environmental conflicts, and when each of them is appropriate;
(d) the ability to interview disputants, design joint problem-solving processes, facilitate meetings, design and conduct interactive training workshops, and evaluate project effectiveness;
(e) marketing and proposal-writing skills;
(f) tools for managing time and stress;
(g) the ability to work effectively independently or as a team member;
(h) an understanding of the professional ethics applicable to dispute resolution specialists;
(i) an understanding of themselves within the context of the cultures and identity groups in which they have developed as individuals, and an ability to communicate effectively with those who come from different backgrounds; and
(j) determination, resourcefulness, and networking skills they will need to draw upon to continue their professional development throughout their careers as dispute resolution specialists.

In the remainder of this chapter, I will discuss these skills in more detail, along with my rationale for prescribing their development. Table 16.1 identifies written sources in which interested individuals may find information pertinent to many of these skill areas.

Table 16.1

ENVIRONMENTAL DISPUTE RESOLUTION (EDR) REFERENCES BY TOPIC
(See 'References' section for code to citations in left column.)

	EDR	Anlys	Tchniqs	Instnlzg	Cases	Ethcs	X-Cult	Trng	Eval
1)									×
2)			×	×		×			
3)	×				×				
4)			×						
5)	×								
6)						×			
7)	×								
8)	×	×		×					
9)	×	×			×				
10)	×		×	×	×				
11)							×		
12)	×								
13)	×								
14)	×				×				
15)			×						
16)				×					
17)	×								
18)			×						
19)	×								
20)							×		
21)							×		
22)			×						
23)	×	×		×					
24)	×	×			×				
25)									×
26)	×								
27)	×								
28)	×	×	×						
29)			×						
30)	×								
31)							×		
32)		×				×			
33)								×	
34)									×
35)					×				
36)							×		
37)								×	
38)						×			
39)	×			×				×	
40)						×			
41)			×						
42)					×				
43)			×		×				
44)	×				×				
45)								×	
46)				×	×				

Legend for Table 16.1

EDR = Environmental dispute resolution in general.
Anlys = Conflict analysis.
Tchniqs = Dispute resolution techniques.
Instnlzg = Institutionalization of collaborative dispute resolution techniques.
Cases = Case studies of collaborative dispute resolution.
Ethcs = Ethical considerations in the use of dispute resolution.
X-Cult = Cross-cultural dynamics in the development and/or resolution of disputes.
Trng = Training people to use collaborative dispute resolution.
Eval = Evaluation of dispute resolution programs.

Familiarity with substantive issues arising in environmental disputes

There is a wide range of thought regarding how much substantive knowledge an intervenor should have. I agree with Cormick (1980) that 'expert' status pertaining to the issues of contention in a particular environmental dispute is likely to be counter-productive because the intervenor is too likely to step over the line into the realm of the technical expert. However, I have found that the highly technical nature of many disputes over environmental quality and natural-resource management calls for intervenors who are at least somewhat familiar with the substantive issues under discussion.

My rule of thumb is that impartial intervenors in environmental disputes should be familiar enough with the substantive issues that their level of technical understanding does not impede discussions. Individuals with a bachelor's or master's degree in environmental studies or natural-resource management, in addition to training in dispute resolution, will have an excellent foundation for an environmental dispute resolution career. Work experience with an organization that tends to become involved in environmental disputes would offer an alternative path to gaining this level of familiarity with environmental issues.

Whether students of dispute resolution gain their knowledge of environmental issues experientially, academically, or through a combination of pathways, they will also need to plan on several hours of background reading related to a particular dispute to effectively facilitate discussions involving a specific set of technical issues. Because environmental disputes in the United States are subject to a substantial volume of federal and state legislation, regulation, and administrative procedure, this pre-intervention reading should include a review of pertinent sections of applicable laws and agency policies and procedures. (*U.S. Environmental Laws* (Bureau of National Affairs, 1986) provides a helpful overview of federal environmental legislation.) The practitioner's background reading should also include any issue or position papers about which discussions between stakeholder groups occurred prior to the request for an impartial intervenor.

   The reader should focus on becoming oriented to: (a) the legal and substantive context of the dispute; (b) the process that would be used to resolve the dispute if the negotiated approach fails (SPIDR, 1991b); (c) the legal standards that would apply if the disputants took their dispute to court (ibid.); and (d) technical terms likely to arise during stakeholder discussions. While the practitioner should certainly not attempt to develop substantive expertise through this reading, he or she should develop a feel for issues regarding which stakeholders may need to consult a technical or legal expert.

Understanding function of conflict in society and when collaborative conflict resolution approaches may be appropriate

Environmental conflicts often involve parties with vastly different levels and types of power with which to affect the outcome of a dispute.[4] While the larger environmental groups have, over the last two decades, professionalized their fundraising and lobbying skills and learned to wield the power of the media and of environmental legislation, many environmental disputes still involve grassroots environmental and citizens' groups with comparatively little clout compared to industry groups and public agencies with jurisdiction over the dispute. Moreover, it appears that an increasing number of environmental disputes will involve the power dynamics associated with racial differences (Commission for Racial Justice, 1987).

   Numerous writers have pointed out that, as a consequence of such power differences, the less powerful parties may find that a conflict-generating strategy will serve their interests more effectively than would negotiations aimed at conflict resolution. (See, for example, Cormick,1980, and Crowfoot, 1980.) Students of dispute resolution should understand that it is fully consistent with the role of the impartial intervenor to assist stakeholders in asking the right questions in their analyses of a possible negotiation strategy. The intervenor's job may include: (a) raising the possibility of negotiations (Murray, 1984); (b) analyzing a conflict to determine whether a collaborative approach would be appropriate; (c) ensuring that each stakeholder has analyzed the dispute from his or her perspective to determine whether a collaborative approach would be the most effective way to serve his or her interests (Cormick, 1980; Fisher and Ury, 1984); and/or (d) helping parties identify and arrange the conditions necessary for all key stakeholders to enter negotiations (Laue *et al.*, 1988).[5] The up-and-coming cohort of environmental dispute resolution specialists need to know, however, that the intervenor's role should under no circumstances include persuading a party to enter negotiations if he or she has determined that negotiations would not be in his or her best interest.

Familiarity with range of dispute resolution techniques available and when each may be appropriate

Those preparing for careers as environmental dispute resolution practitioners must, of course, be familiar with the range of dispute resolution techniques that stakeholders can use to resolve environmental conflicts. These include, but are not limited to, conflict resolution skills training, 'neutral fact-finding', facilitation, mediation, arbitration, mini-trials, the use of settlement judges, and litigation (Millhauser and Pou, 1987; Pritzker and Dalton, 1990).[6] Practitioners-to-be should be forewarned that senior practitioners within the environmental dispute resolution field differ considerably in their terminology, and the differences across specialties and between practitioners and theoreticians differ even more significantly. (See, for example, the different definitions of 'mediation' held by Cormick, 1980, and Burton, 1987.)

Few practitioners are well-versed in all of the above techniques, but they should be able to explain to disputants what each technique is and when it is appropriate. It is essential that practitioners know their own strengths and limitations, and be able and willing to refer clients to other specialists when appropriate.

Table 16.1 identifies written sources dispute resolution students may turn to in an effort to familiarize themselves with the range of environmental dispute resolution techniques available. In addition to reading about these techniques, however, students need practice in their application. Ideally, each student of conflict resolution should take a 3–4-month course devoted primarily to trying out the various techniques available on one another.[7] The course might also introduce concepts of process design, and the final exam could require participants to select, tailor, or develop a dispute resolution approach for a hypothetical dispute.

Would-be practitioners should also look for internship or volunteer opportunities to gain real-life experience with one or more dispute resolution techniques. To the extent that internship or volunteer opportunities are available with environmental dispute resolution specialists, I strongly recommend that individuals seeking careers in this specialty take advantage of them, both to develop a realistic perspective of the arena in which they will be operating and to develop the professional contacts essential for future employment prospects.

However, because environmental disputes tend to involve very high stakes (e.g., public health, the viability of an industry, ecosystem stability, large sums of money, careers, etc.), it is unrealistic to seek one's first 'hands-on' experience as an impartial intervenor in an environmental conflict. Community mediation centers are a more probable source of opportunities, often offering both training and mentorship. Despite the fact that the nature of the disputes are quite different, such experience can be invaluable in 'getting a foot in the door' in the environmental field because it indicates to employers that the student has a certain amount of training, practice, and commitment.

Ability to conduct interviews, design joint problem-solving processes, facilitate meetings, design and conduct workshops, and evaluate project effectiveness

In addition to a conceptual understanding of the universe of dispute resolution techniques, students of environmental conflict analysis and resolution need to develop a functional level of skill in the following areas: (a) stakeholder interviewing; (b) design of joint problem-solving processes; (c) meeting facilitation; (d) the design and implementation of interactive training workshops; and (e) project evaluation. Together, these represent what I would think of as the 'starter set' of skills for the impartial intervenor.

The vast majority of dispute resolution projects with which I have been involved have required interviewing. As with many dispute resolution concepts and techniques, it seems straightforward, but there are subtleties to it that are critical for the usefulness of the results. I recommend that, rather than simply reading about or listening to instructions on how interviews should be done, students should have an opportunity to conduct one or more interviews and receive feedback on them from experienced practitioners and their peers. This could be done in a classroom 'fishbowl' format or by submitting a write-up of an interview for critique.[8] Students can be expected to need coaching on: (a) improving their powers of observation and data-recording; (b) taking responsibility for getting useful data without losing methodological consistency; (c) coping with time limits; and (d) efficient ways of organizing and writing up data.

After mastering interviewing skills, students should be coached through a process design. Many writers have discussed variables to be considered in designing dispute resolution processes (see, for example, Fisher, 1983, and Moore, 1986). Coaching in process design should also include careful attention to the writing and verbal communication skills involved in presenting a draft process design to stakeholders.

A good grounding in both qualitative and quantitative research methods will help new practitioners learn how to design effective dispute resolution processes that will hold up to professional evaluation. Miles and Huberman's 1984 text, *Qualitative Data Analysis: A Sourcebook of New Methods*, is excellent for qualitative approaches. *A Handbook of Biological Investigation* (Ambrose and Ambrose, 1981) is an unusually comprehensible statistics reference which biologists and non-biologists alike should find helpful for quantitative approaches.

Facilitation skills are probably the most-used skills of the impartial intervenor, coming into play in handling disputes from divorces to international natural-resource-management conflicts. Reading about facilitation makes it sound easy (Doyle and Straus, 1984), and many new practitioners perceive themselves to be 'naturals' at it. However, when faced with a roomful of wary or hostile disputants and an agenda full of technical issues, what seemed easy when read as a homework assignment can become overwhelming in the flesh.

Dispute resolution practitioners need a solid grounding in group dynamics (see Mills, 1984, and discussion of the National Training Labs below) and they need to practice facilitation skills. They can do this in the classroom through a fishbowl approach, in fulfilling team projects assigned as part of class requirements, and/or through participation in extra-curricular activities such as student interest groups. Coaching should include: (a) room set-up; (b) flip-chart recording; (c) concisely explaining the process to be used; (d) establishing and enforcing ground rules; (e) paraphrasing and reframing dialogue without losing its meaning; (f) staying impartial; (g) incorporating procedural feedback while avoiding process battles; (h) knowing when and how to encourage discussion and when and how to facilitate closure; and (i) managing time effectively. Only through such practice can new practitioners internalize what it means to be impartial and learn their own strengths and weaknesses as facilitators.

The ability to design and conduct effective trainings in conflict resolution skills is valuable in several ways. First, where disputants have vastly different levels of experience with negotiations, it may be critical to the success of negotiations to provide skills training to the less-experienced negotiators. Second, stakeholders who agree to go through a *joint* training may find it a useful forum in which to float conciliatory gestures. Third, training is the most vital step in helping disputants strengthen their own capacities for resolving conflicts constructively on their own; this is particularly important when the intervenor is working with disputants from a culture different from his or her own, where disputants may have their own approach to dispute resolution (which Avruch and Black in Chapter 9 refer to as 'ethnopraxis') that they simply want to augment, rather than replace. Finally, training often constitutes the bread and butter of market-based practitioner groups.

The skills involved in designing and conducting effective conflict resolution training are quite different from those involved in teaching in an academic setting. Those attending trainings tend to be established professionals looking for pragmatic ways to improve their effectiveness on the job. The trainer must translate theory into exciting, 'bite-sized' pieces, facilitate participants' practice in applying theory to 'back-home' problems, and provide constructive, insightful feedback.

Individuals seeking to develop conflict resolution training skills may find Smith and Christopher (1987) and Robinson and Robinson (1989) helpful. In addition, participation in the workshops and courses sponsored by the National Training Labs (NTL), based in Alexandria, Virginia, offers a very effective way to learn training skills. NTL's eighteen-month, semi-residential course for graduate students who wish to design and conduct trainings for adult learners may be particularly relevant.

Finally, although evaluation is not used as often as it should be, I have included it in my recommended 'starter set' for several reasons. First, I believe the field of dispute resolution needs more evaluation to facilitate its maturation. Project and program evaluation offer an under-utilized potential for developing theory based in the reality of the disputant's world. Second, evaluation is almost always required by funders as a way of ensuring accountability. Third, on the individual level, evaluating our projects is essential if we are to continually improve our effectiveness as impartial intervenors. Therefore, practitioners need to learn the basic concepts underlying evaluation (see, for example, Rossi and Freeman, 1982); their education should include exposure to a variety of ways in which evaluation has been done in the dispute resolution field, from monthly progress reports to case studies to statistically oriented analyses (see, for example, Buckle and Thomas-Buckle, 1986).

Marketing and proposal writing skills

Individuals preparing to practice in the environmental dispute resolution field on a fee-for-services basis will need to develop the skills involved in marketing dispute resolution services and responding to service users' needs with sensitivity and professionalism. They must learn to describe for potential clients in pragmatic and concise terms: (a) the nature of the services they offer; (b) when and why impartial dispute resolution services are useful and when they are not; (c) how these services might be applied to the particular dispute facing the potential clients; and (d) what the anticipated costs and benefits to each client might be if impartial dispute resolution services are used.

Should the potential clients express an interest in further exploring the use of impartial dispute resolution services, the practitioner must be able to write a proposal and develop a detailed budget for the project envisioned. She or he must then be prepared to discuss the proposal orally, modifying it in consultation with the clients.

In all of these discussions, the practitioner must be mindful of the fact that, when providing impartial dispute resolution services, the party or parties who pay for the services may not be the only 'client'. Clients who are members of organizations that regularly employ contractors to perform technical work may be inclined to think that 'he who pays the piper calls the tune'. However, the practitioner must ensure that each party involved understands that an impartial intervenor is accountable to *all* participants in the problem-solving effort. When only one of the stakeholders is paying for dispute resolution services, it may be appropriate to involve the other stakeholders in designing the particulars of the funding mechanism to ensure that the funder does not have undue power over the progress of the problem-solving effort.

Time- and stress-management skills

Making a living in environmental dispute resolution on a fee-for-services basis entails a very stressful lifestyle. It is extremely difficult to manage the pace of projects. A disputant calling for assistance is rarely willing to wait more than a week before meeting with the practitioner to get progress started. Once the process is under way, it tends to acquire a momentum of its own. Typically, an environmental dispute resolution specialist is juggling four or five projects at any given time. Moreover, neither the projects nor the hours fall in a predictable pattern. The hours tend to be long and demanding, and the practitioner should be prepared for frequent travel.

Therefore, I urge practitioners-to-be to take proactive steps to deal with the inevitable stresses of this fascinating profession by learning and using the tools of time and stress management. Tools that I have found to be important at various times include learning to: (a) accurately assess the time a particular task will require; (b) prioritize projects; (c) set manageable daily objectives; (d) screen calls; (e) say 'no' if I do not have time; (f) ask for help when I find myself overloaded, and ask early enough that others can do something to help; and (g) schedule in exercise and 'fun time' when work threatens to consume every free minute.

Ability to work effectively independently or as a team member

Many, if not most, environmental dispute resolution projects are conducted by a team of intervenors, rather than by a sole practitioner. Therefore, new practitioners need to learn the skills involved in developing productive teams. Project 'kick-off' meetings should include discussion of the stakeholders' needs and project objectives, each team member's role, the procedures the team will use for communication, coordination, and internal problem-solving, and any relationship issues that need attention. If the team leader does not bring these topics up, junior members of the team can certainly do so (in a facilitative way). Team members who can communicate their strengths and weaknesses, ask for and give support where needed, and give and receive honest feedback will refine their practitioner competencies much more quickly.

At the same time, individual team members may be expected to work independently a good portion of the time, and need to be prepared to do so effectively. Junior members of the intervention team can distinguish themselves by keeping their eyes on the stakeholders' goal, and sharing responsibility for helping the stakeholders attain their goal, rather than simply doing what the team leader has asked. As tennis player Billie Jean King says, 'You have to want the ball' to excel. In the midst of a dispute resolution intervention – whether it be a training or a mediation – 'wanting the ball' translates into an intense concentration on: (a) the needs of the participants; (b) the support needed by other members of the intervention team; and (c) how the process is working and what possible adjustments are required.

241

This willingness to share responsibility for the project's success must be tempered with judiciousness about how much improvisation can be done without the clearance of the project leader. There may be methodological considerations that limit the extent of improvisation possible (Miles and Huberman, 1984). The team-building discussion that I recommend for the outset of a project should include an explicit discussion of the amount of latitude for improvisation afforded each team member.

Understanding of the professional ethics applicable to dispute resolution specialists

The individual preparing for a career as an impartial intervenor in environmental disputes must have a thorough grounding in the ethics of the profession. She or he should be familiar with the ethical standards of professional responsibility published by the Society of Professionals in Dispute Resolution (SPIDR) in 1991. The subject of professional ethics for conflict resolution practitioners is also addressed by Bacon and Wheeler (1984), Raiffa (1982), and Burton (1987), among others.

However, it is one thing to read a professional code of ethics and another thing to understand and apply that code in: (a) recognizing and disclosing potential conflicts of interest; (b) defining, communicating, and adhering to an appropriate role for an impartial intervenor; and (c) protecting confidentiality where necessary. Students need to explore the implications of the professional codes of ethics discussed in the sources mentioned above through role-play and discussion facilitated by established practitioners.

Understanding one's self within cultural context and ability to communicate effectively with those from different cultures

Intervenors with any hope of being truly impartial in environmental disputes must put in the effort to identify the cultural values, biases, and assumptions they grew up with.[9] Only by raising his or her personal and cultural 'baggage' to an explicit level can an intervenor exercise the conscious control over his or her attitudes necessary to breathe life into the notion of impartiality.

Despite the fact that the intervenor generally stays out of the substance of stakeholder dialogue, the intervenor's role carries a significant amount of power. Stakeholders put a tremendous amount of trust in intervenors precisely because we have trained ourselves not to exhibit the blatant manifestations of bias. They entrust us with a myriad of subtle, but powerful, decisions, such as who to call on in discussions, in what order, and how long to spend discussing a particular issue. Decisions such as these, and our body language in executing them, are vulnerable to distortion in ways that may influence: (a) stakeholders' sense of validation from the intervenor and thus their continued interest in participating; and (b) the respect one stakeholder accords another, and thus the outcome of the dispute.

Cultural 'baggage' also comes into play when practitioners seek to establish their credibility with potential clients. White males still appear to be making the majority of environmental policy decisions in the United States, and those who come from different backgrounds can expect to encounter the same subtle barriers to acceptance here as elsewhere. These barriers are particularly challenging in a field where the hiring decision is of necessity highly subjective. My advice is to: (a) be sure you prepare for meetings; (b) mention your credentials if it seems appropriate; (c) demonstrate your listening skills and facilitative interventions, even in preliminary discussions with the client; (d) display your resourcefulness and creativity as an intervenor; and (e) network with colleagues for support, advice, and professional opportunities.

I strongly recommend that all conflict resolution practitioners be required to participate in an intensive (multi-day) values-clarification/prejudice-reduction workshop prior to entering practice. NTL offers such workshops, as does the Equity Institute in San Francisco. Written sources with which students of conflict resolution may want to familiarize themselves include Kochman (1981), Gudykunst and Kim (1984), and Tannen (1990).

Determination, resourcefulness, and networking skills

Would-be practitioners of environmental dispute resolution must come to grips with the existence of competition for the 'right' to help resolve such disputes. The field of environmental dispute resolution is young (Bingham, 1986), and the market for impartial dispute resolution services still quite underdeveloped. The supply of service-providers appears to greatly exceed the number of disputants aware of our services and willing and able to pay for them.

Thus, individuals planning careers in environmental dispute resolution must pursue their professional development with determination, humility, and an eye out for uncharted opportunities. On more than one occasion, I have heard new practitioners express resentment upon discovering that established practitioners offer few opportunities for bringing junior practitioners aboard. They have expressed disillusionment in light of the fact that the focus of our professional services is helping people work together collaboratively.

However, collaboration rarely happens because it is the 'right' thing to do – it happens when it is in the best interest of all concerned (Cormick, 1980). The career of the dispute resolution professional hinges on the character of the individual(s) involved, in addition to the processes she or he designs and manages. As a result, established practitioners are understandably careful about who they team with and/or employ. Would-be practitioners need to understand this if they are to persuade established practitioners to include them on intervention teams. In addition to letting established practitioners know of her or his availability, a new practitioner must demonstrate to the project leader how she or he would enhance a particular project.

When a new practitioner secures an opportunity to apprentice to an established practitioner, she or he should be one hundred percent reliable in following through on commitments. The next professional opportunity for the new practitioner, as well as for the senior practitioners on the team, will depend on disputants' perceptions of: (a) team members' professionalism, integrity, and style; and (b) whether tangible results were achieved in a reasonable time through the problem-solving process.

Finally, individuals developing careers as dispute resolution practitioners should be aware of key resources that will help them make their professional development a lifelong source of stimulation and satisfaction. For networking opportunities, they should consider joining the Society of Professionals in Dispute Resolution (SPIDR), the Consortium on Peace Research, Education, and Development (COPRED) and/or the National Conference on Peace-making and Conflict Resolution (NCPCR). They may find a subscription to ConflictNet, a national and international electronic networking system for conflict resolution professionals, a cost-effective investment. Regular perusal of journals such as *Mediation Quarterly* and *The Negotiation Journal* is a good habit to develop, along with a selection of organizational newsletters, such as *Resolve* (put out by the Conservation Foundation in Washington, D.C.) and *Consensus* (put out by the Harvard Program on Negotiation).

I would like to conclude by expressing my heartfelt appreciation to the students with whom I have worked at George Mason University's Institute for Conflict Analysis and Resolution for their assistance and thought-provoking questions, and to Dr. Patricia Bidol for her help with my own transition from academia to practice.

Notes

1. Throughout this paper, I will use the terms 'dispute' and 'conflict' interchangeably. While I recognize that some theoreticians make a distinction between these terms on the basis of the depth, significance, and negotiability of the issues involved (Burton, 1988), my experience suggests that the line between a 'dispute' and a 'conflict' is exceedingly nebulous, particularly where natural-resource management and environmental-quality issues are concerned. Moreover, the intervenor's route to the fundamental issues at stake often begins with the more superficial issues.

2. I use the term 'intervention' to refer to actions taken by dispute resolution specialists in general without specifying which technique (e.g., mediation) the specialist is employing. I have borrowed the term from Cormick (1980), who introduced the related term 'intervenor' as an alternative to the popularly used term 'neutral' to convey, among other things, the belief that the dispute resolution practitioner's role is not a 'neutral' one because practitioners seek to alter the dynamics between stakeholders.

3. I use the term 'collaborate' to refer to an approach to negotiations in which stakeholders voluntarily join forces to solve a mutual problem. I do not use this term to mean 'coerce', although it is sometimes inaccurately translated as such when converting from English into other languages.
4. Public agencies typically hold power in the form of decision-making authority, access to essential information, and staffs of technical and legal experts. Industry groups have historically had more financial resources at their disposal than have environmental groups.
5. Alternative frameworks for analyzing environmental conflicts can be found in the following sources: Cormick (1980); Crowfoot (1980); Carnduff and Clark (1980); Marcus and Emrich (1981); Mernitz (1981); Raiffa (1982); Fisher and Ury (1984); and Carpenter and Kennedy (1988).
6. Note 2 above notwithstanding, I use the term 'neutral fact-finding' here to refer to data collection and analysis by an impartial party because this phrase has become an established term of art among environmental dispute resolution practitioners in the United States.
7. University teachers interested in developing dispute resolution courses may wish to review 'Competencies for Mediators of Complex Multi-Party Disputes' (SPIDR, 1991b) in planning their courses' coverage.
8. The term 'fishbowl' refers to a training exercise in which a hypothetical conflict scenario is enacted by several people who are surrounded by a circle of non-participating observers. This is usually followed by a full group discussion of the dynamics experienced and observed.
9. By 'culture', I mean 'a shared way of viewing and practicing life' (Simons, 1989). Thus, I include in the term identity group bonds defined by race and ethnicity, gender, sexual orientation, physical ability, religion, age, and profession.

References*

Ambrose, H. W., III and Ambrose, K. P. (1981), *A Handbook of Biological Investigation*, Hunter Textbooks, Winston-Salem, North Carolina. (1)

Bacon, L. S. and Wheeler, M. (1984), *Environmental Dispute Resolution*, Plenum Press, New York. (2)

Bingham, G. (1986), *Resolving Environmental Disputes: A Decade of Experience*, The Conservation Foundation, Washington, D.C. (3)

Buckle, L. G. and Thomas-Buckle, S. R. (1986), 'Placing environmental mediation in context: Lessons from 'failed' mediations', *Environmental Impact Assessment Review*, 6, pp. 55–70. (4)

Bureau of National Affairs Editorial Staff (1986), *U.S. Environmental Laws*, Bureau of National Affairs, Inc., Washington, D.C. (5)

Burton, J. (1987), *Resolving Deep-Rooted Conflict: A Handbook*, University Press of America, Lanham, Maryland, pp. 27–28. (6)

Burton, J. (1988) 'Conflict resolution as a political system', (Working Paper 1), Center for Conflict Analysis and Resolution, George Mason University, Fairfax, Virginia, p. 2. (7)

Carnduff, S. B. and Clark, P. B. (1980), 'Selected readings on conflict management', prepared in association with the American Arbitration Association and Clark-McClennon Associates; sponsored by the Council on Environmental Quality, U.S.

Geological Survey, and U.S. Department of the Interior, Heritage Conservation and Recreation Service, Washington, D.C. (8)

Carpenter, S. L. and Kennedy, W. J. D. (1988), *Managing Public Disputes*, Jossey-Bass, San Francisco, California. (9)

Clark, P. B. and Emrich, W. M. (1980), 'New tools for resolving environmental disputes: Introducing federal agencies to environmental mediation and related techniques', prepared for U.S. Council on Environmental Quality and U.S. Geological Survey, Washington, D.C. (10)

Commission for Racial Justice (1987), *Toxic Wastes and Race in the United States: A National Report on the Racial and Socio-Economic Characteristics of Communities with Hazardous Waste Sites*, United Church of Christ, New York. (11)

Cormick, G. W. (1980), 'The "theory" and practice of environmental mediation', *The Environmental Professional*, 2, pp. 24–33. (12)

Crowfoot, J. E. (1980), 'Negotiations: An effective tool for citizen organizations?', *NRAG Papers*, Northern Rockies Action Group, Helena, Montana. (13)

Crowfoot, J. E. and Wondolleck, J. M. (1990), *Environmental Disputes: Community Involvement in Conflict Resolution*, Island Press, Washington, D.C. (14)

Doyle, M. and Straus, D. (1984), *How to Make Meetings Work*, Berkley, New York. (15)

Fisher, G. K. (1980), 'The Colorado Joint Review Process – a better way', unpublished paper for Conference on Environmental Permitting sponsored by National Bureau of Standards, Washington, D.C. (16)

Fisher, R. (1983), 'Third party consultation as a method of intergroup conflict resolution: A review of studies', *Journal of Conflict Resolution*, 27, No. 2, pp. 301–334. (17)

Fisher, R. and Ury, W. (1984), *Getting to Yes: Negotiating Agreement Without Giving In*, Penguin, New York. (18)

Gladwin, T. N. (1980), 'Patterns of environmental conflict over industrial facilities in the United States, 1970–78', *Natural Resources Journal*, 20, pp. 243–274. (19)

Gudykunst, W. B. and Kim, Y. Y. (1984), *Communicating with Strangers: An Approach to Intercultural Communication*, Random House, New York. (20)

Kochman, T. (1981), *Black and White Styles in Conflict*, University of Chicago Press, Chicago. (21)

Laue, J. H., Burde, S., Potapchuk, W., and Salkoff, M. (1988), 'Getting to the table: Three paths', *Mediation Quarterly*, No. 20, Jossey-Bass, San Francisco, California. (22)

Marcus, P. A. and Emrich, W. M. (eds) (1981), 'Environmental conflict management: Working paper series', prepared in association with the American Arbitration Association and Clark-McGlennon Associates; sponsored by the U.S. Council on Environmental Quality and the U.S Geological Survey, Washington, D.C. (23)

Mernitz, S. (1981), *Mediation of Environmental Disputes: A Sourcebook*, Praeger, New York. (24)

Miles, M. B. and Huberman, A. M. (1984), *Qualitative Data Analysis: A Sourcebook of New Methods*, Sage, Beverly Hills, California. (25)

Millhauser, M. S. and Pou, C. with the assistance of Bayles, L. A. and Stockton, D. M. (1987), *Sourcebook: Federal Agency Use of Alternative Means of Dispute Resolution*, Administrative Conference of the U.S., Washington, D.C. (26)

Mills, T.M. (1984), *The Sociology of Small Groups*, 2nd edition, Prentice-Hall, Inc., Englewood Cliffs, New Jersey. (27)

Moore, C.W. (1986), *The Mediation Process: Practical Strategies for Resolving Conflict*, Jossey-Bass, San Francisco. (28)

Murray, J.S. (1984), 'Third-party intervention: Successful entry for the uninvited', *Albany Law Review*, 48, pp.573–613. (29)

Pritzker, D.M. and Dalton, D.S. (1990), *Negotiated Rulemaking Sourcebook*, Administrative Conference of the United States, Washington, D.C. (30)

Program on Conflict Resolution (1990), *Researching Disputes across Cultures and Institutions*, University of Hawaii at Manoa, Honolulu, Hawaii. (31)

Raiffa, H. (1982), 'Ethical and moral issues', *The Art and Science of Negotiation*, Harvard University Press, Cambridge, Massachusetts, pp.344–355. (32)

Robinson, D.G. and Robinson, J.C. (1989), *Training for Impact*, Jossey-Bass, San Francisco. (33)

Rossi, P.H. and Freeman, H.E. in collaboration with Rosenbaum, S. (1982), *Evaluation: A Systematic Approach*, 2nd edition, Sage, Beverly Hills, California. (34)

Schneider, P. and Sachs, A. (1983), 'The Patuxent River Clean-up Agreement', *The Environmental Forum*, pp.39–43. (35)

Simons, G. (1989), *Working Together: How to Become More Effective in a Multicultural Organization*, Crisp, Los Altos, California. (36)

Smith, L.E. and Christopher, E.M. (1987), *Leadership Training through Gaming: Power, People, and Problem-Solving*, Kogan Page, London and Nichols, New York. (37)

SPIDR (1991a), Society of Professionals in Dispute Resolution, 'Ethical standards of professional responsibility', Washington, D.C. (38)

SPIDR (1991b), Society of Professionals in Dispute Resolution, 'Competencies for mediators of complex, multi-party disputes', July 1991 Discussion Draft, developed by Environmental/Public Disputes Sector, Washington, D.C. (39)

Susskind, L.E. (1981), 'Environmental mediation and the accountability problem', *Vermont Law Review*, 6, No. 1. (40)

Susskind, L.E. (1983), 'The uses of negotiation and mediation in environmental impact assessment', in A. Porter and F. Rossini, eds, *Integrated Impact Assessment*, Westview Press, Boulder, Colorado. (41)

Susskind, L. (1981), 'Citizen participation and consensus building in land use planning: A case study', in J. Deneufville, ed., *The Land Use Policy Debate in America*, Plenum Press, New York. (42)

Susskind, L., Bacon, L., and Wheeler, M. (eds) (1983), *Resolving Environmental Regulatory Disputes*, prepared for the United States Environmental Protection Agency, Schenkman Publishing Company, Cambridge, Massachusetts. (43)

Talbot, A.R. (1983), *Settling Things: Six Case Studies in Environmental Mediation*, The Conservation Foundation, Washington D.C. (44)

Tannen, D. (1990), *You Just Don't Understand: Women and Men in Conversation*, William Morrow, New York. (45)

Wondolleck, J.M. (1988), *Public Lands Conflict and Resolution: Managing National Forest Disputes*, Plenum Press, New York. (46)

* Parenthetical numbers provide key to reading Table 16.1 in text.

International conference diplomacy: Four principles

International Conference Diplomacy, in my use of the term, refers to international, intergovernmental, multilateral conferences, organized by the secretariats of international organizations, at the behest of member states. The United Nations system, consisting of some thirty-five different organizations, convenes the majority of these conferences. The U.S. State Department, for example, sends official, governmental delegations to over 1000 multilateral conferences a year. This means that some 5000 Americans have an opportunity each year to practice their diplomatic skills in this rather unusual environment. The present chapter takes several aspects of conflict resolution theory, such as the need for small-group interaction to build consensus, and applies these theories to the practical world of international diplomacy.

Unfortunately, because of the rapid turnover in assignments in the U.S. government, approximately twenty-five percent of those Americans selected each year to attend an international conference are attending their first meeting. They enter this new world with little idea as to how international conferences actually work. In an effort to help this situation I developed, several years ago, a practical guide for newcomers to multilateral diplomacy (McDonald, 1984).

It should be recognized that bilateral negotiations and multilateral negotiations are each quite different and require different skills. In the diplomatic sense, bilateral negotiations involve representatives from two countries sitting down and talking. This is what most diplomats normally do throughout their careers. Multilateral negotiations involve diplomatic interaction between official representatives of three or more countries. Aside from the many global and regional organizations within the UN system this would include such regional organizations as the North Atlantic Treaty Organization, Organization for Economic Co-operation and Development, Organization of American States, Inter American Development Bank, Organization of African Unity, Association of South East Asian Nations, which consist of from six to fifty-one member governments.

248

Both parties in a bilateral negotiation usually know a great deal about each other's language, customs, background, and history and have had an opportunity to get to know each other, and the issues, over a period of time. In most instances some sort of a trust relationship has been established and individual strengths and weaknesses have been identified and assessed by both parties. These negotiations are usually handled quietly, informally, behind closed doors, often without an interpreter, usually without a specific time constraint on the negotiation process and usually away from the world's press. The conclusion of the negotiation may be an oral agreement or an exchange of diplomatic notes or even a more formal text signed by the two parties.

The multilateral arena is quite a different scene. For global UN conferences there are usually 2000 or more delegates from 140–150 countries in attendance, operating through interpreters in English, French, Spanish, Russian, Chinese, and Arabic. In addition there can be 400 or so members of the world's press, dozens of nongovernmental organizations and scores of private citizens in attendance. They are all interested in the subject matter under discussion, all want to be kept informed of every detail, and all have the possibility of being present at almost all of the sessions. In addition most conferences have a specific time constraint and are required to begin and end at a given hour on a given day. Identifying the real leadership at such a conference, trying to build some sort of a trust relationship with that leadership, and trying to negotiate consensus in a two-to-three-week time-frame, is extraordinarily difficult.

Very few multilateral negotiations end with the initialing of a draft treaty, which, when ratified by national parliaments, will have the power of law. The vast majority of these international conferences end with the adoption, by consensus, of a Resolution or a Plan of Action which is similar to a Resolution, but longer. Neither has the power of law. They are in fact only pieces of paper forwarded to the capitals of member states, as recommendations for national action. They have no power, in and of themselves, and can be accepted or rejected by member states, who are not required, legally, to take any action at all. Their suasion is moral. If a country has voted in favor of a Resolution or agreed to the text, by consensus, they are morally bound to carry out the recommendations contained in that Resolution.

It is because Resolutions and Plans of Action don't have power that the development of a consensus by the conference is so essential. If a vote is taken on a Resolution, everyone at the conference knows immediately that the recommendations for action contained in the Resolution, are meaningless. States that vote against the Resolution or the Plan of Action, are not required to carry it out and so will not implement the recommendations contained in the document. The moral suasion is gone from the start. If consensus is developed then there will be pressure on all nations present to carry out the terms of the agreement. That pressure can be quite powerful. The goal of

249

all multilateral conferences is therefore to achieve a meaningful consensus. This by no means should be viewed as a lowest-common-denominator effort.

One can see that different skills are needed for different types of negotiations. An international conference diplomat must know how to manage complexity in order to achieve any results in the time-frame given. Preconference and conference organizational skills, as well as negotiating skills, are a prerequisite.

This chapter is written by a practitioner with over forty years of experience in international conference diplomacy and it is designed to be helpful to newcomers to the field. The four principles which are identified here emerged from practical experience. They are intended as guidelines for those who are in the field of multilateral diplomacy or who would like to become better acquainted with the field.

Principle I

'There is a direct correlation between the success of an international conference and the amount of preparation needed to make that Conference successful.'

1. The worst case that I know of, from a U.S. government perspective, was the Sixth Special Session of the United Nations General Assembly, which took place in April–May 1974.

President Boumedienne of Algeria, frustrated by the damage to Third World economies brought about by the OPEC (Organization of Petroleum Exporting Countries)-generated oil-shock of 1973, used Article 20 of the UN Charter to call for a Special Session of the General Assembly in New York. Article 20 states that a Special Session 'shall be convoked by the Secretary General at the request of ... a majority of the Members of the United Nations'. President Boumedienne was also head of the 'Group of 77' (to be explained below) and represented all members from Africa, Asia, and Latin America, a majority of the total UN membership. In his February 1974 letter to the Secretary General of the United Nations, he said his reason for convening this emergency session was to discuss the 'raw materials and development problems' the world was facing. Under the UN rules the conference had to be convened within six weeks of the receipt of the letter by the Secretary General.

Normally it takes the UN Secretariat three years to prepare the documentation for a world conference. Now there was not even time to agree on an agenda, let alone time to prepare some substantive papers to shape the debate. No one could even say whether 'raw materials' included oil.

In April 1974, the General Assembly convened and the delegates learned to their consternation that there was no documentation prepared by the Secretariat because they had no time and no guidance from governments on a hot political issue.

Nature abhors a vacuum. The Group of 77 moved into the vacuum and proposed the creation of a New International Economic Order (NIEO), which condemned the existing international economic order because it did not narrow the economic gap between the rich and poor nations of the world. Their Resolution really set forth all of the G-77's old wishes and frustrations under a new label. They picked up most of the language that had been under negotiation for the previous ten years at UNCTAD (United Nations Conference on Trade and Development) and relabeled it the NIEO. The West was totally unprepared for this move but finally, on 1 May 1974, joined the rest of the world and adopted the two NIEO Resolutions by consensus (McDonald, 1982). Many in the U.S. government regretted that action for the next dozen years.

2. The worst case of international Secretariat ineptitude and lack of understanding of their role in conference preparations that I know of, had to do with the preparations for UNIDO III, the Third World Conference held by the United Nations Industrial Development Organization in New Delhi, India, in January–February 1980.

In this case the Executive Director of the UNIDO Secretariat, based in Vienna, created a secret unit in his organization, without the approval or even knowledge of member states and directed the unit to come up with new ideas and proposals which he planned to surprise governments with, several months before the conference was to take place. In fact the unit spent over a million dollars just developing their ideas. When the document was finally revealed, every member state was shocked, whether they were from the developed or the developing world. The plan called for the creation of seventeen new international organizations, costing billions of dollars to implement, and called for all of them to be managed by UNIDO! The document was so unresponsive to member states' real concerns and so unrelated to what was politically achievable in the practical world, and governments were so angry at not being consulted, that when the conference began, they totally ignored the entire text. It was never mentioned during the course of the three-week meeting by any one of the more than 2000 delegates from 140 nations present at the conference. The Secretariat so offended governments by ignoring their mandate to collaborate with member states that they ended up wasting over a million dollars of governmental contributions and, in addition, had no papers on the conference table for governments to discuss.

Unfortunately, because there was no serious documentation on the table, there was a vacuum here too. The G–77 decided to put forward a draft text they called 'The Havana Declaration'. The radical members of the G-77 had developed this document while meeting in Havana, Cuba, under President Castro's leadership, three weeks before the UNIDO conference opened. Efforts were made by the Western group to develop a counter-text but at the last moment this failed. The politically radical Havana Declaration, called, among other things, for the establishment of two two-billion-dollar industrial-development funds. These funds were to be managed by the Group of 77 but were to be financed by international taxes on the industrial exports of the Western donor countries! The Havana Declaration was finally brought to a vote in the last hour of the conference. It was adopted, over the negative vote of every member of the Western group. UNIDO, as an organization, was almost destroyed by this vote and this document, because the Western countries were so angered that they seriously considered boycotting all future UNIDO meetings.

3. There are many, many examples of excellent, detailed, international preparations which have resulted in very successful conferences. Perhaps the best example, however, is the United Nations World Assembly on Aging, which took place in August 1982, in Vienna, Austria. The UN Secretariat, headed by a knowledgeable and skilled former diplomat, spent over two and a half years preparing for this two-week session. In all there were fifteen international pre-conference meetings before the main event and the documentation prepared for the Vienna conference was outstanding.

The Secretariat first sponsored seven expert nongovernmental meetings around the world, to define the problems and the opportunities facing the aged in every country of the world. Their reports were passed to five governmental regional meetings held in Manila, San José (Costa Rica), Addis Ababa, Amman, and Vienna. This voluminous documentation was then passed to the UN Secretariat in Vienna which drafted a forty-page document, a Plan of Action, containing sixty-five recommendations for national and international action. In addition a twenty-three-nation Advisory Committee was established and held three planning sessions before the conference. In March 1982, 340 participants, representing 159 nongovernmental organizations from forty-three countries, held their own global conference and presented their recommendations to the Vienna Secretariat, for possible inclusion in the draft Plan of Action to be discussed by governments.

By the time the 2000 delegates arrived in Vienna for the big event, they and the 120 governments they represented, felt they were a part of the whole process. They had studied the draft Plan of Action prepared by the Secretariat and were prepared to discuss the substantive issues in the text. Political posturing was at a minimum and the Plan of Action was adopted, on schedule, by consensus. In fact it was adopted by applause, with no reservations on any paragraph and with no explanations of vote called for by any government. A remarkable achievement. Preparation was the key to success.

The 'preparation principle' applies to national delegations getting ready for a conference as much as it applies to international secretariats. I was appointed head of the U.S. delegation to the World Assembly on Aging two years before the conference and immediately started to develop what became a ten-person U.S. secretariat. Sixteen months before the conference a Federal Inter-Agency Committee was established with thirty government agencies and key staffers from the Senate and House of Representatives participating. In addition, a fifty-person nongovernmental organization committee was created and all substantive U.S. government position papers were reviewed by that committee. Six months before the conference, we developed a Scope Paper outlining our goals and objectives and three months before Vienna we had the U.S. delegation list ready for White House approval. Working together as a team meant that we could speak with one voice at Vienna and be enormously effective.

Principle II

'The size and diplomatic level of a delegation to an international conference is in direct proportion to the amount of *domestic* political interest in the subject matter of the conference.'

1. The number of people on a delegation to an international conference and the title and standing, in the bureaucratic hierarchy of the head of the delegation, automatically telegraphs to all other national delegations in attendance, the importance of that conference to the government. Some of the biggest turf battles in government are fought over who will head the delegation to an international conference that has a high priority on the domestic scene. As one small example, a 'treaty' was finally signed, after years of battle, between the U.S. Department of State, U.S. AID (U.S. Agency for International Development) and the Department of Agriculture, as to who would head the U.S. delegation to each of the twice-yearly meetings of the World Food Program, in Rome. The substantive matters on the conference agenda were not nearly as important as the issue of which Washington agency should head the U.S. delegation.

The United States is not alone in having delegation problems however. In 1968, at UNCTAD II (United Nations Conference on Trade and Development), in New Delhi, the U.S. had an outstanding fifteen-person delegation, headed by a skilled professional, who achieved the U.S. goals for the conference. The Japanese had a ninety-three-person delegation, including three cooks. I learned that Japan in fact, had six delegations of fifteen persons each, from six different ministries. They couldn't agree in Tokyo on a Japanese position for the conference and did not trust each other, and so each ministry sent its own team. The Japanese were of course totally ineffective and the laughing stock of the conference. At UNIDO III the West German delegation had somewhat the same problem. They sent a different minister, from a different department, for each of the three weeks of the conference, because they could not agree in Bonn on what policy to follow. They too were completely ineffective.

2. Few people in Washington were interested in the UN World Conference on Technical Cooperation between Developing Countries, (TCDC) to be held in Buenos Aires in 1978, so I was asked to head the delegation, as an Ambassador. I put a small, ten-person, expert delegation together and had a very successful conference. Initially the Third World was quite miffed that the U.S. had not sent a minister to the meeting since every developing country was represented by a minister. This disadvantage was overcome however, because I brought a personal message from President Carter to the conference and he was the only Head of State to make that gesture.

3. The U.S. delegation to the UN World Conference on Science and Technology for Development, in Vienna, in 1979, was headed by a political appointee, inexperienced in conference diplomacy. As a result the U.S. delegation grew to 120 people, many of whom were looking forward to spending a great deal of time shopping in that lovely city. At the first delegation briefing, which took place in Vienna the evening before the conference was to start, there was a revolt and twenty people said they were returning to the U.S. because they had nothing to do. There was great domestic political interest in the conference but the U.S. secretariat for the meeting was inexperienced and did not keep the size of the U.S. delegation under control until it was almost too late. In fact most of the delegation was then put to work and we had a successful conference.

4. In 1980, a U.S. election year, the UN held a World Conference in Copenhagen called the Mid-Decade Conference on Women and Development. The State Department recommended to the White House a balanced, expert, twelve-person delegation. When the White House returned the list it had grown to eighty-seven in number and only included three men. The list contained representatives from every minority women's group one could imagine and practically no one on the list had any UN conference experience. In addition, the head of delegation was a political appointee who did not want to be briefed about the conference. Unfortunately the individual members of the delegation, who squabbled regularly in the U.S., took their disagreements to Copenhagen and squabbled on the conference floor. The result was chaos and ended in the U.S. voting against the Plan of Action, thereby putting the UN's Women's program on hold for five years.

5. We had over 500 applications from people around the country who wanted to be on the U.S. delegation to the World Assembly on Aging. We managed to keep the delegation to thirty people, however, including congressional representation. I had an interesting experience with the White House concerning that delegation list. For all major conferences the Legislative Branch is asked by the Executive Branch if they would like to send two Senators, one from each party and two members from the House, one from each party, as members of the U.S. delegation. On this occasion I had letters

from the leadership of both Houses, nominating their two people, and so I automatically included their names on the list sent to the White House for approval.

Claude Pepper, 'Mr Aging' in the House and also Chairman of the House Select Committee on Aging, was one of the two names on the House list. One can imagine my surprise when I received the approved list from the White House with a thick black line through the name of Claude Pepper! I immediately remonstrated with my contact in the White House but was told that this was a firm decision from 'on high'. I then went to my Assistant Secretary, a political appointee, told him the story and said I was not going to be the one to tell Claude Pepper he was not going to Vienna. Obviously my boss did not want to be that person either so he appealed the decision to his friends in the White House. I was called into his office just before departing for Vienna and told that I had gotten 'my way'. However, I was to be held *personally responsible* for Claude Pepper's actions during his two weeks in Vienna and should insure that he did not get out of line! Of course the Senator was a perfect gentleman and there were no problems.

On my return to Washington, however, I tracked down what had happened. It seems that President Reagan had personally drawn that black line through Claude Pepper's name because he was so mad at him. This matter took place at the height of the Social Security debate and the day before the President had seen the delegation list he had made a speech on the Capitol steps about social security and fifty people had showed up. At the same time, on the other side of the Capitol, Claude Pepper was speaking on the same subject, to 5000 people.

Principle III

'Using the conference structure wisely can be the key to success.'

All major conferences have their own structure defined, well in advance of the meeting, usually in a separate document called 'Rules of Procedure' or in the sponsoring organization's by-laws or constitution. This document will define the role of the plenary session, list the number of committees, identify the officers of the conference, explain how they are to be elected, list their responsibilities, discuss the voting procedure, and even explain who may be an observer and what rights an observer may have. In other words the rules explain how the mechanics of the conference will work. It is one of the most important documents at the meeting and is always ignored by newcomers to the field.

A mastery of the Rules of Procedure is essential. This is also important so that one knows what is not covered by the rules and therefore how far one's flexibility may extend.

The United Nations recognized as far back as 1962 that its membership was growing so rapidly (from 51 nations in 1945 to 179 in 1992), that some

255

innovations designed to encourage more effective negotiations had to be adopted for members to be able to cope with the growth. In that year the 'Group' system was established, by General Assembly Resolution, and applied to UNCTAD. Every member state was assigned to a group. Group A consisted of all Asian and African members. Group B consisted of the developed countries: Western Europe, North America, Australia, New Zealand, and Japan. Group C was Latin America. Group D covered the countries of Eastern Europe. Groups A and C soon realized they had a great deal in common and informally combined forces and called themselves the 'Group of 77', because there was a total of seventy-seven UN member states in the two Groups at that moment in time. Today there are 130 Third World members but they still call themselves the 'Group of 77'. Each Group elected a spokesperson who represented the group's views on the issues under discussion. In fact, Asia, Africa, and Latin America each had an elected representative in addition to the overall G-77 leader. The system was not rigid, in other words individual delegation heads could speak during the conference, but the group leader had considerable power and influence (McDonald, 1990). The group system, in one form or another, is now pervasive across the UN system.

1. The two-week-long TCDC Conference in Buenos Aires, in 1978, offered an excellent opportunity to manage the conference structure, outside of the Rules of Procedure. The rules called for a Plenary and, because of a shortage of UN funds for interpreters, only one committee. That committee, consisting of 800 delegates, was to review a thirty-two-page Plan of Action and recommend its adoption to the Plenary. At the end of the third day they had completed page one. Something had to be created, outside of the Rules of Procedure. A fifty-person, informal working group was established, outside of the Rules of Procedure, consisting of ten delegates from each of the five regional groups and given the task of completing the review of the Plan of Action.

I knew there would be three or four issues that the working group, for political reasons, would not be able to resolve, and so began to work on another change, outside of the Rules of Procedure. It was necessary to apply the theory of small-group dynamics (McDonald, 1990) and try to reduce an amorphous mass of 1900 delegates to a dynamic group of ten, in order, eventually, to negotiate those three or four key issues.

On the fourth day of the conference I met with the Argentinian President of the Conference, an army general with no previous UN experience, and recommended that he invite a small group of delegates to meet with him informally, over coffee, in his office, and talk about the progress of the meeting. He was delighted with the idea but did not know whom, among the 1900 delegates, to invite. I pulled a list of ten names out of my pocket and gave it to the general. It contained the names of the delegates I had identified as conference leaders at that meeting and consisted of two names from each of the five regional groups.

Every conference is different because it consists of different people and takes place at a different moment in history. Every conference develops its own leaders, without regard to either title or country of origin. My list was not selected on the basis of title or nationality but on the basis of demonstrated leadership observed over the previous four days. I hoped the ten would evolve into a small negotiating group and be able to resolve those issues I expected would be forwarded to them by the informal working group, for resolution.

The plan worked. The general, in his capacity as President of the Conference, invited the ten delegates for coffee that first day, and every day thereafter. A trust relationship began slowly to develop. The informal working-group issues were referred to the President, who convened the small group and we remained in constant negotiations for thirty of the last thirty-six hours of the conference. At the last minute the Plan of Action was adopted, by consensus (McDonald, 1990). The change in structure made the difference.

2. Structural change was critical in another case. In 1977 the UN General Assembly appointed a thirty-six-nation ad-hoc committee of member states to try to draft an international treaty against the taking of hostages. The ad-hoc committee met for three weeks in Geneva, Switzerland, in 1977, and again in 1978, with no success whatsoever. The meetings were open to the public, to the press, and to observer delegations from other member states. There were some 500 people crowded into the conference room to listen to the thirty-six appointed members of the ad-hoc committee. They responded by making political speeches to the public and to the press, for home consumption.

In 1979 I was asked to head the U.S. delegation to the third, and probably the last, effort to reach agreement on this critical subject, and proposed a complete change in structure to the ad-hoc committee Chairman. He agreed. At the end of the first thirty minutes of the Plenary session the Chairman announced that the ad-hoc committee was converted into a closed, informal working group. The press, the public, the observer delegations and even the UN Secretariat personnel were excluded, much to their outrage. The whole atmosphere changed very quickly. There were no more speeches by the thirty-six delegations in the ad-hoc committee because no one was there to listen or to record them. The delegates got to work and by the end of the three weeks, reconvened as a Plenary session, right on schedule, and adopted a draft treaty. Here too the change in structure had made agreement possible.

Principle IV

'The level of competence of the Conference President or the leader of the U.S. delegation can often make or break a conference.'

257

1. At the UN Science and Technology for Development Conference in Vienna, in 1979, the Austrian government proposed an Austrian cabinet minister for the presidency and the minister was elected. Unfortunately the minister had no previous international conference experience and literally was not able to cope with the drama of the last hours of the conference. The session was becoming a shambles. Fortunately one of the conference vice-presidents was a parliamentarian from Norway. He stepped in, got us out of the mess, and saved the day.

At the World Assembly on Aging in Vienna, in 1982, the Austrian government announced in advance that they would propose the same minister as President. I was horrified and, with the support of the Austrian Foreign Ministry, tried to derail the appointment. We did not succeed, so we changed the Rules of Procedure at the last minute and put all power in the committee chairmen, thereby avoiding any conflict arising in the Plenary. As indicated earlier, it worked.

The selection of a Conference President warrants the expenditure of a great deal of time and energy by concerned persons because of the importance of that post. It should never be considered as a pro-forma election.

2. The same is true of the selection of the head of the U.S. delegation. Ideally the name of the U.S. leader should be announced six months before the conference opens and all U.S. embassies should be asked to inform the governments to which they are accredited so that those governments can start to focus on the level of their own leadership at the conference. When the United States government takes a leadership role, it sets the stage quite positively. When the U.S. doesn't, the result is usually a negative one.

The effective role of the head of the U.S. delegation at UNCTAD II was mentioned earlier. At UNCTAD VI in Belgrade, in 1983, the head of the U.S. delegation was named one week before the conference was to start; the United States' role was a disaster.

In 1974, at the UN World Conference on Population, in Bucharest, Romania, the U.S. was the world leader in the field of population and family planning and was the world's major financial contributor to the United Nations Fund for Population Activities (UNFPA). The U.S. delegation was led by a skilled member of the Cabinet and it had a very successful meeting. In 1984, at the Second World Conference on Population, in Mexico City, the entire, highly skilled, U.S. delegation was replaced three weeks before the conference and a group of uninformed ideologues took over, on instructions from the White House. Disaster at the conference was finally averted at the last moment when the head of delegation was ordered, by Washington, to join with the rest of the world in adopting the Plan of Action by consensus. However, the White House changed the ground rules on population issues as a result of the Mexico City Conference and, since 1985, has refused to provide funds to the UNFPA. The U.S. is no longer considered to be a leader in this field.

The 1980 Mid-Decade Conference on Women and Development was mentioned earlier. The UN hosted the end of the Women's Decade Conference in Nairobi, in 1985. The head of the U.S. delegation, a political appointee, spent months planning for the conference, hosted a three-day briefing session in Washington D.C., at her own expense, for the thirty-six-person delegation, seven weeks before the conference was to start, and turned the delegation into a cohesive team. She did a brilliant job in Nairobi, where the conference finally adopted the Plan of Action by consensus and truly repaired the poor job done by the United States in 1980, at the Copenhagen Conference on Women and Development.

Conclusion

Conflict resolution theories and diplomatic negotiating practices are often difficult to bring together. Unfortunately, most diplomatic practitioners abstain from reading about conflict resolution theory. Most academics seem to have little interest in finding ways to test their theories, in practice. This chapter has tried to bring these two separate, talented strands a little closer together. If each develops a greater understanding of the needs of the other, then one may well be able to expand the understanding necessary, not only to extend the field of knowledge available to both but also to more effectively resolve international conflict peacefully and eventually bring about a less conflicted world.

References

McDonald, J. W. (1982), *The North-South Dialogue and the United Nations*, Georgetown University Press, Washington, D.C.

McDonald, J. W. (1984), *How to Be a Delegate*, Government Printing Office, Washington, D.C.

McDonald, J. W. (1990), 'Managing complexity through small group dynamics', in J. Burton and F. Dukes, eds, *Conflict: Readings in Management and Resolution*, St. Martin's Press, New York and Macmillan, London.

Part V

Feedback: What does it all mean?

Relating theory to the practice of conflict resolution in South Africa

The problem of resolving social conflict in South Africa can be addressed at a number of different levels and through a wide range of processes. In this chapter I will explore different frameworks through which the complementarity and interconnections of the preceding chapters can be examined and how these insights can provide suggestions for intervention in South African urban governance conflicts.

The assumptions guiding my analysis are that there is a multiplicity of causes for violent social conflict in South Africa, and that a number of intervening factors contribute to perpetuating the conflicts once they become manifest. Furthermore, conflicts at various geographic (e.g., national, regional, and local) and structural (e.g., political, economic, and cultural) levels are closely interconnected. Attempts to change conflict dynamics or address the sources of conflict are of limited use if they are aimed only at one source or one level of conflict manifestation (as is implied in Dennis Sandole's introductory chapter). Such attempts may lead to many partial solutions, but by operating in isolation these individual efforts may be forgoing potential complementarity, and may even be inhibiting each other's potential.

The South African situation seems particularly daunting largely because of this complex entanglement that makes it appear intractable. Social conflicts of every type have become politicized and thus a source of delegitimation of, and challenge to deeper social structures. The intensity of these conflicts has inflicted severe human costs, and highlighted the destructive potential of conflict dynamics. Such social upheaval, however, also contains the seeds of regeneration and growth.

Despite the extreme suffering, there is the sense of potential that is absent in more stable society. The positive functions of conflict have been addressed by a large number of scholars in the field (e.g., Simmel, 1955; Coser, 1956; Curle, 1986). While it is useful to focus on this aspect of the conflict, there are, however, many instances where conflicts have become so encapsulated

263

in their own internal dynamics that they are seemingly impervious to constructive (by any definition) intervention. These conflicts have frustrated attempts by parties to promote either social transformation or integration goals. The intractability of these conflicts is further testimony to the multidimensionality and complexity of their causes and dynamics.

The state of the conflict resolution field

The transition process occurring presently in South Africa is indeed being confronted by conflict resolution bodies at a number of levels. Organizations have been set up to deal with conflict at various geographical and institutional levels. National-level structures (such as that established by the National Peace Accord) recognize the need for problems to be addressed at both the national and the local levels, and locally established initiatives operate with a very clear awareness of the significance of the national political context.[1]

In the United States, where the field has reached a much more advanced stage of development, an abundance of organizations and agencies exist explicitly for the purpose of resolving conflicts. In South Africa the field has very recent origins and is only now experiencing an initial surge of growth. Dispute resolution professionals have not yet established their specialized niches to the same degree, and institutions have not monopolized territories within the field. Amid the confusion, there is thus a dynamic dialogue amongst and between practitioners and theorists in the field which has not (yet) become bracketed into specialized enclaves.

The field has, in South Africa, emerged in the midst of a society struggling to be born. For it to receive social credibility, it has had to address the question (or challenge) about where it fits into this context. Answers that simply address issues of social stability or the alleviation of court congestion are not sufficient. While there is a drastic need for processes that can assist in curbing the level of violence, there is also a questioning of the implications contained in these procedures for the society which they (the procedures) are helping to create. The field is challenged to define what it can contribute with respect to fundamental social change. What values does it affirm or legitimate, what precedents does it set, and whose interests does it serve in the long run? The concept of a general social good is not easily accepted in theory and is treated with suspicion when proclaimed as an institutional goal in such a divided society. So much is being questioned that efforts at resolving conflicts become mired down due to lack of trust in the procedures of transition.

An example that illustrates many of these points is that of the conflict over local-government restructuring. Black[2] and white residential areas in many South African cities are presently exploring their future as united metropolitan systems. The present situation is immensely complex. It involves vast discrepancies in wealth and service provision. Separate political structures with relatively autonomous tax bases exist for different racially segregated neighborhoods. White neighborhoods have local governments that enjoy general credibility, while black local authorities are unpopular, were imposed by the government, and have in many instances been forced to resign because of opposition from their own constituents. Popularly supported 'civics'[3] have engaged white local and regional authorities in negotiations over the interim administration of the townships and the eventual shape of the metropolitan political structure. Progress has generally been painfully slow; some have, however, achieved initial successes, while others have only recently started exploring the options. The process of negotiation is approached with great caution by the black and the more conservative white communities, due largely to the uncertainty of the consequences of being involved in such talks (even when they are only exploratory in nature).

Confrontation has for so long been the central dynamic of efforts to advance social change that cooperative initiatives are seen as potentially very threatening. Proponents of conflict resolution processes have had to defend their advocacy of new techniques which have had little opportunity to demonstrate potential benefits. Previous negotiation efforts (before the advent of the present phase of national reconciliation) had often ended in disillusionment when the central state intervened to reimpose its control (see Swilling, 1988). The power imbalance resulting from the economic disparity between black and white neighborhoods also gave rise to fears of cooptation, even when white local officials were clearly fairly liberal in their ideology (see Atkinson and Heymans, 1988). Before we can justify specific intervention techniques to address these conflicts, it is necessary to examine theoretical frameworks that direct our choice of approach.

Categorizing the field of conflict

The contributors to this book divide the conflict universe into various levels and spheres, making use of different models and categorization schemes to map the field. The progress of theoretical understanding and the development of skilled practice clearly benefit from such schemes. They also contain certain dangers. Classification schemes that separate the field into a number of compartments often translate into artificially autonomous areas of theory and isolated niches of practice. Such compartmentalizations can thus blind us to the connections between these spheres, hampering our ability to explore their complementarity as well as their possible contradictions. They may, however, be utilized specifically to explore these same connections.

All the previous chapters rely on some form of differentiation of levels, spheres, or aspects of conflict and conflict resolution. For some, it is stated explicitly and forms the basis of their analysis (e.g., Sandole, Burton, and Druckman), while for others it is an implicit assumption determined by their theoretical framework or by the *de facto* divisions that exist in the professional field of conflict resolution.

The goal of identifying different levels of conflict is ultimately to discover the appropriate type of intervention process for each. A wide range of approaches has been suggested in the literature, and the chapters in this book borrow from and build on this array. There is an ongoing debate about the appropriate techniques for different forms of conflict. Two questions are raised: What is the appropriate context in which to apply a particular technique? And, what range of techniques are needed to address a particular type of conflict, i.e., is one particular technique sufficient?

Conflicts versus disputes

The identification of levels of conflicts is used for different purposes by the contributors to this volume. The most adamant proponent of the need to differentiate levels of conflict is John Burton (Chapter 4), who argues that there is an essential difference between *conflicts* involving deep-rooted human needs and conflicts that do not (termed *disputes* by Burton). Underlying this distinction lies a model of human nature which differentiates actions and motivations which strive for the satisfaction of ontological human needs from those that seek to satisfy other interests, which are presumably culturally or individually specific. It is further suggested that ontological needs are pursued at (almost) any cost, while other interests are compromisable and only pursued given a rational cost–benefit analysis. The distinction of this analysis thus arises from a particular psycho-biological understanding of human nature that applies across all cultures (see Burton and Sandole, 1986).

Burton's clean separation of conflicts and disputes translates into two separate forms of intervention: analytical problem-solving workshops for conflicts, and traditional power-based bargaining, authoritative third-party intervention or conflict 'management' for disputes (see Burton and Dukes, 1990). This discrete categorization system thus has important consequences for how we deal with conflict. By labeling something a dispute (i.e., as not being connected to the satisfaction of a basic need), it may become relegated to power-based processes. This effectively depreciates the significance of the issues that are then settled to the detriment of the powerless.

The flaw in this analysis is not its identification of human needs as a source of conflict; rather, it is the analytical independence of the causal domains (needs and interests), and the autonomy of spheres of practice (problem-solving workshops and alternative dispute resolution). If human needs are seen as an aspect (present to a greater or lesser degree) of many real-world conflicts, rather than the defining characteristic of conflicts, processes to deal with this aspect of the conflict can be used in a complementary fashion along with other processes.

An alternative avenue for exploring the connection between the levels of conflict from a human-needs perspective is to develop a more integrated model of human nature that does not neatly separate our motivations into needs satisfaction versus interest satisfaction. While not denying the possibility of discerning different sources of motivation, one can still question the assertion that they act independently from one another in shaping our actual goals and actions.

Human consciousness and cultural systems fuse different aspects of our nature and external stimuli into a coherent framework for viewing the world. It would be simplistic to expect people to be able to separate their worlds of meaning into a binary scheme of deep versus superficial needs. The contribution of Avruch and Black in this book (Chapter 9) contributes greatly to an appreciation of the need to understand the cultural framework of meaning in order to make sense of actors' goals and behavior. It is thus only through a cultural analysis, they argue, that mutual understanding and appreciation of respective positions can be arrived at.

Preserving the analytical and practical importance of deeply rooted human needs and their effects on conflict dynamics suggests the need to incorporate processes that address them.[4] Moreover, if we conceive of human needs as a factor present (in varying degrees) in a range of conflicts, techniques that deal with them should be more widely used than Burton's model suggests. It should, however, not be seen as the singular answer to a particular conflict.

A perspective that builds on a classification scheme similar to that of Burton is Wallace Warfield's chapter on public policy conflict (Chapter 12). Warfield also perceives the necessity to identify deep-rooted needs such as identity and security that cannot be dealt with through rationalistic approaches. He contrasts these with resource-distribution issues that can be dealt with through a bargaining approach. While recognizing a linkage between the two, Warfield stresses the need to use particular techniques in dealing with culturally based needs. Policy conflicts between minority identity groups and public organizations, Warfield argues, contain both elements, and therefore need a dual approach (neither of which is incorporated in present organizational decision-making styles).

South African application

Relating these ideas to the local-government conflict previously mentioned, there is clearly a dimension of deep-rooted human needs present in the conflict. Regardless of how they are defined, in situations of political turmoil and economic uncertainty, basic human needs become closely tied to political control of one's neighborhood. Many black residents (particularly squatters) still face great uncertainty regarding their ability to even meet basic subsistence needs. Black citizens have been denied the right to participate in decision-making regarding the governance of their own neighborhoods and the broader metropolitan areas (in which they form majorities). White citizens, on the other hand, face what they perceive as being a threat to the control and cultural identity of their communities. They are searching for a sense of local security in a context of national insecurity.

A needs-oriented approach to this conflict would suggest that the problem be jointly analyzed by the parties in order to examine their respective positions and to determine needs that lie at their foundation. One should specifically avoid a bargaining approach which assumes that parties can trade off their interests to arrive at a settlement that may compromise their fundamental needs. Irrespective of the balance of power, a settlement that fails to address such needs will not end the conflict.

Innovative solutions that address the basic needs of all the parties need to be discovered. This discovery requires the involvement of all the parties in a joint analytical process (probably facilitated by a third party). Bargaining procedures can only be applied to those aspects of the conflict in which basic values of either party are not threatened. The basic needs that parties feel are being threatened or denied, probably vary depending on the contrasting contexts faced by each community. The process of bringing these to the surface would require the parties' active involvement, rather than an academic's isolated analysis. And, rather than imposing a theoretically designed model of what is or is not a basic need, parties should be involved in a culturally sensitive search for a mutual understanding of how various goals and actions are valued and linked to deeper needs and contextual demands.

Richard Rubenstein's chapter on class conflict (Chapter 10) raises a very important caution regarding the common inclination to treat economic issues as essentially less deep-rooted (or less needs-based) than conflicts over political or cultural identity. It is only under specific political circumstances (a generally accepted social contract) that parties can address economic issues through consensual normative and institutional frameworks. In South Africa, insufficient consensus exists for economic issues to be treated as such a subordinate, interest-based aspect of the problem. The economic system that forms a fundamental basis of the urban structure must also be subjected to a needs-analysis, and its relation to communal identity examined.

Nested spheres of conflict

Another framework that underlies many approaches to intervention-technique selection is a system-levels-based model. The clearest explication of this approach is that of Maire Dugan (forthcoming), who identifies four levels (or nested spheres) of conflict: (1) conflict of interpretation, (2) relational conflict, (3) organizational conflict, and (4) system-wide conflict. Each successive level contains manifestations of the prior level. A conflict of interpretation could thus be a manifestation of any of the deeper levels, or it may simply exist on its own. A system-wide conflict, however, manifests itself at all three other levels as well.

The distinction developed by Dugan is based on a structural analysis of human interaction systems. Systems are examined in terms of their location within each other. A certain system dynamic or characteristic (e.g., conflict) has effects on the systems contained within it (more conflict).

Coming from a social-systems perspective, Dugan's model suggests different forms of intervention for each of the four levels identified and thus, because they are nested, a multi-pronged approach for deeper levels of conflict. The connections between the levels of conflict translate into a prescription for complementary forms of intervention. Certain approaches are designed to fit particular levels. As long as we are able to see where in the scheme specific techniques fit, and not apply them to inappropriate levels or expect them to be sufficient in themselves, such a narrowing of focus can be very beneficial to the development of the field.

This, it seems, is illustrated by the chapter by John Warfield (Chapter 5) who focuses on resolving disagreements regarding methods of accomplishing a task. If one locates this analysis within the framework developed by Dugan it can be regarded as providing valuable insight into how one could approach conflicts of interpretation. Addressing this level of conflict is often a central aspect of resolving a particular issue in contention. It is very often, however, only a partial solution, and requires complementary techniques that address other deeper levels of the conflict.[5]

Another argument for examining the connection between levels is presented by Joseph Scimecca's critique of alternative dispute resolution (ADR) (Chapter 14). He advocates the need for a broader conflict theory to undergird ADR practices, arguing that the disputes handled by these processes arise from system-wide structural conflicts. Using Dugan's terms, interpersonal conflicts should thus be analyzed as nested manifestations of deeper levels of conflict. Scimecca's critique rests on a structural analysis that sees the decisive factor in a conflict as the power distribution inherent in social stratification systems. The influence of this structural phenomenon is viewed as affecting both interpersonal disputes and broader intergroup conflicts. The need to see the commonality (especially the influence of power) between the different levels of conflict is thus emphasized. Scimecca thereby offers a critique of the isolation of certain categories of conflict that have emerged in the practice of conflict resolution.

Paralleling Dugan's nested model is Daniel Druckman's distinction between different sources of conflict (Chapter 2), namely interests, understanding, and ideology. His distinctions also lead him to examine the ways in which these types are connected. He identifies the need to examine how the different types of conflict reinforce each other or interact to add a new dimension to a problem. It is also suggested that conflicts can translate into new forms, thus becoming either more amenable or more resistant to attempts at resolution. It is thus important to note that escalation of a conflict does not simply involve greater size or intensity, but may add a new dimension that requires an expanded repertoire of approaches. Such evolutionary analyses of conflict dynamics also need to be incorporated into the models previously examined.

Hugo van der Merwe

South African application

The influence of the broader apartheid structure – a manifestation of Galtung's structural violence (1969) discussed by Sandole (Chapter 1) – is clearly influential in shaping conflicts of interpretation, relationships, and organizations at every level of South African society. One cannot deal with these micro-processes as if they can be fully resolved independently from the broader social context. The conflictual social system has a very direct impact on the way people come to define their interests and their ability to pursue them at a personal level. The authoritarian control of the apartheid system impacts on almost every aspect of people's daily lives. Even in situations where conflicts start off as simple miscommunications, they can rapidly escalate in intensity when parties commission broader systemic forces to bolster their positions. The system of racial classification and segregation has deeply affected the way individuals understand and relate to members of other racially defined groups. It is not simply a cultural difference, but also an awareness of being radically differently positioned in an externally determined social hierarchy.

Resolving an interpersonal conflict must at some level depend on acceptance of legal parameters, common values, or the legitimacy of structurally determined bargaining power. If these structurally shaped constraints are themselves subject to intense debate, the possibility for interpersonal conflict to be effectively treated in isolation from the broader context is small. In South Africa, the apartheid structures have been delegitimated and thus cannot serve as mediating forces. New alternative sources of power and legitimacy are, however, not yet firmly established and universally accepted, even within seemingly homogeneous communities. Organizations that address these conflicts thus have to depend on specific power structures, value systems, or legal codes within which to frame the resolution process. Conflict resolution forums in the townships have, for example, typically depended on the civics as sources of authority and the Freedom Charter[6] as a source of principles. This reliance on alternatives has the effect of legitimizing a newly emergent (or locally dominant) set of values and social structures. The forums negotiating local-government restructuring have in some cases arrived at broad principles of agreement, such as democratic structure, a non-racial universal franchise, a single tax-base for a whole city, and the need for devolution of power. Whether this provides a sufficient basis within which to then concentrate on more substantive issues remains to be seen.

Contingency models

Some theories of conflict intervention take the evolutionary perspective of conflict as the basis for determining intervention strategies. Christopher Mitchell (Chapter 6) mentions the need for contingency theories which link particular techniques to specific stages of the conflict process. Conflicts can be seen as progressing through a sequence of stages, each requiring intervention techniques appropriate to its specific dynamic and position within the developmental course of a conflict. The question of timing of different approaches thus becomes the focus of analysis (see Kriesberg, 1981; Fisher and Keashly, 1991). Wallace Warfield (Chapter 12) also contributes to this analysis by calling attention to the need for trust-building mechanisms in situations of intense conflict or crisis. He asserts that this phase of conflict intervention must be connected to transformational change at the causal level, and that without such linkage they would merely amount to a 'veneer of tranquility'. A further element of this sequential approach addressed by Warfield, is the transitional need for cultural role interpretation in situations where relationships are badly strained and communications are traumatized.

South African application
In many cities the post-1990 negotiations only managed to sprout after a lengthy period of exploratory talks and tentative agreements. In some cities relations between civics and white authorities have reached a fairly cordial level after an initial period of animosity and distrust. A further aspect of this transitional stage is the role of the development of a deeper understanding of respective fears, goals, and interests. Earlier negotiations (pre-1990) had been complicated by a lack of familiarity with the way in which the structures of the respective parties operate. Unrealistic demands were made, based on ignorance of the functioning and goals of one's adversaries. The process of negotiation was also a new experience with which the parties first had to gain familiarity and confidence. Intervention processes that could serve this phase more directly include: negotiation training, education workshops on the various parties' structures and means of operation, and analytical workshops to examine the underlying causes of the conflict and to explore the range of resolution options. The parties have often been thrown together in negotiation forums for which they were/are ill-prepared. This has particularly impaired the negotiation ability of the civics because they have had little exposure to the processes of official governance, but both parties have been affected by the resulting lack of progress. If such transitionary processes involve joint actions (e.g., shared training forums), they can themselves also play a role in promoting trust and in developing parties' familiarity with cooperative endeavors.

In many cities, conflict over governance restructuring is still very intense, with little prospect for the emergence of cooperative forums. Anger, fear, and suspicion are still mounting over issues such as: the disconnection of water and electricity services by the white authorities, township boycotts of service charges, and consumer boycotts of white-owned shops. Crisis-intervention approaches are needed in such cases to establish some initial calm before any official processes can get off the ground.

Social structures

Another social-systems-based distinction used in many of the chapters is one that has been fundamental to academic disciplinary boundaries: that between social structures, e.g., political, cultural, and economic structures. The emphasis in most of the conflict resolution literature has been on the political sphere, namely the design of new constitutional systems that would restructure the relationship between the conflicting parties in such a way that their interests can be pursued in a regulated institutionalized setting. (See especially Lijphart, 1986 and Horowitz, 1991 for examinations of constitutional options for South Africa.)

Contributors to this volume have highlighted the need to examine the cultural sphere and the way it relates to the political and economic spheres. Mary Clark (Chapter 3) provides valuable insights into the cultural paradigms that cause human deprivation and proposes a conflict resolution process that involves exploring healthier worldviews that are more attuned to the basic human needs of social bonding and sacred meaning. Elise Boulding's analysis of culture and political systems focuses on the environmental parameters of which these systems need to become cognizant (Chapter 13). Both these contributions address the link between the cultural, political, and economic spheres. Clark stresses the opposition from the political and economic elites as major impediments to cultural change, and Boulding points to the mutually reinforcing link between warlike cultural images and existing (nation-state) political structures. The interdependence of these systems is emphasized: one cannot bring about fundamental social change without addressing all three. They form a coherently intertwined basis for the present conflict-generating system, sustaining their interactive perpetuation. Clark and Boulding also suggest, as a remedy, the need for smaller political–economic units which would be more capable of satisfying environmental and psychic needs, and which would allow for greater freedom in the search for innovative cultural paradigms.

South African application

The existing local-governance system is a subsystem of the broader apartheid system. It embodies specific cultural values, political structures, and an economic order that reinforce each other and deprive urban residents of basic human needs. Transforming this system requires more than a simple restructuring of political institutions. Underlying economic disparities and cultural divisions have become so entrenched that their dynamics are capable of relatively independent self-perpetuation. Each of these systemic foundations of apartheid needs to be addressed in its own right, as well as in conjunction with the others. Analyses of urban social movements (e.g., Castells, 1983) caution us about the limitations of processes that only address one aspect of the urban system, and which, therefore, cannot fundamentally transform it.

Alternative systems that replace the crumbling apartheid structures also have to be examined, and evaluated for their ability to meet human needs. The debate over imported models that have proven unsatisfactory in many other countries needs to be transcended, and options that answer expressed needs of local communities need to be explored with greater inventiveness.

The dynamics of the conflict have, however, also generated their own culture and institutionalized structures. The culture of violence involves the growing immunity of South African society to the horrors of violence. Violence becomes such a common response to conflict that people see it as the norm, and find it difficult to conceive of dealing with conflict differently. This cultural dynamic is, however, only a contributing factor. The causal aspect involves the institutionalization of violence as a 'functional' response to a situation (from the perspective of certain groups).[7] Aggressive behavior becomes necessary for personal and group survival in a situation where cooperative or conciliatory behavior is treated as a sign of weakness, and where basic survival needs are not assured. Criminal violence reaches such proportions that perpetrators do not have to fear being caught or punished. Revenge (and counter-revenge) becomes a common response to grievances because other forms of justice are not obtainable. Such spirals, however, serve the interests of those dependent on coercion and community discord as sources of power. Reconciliation between adversaries themselves (not just their representatives), recourse to authoritative intervention, and the alleviation of economic deprivation are all needed to reverse this dynamic and transform the cultural inclinations that facilitate it.

The evolution of new cultural paradigms is a process that cannot be imposed or engineered from above. It has to grow out of the day-to-day experiences of the members of a community. A new cultural logic has to be cultivated, and be supported and engendered by new political and economic structures.

Conclusion

In this chapter, my intention has been to emphasize the need for a range of models that draw attention to different dimensions of conflict. A recognition of this multidimensionality should sensitize us to the limitations of specific approaches that offer only partial solutions, and which therefore need to be complemented by other intervention techniques. The complexity of the South African situation cannot be overemphasized when intervention processes are evaluated.

The strategies proposed in this book are all relevant to South Africa, but need to be carefully considered in relation to their specific contextual application. Rather than a 'carpet-bombing' approach (a phrase with appropriately negative connotations) that tries everything in the hope that somewhere the right strategy is hit upon, strategies have to be considered on a contingency basis, each connected to a specific contextual imperative.

There is a legitimate fear among many in South Africa of the country being used as an experimental laboratory in which new techniques can be demonstrated. Contributions to this book make very clear that intervention techniques should be carefully attuned to the specific conflict and its dynamics. Resolving a conflict requires not only good tools, but also careful consideration of which of the many tools can be (and need to be) utilized to deal with a specific problem. The contributors to the book make a major contribution to advancing our understanding of how to approach this problem.

Notes

1. Local organizations and forums such as the Community Dispute Resolution Resource Committee and the Witwatersrand Metropolitan Chamber operate with a very clear awareness of the limitations imposed by the national political context.
2. The term 'black' is used in the inclusive sense to refer to all those not classified as 'white'.
3. Civics are grassroots community organizations that emerged in black townships to address both political and local civic concerns. They have usually been aligned with the African National Congress (ANC).
4. John Murray's contribution (Chapter 15), for example, deals with a conflict that may appear to some as simply an interest-based dispute, but he emphasizes that there are deeply held beliefs and values at stake that require an approach that does not assume conventional bargaining over positions as a viable solution.
5. Benjamin Broome's chapter (Chapter 7) on relational empathy also fits very neatly into this classification scheme.
6. The Freedom Charter is a document that spells out various principles for the structuring of a democratic non-racial South Africa. It is accepted mainly by organizations aligned with the ANC.
7. The structural violence inherent in the present political and economic system is, furthermore, the context within which these cultural dynamics develop. The cultural logic of violence is, in part, provided by the apartheid ideology itself.

References

Atkinson, D. and Heymans, C. (1988), 'The limits and possibilities of local initiatives for change: The case for participatory planning', *Politikon*, 15, pp. 31–44.

Burton, J. W. and Dukes, F. (eds) (1990), *Conflict: Readings in Management and Resolution*, St. Martin's Press, New York.

Burton, J. W. and Sandole, D. J. D. (1986), 'Generic theory: The basis of conflict resolution', *Negotiation Journal*, 2, pp. 333–344.

Castells, M. (1983), *The City and the Grassroots: A Cross-Cultural Theory of Urban Social Movements*, University of California Press, Berkeley.

Coser, L. A. (1956), *The Functions of Social Conflict*, Free Press, New York and Collier-Macmillan, London.

Curle, A. (1986), *In the Middle: Non-Official Mediation in Violent Situations*, St. Martin's Press, New York.

Dugan, M. A. (forthcoming), *Making the Connection: Peace Studies and Conflict Resolution*, Sage, Newbury Park, California.

Fisher, R. J. and Keashly, L. (1991), 'The potential complementarity of mediation and consultation within a contingency model of third party intervention', *Journal of Peace Research*, 28, pp. 29–42.

Galtung, J. (1969), 'Peace, violence and peace research', *Journal of Peace Research*, 6, pp. 167–191.

Horowitz, D. L. (1991), *A Democratic South Africa?: Constitutional Engineering in a Divided Society*, University of California Press, Berkeley.

Kriesberg, L. (1981), *Social Conflicts*, Prentice-Hall, Englewood Cliffs, New Jersey.

Lijphart, A. (1986), *Power-Sharing in South Africa*, Institute of International Studies, University of California, Berkeley.

Simmel, G. (1955), *Conflict and the Web of Group Affiliations*, Free Press, New York and Collier-Macmillan, London.

Swilling, M. (1988), 'Beyond local option: Coercive co-option or democratic transition?', *Reality*, 20, pp. 23–25.

Epilogue   *Dennis J. D. Sandole*

Future directions in theory and research

In reviewing the contributions to this volume in terms of the question I posed in my introductory chapter, 'Do we have anything to say about, or to offer the parties in, protracted, violent conflict situations?', it seems to me that parts of some very important 'blanks' have been 'filled in'. Still, *not* surprisingly, 'blanks', or parts of them, remain, thereby providing opportunities (if not 'imperatives') for future research.

Some years ago John Burton and I (1986) argued that a 'paradigm shift' was in progress in how people, *at all levels*, dealt with conflict, away from *Realpolitik* (competitive) and toward *Idealpolitik* (cooperative) modes of conflict resolution – a view which Francis Fukuyama (1989, 1992) might argue is compatible with his thesis that 'the end of history' is upon us.

While such 'paradigm shifts' may accurately describe changes in East–West relations, they clearly do not reflect what is taking place *within* parts of the West (e.g., Northern Ireland, Los Angeles) and the East (e.g., the former Yugoslavia and former Soviet republic of Azerbaijan). People in those (and other) areas are, in Fukuyama's terms, 'still *in* history'. To what extent do the various contributions to this volume address the question 'Why?', or more specifcally:

(a) Why/how did the violence in Northern Ireland and Los Angeles, and the wars in Croatia and Bosnia-Hercegovina, and Nagorno-Karabakh occur?
(b) How could such violent conflicts have been prevented?
(c) Once under way, how could they have been 'short-circuited' and their violent manifestations terminated ('negative peace' – see below)?
(d) What do we (the U.S., Irish, and British governments, and local political and civic leaders; the United Nations, NATO, and European Community; and Serbian, Croatian, Slavic Muslim, Armenian, and Azeri political and civic leaders; and conflict analysts, conflict resolution theorists and practitioners, peace researchers, and 'concerned others') do now?
(e) What are the 'lessons' for 'ethnic time-bombs' elsewhere?

Some concepts, potentially relevant to some of these questions, come immediately to mind, for example, Kevin Avruch and Peter Black's (Chapter 9) *ethnotheories* and *ethnopraxes*; Benjamin Broome's (Chapter 7) 'third culture', or *relational empathy* ('shared meaning') which, for him, 'is essential for successful conflict resolution'; and Joseph Montville's (Chapter 8) 'healing and reconciliation process', comprised of acts of *contrition* and *forgiveness*.

Taking these insights as points of departure, further research is then needed on how to translate 'ethnotheories' and 'ethnopraxes' into synergistic, collaborative, problem-solving *wholes*: '*meta*-ethnotheories' and corresponding '*meta*-ethnopraxes' that bridge the otherwise irreconcilable *Weltanschauungen* and approaches of 'warring factions'. In effect, further research is required to understand the dynamics of 'paradigm shifts', from Mary Clark's (Chapter 3) 'pathological' to 'healthy cultural worldviews' and corresponding institutions, and from Elise Boulding's (Chapter 13) 'military to diplomatic preparedness' and 'national' to 'common security'.

Further research is also needed to understand where 'relational empathy' fits in to the dynamics of 'paradigm shifting', as well as how to facilitate its development among conflicting parties, especially during or after a process of *brutal* efforts to suppress one another. Of relevance here are some thoughts I have expressed elswhere on 'the intrapsychic effects of and contributions to conflict at other levels' (Sandole, 1987, p. 296):

Once individuals in conflict – whether at the interpersonal, intergroup, interorganizational, international or any other level – start to express themselves through the conscious defenses ... they may become brutalized, unable to view their 'enemies' as anything but despicable subhumans. Under such circumstances, which can lead to an extension of the conflict beyond the lives of its original participants, potential third parties who wish to intervene effectively must be able to operate at the intrapsychic as well as interparty levels. Unless the first is dealt with adequately, the second may only worsen. This is a challenge for all concerned.

Accordingly, further research is needed on how, and under what circumstances, acts of 'transactional contrition and forgiveness' can be *meaningfully* articulated by conflicting parties or facilitated by third parties, in order to launch a 'healing and reconciliation process', especially among people who have been brutalized by each other. Appropriate apologies, under appropriate conditions, might lead to 'relational empathy' which could facilitate the development of a 'meta-ethnotheory' and 'meta-ethnopraxis' in conflict resolution, further facilitating the 'paradigm shifting' to 'healthy' 'common security'.

I am here reminded, however, of a local politician from Northern Ireland who asked me, 'How can you expect a man whose relatives have been blown to bits, to accept apologies from those who have confessed to committing the terrible deeds?' Further research is clearly needed, therefore, into how

277

intense emotional resistance to reconciliation can be overcome: what would it take for an apology to 'work'?

Difficult though it may be, empathy can be developed, even under (or perhaps because of) the threat of what Bryant Wedge and I (1982) have referred to as 'globicide'. In this regard, Ralph K. White (1983) has argued that the continuation of the Cold War and the threat of nuclear annihilation were fed by the superpowers' 'woeful lack of empathy' for each other. Now that the Cold War 'seems' to be a thing of the past, perhaps its demise should be studied to ascertain whether empathy played a role in that process and, if so, how; also, how empathy could be applied to other, similar conflict situations or systems.

All of this relates to John Burton's (1984) definition of the individual as the main unit of analysis at all levels, and to Daniel Druckman's (Chapter 2) 'person variables' (e.g., 'attitudes, values, or cultural styles'). Here I recall Druckman's finding that the research literature is not clear on the 'enhancing and moderating effects of the situation on the expression of person variables'. In some cases, 'person variables' are revealed, 'loud and clear'. In other cases, they are 'hidden' – either showing up not at all or in relatively insignificant ways. This, especially the 'hidden' part, is compatible with my own research experience (see Sandole, forthcoming). Clearly, further research needs to be conducted in this area, especially given the apparent significance of some individuals (e.g., Hitler, Stalin, Saddam Hussein, Milosevic) in the initiation, escalation, and 'controlled maintenance' of some conflict situations or systems, plus that of others (e.g., Brandt, Gorbachev) in conflict resolution.

Whether 'person variables' are revealed to be significant or not, may depend upon the levels of environment with which individuals are interacting. Given the operative framework in my introductory chapter, individuals can interact with any or all of four levels: individual/interpersonal, societal/national, international/transnational, and global. Perhaps the more comprehensive the level, the more 'hidden' the 'person variables'.

This raises (as in my introductory chapter) the issue of how comprehensive theory ought to be – how far we ought to cast our net to catch the significant factors in violent conflict initiation and escalation and in conflict resolution. This also raises (again) the issue of 'paradigms'.

Thomas Kuhn (1970, Ch. 4) tells us that paradigms are, to various degrees, comprised of four fundamental components:

(1) *metaphysical*: the paradigmatic community's (*agreed*) sense of a 'legitimate' or otherwise appropriate subject-matter;
(2) *theoretical*: the community's sense of appropriate explanations for the behavior of that subject-matter;
(3) *instrumental*: the community's sense of appropriate methods for conducting further research into the behavior of its subject-matter (and in

the case of conflict and conflict resolution, sense of appropriate methods for intervening into conflict situations and systems); and

(4) *methodological*: the community's sense of appropriate questions that require answers (such as those I posed above, concerning Los Angeles, Bosnia-Hercegovina, etc.).

Clearly, the 'field' of conflict and peace studies (CAPS) is not (yet!) a 'paradigmatic community'. There is no agreement on even the basic, metaphysical level. According to John Burton (Chapter 4), for example, there are profound differences between 'conflict' and 'disputes'; whereas for Marcelle DuPraw (Chapter 16), the two terms can be used interchangeably.

Although Johan Galtung (1969, p. 190) argues 'emphatically, that a discipline fully satisfied with its own foundations and definition is probably a dead discipline', some of the rest of us may be concerned that we cannot agree, either on what we are studying or in what it is that we are intervening. And given Burton's distinction between *conflict management, settlement, resolution*, and *provention* (also see Burton, 1990 and Burton and Dukes, 1990), perhaps some of us are also unclear about what we are, or should be, doing when we do intervene, especially in situations where the parties are 'emotionally wounded'.

Here it would be useful to have others (e.g., Serbs, Croats, Slavic Muslims, Armenians, Azeris, Palestinians, Israeli Jews, Tamils, Sinhalese, and others) do what Hugo van der Merwe did in Chapter 18, and attempt to answer the question, 'What do all the contributions to this volume say to me as a South African (Palestinian, etc.), that is relevant to understanding *and* resolving the conflicts in my part of the world?' (It might even be useful to build a conference around such presentations, with the participants sharing their various applications of specific concepts to aspects of different conflicts ('concepts in action'), and perhaps experiencing helpful *commonalities across cases*.)

Implicit here is an interesting distinction – between what Abraham Kaplan (1964, pp. 32–33, 139–143) labels *act meaning* and *action meaning*. The former refers to the meaning of acts and events as perceived by actors (e.g., parties to conflicts), while the latter refers to the meaning of actors' behaviors and events in their environments as perceived by observers (e.g., third parties: analysts, facilitators, etc.). Further theory development on the etiology of violent conflict must take into account 'act' as well as 'action meaning', addressing along the way one aspect of the 'instrumental' aspect of paradigms: the orientation of community members toward research methods.

Some theorists/researchers are *quantitative*, while others, like practitioners, tend to be *qualitative* in research methods orientation. This should not be a major problem for the field – the 'quantifiers' can continue their efforts to tap into 'action meaning' (and sometimes 'act meaning' as well), while the qualitative-oriented theorists/researchers and practitioners can continue (via Max Weber's *Verstehen* (see Kaplan, 1964, pp. 142–143) and other methodologies) to delve into 'act meaning'.

Whether our contributors who are primarily theorists/researchers have adequately incorporated insights from practice (to the satisfaction of practitioners), lest they not be seen as 'relevant' (in this regard, see Easton, 1969), it is clear that 'practice' (the remaining aspect of the 'instrumental' component of paradigms) means different things to different people. It is not only that some of us may be concerned with 'settlement', others with 'management', and still others with 'resolution,' and perhaps a dedicated minority with 'provention', but also that we cannot − even as close colleagues − agree on what some of these terms mean (apropos 'conflict management', for example, see Sandole, 1986, p. 120).

And whether our contributors who are basically practitioners have satisfied Joseph Scimecca's (Chapter 14) call for the practice of conflict resolution, specifically 'alternative dispute resolution' (ADR), to be 'undergirded' by a 'theoretical base', lest they not be seen as 'true professionals' (but instead, as agents of 'social control'), it is clear that theory (the *theoretical* component of paradigms) also means different things to different people. And here there is a need for further research − to explore, for instance, not only whether *needs* (and which ones) do or do not play a role in conflict, but to develop *comprehensive* explanations of conflict initiation and escalation, plus corresponding approaches to conflict resolution *and* prevention. Daniel Druckman's (Chapter 2) own unique contribution to 'further directions in theory and research' (his 'next steps in the accumulation of knowledge'), Christopher Mitchell's (Chapter 6) provocative distinction between 'micro', 'meso', and 'macro'-level theory, plus the four-part framework and corresponding discussions in my introductory chapter, are useful points of departure for further research, not so much for generating agreement on what the 'right' theory is, or ought to be, but on mapping out a fuller sense of what makes conflict 'tick' as well as a fuller sense of how to deal with it. This should include, on both the initiation/escalation and resolution/provention sides, a search for the possibility of dynamic *interactions* between the relevant variables. As Druckman (Chapter 2) says in his conclusion, 'Much remains to be learned about the way that different sources of conflict *interact* over time and in various ... contexts', as well as in understanding how 'debate and bargaining processes', plus other variables (including person and situation), '*interact* in determining the outcome of diverse cases' (emphasis added).

As I implied in my introductory chapter, a comprehensive theory of conflict and conflict resolution should include Galtung's (1969) concept of 'structural violence'. Such a theory should also include the distinction between 'positive' and 'negative' peace, which corresponds to Galtung's distinction between structural and personal violence. Negative peace refers to the *absence of personal violence*, while positive peace refers to the *absence of structural violence* or, more 'positively', the *presence of social justice.*

In line with the 'contingency model' thinking of Fisher and Keashly (1991), some conflict situations may require a 'negative peace' kind of response, at least in the short run, e.g., getting the parties to a violent conflict 'to the table' to negotiate a cease-fire and agreement for the dispatch of peacekeeping forces, perhaps in order to facilitate the initiation of *cooperative* approaches to dealing with the problems underlying the conflict. 'Negative peace', therefore, may be a preliminary step toward 'positive peace'. 'Positive peace' may also be necessary to prevent further outbreaks of 'personal violence' (and the further need, therefore, for 'negative peace').

Given the potential linkages between personal and structural violence, and therefore, between negative and positive peace, it is interesting to note that much theory and practice in conflict resolution concerns *negative peace*: the prevention (*proactive*) or reduction and elimination (*reactive*) of violent means for dealing with conflict. This is an honorable objective and again, in the short run, it may be a necessary preliminary to doing anything else. And as Galtung (1969, p. 190) says, 'there is a tendency to focus on negative peace because consensus is more easily obtained'. In any case, many third parties are not politically or otherwise appropriately positioned to facilitate the structural changes (at the societal/national, let alone international and global levels) necessary to bring about positive peace. That notwithstanding, an approach to peace that ignores the positive (and therefore, the potential structural) element, may be counterproductive and ultimately self-defeating — the use of violence to stop violence may only serve to fuel and to sustain those *negative self-fulfilling prophecies* (NSFPs) I mentioned in my introductory chapter. Hence, commenting on the 'post-[Los Angeles] riot rise in gun sales', Coleman McCarthy (6 June 1992), tells us that:

Those who carry loaded guns for self-protection keep widening the circle of violence: They are ready to shoot people who shoot people who were shot at by people other people shot at after they were shot at. All in the name of self-defense.

Various contributors to this volume imply the distinction, and make clear the connection, between negative and positive peace. John Burton (Chapter 4), for example, introduces us to conflict *provention*, which is concerned explicitly with the elimination of structural violence and the pursuit of social justice. Richard Rubenstein (Chapter 10) expands upon, and provides concrete examples of, 'provention' as an orientation relevant to relieving the structural violence that gives rise to the kinds of conflicts that will probably come, more and more, to characterize industrial societies. Mary Clark (Chapter 3) talks about the need to transform our 'pathological worldviews' and institutions into their 'healthy' cultural and institutional opposites, where structural violence would be effectively eliminated: where the 'psychic needs shared by all humans for social bonding and sacred meaning' can be met.

Alvin and Heidi Toffler (1992, pp. 14, 16) suggest a connection between structural violence and future conflicts in industrial societies, where 'psychic needs' will tend to be met for fewer and fewer people. They argue that the Los Angeles riot of April–May 1992 was not a unique event and that, barring appropriate 'paradigm shifts' from *Second-* to *Third-Wave* thinking and corresponding institutions (see Toffler, 1981), we are going to experience *more of the same*, abroad as well as in the United States:

the explosive charge that powered the Los Angeles riot is not a local, nor even an American phenomenon. It is a global event linked to a *basic redistribution of economic and political power*. It has its roots not merely in [a dangerous new kind of] *racism*, but in the technosocial revolution [the *Third Wave* of change] now sweeping across the earth ... with direct [implications for] ethnic or race relations (emphasis added).

How should 'further research' into the remaining 'blanks' (or parts of 'blanks') be structured? One approach (which is being pursued at our Institute for Conflict Analysis and Resolution) is to develop long-term projects around protracted, violent conflict systems, *locally* (e.g., Washington, D.C.), *nationally* (e.g., Los Angeles), and *internationally* (e.g., Nagorno-Karabakh), involving appropriately trained persons (e.g., students and faculty from university conflict resolution programs) in various roles (e.g., analysts, facilitators). Without turning or otherwise framing these conflicts into the kinds of 'experimental laboratories' that van der Merwe (Chapter 18) mentions as a fear among some in South Africa, these projects could, *ethically*, provide the same kinds of opportunities that Mitchell (Chapter 6) associates with problem-solving workshops:

greater opportunities for theory development in the threefold sense of hypothesis *generation*, theory *testing*, and theory *use*, than have previously been available to students of the 'art' of facilitated and collaborative problem-solving in protracted and deep-rooted conflicts (emphasis added).

In my 'problem-solving' activities, I tend to distinguish between *research problems* and *practical problems*. The former are concerned with finding answers to fundamental questions, such as 'Why do people kill others who *involuntarily* belong to certain ethnic, racial, religious, or other "outgroups"?', while the latter deal with taking that knowledge (assuming it exists) and attempting to influence decision-makers who preside over the political process at various levels; in effect, enacting Burton's (1991) '*consultative* role of the professional in conflict resolution' (emphasis added). By establishing and maintaining contact with decision-makers at the local, national, and international levels, the projects referred to above could facilitate the resolution of 'practical' as well as 'research problems'.

Bridging the gap between the 'academic' and the policymaker, however, is no easy task; for example, at the international level:

Few diplomats, negotiators, and arms control policymakers have seemed to find much utility in scholarly, theoretical writing, and scholars [have] tended to be unlikely to interest themselves in the [governmental] practitioners' experience (U.S. Institute of Peace, April 1991, p. 4).

However, some of the contributors to this volume are already in 'both worlds'. The 'trick' now (and an anticipated outcome of this volume) is to further integrate, and expand the connection between, theory and practice, further facilitating the likelihood of policies aimed at 'provention' (*positive peace*) as well as management, settlement, and resolution (*negative peace* 'and beyond'), at *all* levels. A 'challenge for all concerned'.

References

Burton, J. W. (1984), *Global Conflict: The Domestic Sources of International Crisis*, Wheatsheaf Books, Brighton.

Burton, J. W. (1990), *Conflict: Resolution and Provention*, Macmillan, London and St. Martin's Press, New York.

Burton, J. W. (1991), 'Problems of leadership', unpublished manuscript, Institute for Conflict Analysis and Resolution, George Mason University, Fairfax, Virginia, April.

Burton, J. W. and Dukes, F. (eds) (1990), *Conflict: Practices in Management, Settlement and Resolution*, Macmillan, London and St. Martin's Press, New York.

Burton, J. W. and Sandole, D. J. D. (1986), 'Generic theory: The basis of conflict resolution', *Negotiation Journal*, 2, pp. 333–344.

Easton, D. (1969), 'The new revolution in political science', *American Political Science Review*, 63, pp. 1051–1061.

Fisher, R. J. and Keashly, L. (1991), 'The potential complementarity of mediation and consultation within a contingency model of third party intervention', *Journal of Peace Research*, 28, pp. 29–42.

Fukuyama, F. (1989), 'The end of history', *The National Interest*, Summer, pp. 3–18.

Fukuyama, F. (1992), *The End of History and the Last Man*, Free Press, New York.

Galtung, J. (1969), 'Peace, violence, and peace research', *Journal of Peace Research*, 6, pp. 167–191.

Kaplan, A. (1964), *The Conduct of Inquiry: Methodology for Behavioral Science*, Harper and Row, New York and London.

Kuhn, T. S. (1970), *The Structure of Scientific Revolutions*, 2nd edition, University of Chicago Press, Chicago and London.

McCarthy, C. (1992), 'The perils of packing a gun', *The Washington Post*, 6 June, p. A23.

Sandole, D. J. D. (1986), 'Traditional approaches to conflict management: Short-term gains vs. long-term costs', *Current Research on Peace and Violence*, 9, pp. 119–124.

Sandole, D. J. D. (1987), 'Conflict management: Elements of generic theory and practice', in D. J. D. Sandole and I. Sandole-Staroste, eds, *Conflict Management and Problem Solving: Interpersonal to International Applications*, Frances Pinter, London and New York University Press, New York.

Sandole, D. J. D. (forthcoming), *The Genesis of War: Mapping and Modelling of Complex Conflict Processes*, Lynne Rienner Publishers, Boulder, Colorado.

Toffler, A. (1981), *The Third Wave*, Bantam Books, New York and London.

Toffler, A. and Toffler, H. (1992), 'L.A.'s lessons for the world', *World Monitor* (The Christian Science Monitor), 5, June, pp. 14, 16–18.

Dennis J.D. Sandole

United States Institute of Peace (1991), *United States Institute of Peace Journal*, April, pp. 3–4.

Wedge, B. and Sandole, D.J.D. (1982), 'Conflict management: A new venture into professionalization', *Peace and Change*, 8, pp. 129–138.

White, R.K. (1983), 'Empathizing with the rulers of the USSR', *Political Psychology*, 4, pp. 121–137.

Contributors

Kevin Avruch, Ph.D., Associate Professor of Anthropology and member of the Faculty Liaison Committee of the Institute for Conflict Analysis and Resolution, George Mason University. He is the author of numerous works on culture and conflict including *Conflict Resolution: Cross-Cultural Perspectives* (1991) which he co-edited with Joseph Scimecca and Peter Black.

Peter W. Black, Ph.D., is Professor of Anthropology at George Mason University. A specialist in Micronesian cultures, he is a member of the Faculty Liaison Committee of the Institute for Conflict Analysis and Resolution, and author of numerous works on culture and conflict including *Conflict Resolution: Cross-Cultural Perspectives* (1991) which he co-edited with Joseph Scimecca and Kevin Avruch.

Elise Boulding, Ph.D., is former Secretary General of the International Peace Research Association. She is also Professor Emerita of Sociology at Dartmouth College, and previously Visiting Professor at the Institute for Conflict Analysis and Resolution, George Mason University. She has written numerous works, including *Building a Global Civic Culture: Education for an Interdependent World* (1988), and an edited volume entitled *Peace Culture and Society: Transnational Research and Dialogue* (1991).

Benjamin J. Broome, Ph.D., is Associate Professor of Communication and a member of the Faculty Liaison Committee of the Institute for Conflict Analysis and Resolution at George Mason University. He is widely published in interpersonal and intercultural conflict (articles in, e.g., the *Journal of Conflict Resolution, International Journal of Conflict Management, International Journal of Small Group Research,* and *International Journal of Intercultural Relations*). He regularly conducts group problem-solving sessions with various Native American Indian tribes, including the Comanche, Apache, and Cheyenne/Arapaho.

Brack Brown, Ph.D., is Associate Professor of Government and Politics and a member of the Faculty Liaison Committee of the Institute for Conflict Analysis and Resolution at George Mason University. Among his various publications is the book, *The Search for Public Administration* (co-authored with R. Stillman II).

Contributors

John W. Burton, Ph.D., D.Sc., is Distinguished Visiting Professor and former Director at the Institute for Conflict Analysis and Resolution at George Mason University. One of the major figures in the theory and practice of international conflict resolution, he was an Australian delegate to the United Nations Charter Conference in 1945, and was appointed Permanent Head of the Australian Foreign Office in 1947 and Australian High Commissioner to Ceylon (Sri Lanka) in 1951. He has also been a Jennings Randolph Distinguished Fellow at the U.S. Institute of Peace in Washington, D.C., and author of many works, including *International Relations: A General Theory* (1965), *Systems, States, Diplomacy and Rules* (1968), *Conflict and Communication: The Use of Controlled Communication in International Relations* (1969), *World Society* (1972), *Deviance, Terrorism and War: The Process of Solving Unsolved Social and Political Problems* (1979), *Global Conflict: The Domestic Sources of International Crisis* (1984), and most recently, the four-volume *Conflict* series (1990).

Mary E. Clark, Ph.D., is the Drucie French Cumbie Chair in Conflict Resolution at the Institute for Conflict Analysis and Resolution, George Mason University. She was named first U.S. 'Professor of the Year' in 1981 by the Council for Advancement and Support of Education. A biologist with deep philosophical interests, she is the author of two editions of a biology textbook, *Contemporary Biology* (1973, 1979), and of *Ariadne's Thread: The Search for New Modes of Thinking* (1989).

Daniel Druckman, Ph.D., is a Principal Study Director at the National Academy of Sciences, Washington, D.C. He is also Adjunct Professor of Conflict Resolution at the Institute for Conflict Analysis and Resolution, George Mason University. He has written widely in the field, including his edited volume, *Negotiations: Social-Psychological Perspectives* (1977) and his co-authored books on *Nonverbal Communication* (1982) and *Political Stability in the Philippines* (1986), plus book chapters and many articles in various journals.

Marcelle E. DuPraw, M.S., is an independent environmental and cross-cultural conflict resolution specialist. She has experience in mediation, facilitation, training, and dispute resolution system design, having served in a number of capacities in the field, including Associate at the Conflict Clinic, Inc., at George Mason University, and Senior Associate in Conflict Management for ICF. She is the author of several articles, including, 'American/Soviet consultations on environmental and ethnic dispute resolution' (1991).

Herbert C. Kelman, Ph.D., is Richard Clarke Cabot Professor of Social Ethics at Harvard University and Chair of the Middle East Seminar at the Harvard Center for International Affairs. He has worked with John Burton and developed his own 'interactive problem-solving' approach to bringing Palestinians and Israelis (among others) together to explore the problems underlying their conflict. Currently President of Psychologists for Social Responsibility (PSR), he has also been a Jennings Randolph Distinguished Fellow at the U.S. Institute of Peace in Washington, D.C. The most recent of his many published contributions to the field are his co-authored *Crimes of Obedience: Toward a Social Psychology of Authority and Responsibility* (1989) and 'Applying a human needs perspective to the practice of conflict resolution: The Israeli–Palestinian case', in John Burton's edited *Conflict: Human Needs Theory* (1990).

286

Ambassador **John W. McDonald**, J.D., former President of the Iowa Peace Institute, spent 40 years with the United States Department of State. He has been active in many multilateral negotiations, often as the chief United States representative. He is currently Bryant Wedge Visiting Professor and a Senior Associate with the Institute for Conflict Analysis and Resolution, George Mason University, and has published a number of works including the co-authored *Multitrack Diplomacy: A Systems Guide and Analysis* (1991), co-edited *International Negotiation: Art and Science* (1984), and *Conflict Resolution: Track Two Diplomacy* (1987).

Christopher R. Mitchell, Ph.D., is Professor of Conflict Resolution and International Relations and Director of the Institute for Conflict Analysis and Resolution, George Mason University. A long-term colleague of John Burton, he is the co-editor of *New Approaches to International Mediation* (1989), and author of *The Structure of International Conflict* (1981), *Peacemaking and the Consultant's Role* (1981), and *Gestures of Conciliation* (forthcoming).

Joseph V. Montville, A.M., a former career diplomat, is Senior Consultant on Conflict Resolution at the Center for the Study of Foreign Affairs, Foreign Service Institute, U.S. Department of State. He is also a Senior Associate with the Institute for Conflict Analysis and Resolution, George Mason University. His recent published works include the edited *Conflict and Peacemaking in Multiethnic Societies* (1990), and the two co-edited volumes, *The Psychodynamics of International Relationships* (1990).

John S. Murray, J.D., is former President and Executive Director of the Conflict Clinic, Inc., at George Mason University. He is presently a private consultant in conflict resolution, specializing in process design, facilitation, and training services, both nationally and internationally. He has worked most recently with environmental protection, economic development, and ethnic conflict in the Baltic States and the Middle East. Among his many published works is a coursebook for law students entitled *Processes of Dispute Resolution: The Role of Lawyers* (1989).

Richard E. Rubenstein, M.A., J.D., is Professor of Conflict Resolution and Public Affairs, and former Director of the Institute for Conflict Analysis and Resolution, George Mason University. He has authored a number of works on political violence, including *Alchemists of Revolution: Terrorism in the Modern World* (1987).

Dennis J.D. Sandole, Ph.D., is Associate Professor of Conflict Resolution and International Relations at the Institute for Conflict Analysis and Resolution, George Mason University. A former William C. Foster Fellow with the United States Arms Control and Disarmament Agency, he is currently a NATO Research Fellow. His published works include the co-edited volume, *Conflict Management and Problem Solving: Interpersonal to International Applications* (1987) and *The Genesis of War: Mapping and Modelling of Complex Conflict Processes* (forthcoming).

Joseph A. Scimecca, Ph.D., is Professor of Sociology at George Mason University, and a former Director of the Institute for Conflict Analysis and Resolution. He is the author of numerous books, including *Society and Freedom: An Introduction to*

Humanistic Sociology (1981), and co-editor with Kevin Avruch and Peter Black of *Conflict Resolution: Cross-Cultural Perspectives* (1991).

Hugo van der Merwe is a Ph.D. student and former Research Assistant at the Institute for Conflict Analysis and Resolution, George Mason University. He is a former Senior Research Assistant at the Centre for Intergroup Studies at the University of Cape Town, South Africa.

John N. Warfield, Ph.D., University Professor and Director of the Institute for Advanced Study in the Integrative Sciences, George Mason University, has taught in the past at the Institute for Conflict Analysis and Resolution. He has authored many publications, including a recent two-volume work entitled *A Science of Generic Design: Managing Complexity through Systems Design* (1990).

Wallace Warfield, M.A., former Senior Associate with the Conflict Clinic, Inc., at George Mason University, is currently Practicum Coordinator for the Applied Practice and Theory Program at the Institute for Conflict Analysis and Resolution. He is also a former Distinguished Visiting Fellow at the Administrative Conference of the United States and Acting Director of the Community Relations Service of the U.S. Department of Justice, plus President of the Society for Professionals in Dispute Resolution (SPIDR). He is the author of several recent articles, including 'The implications of ADR processes for decision making in administrative disputes', *Pepperdine Law Review* (1989).

288

Index

Index

Brandt, Willy, 19, 117–18
Breger, M., 171
Brezhnev, Leonid, 117
Broome, Benjamin J., 97–107, 274 n.5, 277
Brown, Brack, 158–73
Brown, L. David, 167, 170
Brundtland Report (1987), 194, 203
Bruner, Jerome, 48
Buber, Martin, 107 n.2
Buie, D.H., 99, 102
Buntz, G.C., & B.A. Radin, 170
bureaucracy
  and nation-state, 165–8
  see also organizations, public
Burleson, B.R., & S. Bingham, 100
Burton, John, 6, 67, 75, 97, 242, 276, 278, 282
  and authoritarianism, 168–9, 172
  conflict resolution as political philosophy, 55–64
  and human-needs theory, 14, 20, 59–60, 165, 213–14, 266–7
  and levels of conflict, 14, 15, 16, 265, 266, 279
  and problem-solving approach, 78, 114, 140
  and provention, 60, 63–4, 281

capitalism
  crises, 62–3
  and imperialism, 16–17
  and interest groups, 152, 214
Carr, E.H., 4
Carroll, Raymonde, 134–6
Casmir, F.L., 104
Casmir, F.L., & N.C. Asunción-Lande, 104
Caspary, W.R., 85, 90
change
  and conflict, 5, 167, 216, 230, 264
  cultural, 48–50, 52–3, 63, 123–4, 204–5, 272–3
Choucri, Nazli, 7, 17, 21
Christakis, Alexander N., 71
Churchill, Winston S., 116
civil rights movement, and public policy, 178, 185

'civics', in South Africa, 265, 270, 271
Clark, Mary E., 20, 21, 43–53, 272, 277, 281
class
  conflict, 148, 153–6, 214
  interests, 149–53
client group, and public policy conflict, 176–90
coercion
  by state, 45, 50, 57, 166
  in conflict resolution, 146
cognition, and affect, 100–1
cognitions
  alternative, 27–8, 44–5, 51–2, 140–1
  see also equilibrium, cognitive
cognitive therapy, 123
Cohen, Raymond, 139, 142
commitment, of intervening agent, 68, 70
communication
  and empathy, 97, 103, 104–7
  facilitated, 229–30
communism, crises, 62–3
competition
  in conflict resolution, 4, 5–6, 21, 29, 31, 35–6, 276
  in evolution, 48–9
  in public policy conflict, 182–3
compromise, willingness for, 27, 29, 31, 37, 218
concession, and bargaining, 29–30, 33
conferences, international
  delegation size, 253–5
  and diplomacy, 248–59
  leadership, 257–9
  preparation, 250–3
  structure, 255–7
confirmation, in problem-solving workshops, 85, 115
conflict
  aggressive manifest conflict process (AMCP), 7, 13–14
  analysis, 154, 214, 228, 232
  context for, 35–7, 38
  definition, 6–7, 55–6
  domestic, 56
  ethnic, 57, 112–25, 148, 276

290